Denver's Histor

A Nosta

To Bob
with best wishes
Theodore A. Borillo

Denver Public Library Western History Collection - No. X-24657

DENVER'S HISTORIC ELITCH THEATRE

A Nostalgic Journey

(a history of its times)

by

Theodore A. Borrillo

ISBN-10: 0-9744331-4-4
ISBN-13: 978-0-9744331-4-1

Graphic Design by David Robison
Arvada, Colorado

Printed in the United States

I have never met but one man in my life
whose suppressed ambitions had not included a
desire to act . . . And if there is a woman living
who has not been similarly ambitious she is not
numbered in my circle of acquaintances.
Which accounts for the amazing interest the
theater holds for our people.

BURNS MANTLE
Drama Critic
Denver Post, August 3, 1924
(Amusement Section)

History Colorado - # 10038867

John & Mary Elitch

Denver Public Library Western History Collection

DEDICATION

This book is dedicated to
the memory of
John and Mary Elitch
founders of
Denver's Elitch Theatre

and to

the many actors, actresses, directors, stage managers, scenic designers, staff and crew, members of management and the devoted Denver audiences, all of whom contributed to making Denver's Elitch Theatre the oldest continuous summer theater in America

and to

my children, Christopher, Angela, Matthew and Thomas (a fine and devoted actor)

and

in memory of my wife, Elfriede.

CONTENTS

Year By Year

References to subheadings listed within a chapter are some but not all of the chapter subheadings

PREFACE

My love of theater began long before I ever heard of Elitch Gardens. It began in a small enclave in the Bronx where I was born and lived among Italians, my parents among them, and where I spoke Italian before I learned English. Italian immigrants gave up a great deal in coming to America, as most did not know how to read or write or converse in English.

Fortunately, however, they were able to be entertained by Italian radio programs and, even more important, live theater in the Tremont area of the Bronx. Many well-known Italian actors, actresses, singers and comedians provided excellent entertainment for my parents and, yes, for me. I learned to appreciate theater from those Italian stars that sang and performed for these immigrant people and their children. And as I listened to Gilda Mignonette, Carlo Buti, Nicola Paone, Clara Stella, Sandro Giglio, Joe Masiello and others, I learned the value of theater in enhancing the lives of others.

My appreciation for the theater and those who make it work has never left me to this day. And so I acknowledge those Italian performers that made me love the theater. You can imagine how thrilled I was in the summer of 1969 to watch Joe Masiello's son play the lead role in the musical *Pal Joey* at the Elitch Theatre.

This love of theater broadened significantly during my life in New York City during the big band era. Broadway was a poor man's paradise. I was a constant patron at Broadway's many plays (that were later produced on the Elitch stage), as for example, the wonderful *Sabrina Fair* in 1953, with Margaret Sullavan, Scott McKay and Joseph Cotton. In 1958 I saw Henry Fonda and 26-year-old Anne Bancroft in *Two for the Seesaw.* I recall as a young man in 1951 waiting outside the stage door to catch a glimpse of Barbara Bel Geddes leaving the theater after a performance of *The Moon is Blue.*

When I attended the City College of New York, I was a member of Theatron, an organization that presented plays at the College. I was a member but not an actor. I helped with the advertising and other non-acting chores. I remember attending the radio broadcast of *Songs for Sale* hosted by Jan Murray and staffed with two young and gifted singers, Rosemary Clooney and Richard Hayes. My purpose in going was to invite Jan Murray to appear at the College to receive an award.

In choosing to write *Denver's Historic Elitch Theatre - a Nostalgic Journey,* clearly, the memories of the theater from those early days in the Bronx constituted the beginning of a truly wonderful nostalgic journey. I am not an outside writer looking in on the subject; rather, I am one who has been totally engrossed in my love for the theater and those who make it possible. How fortunate, in my move west from New York City, that I found a home in Denver, Colorado where one of America's greatest and most respected and inspiring playhouses was located, a place where the world of theater focused its attention every summer - Elitch Theatre. I was a regular patron of Elitch Theatre. I miss its seasons. It is important to preserve the history and memories of its seasons, as I have tried to do in this book, year by year.

Those who love the theater, as well as others, will recognize those summer days and nights at Mary and John Elitch's Gardens and their Theatre and hopefully will enjoy this nostalgic journey as much as I have enjoyed the research and preparation of the manuscript.

I never acted, nor do I believe I would have been significant in any attempt to act. I became a lawyer instead. Some people look upon lawyers as "actors" so there is some consolation for me in my chosen profession. This background is the source of my love and inspiration, both of which are necessary when undertaking a project of this sort. I acknowledge those lovers of the theater who continue to inspire me with every play I read, with every play I see. And, most of all, I thank you for your interest in this nostalgic journey.

Theodore A. Borrillo
Littleton, Colorado
October 2012

Chapter One

(August 30, 1987)

The Last Performance

On Sunday, August 30, 1987, the boards of the stage of the Elitch Theatre, upon which a world of famous actors and actresses entertained decades of audiences, hosted their final performance. The Theatre had come a long way since May 1, 1890, its opening day. The ghosts of John and Mary Elitch must have watched in the wings as the Theatre approached its final scenes, its final applause, its final curtain call, its final moment. It was a farewell evening, a dream fulfilled and an uncertain future. It was goodbye. All that would remain would be nostalgia - events, memories and moments to be remembered, to be recounted, to be shared, to be never forgotten.

The final play was *Nunsense,* a musical comedy "based on the premise that everything is funnier when performed by women in habits." The musical, which takes place during a fund-raising talent show by the Little Sisters of Hoboken, presented the audience with nuns as gourmet cooks, country-and-western singers, tap dancers, ventriloquists and movie stars.

Nunsense began the season, and by popular request, it was selected to return for a special engagement for the final two weeks of the season. It was as if the audience didn't want to let go but wanted to delay the Theatre's goodbye, to delay its end, for two more weeks.

It was fitting that the final play of the near-century-old Theatre starred Mary Jo Catlett, whose stage appearance began in her native Denver with the Windsor Players, and it was at the Elitch Theatre playing Agnes Gooch in *Auntie Mame* in the mid-60s that she earned her Actors' Equity card. She completed her study of theater at Loretto Heights College in Denver, and following graduation, she went to New York where, within a year, she made her Broadway debut in the role of Ernestine in the original *Hello Dolly!* with Carol Channing. In 1985 Ms. Catlett fulfilled a fantasy by coming back to the Elitch Theatre to star in *Harvey.* Ms. Catlett said that to return once again to the Elitch Theatre in the play *Nunsense* is "the best habit one can have."

Although Ms. Catlett complimented Denver audiences as "the best because they listen and react and really enjoy theatre," the final performance was a sad farewell to Denver's romance that began a century before with a Theatre that was loved by all who came to know her. And so it was that the long history of one of America's most prestigious summer theaters came to an abrupt end.

The Theatre now sits in silence, a haunting presence harboring a lifetime of memories, an old wooden building now surrounded by a highly populated housing development and business district. The shell of the building has been preserved. Its empty stage and seats continue to stand, alone and in darkness, a continuing reminder of those golden summers when hundreds awaited the opening of Elitch Theatre.

The history of Elitch Theatre embodies the love story of John and Mary Elitch. It echoes the love of those actors and actresses who brought theater into our hearts. Elitch Theatre became the oldest continuous summer theater in America. In many ways, it was a pioneer among the annals of theatrical history. Cecil B. De Mille, renowned film producer and director, described the famous Theatre as being "what all actors and actresses consider one of the greatest cradles of drama in American History."

Whitfield Connor, former actor, executive director and general manager of the Elitch Theatre for many years, said it best. He stated:

> In a world too often given to dismissing the great traditions which have made us strong, it is comforting to know that every professional in the theater is proud to be able to say, "I have played Elitch's."

Chapter Two

(1872 - May 1, 1890)

The Early Years
The Opening of the Gardens
The Theatre Building
The Management Policy

The Early Years

The story of John and Mary Elitch is a love story, despite the fact that their backgrounds consisted of opposites. Mary was a Northerner, born in Philadelphia, Pennsylvania. John was born in the South in Mobile, Alabama. Mary's mother was Lutheran and her father was Presbyterian. John was rooted in Roman Catholicism. Mary's heritage was German, her father insisting that it be spoken in the home. John was a blue-blood American, a direct descendant of Stephan Hopkins, a signatory to the Declaration of Independence. Yet, as in many cases of opposites, love triumphed and sustained them in marriage.

Mary Elitch was born Mary Elizabeth Hauck on May 10, 1856. As the oldest of six children, she developed a strong sense toward social interaction and needs. She moved with her parents to California while still in her early childhood years and grew up on an estate near San Jose, where her father raised horses and fruit. She was strictly reared and educated by her parents. Mary was placed in the Convent of the Sisters of Notre Dame in San Francisco, where she lived as a boarding pupil. She came to revere the sisters and requested to become Catholic, which faith was to become an important part of her life. Her parents honored her request, and Mary became a member of the Catholic Church.

> At sixteen, when most girls were beginning to snug their slim waists into stays, cast an innocently flirtatious eye at the local swains, and embroider pillow slips for their hope chests, Mary's mother became a semi-invalid, and Mary had to assume the full responsibility for their home.
>
> She studied with her father evenings in lieu of the Convent she had been attending, gardened among her mother's flower beds afternoons, and learned to speak fluent Spanish from the imported ranch help. Her only outside contact was church, which her father let her attend regularly in San Jose each week. It was at Sunday School that she met John Elitch.[1]

John Elitch was tall, dark and attractive with black curly hair and a mustache. He was six years older than Mary, having been born on April 10, 1850. By the time he was 12 years old, he was with his family in Santa Clara, California, where he later attended Santa Clara College. After his attendance at college, John worked with his father in the restaurant business.

Mary responded to John's interest in her, and, after Sunday church services, she would allow him to accompany her to a point close to her home. She was resolutely against John meeting her father, explaining apprehensively that "it would be the end!"

John courted Mary with daily notes delivered to her by her 10-year-old brother Edward, who was bribed with a dime to deliver the notes and return Mary's answers. At last, a note from John read, "I'm going to San Francisco for a job; will you marry me when I come for you?" Edward delivered Mary's scribbled note to John; the answer was "Yes."

John got a job in a restaurant and started saving his money. Finally he returned to Santa Clara, and Edward carried the news to Mary. John arrived to marry her. Mary knew that a marriage to John would incur the wrath of her stern and protective father.

Without her father's consent, Mary and John eloped and were married in San Jose in May of 1872. Mary was 16 and John was 22. As Mary had feared, her father disowned her. Later, however, as most fathers would, he forgave her for her hasty marriage, and upon his death in 1882, he left Mary a share of his estate.[1]

After their marriage in 1872, John and Mary settled in San Francisco where John opened a restaurant in the California Theatre building, which was frequented by actors and actresses and other members of the theatrical world. To John Elitch, it was an attractive world. It was there that John first became interested in the theatrical profession.[2] From time to time, John took part in amateur theatrical performances.[3]

Until her marriage to John Elitch, Mary had not seen the interior of a theater. John took Mary to see her first play, *The Streets of New York* with Frank Mayo, at the California Theatre in San Francisco. The experience was memorable and made Mary determined to become, in some manner, identified with theater.

During the silver jubilee celebration of Elitch Gardens in 1914, Mary Elitch wrote an article for the *Denver Post* sharing her memories of those early days. She wrote:

> It may be something of a surprise to those people who have known me through a whole quarter of a century as the theatrical manager to learn that I never saw a play - was never inside a theater - until a comparatively short time before I opened Elitch Gardens.
>
> *The Streets of New York* was the first theatrical performance I ever attended. Frank Mayo, beloved by another generation, was the star. One evening my husband took me downtown, saying he had a treat in store

for me. We went to the old California Theatre - since destroyed by the earthquake; and there I saw my first play.

I will never forget that performance. My love for the theater began that evening as I watched Frank Mayo act, and it has never left me.[3]

Frank Mayo was later to become a beloved friend of John and Mary Elitch. Mayo's daughter, Deronda Mayo, later played at the Elitch Theatre during the 1901 season.[4] Almost a century later, *The Streets of New York* was presented at Denver's Elitch Theatre in 1980, with Farley Granger playing the lead.[5]

John's love of the theatrical world continued to grow, and he told his friends that his ambition in life was to become "an amusement manager." His first opportunity came in 1878. On May 28, 1878, after several years in San Francisco, John sold his restaurant there and invested most of his money in a traveling show company, which turned out to be a poor investment. His entire investment was lost.[2]

In 1880, John and Mary looked to Denver to begin over. They arrived in Denver during the summer of 1880, without money and without friends, but with a desire and willingness to work. John secured a job as a cook in the Arcade restaurant, located at Larimer and Sixteenth Streets. The following year, the Elitchs learned that silver was discovered in Durango. In the spring of 1881, they took the savings that they had accumulated across the snowy San Juan Mountains and opened a restaurant in Durango in time to feed the spring prospectors. It was a prosperous year for them. By the winter of 1881, they had earned $4,000.00, a decent profit. John, again moved by the lure of the theater, returned to the warmer weather of California and again invested in a traveling stock company and once more lost his investment.[2]

John returned to Denver in 1882 and, with the financial assistance of a friend, opened an oyster and chop house at 16th and Curtis Streets. While it was popular and prospered,* ultimately, its accommodations became inadequate and John set out for another enterprise. Finally, on August 6, 1886, John Elitch opened his Elitch Palace Dining Room, located at 1541 Arapahoe Street. It was described as "the finest and most complete restaurant between Chicago and San Francisco, and equal to the finest in any of the larger cities." It was lavishly decorated and attracted star performers who were appearing at the Tabor Grand Opera House, as well as newspaper editors, politicians and other Denver society leaders. The dining room was the largest in Denver, comfortably seating two hundred persons.[6]

While in Denver, John Elitch became active in civic affairs. Being devoted to athletics, he was one of the founders of the Denver Athletic Club, which took the old Baptist Church at 18th and Curtis Streets as its clubhouse and gymnasium, the

* It was reported that John had netted about $1,000.00 a month. *Denver Republican,* Mar 11, 1891, p. 1.

congregation having erected the larger First Baptist Church on Stout Street.[7-1]

In 1887, John and Mary purchased the 16-acre Chilcott Farm in the town of Highlands, five miles from the heart of Denver, for the purpose of raising vegetables and small fruits for the restaurant.[7-2]

> In 1862, President James Buchanan signed a bill creating the Colorado Territory and appointed William Gilpin as its first territorial governor. Shortly thereafter, a woman named Martha Hager arrived in the Territory with her husband and sons. This frontier family settled in the mountain town of Empire, which served as a food distribution center for the local Ute Indians. Unfortunately, some drunken renegades butchered her husband one dark night so Martha moved her sons to the safety of Denver, where she met and married William Chilcott. He talked her into homesteading a farm five miles to the west of the town. The land contained good water and a small lake, and Martha soon planted numerous trees - cottonwoods for shade and an apple orchard for taste.[8]

The town of Highlands began as an elite suburb of the unsavory Denver in 1875. Highlands "prided itself on its clear air, beautiful gardens and tree-lined streets and, in particular, its high moral standards." Denver first tried to annex the town in the 1880s, but the people voted it down, not wanting it to become part of the "dirty, crowded, smoggy, crime-ridden, sinful city of Denver." Ultimately, the financial state of the Highlands caused it to give in. The lack of an adequate tax base, a treasury impacted by the Silver Panic of 1893 and needed infrastructure investments left the town with little choice. Finally, on June 22, 1896, the population of 8,000 voted to annex the town to Denver, with a promise from the city to facilitate transportation between the Highlands and Denver.[9]

In 1888, John Elitch sold his Palace Dining Room.[10] The original name of the restaurant was retained until 1890, when it was renamed the Tortoni Dining Parlors, or "Tortoni" for short. The "Tortoni" established itself as one of the finest establishments of its kind in the West. Like John Elitch's restaurant, it attracted patrons from all walks of life, but especially noteworthy was a group known as the "Sacred 36," who were classified as "The Smart Set" among the "Who's Who in Denver Society." Upstairs were dining rooms "where men of wealth often met, and deals involving millions were consummated. Political campaigns were planned behind locked doors." [11] Denver's "Newspaper Alley" was close to Tortoni's back door, so the restaurant became a favorite gathering place for newspaper men, journalists and writers of the day, including Gene Fowler and Eugene Field.* The restaurant continued to operate until December 31, 1915, its 30th year. Prohibition caused

* A branch of the Denver Public Library located at 810 South University Boulevard is the Eugene Field Branch.

the end of this operation as well as so many other similar establishments, which were presumably "weakening the moral fiber of mankind" by serving alcoholic beverages.* In 1963, the block at Arapahoe Street that housed the restaurant was demolished. The Federal Reserve Bank and parking lot now occupy this space.

The Decision to Convert the Chilcott Farm

After selling his Palace Dining Room, John Elitch, with Mary, decided to convert the Chilcott farm into a beautiful place for families to gather and, of course, "We'll build our theatre."

> Occupying the comfortable farm house that was located in the orchard, they eagerly planned and worked together, for, though John had his own conviction of the great emprise, Mary held the vision beautiful. No stone was laid, no tree planted or trimmed, no path projected, without her complete and joyful approval.[12-1]

Mary Elitch had a great love for animals and she and John decided to acquire a few animals to form the nucleus of a zoo within the gardens. She acquired the animals from a man named Adam Forepaugh, who operated a zoo in San Francisco. A bandstand was constructed within the gardens, as well as picnic areas. The gardens had other accommodations as well, such as a cafe that served sandwiches, pastries, and light liquid refreshments.

While in California, John and Mary had become friends with Charles W. Goodyear and Charles E. Schilling, experienced vaudeville performers, and the Elitchs invited them to assist in the operation of the Theatre. Goodyear and Schilling arranged for several vaudeville artists to participate in the Theatre's first program.

John and Mary Elitch's labor of love progressed, and on May 1, 1890, the gates of the gardens were opened to the public, and their dream became a reality.

Colorado was declared a territory in 1861 and achieved the status of statehood in 1876. The westward expansion of people was directly linked to the discovery of gold and silver. Mining camps were sprinkled about many areas of Colorado. By 1870, the population of Denver was the highest with Central City second. By 1880, Leadville was second to Denver.[13] In 1870, the population of Denver was estimated at less than 5,000 people, but by 1880, it had increased to 34,629 inhabitants.[14-1]

> By 1880 (Denver) real estate values were advancing substantially and swiftly. Three important buildings completed during 1880-1881 were the Windsor Hotel, City Hall and Union Station. Other significant improvements included the establishment of the first telephone exchange in 1879 and the installation of electric street lights in 1883.[14-2] More than

* In lively days, the name "Tortoni" was worked into the floor in front of a fireplace near the bar, using gold pieces of various denominations. Later when times were tough the gold pieces were dug out with a chisel. *Denver Post*, Mar 19, 1932, p. 4.

> six hundred miles from the nearest railroad point, Denver was the trading center for a dozen flourishing mining camps within a radius of a hundred miles. Consequently, it experienced the mushroom growth that accompanies any town so situated.[14-3]

By 1890, the population of Denver had increased to 106,713. The city of Denver had expanded with the construction of "several new railroad extensions including the Missouri Pacific, the Rock Island, the Santa Fe, the Colorado Midland and the Denver and Rio Grande - all serving Denver and the last two pushing into and across the mountains." [14-4] Denver had become the established center of the Rocky Mountain Region.

The Opening of the Gardens

On May 1, 1890, the scheduled opening of the Elitch Zoological Gardens and Amusement Park was chilled by showers that threatened to dampen the spirits of all who came. Notwithstanding this, a large crowd attended the opening of the park.

A short time prior to the opening day celebration, city officials had installed and opened a steam train line from downtown Denver to the Gardens. The line began at the end of the old cable system at Thirteenth and Galapago Streets and ran to Thirty-eight and Tennyson Streets.[15]

Mary Elitch vividly described the event as follows:

> When the momentous day of opening arrived, I was filled with grief and disappointment, for rain was falling. Mr. Elitch was nearly as sorrowful as I, for we had made great preparations for the opening and it seemed doomed to dismal failure. Looking back through the vista of years, I am sure my sorrow was for him far more than for myself. I remember I prayed very fervently for a cessation of those May showers. As we stood in our doorway, trying to encourage each other, a horseman dashed up to the gates. Excitedly hailing Mr. Elitch he announced that all of Denver was moving over to Elitch; that the train, packed to capacity, was laboring up the hill from the river; that coaches, carriages, delivery wagons, farm wagons, people on bicycles and people afoot were headed for our opening. We then realized that Denver was ready for what we had to offer, and her people cared not for showers; but even as we bustled about in last-minute excitement, the glorious sun broke through the clouds.[12-2]

The rains ceased suddenly as the crowds neared the Gardens. Then as Wolfe Londoner, Mayor of Denver, turned the key in the garden gates and flung them wide, the Elitch Zoological Gardens and Amusement Park was officially open. The great crowd swept into the place like a tidal wave, and the celebration began.

Men shouted and danced and tossed their hats into the air. Women laughed and cheered and hugged their friends. Mary Elitch then dedicated the Gardens to clean amusements, to the joy of little children and the recreation of all people. Mary Elitch became "the first woman in the world to own and manage a summer and zoological resort." [16] Until the opening of the Denver City Park Zoo, Elitch was the only zoological gardens between Chicago and the West Coast.

Among other things, the Gardens also contained a lake, picnic grounds, rides, games and concession stands.

Phineas T. Barnum of circus fame was present,* as were Mr. and Mrs. Stratton, known to the public as General and Mrs. Tom Thumb (famous midgets), Senator H. A. W. Tabor, Governor John L. Routt and ex-Governor John Evans. Eugene Field, the poet and colorful reporter for the *Denver Republican,* was also present as were James O'Neill and Nat Goodwin, leading actors of the day.

Following an elaborate picnic, the doors of the Theatre opened for the public to enjoy free vaudeville performances. When the curtain of the Theatre rolled up, Mayor Londoner made an opening speech in which he touched upon the magnificence of the Theatre and the gorgeous elegance of the grounds as "first class in every particular." He described the resort as a place "where the mothers and children could come to spend a quiet day free from household cares and worryings, and a place where the working man and his family could come on Sundays." [17]

The program that followed was greeted with storms of applause, and frequent encores showed plainly that everyone was satisfied. The program included Miss Minnie Zola, the little athletic wonder, Van Auken and La Van, champion triple horizontal bar performers of the world and Miss Rosa Lee, the gifted and refined balladist, just to name a few. Charles Goodyear, comedian, and Charles Schilling, the quaint, comical musical genius, also performed. Vaudeville acts by notable performers continued throughout the summer.[12-3]

Mary recalled in her memoirs:

> While we were ambitious, and a great vision was cherished, John Elitch and I did not really dream, that day when we witnessed the acts on our stage, what Elitch Gardens and its Theatre might become in the life of Denver, and to the profession.[12-4]

The Theatre Building

The Theatre was built in 1890. W. L. (Billy) Heckart owned a pool hall and lunch room at 38th and Tennyson. He and his carpenter father built the Theatre.[18]

* "It was at this time that a section of land adjacent to Denver was being developed. The real estate people back of the project honored Mr. Barnum by bestowing his name upon the tract, which today is a closely settled community and still bears the name of the great showman." Dier at p. 24.

The architecture of the Theatre is sort of a "resort" design. It is a plan which was fairly prominent at seaside resorts and mountain retreats in the early 1900s. Its frame architecture is something that is not now very often found.

The building was circular in design, with a canopy or tent-like covering, and twelve sides, two of which were left open as entrances. In describing the opening day activities at the Gardens, Mrs. Elitch mentioned the building briefly:

> The sides of the Theatre were not enclosed, and those who could not obtain seats inside stood about under the trees, from which vantage points good views of the stage were possible.[19]

Before the commencement of the 1891 season, a permanent roof was built over the entire Theatre, and the sides were enclosed.

From time to time, there were remodeling projects that resulted in a change of the seating capacity, the drop curtain and the space accommodation of dressing rooms, just to mention three. However, except for the enlargement of the stage by the addition of a backstage area in 1954, the original building in appearance has remained essentially the same since its 1890 original design by Charles Herbert Lee and Rudolph Liden, Denver architects at the turn of the 20th century.

In 1930, a few months after Arnold B. Gurtler assumed the management of the Theatre following the death of John M. Mulvihill, Gurtler recognized the desire of patrons of the Theatre that it retain its original charm and flavor. In an article for *Billboard* magazine, Gurtler's sentiments were expressed:

> Like the "Church Around the Corner" and Henry Ford's "Little Red Schoolhouse," there is another building in America which has not been affected by modernism. Elitch's frame theatre building has remained unchanged through the years ... This old Theatre is so dear to the heart of the public ... that its quaintness and charm are looked upon as something to be preserved as a priceless heirloom. Someone once asked me why I didn't dismantle the old building and put a modern structure in its place. The expression of amazed chagrin which came over my face made the person feel as if he had committed a grave breach of etiquette. Anyone who has beheld the charm of this historic old playhouse at the end of a winding path through the apple orchard would readily appreciate the sentiment attached to it. Truly it is in striking contrast to the throbbing scene near-by -- the thoroughly modern spectacle of an up-to-date amusement park.[20]

The original drop curtain at Elitch displayed scenes of Elitch Gardens, with Denver and the Rocky Mountains in the background.[14-5] It was replaced in 1894 with a curtain that displayed the following verse below a pictured cottage:

Ann Hathaway's cottage
A mile away
Shakespeare sought
At close of day

The curtain was painted by Charles F. Thompson Scenic Company studios of Los Angeles. Denver business proprietors purchased advertising to display on the backside of the curtain, tempting the performers. For example, J. H. MacCraken of "Saddle & Light Livery" at 1413 Broadway offered "Horses called for and delivered, riding tonight." Haberl Jewelry Co., manufacturing jewelers, offered "special prices to the profession."[21]

The new curtain with "Ann Hathaway's cottage" remained with the Theatre through its last performance in 1987.

The Theatre's outer lobby became a photo gallery of stars who had played there over the years, among them being Douglas Fairbanks Sr., Tyrone Power, Harold Lloyd, Sylvia Sidney, Sarah Bernhardt, Minnie Maddern Fiske, Edward G. Robinson, Fredric March, Florence Eldridge, Barbara Bel Geddes and Grace Kelly. During the winter of 1954, the Theatre's electrical layout and plumbing system were changed, and the stage was enlarged by the addition of a backstage area, the plan being "to give the Theatre one of the finest stages in America."[22]

The result was a stage with a 32-foot opening, a 40-foot depth, and the ability to accommodate 5 sets. It has been said that "the stage area at Elitch is vast and can accommodate the most ambitious scenic projects."[23]

The Theatre reportedly had "1,419 seats ... without counting the boxes." * [24] The boxes accommodated from 48 to 60 persons, depending on the number allowed within each box.[25]

Elitch Gardens was more than a theater. It was an amusement park and playground, a zoo and gardens, a family atmosphere, a place of comfort removed from the tension of the inner city. The Theatre was to touch the lives of many, both actors and audience, for almost a century.

The Management Policy

Newspapers advertising the opening of the Gardens identified the management policy that would embrace its patrons. The Gardens would be "a strictly respectable family resort" - "a place to take your wives" and "a place to take your children." No intoxicating liquor would be sold on the grounds. Persons obviously under the influence of alcohol would not be allowed entrance nor would any other "objectionable or improper characters." With regard to the Theatre, the artists and acts presented had to be acceptable to mixed audiences, and nothing of a vulgar

* There were 32 rows of seating downstairs and 9 rows of seating in the balcony. Seats in the balcony were added during the remodeling process before the 1891 season. Levy at p. 184.

nature would be tolerated on the stage. In essence, newspaper ads promised that the resort would be "the greatest feature Denver has ever had" and that it would be "far surpassing any resort of its kind in America."[26]

Years later, in an article in the *Rocky Mountain News* that reflected on the memories of Elitch, Mary Elitch was quoted as having said:

> I can say with a consciousness of truth that no girl was ever exposed to temptation in my Gardens and I know that while I may not have turned any boy or girl from evil associations outside my gates, no evil influence was permitted to reach them within.[27]

Children's Day

While John and Mary were without children in their marriage, Mary was to become a mother figure to the many children who were to visit the Gardens.

During this first season, Mary Elitch inaugurated an event that was to continue into the next century at Elitch. She established "Children's Day," a special outing every Tuesday for "the children of Colorado" during which they enjoyed educational and other activities at the Gardens.

An article from the *Chicago Record-Herald* commented on the weekly event.

> Every activity for the interest, pleasure and education of the little visitors is furnished, and Mrs. Elitch, who is a child again with the children, personally conducts or participates in the games and classes. Animal study is pursued with the animals in real life for illustration; Indian days -- with real Indians to teach the boys and girls how to decorate their wigwams and tepees; and classes in nature study and elementary botany to help the children understand the many fine trees and beautiful flowers are conducted; there are also dramatics and folk dancing for the children.[12-5]

So important did Children's Day become to Colorado that Mary Elitch published a free weekly newspaper known as the *Child's Companion* in which coming events were described and news of the Gardens was conveyed to the readers.[12-5]

In March of 1932, in the "Foreword" to Mary Elitch's memoirs by Caroline Dier, Burns Mantle wrote:

> Among all the tributes that have been paid, and will be paid, to the Lady of the Gardens, there is none finer, to me, than that which followed her establishment of Children's Day. Immediately, without other or further guarantee, thousands of city parents brought their young hopefuls to the gates of the Gardens, paid their way through and forgot them until closing time. They knew they would be safe there - as safe as they would be at home, and much happier.

Throughout the years, "Children's Day" remained a source of great pride for Mary Elitch.*

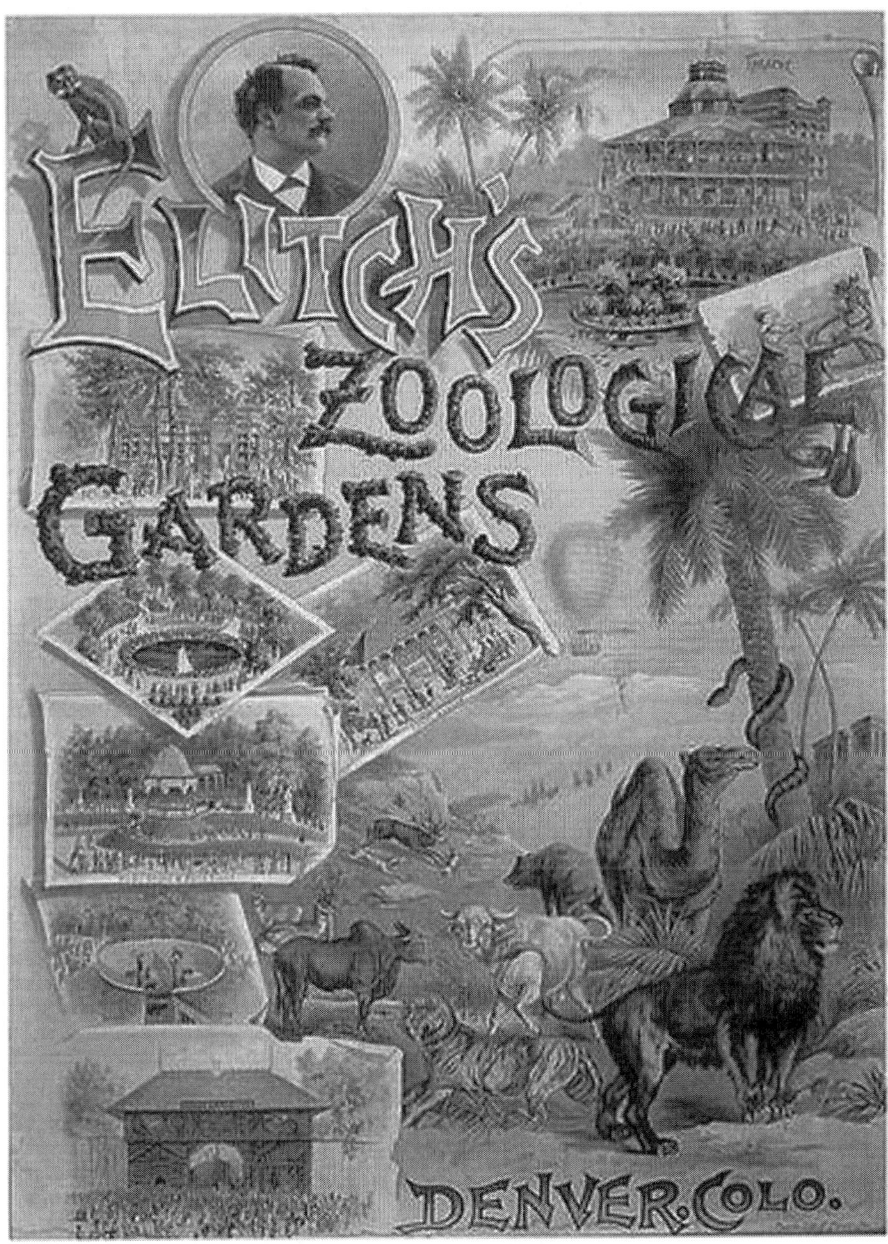

Poster advertising the opening of the Gardens

* E.g., The Elitch Theatre program for the week commencing Jun 12, 1904, p. 3, stated, "Tuesday is Children's Day, when Mrs. Mary Elitch Long cuts the regular charges for children in two. It is 5 cents everywhere and for everything for the little ones."

Denver Public Library Western History Collection

Mary Elitch with her goats

History Colorado - # 10039847

Mary Elitch with her lion cubs

Chapter Three

(1891)

The Death of John Elitch
The Elitch Gardens Amusement Company
The Lighting at the Elitch Theatre
Manhattan Beach

The Death of John Elitch

The 1890 opening season of the Gardens was economically successful. John and Mary Elitch netted $35,000.00.[1] When the season came to an end, John Elitch, together with Charles W. Goodyear and Charles E. Schilling (both of whom had appeared in vaudeville bills at Elitch Gardens throughout the summer), decided to organize a company known as the Elitch, Schilling and Goodyear Minstrels. The company decided to play the theatrical circuits in winter and Elitch in the summer, with Thomas Long as their manager. The troupe secured bookings between Denver and the Pacific Coast for the ensuing winter season.[2]

Before leaving Denver, the company played a successful week's engagement at a local theater. Following the troupe's debut, the *Denver Republican* predicted a success for the new venture. According to the critic:

> Mr. John Elitch was in his best humor last night, and he stood at the entrance of the Fifteenth Street Theater, a typical show proprietor in appearance, and had a pleasant smile for all of his friends and patrons. Well might he have appeared pleased for the evening witnessed the debut and putting on the road a minstrel show that he has spent thousands of dollars in equipping and many months in drilling and training for public appearance.[3-1]

The minstrel troupe's new venture began by touring Peter McCourt's Silver Circuit in Colorado and then the Pacific Coast that winter, before opening at the Alcazar Theater in San Francisco in March of 1891.[3-2] The minstrels were successful. Mary, by now imbued with the "feel" of the theater, was trouping with them. And so it happened that she was backstage when, without warning, John suddenly collapsed. He was taken to the Hotel Melville at the corner of Market and Turk streets in San Francisco, the "headquarters" for Denver visitors to the city, where John Elitch stayed and where he always felt at home. A few days later, on March 10, 1891, he died, his illness reportedly "taking the form of quick consumption, complicated with pneumonia." His obituary stated that John Elitch was "the same brave, genial John to the end," and "before death came gave a cordial hand-clasp to those to whom he was too weak to speak."[3-2] John Elitch was 41 years old.

Melville Herman, keeper of the Melville Hotel and an old friend of John Elitch, recalled the onset of his symptoms shortly before his death. A news article stated:

> Mr. Herman, talking of his death today, said that when John first arrived last month, and spat blood when he came up stairs, he told him he ought not to risk his life by staying with the minstrel company, but John replied, "Oh, I'm strong and will soon shake off this cold." He didn't take care of himself, however, and rapidly grew worse.
>
> "From the first day he took to his bed," added Mr. Herman, "I saw there wasn't any hope for him, and his wife saw it too, but she humored the dying man, and agreed with him when he said he would soon recover. Yesterday (on March 10th) about noon he called me in and asked me for God's sake to send for the doctor, as he was suffering terribly.
>
> "When the doctor came, he said: 'Well, doctor, how am I?' The doctor replied: 'I won't deceive you; you are a very sick man, and if you have any arrangements to make you had better make them now.'
>
> "'Well,' replied Elitch, 'can't a man live with one lung?'
>
> "'Yes,' was the reply, 'but not with two diseased lungs such as you have got.'
>
> "He gave John Elitch something to quiet the pain, but hemorrhage came on soon after and in a few minutes John lost consciousness and passed away.
>
> "The doctor called his complaint gangrenous pneumonia, and said it was a wonder he lived as long as he did, for the membrane of his lungs was all diseased." [3-3]

The news of Elitch's death created great sorrow, for he had spent his boyhood and young manhood in San Francisco, "and everyone liked him for his genial, whole-souled ways."[3-3] On the following day, March 11, 1891, the *Rocky Mountain News* carried the story on page 1, as follows:

> The veteran restaurateur and showman, John Elitch of Denver, Colorado, died at the Melville Hotel in San Francisco last night of a complication of diseases. He came to this city with his company, the Elitch, Schilling and Goodyear Minstrels, but was compelled to take to his bed immediately. There was no hope of his recovery from the first, the attending physician warning his friends and relatives to be prepared for the worst. John Elitch was even better known in San Francisco and other California towns than he was in Denver, he having been born at San Jose in California. His wife was with him at the time of his death, having been summoned to his bedside as soon as his illness was known

to be serious. His end was very peaceful, being much like falling asleep.

When the Elitch Theatre was being built in 1890, John Elitch fell through a partially completed floor, injuring himself severely. Elitch never completely recovered from the fall, and it was believed that may have contributed to his death in California in 1891.[4]

His remains were taken by train to San Jose, where funeral services and burial were held on March 13, 1891. A large delegation of actors and friends attended the funeral service at the Roman Catholic Cathedral in San Jose.[3-3] In 1897, his body was removed from California, brought to Denver, and was buried in Fairmount Cemetery on September 17, 1897, where he now rests beside Mary Elitch Long. Mary had John's profile, "with the curly hair and mustache, carved onto his tombstone."[5]

The Elitch Gardens Amusement Company

After John's death, Mary did not have enough money to run Elitch Gardens. Yet, she was determined to continue the dream of the Gardens and the Theatre.

In *The Lady of the Gardens,* a book that contains some of her memoirs, Mary Elitch is quoted as saying:

> The death of my husband left me with our great venture still something of an experiment, in spite of its one successful season; but having been imbued with his vision, and knowing his ambitions for the enterprise, I determined to carry on and so undertook the entire management myself.
>
> The decision was arrived at while in San Diego, where I went after the burial of my husband. I then returned to Denver to take up my life work. Never shall I forget the spring morning, standing before the door of our home, surrounded by the trees and beautiful shrubbery and garden beds my husband had so happily placed. While the birds were outlining their summer plans in the trees above me, I told myself, as this was to be my life work, I might as well begin.* [6-1]

Throughout her life, Mary Elitch was a faith-oriented person. In years to come, Denver residents would witness her kindliness, her sensitive love of beauty, her passion for animals and children, and her family values. Her task of management had to begin.

> I looked around to see how I could begin. Some sticks holding up the sweet peas had fallen down and I told myself I could begin with them. So it has been ever since. I've always done the nearest thing. But first

* The title "Lady of the Gardens" was given to Mary Elitch by Frank W. White, drama critic and editorial writer of the *Denver Post,* soon after the death of her husband, when she assumed the entire responsibilities of the Gardens. Dier at p. 32.

> I looked up to God and asked Him for His help. One must never rage and demand things either of life or God. Be receptive. Be ready and everything that comes will find its place and be the best thing for you.[7]

The need for money to manage the Gardens was resolved on April 25, 1891. Nine prominent Denver businessmen reached an agreement for the transfer of Elitch Gardens to a corporation to be formed by them for the sum of $250,000.00. By May 4, 1891, the articles of incorporation were filed and the Gardens were transferred to The Elitch Gardens Amusement Company and its stock was capitalized at $300,000.00. A. B. McGaffey, of Porter, Raymond & Company, was President, S. A. Joseph, President of the South Denver Electric Light and Power Company, was Vice-President, and William P. Macon, Attorney at Law, was Secretary and Treasurer.[8]

At the same time, they placed upon the market a limited number of 100,000 shares of stock at one dollar per share.[9-1] The advertisement informing the public of the availability of stock read in part:

> No stock sold to a single individual in excess of 1,000 shares. The personnel of the directorship and management of the company (every one of them reputable, high-up business people) practically insures a profit triple that of the $35,000 gained last year. Subscribe now before shares reach the double-up limit.[9-1]

The corporation hired Charles Schilling to act as manager, which position he accepted. Mary Elitch remained with the Gardens in an administrative capacity and participated in their management.

A full-page advertisement was carried by the *Rocky Mountain News* in large bold print, urging the purchase of shares by the Denver public. The directors of the company explained:

> A handsome return for their money is vouchsafed to all who invest, for this institution is bound to pay its stockholders, and for the following reasons: Last year, which was the first of its public existence, it netted to its owner the sum of $35,000, which, taking into consideration the fact that it was a new business with its originators, struggling for existence and popular recognition, and laboring under the inevitable disadvantages and impediments that must confront every new enterprise of the kind, was certainly a most remarkable revenue.[9-2]

The prospectus prepared and issued by The Elitch Gardens Amusement Company stated:

> In the short season of five months, the Gardens returned to the proprietor a net profit of $35,000, although then laboring under three serious disadvantages, viz.: first, but one mode of public street transportation, i.e., the Berkely motor line connecting with the Fifteenth

Street Cable; second, the fact that last year the improvements were not complete until August; third, a deficiency of lighting accommodation.

The prospectus then went on to emphasize the increased street car facilities and electric lights.

> Last year the Gardens could only be reached by one line of transportation, which, while it carried during the three summer months 450,000 persons, had to refuse as many more on account of insufficient transportation facilities. This disadvantage has been remedied by the building of the West End Electric Railroad, and the conversion of the former motor line into an electric line, and there are now sufficient facilities to transport to and from the Gardens 100,000 persons daily.
>
> Last year the Gardens were open only in the daytime, but now electric lights have been put in, which will render the grounds as light as day, and people can enjoy the attractions of the place until late in the evening.
>
> It is reasonable to presume that with the increased transportation facilities and the receipts from night performances that the profits from the Gardens this season will be far in excess of those of last year.[10]

The newspaper advertisement echoed the benefits from the prospectus and then identified the list of property owned exclusively by the company as follows:

> 16 acres of land, 600 fruit trees, 1500 twenty-year old shade trees, $8,000 water works, theater, seating capacity 1,600, restaurant, two animal houses and corrals, three green houses, $8,000 bear pit, (followed by a list of animals housed at the zoo, including, among many others) 1 male African lion, 1 female African lion, 1 male mountain lion, 3 cub mountain lions, 1 dromedary, 1 female camel, 1 sacred bull, 1 buck elk, 1 doe elk, 1 water buffalo ... 5 Angora goats, 6 native goats ... 14 tame rabbits ... 8 monkeys ... 1 South American parrot, 1 Mexican parrot, 2 gray squirrels.[9-2]

In an effort to lessen the impact of the competition from the Manhattan Beach summer resort, which opened in 1891, admission prices were reduced. The Company again presented a number of vaudeville acts, as well as the Boston Opera Company at mid-season for six weeks of popular productions of light opera. The season was financially successful.

The Lighting at the Elitch Theatre

Elitch Theatre was equipped with gas appliances in 1891 for lighting on the stage and throughout the Theatre. The addition of gas lighting permitted evening as well as matinee performances.

> Small shades were installed for the footlights which interfered in no way with the view of the stage from any part of the auditorium but

which furnished a perfect protection from the glare of the lights.

Although the management installed electricity at the main entrance and along the walks of the Gardens in 1891, it was not until 1899 that new electrical equipment replaced the original gas fixtures in the theatre.* [11]

Manhattan Beach
A Rival Summer Amusement Park and Theater
A Brief History (1891-1914)

The economic success of Elitch Gardens in its opening season more than likely was the stimulus for the opening of the rival amusement park which was to become known as Manhattan Beach. The park opened on or about June 27, 1891.** It had a large theater and was located on the north side of Sloan's Lake in west Denver.

In 1860, Thomas M. Sloan, while drilling an irrigation well on his farmland in west Denver, tapped an artesian spring and the ensuing gush of water filled up 200-acres of the farmer's land. The body of water became known as Sloan's Lake.[12] In 1866, Thomas Sloan filed homestead papers on the area and received confirmation from President Andrew Johnson on December 13, 1866. Thomas Sloan died in 1873 and his estate became mired in legal claims and confusion for many years.

In the winter of 1889, an enterprising pioneer settler, a German immigrant named Adam Graff, "had established a successful ice business by sawing out neat squares of ice from the frozen lake during winter months." While sawing away on the ice, "his thoughts turned to summer, and another use for the lake." [12] Adam Graff, together with Steinke & Company, joined together in purchasing the Sloan's Lake property and opened a resort in April of 1890.

> It was called Sloan's Lake Resort ... One of the major attractions ... was a steamship, a converted coal barge, which had been hauled in from Mississippi to carry passengers on sightseeing tours around the lake. The ship was called the *City of Denver,* and a ride on it cost 25 cents.
>
> The Sloan's Lake Resort was limited in its attractions, and the dream ended a year later when most of the facilities burned.[12]

As a result, Graff and Steinke & Company were induced to sell the property. In April of 1891, new owners purchased the property and the remains of the facility. The purchasers were Eugene Booth and other eastern capitalists and George G. Darrow, J. E. Sackett and John Howard. The new owners decided to incorporate as the Southern Investment Company, and announced that a summer amusement

* "As early as 1870 gas, manufactured from coal, was used for illuminating Denver homes and public buildings ... Thomas A. Edison gave the world the electric lamp in 1879 ... Keen competition now developed between the gas company and the electric company, each claiming superiority for its own utility." Hafen and Hafen, *The Colorado Story* (The Old West Publishing Company 1953), pp. 373-374.

** Newspaper accounts vary on the date in June that the park opened.

park resort and theater would be immediately erected. It was to be called Manhattan Beach.[13-1] Construction of the park commenced promptly and rapidly. Tons of sand were brought from California to provide a beach. The theater was a large circular building resembling Shakespeare's Globe Theater.[12]

On July 13th, the Wilbur Opera Company opened a season of comic opera at the Manhattan Beach theater.[13-2]

> Manhattan Beach was beautifully landscaped, with elaborate gardens. One fountain had a central jet 100 feet high. The several buildings included a large theater, a menagerie building 270 feet long, several smaller animal houses, an open-air cafe, roller skating rink, dance pavilion, bath house and boat dock.
>
> Two bands were featured on shore, in addition to one aboard the *City of Denver* (the ship that cruised the lake).*
>
> The theater was the biggest attraction at the park. Many famous performers appeared there.[14]

The seating capacity of the theater varied from 2,000 to 3,000 seats - clearly, much greater than the Elitch Theatre.[15] The acoustic properties of the theater were said to be "perfect and only equaled in this country by the Mormon tabernacle at Salt Lake City."[16]

> After Denver staged a big clean-up campaign against gambling, after-hours drinking and wild wily women, a high board fence was erected along Sheridan Boulevard to separate the wholesome festivities of Manhattan Beach from the questionable activities offered by Edgewater's waterfront.[17]

In an effort to lessen the impact of this rival competition, the Elitch management reduced admission prices and suddenly offered the Boston Opera Company in popular productions of light opera at its theater, in addition to vaudeville acts.** Crowds were also attracted to Elitch by various acrobatic and animal acts performed outdoors, as well as by the famed balloonist and aerialist, Ivy Baldwin.

In 1892, rumors were afloat of a consolidation between the two North Side summer resorts; however, both companies denied that any consolidation of the two companies had been made.

> They said, however, that an agreement had been entered into between the two companies placing both on an equal basis as to charges for admission to the resorts and to the two theaters.

* In 1905, the *City of Denver* sank after suffering severe damage in a heavy windstorm. However, all individuals aboard were brought ashore safely.

** The Boston Opera Company. in mid-season, presented performances from a selection of light operas, including Gilbert and Sullivan's *The Pirates of Penzance, Patience* and *Isolanthe.*

Commencing on Tuesday, July 26, the price of admission at both the Gardens and the beach will be 25 cents for adults and 10 cents for children over 10 years old. The theaters at both places will make a charge for reserved seats of 25 cents for parquet seats and 15 cents for dress circle seats. The balcony circle in both theaters will be free - no charge whatever.

The reasons for making a charge for reserved seats, in addition to the gate entrance, are several. In the first place there has been considerable complaint from persons wishing to engage seats for picnics, parties, etc., that they have been unable to do so, and to procure seats where they were all free, as they have been heretofore, that they were compelled to enter the theater much earlier than they desired if they wished to secure seats. Then if the seats were vacated between the acts, they had no assurance of finding them vacant on their return.

No other resorts in the country furnish so much entertainment and of such a high character for so little money, and they feel that the public will sustain them in the change, especially when they bear in mind that they have over 1,000 free seats, and good ones, in each theater.[13-3]

While the initial season was profitable for the Southern Investment Company, the resort failed to produce the profits expected for the 1892 season. Competition between the two theaters lessened during the 1893 season when Elitch presented a season of plays by the Frank Norcross Stock Company, while Manhattan Beach continued with light opera. The profits of Manhattan Beach improved that season owing to the lack of competition in its opera presentations, as well as to an improved company. In the summer of 1894, the management of Manhattan Beach turned towards dramatic presentations, such as *School,* a comedy by T. M. Robertson, and *The Open Gate* by Haddon Chambers.[18]

Inasmuch as the owners of Manhattan Beach lacked the expertise necessary to obtain and arrange the talent needed for its theater presentations, they enlisted others to manage the theater. Stock companies were engaged. In 1900, an arrangement was made whereby Mary Elitch would lease and manage the theater at Manhattan Beach, for which she paid a rental fee.

The news that Mary Elitch would operate both the Manhattan Beach and Elitch Gardens theaters was first announced in the *Denver Post* on January 28, 1900.[19] Walter Clarke Bellows directed the stock companies at both theaters during the 1900 season. Mary Elitch and her manager, Thomas D. Long, were satisfied with the new arrangement. An article in the *Denver Post* pleasantly noted that Manhattan Beach and Elitch Gardens "will no longer be rival resorts, but friendly ones ..."[19]

In November of 1900, Mary Elitch and Thomas Long married, and after a long honeymoon, returned to Denver where they operated both theaters for the second successive season. The *Denver Times* commented favorably about Mary Elitch's participation in the 1901 summer season.

> Manhattan Beach will open next Saturday night. Mrs. Elitch Long has determined upon a season of comic opera and musical comedy and to that end has brought to Denver one of the best and most evenly balanced singing organizations which has been heard here for many a year.
>
> The latest venture of Mrs. Elitch Long is one of the most pretentious order and will be upon the same complete scale as the dramatic productions at the Gardens. The organization will be known as the Elitch Long Comic Opera Company, and the management have every confidence in their belief that they will make it an honor and a credit not only to themselves but to Manhattan Beach throughout the summer season.[20-1]

The 1901 season was launched by a production of *The Wizard of the Nile,* and the review stated that, "It was a hazardous undertaking for Mrs. Elitch Long to put on an opera company at Manhattan Beach ... (However, the company) possesses many excellent qualities and ... it seems certain to revive popular interest in Manhattan Beach."[20-2] As to the 1901 season, Mary Elitch was quoted in her memoirs as follows:

> This had been a noteworthy summer, from point of attractions, and a very busy one; for Elitch management was not confined to the Gardens. The Elitch-Long Comic Opera Company opened at Manhattan Beach on June 29th, with Florence Wolcott, prima donna, and Frances Graham, contralto. The first opera sung was *The Wizard of the Nile.*
>
> Some of the favorite operas presented were *The Idol's Eye, Girl from Paris, Manila Bound, Madeleine, or The Magic Kiss* and *Lady Slavey.* A special corps of scenic artists was brought from Chicago and Milwaukee, and rich and elaborate costumes ordered from San Francisco. Everything was done on the same pretentious and lavish scale dictated by the policy of the Gardens.[6-2]

While Manhattan Beach continued to "compete" with Elitch Gardens, the bonds between the audiences at Elitch Gardens and Mary Elitch and her commitment to bring the best for their entertainment and a wholesome environment for families favored the Gardens. Many who attended Manhattan Beach were primarily interested in bathing, swimming and boating.* [21]

The summer competition with Manhattan Beach ended in 1908 when a fire occurred the evening after Christmas in the theater[22] and the blaze swiftly became

* The *Denver Republican,* Jul 20, 1902, p. 17, noted that "The close, sultry weather the past week has made Manhattan Beach a veritable Mecca, the boating, bathing and fishing being counted among the chief attractions."

a raging inferno that burned the theater to the ground, as well as other buildings and most of the resort.* The heat from the fire was so intense that it buckled glass windows in nearby Edgewater homes.[17]

In 1909, another resort opened as Luna Park under new management. The park added two roller coasters and attempted to again rival the already famous Elitch Gardens. The theater was never rebuilt and the public began to lose interest in the amusement park. In 1910, another steamboat was christened and known as the *Frolic* for the pleasure of crowds at Luna Park. By 1912, the name of the park was changed back to Manhattan Beach, but the park had had its day. It could no longer meet the competition of its longtime rival, Elitch Gardens, and it closed its doors in 1914.[23] By 1920, the area around Sloan's Lake that housed the amusement parks reverted to marsh and cattails.[24] Sloan's Lake is now owned by the City of Denver and is a municipal park. Over the ensuing years, Sloan's Lake has been revamped and opened for boating and other water recreation. In 1953 a plaque was erected on Sloan's Lake as a reminder of those thriving summer days of yesteryear. Today, Sloan's Lake encompasses 176 acres and is the largest lake in Denver.

Manhattan Beach's "City of Denver" boat on Sloan's Lake

* *Jefferson County Sentinel,* Dec 29, 1966, p. 17. The cause of the fire is not known. There was speculation which included "a few whispers of arson. Some thought a transient vagrant sought shelter in one of the buildings and built a fire to keep warm. Others claimed that defective wiring and a high wind combined to create the holocaust."

Chapter Four

(1892 - 1898)

The Silver Panic of 1893
Elitch Gardens Placed Into Receivership
Mary Elitch Reacquires the Gardens
The Second Stock Season
Thomas Edison's Kinetoscope and Vitascope
Resident Stock Company
Mary's Abiding Love for John Elitch

The 1892 Season

The 1892 season at Elitch Gardens offered a wide variety of vaudeville entertainment in the Theatre and the park. For example, among the vaudeville acts were Eldora, the ideal juggler; Miss Vivian performing the La Serpentine dance, "which she had the pleasure of offering in all the principal cities of the United States"; and Al Newton, the most marvelous manipulator of Indian clubs, performing astounding feats of dexterity and skill as to seem almost miraculous.

The management at Elitch also presented seventeen weeks of light opera by the Aborn Opera Company, including *The Merry Widow Waltz* by Johann Strauss. Newspaper articles indicated that the season of light opera was successful.

Denver's telephone directory for the year 1892 revealed that Elitch Gardens provided telephone service for its patrons. There were only 1700 telephones in Denver, and the progressiveness of Elitch in providing telephone service was appreciated by its patrons.[1]

Ivy Baldwin

A very popular attraction at Elitch Gardens was Ivy Baldwin. From 1890 to 1907, he made a balloon ascent every Saturday and Sunday. He varied his balloon routine by doing stunts on a trapeze as he ascended. In 1902, for the first time, Ivy Baldwin parachuted to earth from the balloon. One Fourth of July as he slid down the rope of the balloon, his suit caught fire, and he spent the next week recovering from his burns. For the occasion, Baldwin had ordered an asbestos suit to avoid this risk, but it failed to be delivered on time for his performance.[2]

The 1893 Season

The corporation known as The Elitch Gardens Amusement Company operated the Gardens through the summer of 1893. The corporation employed the Frank Norcross Company, a stock company organized in New York by actor-director Frank Norcross. It was the first full-length season of summer stock in the history of Denver. It was a challenging and brave undertaking.[3-1] In addition to the twelve plays, there were a total of eight one-act plays presented in three separate programs. The first stock play presented at Elitch was *Nancy and Company* by Augustin Daly. It opened on June 10, 1893.

On July 17, 1893, the Norcross Company presented the three-act comedy *Our Boys* by H.J. Byron that had run in London for over 1,300 nights.[4] Vaudeville performers were at times presented between acts of the plays. Thomas W. Robertson (1829-1918), an English playwright, authored four of the plays presented at Elitch, namely, *Caste, Home, Ours* and *School. Caste* "told how an officer, who is a marquise's son, proves by his devotion to the instinctively well-bred daughter of a common drunkard that social class is no barrier to a happy marriage."[5-1]

> The production of *Caste* led to one of the American theatre's most-celebrated law cases. Lester Wallack had expected to premiere the piece in New York as he had earlier Robertson works, but before he could open his season, (actor and producer) W. J. Florence brought out an unauthorized production. Wallack attempted to obtain an injunction, but Florence argued successfully that "in the absence of international copyright" he had done no wrong, since a quirk in the law allowed anyone who could memorize a play to produce it. Florence claimed he had done just that and was upheld.[5-1]

The Silver Panic of 1893

The economic good times that Denver and the Far West were enjoying for several years abruptly ended in the summer of 1893 with the repeal of the Sherman Silver Purchasing Act. The Act, passed in 1890, authorized the government to purchase 4.5 million ounces of silver monthly and thereby increased the monthly coinage of silver by 125%, boosting the price of silver considerably.[6] In 1892, Grover Cleveland, a man who firmly believed in the gold standard, was elected President. On March 4, 1893, Cleveland was installed as President.

> The administration was not three months old when a series of bank failures and industrial collapses inaugurated the panic of 1893. The treasury's gold reserve was depleted by an excess of imports and by liquidation of American securities in London after a panic there. Gold was subject to a steady drain by the monthly purchase of useless silver required by the Silver Purchase Act of 1890, and by the redemption of greenbacks which by law were promptly reissued and formed an "endless chain" for conveying gold to Europe.[7]

The panic had its immediate effect in Colorado, it being a "silver" state.

> When nine banks closed in Denver within two days, the height of the "Panic of 1893" was reached - July 18, 1893. This catastrophe coincided with the opening of the sixth week of the Norcross engagement at Elitch,

and the economic chaos in the city, as well as in most of the entire country, hardly inspired citizens to think of entertainment and theatre going.[3-2]

Within a period of four days, the price of silver dropped from eighty-two cents an ounce to sixty-two. Investors panicked as the price dropped even more. By midsummer of 1893, a full 90% of Leadville's labor force was out of work.[8] Prosperous citizens became bankrupt. Many seats at the Elitch Theatre remained empty.

Elitch Gardens Placed Into Receivership

Because of the sharp decline in attendance, Norcross left the company before the end of the summer, reporting that he had lost over one thousand dollars on the season.

After Norcross left, Adolph Bernard, the stage manager under Norcross, directed the company during the final three weeks of the season, presenting two old stock favorites, *Home* and *Snowball,* as well as a program of one-act plays. Bernard successfully completed the season, and his workmanlike approach was recognized by the cast in a letter presented to him, along with a gift. In part, the letter read:

> With this note we hand you a trifling testimonial of the very high appreciation and regard in which you are held by your colleagues ... For fifteen weeks we have been associated in our different capacities and ... we have seen and entirely appreciated your honesty of purpose, your tireless energy, your sterling worth and your intelligent, well-directed and successful efforts for the common good.[9]

Notwithstanding the successful emergency efforts of Adolph Bernard, the attendance at Elitch and at other places of amusement dropped substantially, and by the middle of August the Gardens were placed into receivership.[10]

The 1894 Season

Mary Elitch Reacquires the Gardens

In April, 1894, Mary Elitch reacquired ownership of the Gardens by a purchase under a deed of trust for $150,000.00.[11-1] With Mrs. Elitch as sole owner, the Gardens returned to presenting vaudeville programs for the summer. Advertisements and programs carried the title, "Elitch's Zoological Gardens and Grand Pavilion Theatre."[3-3]

Among the many vaudeville acts appearing that summer were The Brothers Borani, the famous and marvelous disappearing demons from the Follies Bergere in Paris, with all their costly and magnificent stage setting. And there was Professor Sherman's herd of educated goats; Berkely and Howard, sketch artists; Sandow, the strong man; Emma Francis, contortionist; The Stone Brothers, acrobatic comedians; Melville, aerialist; Halton, cannon ball performer; and Cunningham and Grant, song and dance team. Charles W. Goodyear appeared "with a few stories, some of which are old, cold, and a few that have not been told." Master Charles Carter added to the entertainment, "the most wonderful of modern prestidigitators in a series of marvelous conjuring feats, and sleight of hand manipulation." Charles Schilling appeared as the "musical comedian."

Charles Schilling [12]

Charles Schilling had managed the Gardens during its opening season in 1890 and again during 1891 following the death of John Elitch. After Mary Elitch reacquired ownership of the Gardens, Schilling was again engaged as manager for 1894 and 1895. He was Treasurer from 1897 through 1899. During the summer of 1898, Schilling married Mary Elitch's sister, Anna Hauck. Mr. Schilling later became involved in business in California, setting up home in Los Angeles, where Mrs. Schilling continued to reside following his death.

The 1895 Season [11-2]

Every winter it was the practice of the Elitch management to devote time and money to improving and beautifying Denver's popular family resort. The 1894-95 winter season was no different. During the summer season of 1895, there were more flowers, more shade trees and more ground than ever before. In addition to the 20,000 extra plants scattered about, "an acre and a half of ground has been added, a grove of pine trees set out, new walks laid, new fences built, and the new summer house erected makes the new part the prettiest corner of the grounds." A new and popular feature was the fish pond, which was kept well stocked with different varieties of fish, from black bass to carp.

Realizing that many of those who made the trip to the Gardens did so on bicycles, the management had a long railing built just inside the gate, "where wheels will be checked free of charge, and cyclers may enjoy the performance in the Theatre or the pleasures of the grounds without fear of finding their wheels missing when ready to return." The Theatre was "entirely remodeled and enlarged and is claimed to be the most beautiful summer resort theater in the United States."

The season of 1895 began with six weeks of vaudeville programs. Among the acts were Ford and Lewis, burlesque acrobats; Jerome and Alexis, the "Human Frog"; Martin's Dog Circus; Stack and Milton, horizontal bar act; Harry Sefton, dancing spider; Reto, contortionist; Granjeau and May, wire performers; Coogan, Ben Mowat and Son, club-swingers; and Rand and Tafe, the "greatest break-neck act before the public." However, when box office receipts dwindled, Mary Elitch abandoned the vaudeville programs and engaged the Dunbar-Pyke Opera Company, a light opera organization which originated in Boston and was touring the West on its way to California. Because of previous commitments, however, the company was able to remain at Elitch for only six weeks. Since other companies were not then available, the managers concluded the season with four weeks of vaudeville, which included Charles Schilling's minstrels; Damora, acrobat; Sato, juggler; Price Paul, ventriloquist; Charles Goodyear and Al Leach; and Meeker and Mack, comedians.

By 1895, the worst of the depression caused by the Silver Panic of 1893 was over. As individuals gradually recovered from the crash, suburban areas began to develop, increasing both the size and population of the Denver area.[3-4]

The 1896 Season

The Second Stock Season

In 1896, the second stock season was a slight roller coaster ride with a positive ending. It was described concisely as follows:

> In 1896, Mrs. Elitch signed J. H. Huntley to direct a resident stock company, headed by Jennie Kennark (who had been leading actress at Manhattan Beach the previous season) in a series of popular melodramas. The season opened with *Rosedale,* a Lester Wallack success. After six weeks of melodrama, however, and a few unsatisfactory notices, the organization of the company was changed. Huntley, who was not very popular with audiences or with newspaper reviewers, was replaced by Walter Edwards, leading man at Manhattan Beach in 1895. Since there had been criticism against the type of plays being offered, the plays under the direction of Edwards were lighter – more comedy-drama and comedy and less melodrama.[3-5]

Huntley left the company on July 11, 1896. Walter Edwards became director on July 12, 1896. Theatergoers and drama critics approved of the change to Edwards and of the new play selections. The first play directed by Edwards was J. K. Tillotson's *A Gilded Crime.* The newspaper review carried the following comment:

> *A Gilded Crime* seemed to please the audiences greatly ... Walter Edwards' presence has strengthened the company materially ...* [13-1]

Maude Fealy, who was to become a well-known Denver actress, made her debut in the Theatre during this season, playing children's roles.[13-1] She first appeared during the week of July 19th in Henry C. De Mille's *The Lost Paradise.*

Among the many other plays presented during the season were Richard Blanchard's *The Galley Slave,* William Haworth's *Ferncliff* and Steel MacKaye's *Hazel Kirke. Hazel Kirke* was written in 1880 and was "among the very first plays to send out road companies, five of them touring while the original production remained in New York."[5-2]

* Walter Edwards appeared at Elitch Theatre as an actor with the Elitch company during the 1897 and 1898 seasons and later in 1912.

Thomas Edison's Kinetoscope and Vitascope

Beginning in 1892, Thomas Edison's invention of the Kinetoscope enabled people to see "moving pictures" in penny arcades or peep shows. Simply stated, one would drop a penny into a slot on the machine, peep through an opening, crank the machine, and a light would flash on to illuminate a series of scraps of film that would turn in sequence for a minute. You could see, for example, "Fatima wiggle her torso or a small boy squirt the garden hose on a well-dressed gentleman."[14-1]

> The Kinetoscope was as far as Edison considered it expedient to take his new invention. Pleased with the flood of pennies that flowed in from the peep show parlors, he feared that if he were to project his images so that more than one person could see them at a time, the audience would soon be exhausted. But the pull of "living pictures" magnetized a host of would-be Edisons here and abroad. By 1895, the Kinetoscope had a lively imitative competitor in the Mutoscope, and strenuous efforts were being made by a score of mechanically-minded men to combine the Kinetoscope principle with that of the magic lantern, so as to throw a larger-than-life-size picture on a sheet or on some other white surface.
>
> Prodded by the many imitators who threatened to reap the rewards of his ingenuity, Edison finally sanctioned the projection of his tiny film images on the rudimentary equivalent of today's theater screen.[14-2]

Edison's enhanced invention became known as the Edison Vitascope. The first public performance of the Vitascope was held on April 23, 1896 in the famed Koster and Bials' Music Hall in New York. It was indeed a new and exhilarating experience for the onlooker.[14-3]

On August 14, 1896, Mary Elitch introduced guests of the Gardens to the Edison Vitascope, allowing astonished locals to be the first in the West to share the experience of seeing moving pictures on a screen, an experience that was the precursor to movies as we known them today. The scenes shown were the Leigh sisters in their umbrella dance, breaking waves on the sea and a boxing match.[15]

The second picture represented the breaking of waves on the sea shore. The effect was simply marvelous. Wave after wave came tumbling on the sand, and as they struck and broke into tiny floods just like the real thing, some of the people in the front row seemed to think they were going to get wet and looked around to see where they could run to in case the waves came too close.[15]

The promise by Mary Elitch to introduce the patrons of the Gardens to the Vitascope was the subject of a very favorable article in the *Daily News*.

> There is one thing noticeable about the management of Elitch, and that is the striking manner in which it keeps its promises. The management

of the Gardens does not believe that promises are like pie crust, easily broken, or that they are made to be broken. It believes in keeping religiously every promise made to the public ...

As in the case of the Vitascope, a great many wondered what it was when the management advertised the only Edison Vitascope to be exhibited in Denver. Thousands have seen for themselves during the past week, and it is safe to say that it has more than justified all the good things said concerning it in advance of its appearing here.

Commencing this afternoon several new pictures will be shown, and, by request, the ocean scene from off the coast of Dover, which made such a hit the first week of the Vitascope, will be reshown.[13-2]

The 1897 Season

Improvements in the Gardens

Once again, improvements were made by Mary Elitch in the Gardens for her patrons to enjoy. Rustic benches were scattered plentifully throughout the grounds for sweetheart couples to enjoy. Stone walks took the places occupied by the gravel ones of other years, with those from the entrance to the Trocadero and Theatre being the most noticeable. A rustic bridge was built over a little waterway near the greenhouses. New fountains and fish ponds were added. The gardener set out 35,000 plants, and their effect in bloom was ideally beautiful. Not the least of all was a baby monkey born in the Gardens' zoo that the children were happy to see.

The Theatre building had twelve new fashion boxes in its auditorium, and the settings of the stage were almost entirely repainted.[16]

Resident Stock Company

Mary Elitch decided to establish a resident stock company plan at Elitch. This proved to be far more successful and dependable than the rather haphazard booking of individual vaudeville acts. Until 1899, vaudeville performances were sometimes presented between acts of plays. Beginning with 1901, vaudeville was eliminated at Elitch.

From 1897 until she relinquished control of the Theatre management in 1915, Mary Elitch followed the policy of having a resident stock company for a full season, augmented with occasional guest stars. The season usually began in June and continued through the first week of September. For the most part, actors of the resident company, numbering between ten and eighteen, were engaged for the entire season and were seen in nearly every production of the summer.

The company of actors, each well-known as a special stock character type, was recruited and cast in New York or Los Angeles and brought to Denver to play in ten plays.

The summer cast consisted of a leading man and a leading lady, a character actor and actress for older parts, a juvenile ingenue, a first and second business man and a first and second business woman, a comic, perhaps a "soubrette" (a coquettish male or frivolous young woman in comedies), and so forth. If minor supporting players or extras were needed, they were selected from the list of local amateurs (usually supplied by the acting schools of Margaret Fealy and Robert Bell) or from former professional actors who had moved to Denver to make their home.

If a leading player had to depart for New York or Hollywood in the middle of a season, as would occasionally happen, a "star" was engaged to replace him or her.

Louis Calhern (1895-1956), the formidable actor of stage and screen, received his early experience in theater playing stock in New York and St. Louis. He valued the experience, stating:

> Principles grounded in the minds of students in schools of dramatic art are of inestimable value, undoubtedly, but unless one gets actual experience with the hard knocks that are inevitable, which only comes from playing before an audience, all the instruction in the world will be of no advantage.
>
> I believe in stock companies. It is intense, laborious work, for, while actors are appearing in one play, they are rehearsing another and probably studying a third. I grew up in stock and there I learned much that I know about acting. I played many parts with considerable variety in character, mood and period.[17]

Many excellent actors, like Louis Calhern, enhanced their acting ability and careers with stock company experiences. The stock experience made for versatility and resourcefulness, provided training for memory and developed in the actor the self-confidence needed to meet the challenges of a theatrical career.

The early theater stock companies in America were essentially localized. They were staffed by a permanent resident company which acted exclusively in that theater and who lived in the community. Each theater with its company was an independent entity, for there was no inducement for it to establish a business relationship with other theaters. In general, actors' ambitions were satisfied if they could advance from utility man to leading man.

For many reasons, the local stock company gradually faded away.

> Even the actors and actresses, well-liked and admired as they usually were, eventually grew somewhat wearisome. They were so well-known in the community in their private capacities that John Doe as Hamlet was never wholly the melancholy Dane, for there was always something of friend John showing through the make-up.[18]

Another disadvantage of a small local company was its inability "to mount a sufficient variety of plays, and miscasting and hasty productions are sometimes inevitable."[19] The local summer theaters then began to look to New York (and later, also to Los Angeles) each year for actors to make up a resident stock company for the summer season.

For many reasons, with each passing season, the lure of playing at Elitch Theatre continued to grow. Jennie Eustace, one of the cast members of the 1912 Elitch-Long Stock Company, expressed her feelings about appearing at Elitch.

> When I was asked to come to Elitch Gardens for the summer, I think I was the most delighted player on Broadway.
>
> Now, imagine a player who has worked hard in New York for season after season without any sort of vacation except, possibly a couple of weeks in June or July at the seashore. For an opportunity to get out here to your Colorado and just lounge about a place like Elitch Gardens the player would almost trade all his worldly possessions. Elitch is famous all over the country for its restful beauty.
>
> Among all the players I know, I don't believe there is one - no matter what his or her prominence - who would not shout for joy at receiving an invitation from Mrs. Long to join the Gardens Stock Company for the summer.[20-1]

Clarence Handyside, another 1912 cast member, appearing for the second straight season, and who had long been a favorite in New York, expressed his sentiments about leaving.

> There is always a touch of real sadness about this breaking up of the summer stock company. The relationships one forms at this time of the year are closer than those formed by the members of companies on tour in the winter. There the actors are traveling all the time and are stopping in different hotels, so that they seldom see each other except at the theater. Here we are just like one big family. This is particularly true here at Elitch Gardens.
>
> Mrs. Mary Elitch Long looks after her family of summer players with such care - finding them delightful homes, promoting fine friendships, arranging many pleasures for them - that the work here doesn't seem like work at all, but just one long, pleasant outing. The actors are thrown together so constantly that they get very fond of each other, and used to the little family circle.
>
> When the last curtain shuts us from the audience, and we gather on the dimly-lit stage for the last time to say good-bye, there are lumps in every throat, and tears in every eye.

> The summer here at the Gardens has been delightful during every moment. The players have been more than congenial, and Mrs. Long and the Denver public more than kind. None of us want to go away.[20-2]

On May 30, 1897, Mary Elitch opened the season with the play *Helene,* by Martha Morton. James O'Neill, father of playwright Eugene O'Neill, who had visited the Theatre during its construction, came back to be the leading man during the 1897 season. James O'Neill had known John Elitch in San Francisco and honored a promise he had made to him that "I'll come back and play on that stage whenever you say."[21]

Mary's Abiding Love for John Elitch

Mary's love for John Elitch never left her. At the season's end, his remains were moved at her request from California to Denver and on September 17th, John Elitch was buried at Fairmount Cemetery, where he now rests beside Mary, his lovely Lady of the Gardens.

The 1898 Season

The summer of 1898 was the second season that Elitch had its own resident stock company. George Edeson returned as director of the season's plays.

Notwithstanding the gallant efforts of Mary Elitch, the second season of a resident stock company was not without growing pains. Frank W. White, the drama critic for the *Denver Post,* felt that the Elitch company of actors was not as strong as it might have been.[22] Overall, however, the season resulted in good attendance at the Gardens and a better profit. The summer of 1898 was unusually hot and this encouraged a night out at Elitch in the cool air of the mile-high city.

In addition to live theater, patrons were attracted by entertaining vaudeville acts. Vaudeville acts were performed during the last several weeks of the season and, on occasions, at matinees and between the acts of a play. The matinees during the season were held free of charge.*

* The matinee performance was introduced to American audiences by Dion Boucicault (1822-1890), the great actor who appeared for more than fifty years on the English stage. The first matinee performance in America was presented in New Orleans. His son, Aubrey, would be among the cast of players at the Elitch Theatre during the 1903 season. Dier at p. 81.

Mr. Boucicault first tried the matinee performance in London, and when it met with immediate success, he decided to introduce the idea in America. *Denver Post,* Jul 7, 1901, p. 14.

Ivy Baldwin's Ascension Balloon

Walter Edwards (1912)

Chapter Five

(1892 - 1898)

The Theatrical Syndicate
Actors' Equity Association

The Theatrical Syndicate

No writing of theatrical history should omit reference to the formation of the Theatrical Syndicate, its sensible good intentions, and later its stranglehold on theatrical decisions.

Gradually, prior to 1900, summer theaters across the country began to grow in number and sought performers for their seasons. New York City was initially the site of their search. Theater managers in large numbers poured into the city in the middle of June, after the close of the Broadway theatrical season, to negotiate deals.

> Union Square was then the theatrical center of the city, and it was here that the managers of theaters and the managers of attractions met, negotiated and consummated their agreements. Permanent theatrical offices were at first virtually unknown, and the business was conducted almost entirely in the street, on the park benches or in the lobbies and barrooms of the hotels which served as the headquarters for the visiting theatrical people. Managers of theaters rushed about looking for the managers of the attractions they wanted to book, while they dodged the less desirable offerings; the attractions sought the theaters they were anxious to play and remained cold to the others until driven toward them by lack of anything better. Every company manager boasted of the drawing power of his star and his production. Every theater manager talked of the attendance records which his house had rolled up during the previous season. Disengaged actors were there too, all of them stars in the telling, besieging the managers for engagements. Rumor and gossip filled the air.[1-1]

This method of doing business was casual. Written contracts between actors and theaters were rare in those early days of booking. This often had chaotic consequences. For example, if the manager of an actor received a better offer, he would simply notify the theater that the actor would not be able to appear at the scheduled time. An actor might have agreed to three different contracts with the hope that one would materialize.

As a result, in 1895, the Theatrical Syndicate was formed, and "its ostensible purpose was to bring order to the chaotic booking practices then prevalent in the theater." Within a short time, however, the Syndicate negotiated agreements with virtually all major legitimate theaters, not only in New York City, but also in the rest of the country, to structure the business of theater. In this manner, the Syndicate gained control of such theaters and monopolized the theatrical industry. It was "in a position to dictate script choices, production styles, salaries, royalty agreements, ticket prices and even advertising rates."[2] As a result, the Syndicate forced actors and rival managers to accept financial terms and booking arrangements dictated by the Syndicate. It determined what plays would be produced and available and also what touring companies would bring them. Indeed, the Syndicate maintained "a practical stranglehold on the American theater."[3-1]

Prior to the creation of the Theatrical Syndicate, Peter McCourt (1859-1929), the brother of "Baby Doe" Tabor, exercised significant control over entertainment presented to theatergoers in Colorado.[4] As the railroads and the miners traveled west to Colorado, in the late 19th century, McCourt began signing up theaters throughout the front range of Colorado as their booking agent in order to entice East Coast theatrical attractions to travel to Colorado to the various cities along the "silver (entertainment) circuit" rather than perform in only one city, like Denver. McCourt had a virtual monopoly on which groups were booked and where they played throughout Colorado. However, his influence lessened over the years, as the New York Theatrical Syndicate and later the Shubert brothers gained control over nationwide theater bookings.[5]

By 1901, the Theatrical Syndicate controlled the following four theaters in Denver: Broadway, Lyceum, Denver (Wonderland) and the Tabor Grand Opera House. However, the theater at Elitch Gardens operated from its beginning as an "independent" theater and did not succumb to any involvement with the Theatrical Syndicate. It was and remained the only "independent" theater operating in Denver during the years of the New York Theatrical Syndicate monopoly. As to the availability of Broadway plays for Elitch to present, the study by Edwin Levy has the following comments:

> Because of the fact that the New York Theatrical Syndicate controlled the production rights of many plays of outstanding literary and dramatic quality, these works were not available to Elitch until long after the original Broadway presentation. Nevertheless, there is evidence to substantiate the fact that the "popular" successes were sometimes presented at the Gardens within a few months after the New York premieres.[6-1]

Actors who opposed the Syndicate often found themselves unable to get work in suitable theater venues, touring the country performing in rundown auditoriums, gymnasiums and tents. Certain managers and actors who had individual drawing power, such as David Belasco, Minnie Maddern Fiske, Sarah Bernhardt, Richard Mansfield, Joseph Jefferson and Henrietta Crosman rebelled against the Syndicate. [6-2]

In the summer of 1902, the Independent Booking Agency organization was created in opposition to the Syndicate to establish a rallying point for the independent movement of managers who desired to control their own bookings.[1-2]

> As the only "Independent" theater operating in Denver during the years of the New York Theatrical Syndicate monopoly, Elitch Gardens attracted, between 1903 and 1908, the touring companies of several staunch opponents of the Syndicate: Henrietta Crosman, Minnie Maddern Fiske, Sarah Bernhardt and David Warfield. The appearances of these players greatly enhanced the reputation of the Gardens during a period when Denver audiences were almost completely dependent upon the whims of eastern managers for theatrical entertainment.[6-3]

As the reputation of Elitch grew, the Theatre's ability to attract actors was greatly enhanced. The relatively pleasant summer climate of Denver proved a stimulus to actors who desired a change of scene from the hot summer weather of theaters in the larger cities of America, such as New York, Boston and Philadelphia.

> (As time went on), the Syndicate was blamed for much that ailed American theater and drama. Conceived as a purely business enterprise, the Syndicate had no interest in theater as an art form. Plays, actors, and designs were valued strictly in economic terms. Playwrights and composers, if they wished to sell their work, were required to produce standardized comedies, melodramas and operettas that conformed to the proven formulas. Actors were regarded as interchangeable commodities and allowed little or no range, expected to play the same type or even the same role for years on end.[2]

The opposition of actors had some effect on the Syndicate. The monopoly was broken by an organization built by the Shubert brothers who, beginning in 1900, created a nationwide network of their own theaters. By the time of World War I, "the Shuberts had supplanted the Syndicate as the dominant force in American theater, forming a mini-monopoly of their own." However, in later years "they often gave substantially reduced rents to struggling, worthwhile attractions and kept many theaters in the legitimate fold that might otherwise have been lost to movies or burlesque." In 1973, the various interests of the Shubert brothers' companies were restructured as the Shubert Organization which continues to own and operate many Broadway houses, as well as others in large cities in America.* [3-2]

Actors' Equity Association

The Actors' Society of America was formed in 1895 in an effort to standardize contractual obligations between performers and producers. Following the

* For a history of the Shubert Brothers and their role in show-business see Stagg, *The Brothers Shubert* (Random House 1968).

death of its leader, Louis Aldrich, the influence of the group declined until it was finally dissolved in 1912.[3-3] Following the dissolution of the group, Actors' Equity Association was founded on May 26, 1913 by 112 actors in New York City. They recognized the need for "equity" in the relationship between actors and producers.[1-3]

The first president of the union was comedian Frank Wilson. George M. Cohan, composer, actor, director and producer, was opposed to the union, stating, "I will drive an elevator for a living before I will do business with any actors' union." A sign later appeared in Times Square reading, "ELEVATOR OPERATOR WANTED. GEORGE M. COHAN NEED NOT APPLY."[7]

Some of the long list of abuses regularly suffered by actors included the following:

> A lack of standard contracts, irregular wage payments and frequently no payment for work performed, unlimited rehearsal periods without pay, the stranding of road companies that closed suddenly with no provisions for sending actors home, the need for actors to provide their own transportation and wardrobe without compensation, the ability of managers to fire actors at will, and the lack of recourse for actors to challenge management short of prolonged and costly legal battles.[8]

The concept of Actors' Equity made slow progress, and in 1919, the actors went on strike, closing virtually all the Broadway theaters. The public, becoming aware of the indignities suffered by actors, wholeheartedly supported them. Equity prevailed as a viable organization, and theater managers acceded to the demands of "equity," and the unfair exploitation of the actor came to an end.

The contract benefits of Equity now include the following:

> Minimum salaries (negotiated rates, overtime, extra pay for additional duties, free housing or per diem on tour); work rules (length of day, breaks, days off, safe and sanitary conditions); health, pension and 401(k) benefits; dispute resolution (including recourse to impartial and binding arbitration); just cause (penalties for improper dismissal); bonding (guaranteeing payments to the Actors if producer becomes insolvent or defaults); and Supplemental Workers' Comp insurance, which provides additional compensation over-and-above Workers' Comp if you're injured on the job.[9]

The Elitch Theatre ultimately became an Actors' Equity Association theater and had to employ Equity actors and abide by Equity rules. An Actors' Equity theater was permitted to employ a certain percentage of non-Equity performers and negotiate with them on an independent basis.

Chapter Six

(1899 - 1902)

Selecting a Director
Henrietta Crosman
Theater Etiquette
Advice to Aspiring Actresses
Eloquence of Actors and Actresses
Marriage of Mary Elitch to Thomas D. Long
Blanche Walsh and Rose Coghlin
Mary Elitch and Thomas Long Circle the Globe
Improvements to the Theatre
The Shakespearean Plays

The 1899 Season

Selecting a Director

Mary Elitch obtained the services of Thomas D. Long as business manager. Charles Schilling was retained as treasurer, and the word "zoological" was dropped from the title of the resort, which has since been known as "Elitch's Gardens."

As Mary Elitch became more and more aware of the needs of Elitch Theatre for it to achieve success, she knew that the selection of a director was a critical element in the success of the performance of plays. In this regard, Mary Elitch engaged Walter Clarke Bellows as director. His tenure continued through the 1908 season. Bellows was well-known and respected in Denver, having previously been a director at the Broadway and Lyceum Theaters. He had also been stage manager for Charles Frohman at the Lyceum Theater in New York during the 1896 and 1898 seasons.

> For the most part, theater is not seen by spectators as fragmented but as a single experience. Though made of many parts, a theater event should form a complete picture. This is not a simple matter. Theater is one of the most complex of the arts, involving not one or two elements, but many simultaneously: script, performance, costumes, scenery, lighting and point of view. These diverse elements - a mixture of the tangible and intangible - must be brought together into an organic whole.[1-1]

It is the director's responsibility to bring the many elements of theater together on stage. For example, he or she is particularly responsible for the performers' interpretations of their roles.

> During the rehearsal period, the director must make certain that the actors are realizing the intention of the playwright, that they make sense of the script and bring out its meaning. Also, the director must ensure that

the performers are working well together and must help them overcome any personal problems they have, such as insecurity about a role or fear of failure.* [1-2]

The director must also decide on *blocking* the play, that is, establishing the places where actors move and position themselves on stage. The director guides the performers to make the best use of stage space. For example, a fireplace, with its sense of warmth, can become an area to which a character returns for reassurance.

> If one performer hides another at an important moment, if a crucial gesture is not visible, if an actor makes an awkward movement, if an actress cannot be heard when she delivers an emotional speech, the director points it out. Also, the director underscores the meaning of specific scenes through visual composition and stage pictures, that is, through the physical arrangement of performers on stage. The spatial relationships of performers convey information about characters. As an example, important characters are frequently placed on a level above other characters: on a platform or step, for instance. Another spatial device is to place an important character alone in one area of the stage while grouping other characters in another area. This causes the eye to give special attention to the character standing alone.[1-3]

In essence, the director represents the eye of the audience. He must be able to see the production from the theatergoer's point of view and direct the production toward the playwright's intended effect. In this role, the above examples are but a few of the many concerns of a director. There are others.[1-4] Over the years, in this regard, the Elitch management had been fortunate in their selection of directors.

As director, Walter Clarke Bellows was also responsible for the selection of the plays to be performed and the cast. That summer, Bellows decided to present *Cyrano de Bergerac* in Denver for the first time. The play by Edmond Rostand had premiered in Paris on December 28, 1887. The cast of *Cyrano* called for 76 speaking roles, with extras added, for about one hundred people on stage. This did not deter Bellows from accepting the challenge. Mary Elitch described the rehearsals and the success:

> Rehearsals appeared like nothing but an amazing mix-up of professionals and amateurs. The task of assembling this enormous crowd of people into the smoothly functioning company that thrilled the record attendance at every performance was bravely tackled and effectively and brilliantly accomplished. It was indeed a triumph of

* In the Clifford Odets play, *The Country Girl,* the plot centers around the director's efforts and challenges to overcome the insecurity and fear of failure of Frank Elgin, the lead character in the play he is directing. The movie version (1954) of the play cast William Holden as the director, Grace Kelly (received an Oscar for best actress), and Bing Crosby as Frank Elgin.

tremendous labor and surprisingly successful results.[2-1]

During rehearsals, Bellows was known to be mild-mannered and rarely became excited in guiding the company. He was patient and understanding of inexperienced actors.

Ray Southard, an actor who appeared in several productions staged by Bellows during the years 1899-1908, in an interview with theater director Edwin Levy of the University of Denver, recalled that Bellows planned all of the major movements before rehearsals began. Southard stated:

> There was never any wasted time at rehearsals. He was always careful to explain why certain business was called for, and if there was any question about the reason for a movement or a bit of action, he could always give us a good reason for it. He developed a great deal of confidence in the actors. Sometimes, however, he would get up on the stage and act himself, if someone wasn't "getting" what he was driving at. Bellows himself couldn't act enough to keep warm, but he could give the actors a good basis to build on.[3]

Bellows also initiated a policy of outdoor rehearsals in a secluded garden spot near the Theatre building, whenever feasible and practicable. He observed that actors seemed to work better in comfortable surroundings, away from the confines of a stock theater. Actors expressed pleasure at "rehearsing a play in the brightness and warmth of Colorado sunshine, with the greensward instead of boards for a stage and trees for a background."[4-1]

Bellows also impressed upon the actors the importance of an actor's first entrance on stage. "It must be effective; it is remembered longer than anything else immediately following," he contended. Further, he believed the most striking entrances were made "well upstage" and "from an elevation."[4-2]

During the winter months, the Theatre had undergone a number of changes. Formerly, there was only one exit from the lower floor, but this was changed to three, one in the center and one on either side. A ladies retiring room was provided. New boxes were built and were so placed that every move of the performers could be seen. To the right and left of the stage, two Venetian screens provided a pleasing effect. Every piece of scenery was new. Moreover, an artist was engaged to continually prepare scenes that were to harmonize with each play presented. The seating capacity in the Theatre was increased by over 200.[5-1] New electric equipment replaced the original gas fixtures in the Theatre.[4-3]

The plays selected for the season provided another banner year for theatergoers. The season opened with *The Charity Ball* by David Belasco and Henry C. De Mille. On July 19th, a record crowd witnessed the play *Madame Sans Gene* by Victorian Sardou. It was reported to be "the greatest Wednesday in the history of the resort."[6]

Victorien Sardou was one of the most successful French dramatists of his day. The season also featured *Diplomacy,* another of Sardou's plays. Elitch's resident stock company was busy with these and other plays. The female lead for the season was the well-known Henrietta Crosman.

Henrietta Crosman

Among the many performers that had graced the stage at Elitch, Henrietta Crosman's return was welcomed as one of Denver's favorites. The *Denver Times* had this to say:

> Miss Crosman came to Denver several years ago and became, and is now, one of the most popular players who ever visited the West. Her name alone is sufficient to give any company the stamp of excellence. Twice since her first visit has she returned, once to a stock organization and last season as a star.[5-2]

Henrietta Crosman (1861-1944) was born in Wheeling, West Virginia and made her first appearance on stage in 1883 as Lily in *The White Slave.* She began to receive more important roles until her final New York appearance in *Thunder in the Air* (1929). She continued to act, however, until shortly before her death. In the book *Sixty Years of Theater* she is described as "an exceedingly bright and capable performer, of considerable range and much technical expertness."[7-1] She returned to Elitch Theatre with her own company in 1903.

Theater Etiquette

From time to time, the Elitch management reminded its theatergoers to arrive at the Theatre before the opening of the play and discreetly urged women to remove their hats as they had become so large that those sitting behind them could not see. The following caveat appeared in the Elitch Theatre program for the week of June 3, 1899:

> The curtain will rise promptly at 2:10 for the matinee and 8:10 for the evening performances. It is hoped by the management that patrons will be in their seats before the curtain rises - thus avoiding the disturbing of others after the play has commenced. This frequent evil will be somewhat abated if our patrons will remember that such impoliteness more often arises from thoughtlessness than from bad breeding. * [8]

Hats became a contentious issue, and "decorously worded notices appeared in programs, suggesting that a lady's crowning glory was her hair - not her hat."[9]

The 1900 Season

Mary Elitch expended whatever effort and expense necessary in welcoming the twentieth century by making the 1900 season as successful as possible. She selected

* This caveat appeared from time to time in Elitch Theatre programs.

sixteen excellent plays that included among them William Shakespeare's *As You Like It,* Henrik Ibsen's *A Doll House,* Madeleine L. Ryley's *A Coat of Many Colors* and Clyde Fitch's *The Moth and the Flame.* Because of the number of plays presented, the cast had more leading actors than in later years, as well as guest stars that joined the company.

In presenting the play *As You Like It,* the rear wall of the Theatre building was temporarily removed so that the stage could extend out beneath the trees producing the ultimate achievement of forest and pastoral scenes. Clearly, in the words of Mary Elitch, it "was a masterpiece of staging and theatrical art."[2-2] *As You Like It* was the first Shakespearean play to be presented at the Elitch Theatre.

Among the great performers engaged by Mary Elitch to appear at Elitch was Blanche Bates. In a recent appearance in the role of Miladi in the New York production of *The Three Musketeers,* "her magnificent interpretation of Dumas' polished adventuress, lithe and sinuous in her movements, fierce and sensual, full of fascination and craft, tempestuous in temperament and emotion, made her the most notable figure upon the New York stage and the undisputed heroine of the theatrical season." Extraordinary inducements were offered to her by Mary Elitch to cause her to cancel her European holiday and to cable from London her acceptance of the Gardens invitation.[10-1]

Blanche Bates appeared at Elitch following her successful New York appearance as Cho-Cho-San in *Madame Butterfly.* Having been born in Portland, Oregon, Blanche Bates loved the West. Moreover, she loved Denver so well that she built herself a home on Inspiration Point in the northwest part of the city.[11]

On July 17, 1900, Elitch Theatre celebrated its fifteen hundredth performance from the installation of a stock company at the resort. The occasion was made a memorable one by Mrs. Elitch. The festivities included music all day by the well-liked Adelmann orchestra and at night by a magnificent display of fireworks. It was estimated that about 12,000 people joined in the celebration.[10-2]

Advice to Aspiring Actresses

In an article that appeared in the Denver Post, Blanche Bates offered advice to young aspiring actresses.

> You want me to tell you what a girl must do and what a girl must be to really do something worthwhile in this business? ... She must sacrifice everything for her work. She must give up home, friends, family, society, sweethearts, fun of all kinds. She must give up eating, she must give up drinking - at least, regularly ... She must be physically perfect to be able to endure the strain of work. She must be beautiful, she must be talented beyond the average actress, she must be patient, enduring, long-suffering, industrious, good-natured and young - and then - she must

forget completely that she is anything but a very ordinary, hard-working actress. She must be madly and irrevocably in love with her work.

> An actress must love her work more than anything else in the wide world, and be willing to walk right over everything else in the world for it. She must feel every part that she plays as if it were herself who was passing through the experiences of her character ... She must forget heaven and earth, herself and all her surroundings in her part, and she should never attempt to play a part that she cannot feel ... Your audience gets from you just what you give it. If you give people nothing more than lines they will get nothing more than lines. They will not know just what is the matter, but they will know that something is wrong.[12-1]

Eloquence of Actors and Actresses

Theatergoers are sometimes startled by speeches given by actors and actresses upon their receipt of an Oscar or Tony Award that do not seem to measure up to the eloquence displayed by them in the theatrical performances for which they are being honored.

Blanche Walsh, an accomplished actress, brought some understanding to the subject in a speech she delivered in New Orleans at the turn of the 20th century to a large company of women, in which she defended the heroines in the plays of the successful French dramatist, Victorien Sardou (1831-1908). The following were her initial comments:

> I must preface this informal talk by first asking your indulgence. This is my initial attempt at a speech, and it is with some diffidence that I essay it. One is apt to imagine that the flow of rhetoric from a professional - an actress - is as easy as breathing; the fact is overlooked that in the portrayal of our various roles, utterance is put into our mouths by the playwright, easy enough under these conditions to be poetical - rhythmical - versatile or humorous. So in the endeavor to say something to you I have made an unpleasant discovery. I find I am no essayist, no orator, that to clothe one's thoughts in fitting garments is no easy task.[12-2]

Notwithstanding the prefatory remarks by Blanche Walsh, her speech was excellent, thought-provoking and well-received.

Frederick Perry

Frederick Perry was a member of the cast in 1900 and 1904. The story is told that on one occasion he arrived late for a matinee performance, "and with his mind elsewhere, sensed he was not alone as he arrived at the stage door. Turning, he found himself face to face with Sam, a large black bear who had escaped from the Elitch Zoo, and who fancied the actor for lunch. Perry skipped through the door just ahead of Sam, and a few moments later was performing on stage. Audience members at that performance noted that the actor seemed just a bit off his stride."[13]

Marriage of Mary Elitch to Thomas D. Long

On November 21, 1900, Mary Elitch became the bride of Thomas D. Long in a quiet and simple ceremony at the cottage in the Gardens.* A few intimate friends and relatives of the parties were present. Father William F. O'Ryan performed the wedding ceremony. Burns Mantle, the well-known drama critic and friend, was best man. At the time of the wedding, Long had been manager of Elitch Gardens for three years, and it was largely through his able and far-sighted direction that marked improvements in the Gardens had been accomplished. The newlyweds left for a trip to New York City and other Eastern cities. Most of the winter was spent in New York before returning to Denver.[10-3]

At the wedding reception held for them upon their return, the toast given by Burns Mantle was as follows:

Here's to Tom and Mary Long
Where hearts are right and never wrong;
And this is the burden of our song:
May Tom have Mary Elitch Long

The 1901 Season

The Winter Before the 1901 Season

Mary Elitch spent the winter of 1901 in Washington D.C. where she, Walter Bellows and Thomas Long operated the Lafayette Square Theatre. When the Gardens opened for the 1901 season, patrons noticed that a beautiful fountain had been added, and new animals had become part of the zoo, among them a family of monkeys, an Egyptian camel and baby mountain sheep. New and elaborate electric lighting gave added brilliance to the grounds and buildings. The citizens of Denver welcomed the new summer season.[2-3]

By 1901, the popularity of Elitch Gardens and its Theatre was of national interest. Again, the play selection was excellent. It included Oscar Wilde's *A Woman of No Importance,* J. M. Barrie's *The Little Minister,* Victorian Sardou's *La Tosca* and Tom Taylor and Charles Reade's brilliant comedy *Peg Woffington.*

Various star performers were engaged for the season to play leading roles for periods of several weeks, supported by the strong resident company. Among the star performers were Blanche Walsh, Rose Coghlan and Maude Fealy. Edward Morgan was selected to play the feature role in *The Only Way.*

The season was a profitable one.

* For many years prior to his assuming the management of Elitch Gardens, Thomas Long "had charge of the retail department of Mr. Scholtz's drug business, and in this position, by a uniform courtesy and a naturally magnetic personality, he made many friends." *Denver Times,* Nov 21, 1900, p. 2

Blanche Walsh

Blanche Walsh came to Elitch for a four-week engagement, beginning with the play *Under Two Flags.* In *Romeo and Juliet,* Blanche Walsh played Romeo and Maude Fealy played Juliet. It was said that when she is "really interested (in a part), there is not a woman on the stage who plays with the same fire and intense realism of Blanche Walsh."[12-3] The attendance "during Miss Walsh's engagement was record-breaking, the receipts were large, and the management was accused of unheard of liberality when it became public that Miss Walsh was receiving a weekly salary of $750."[2-4]

The *Denver Post* commented on the increased attendance at the Theatre.

> No place of amusement in Denver has ever drawn and continued to draw such enormous crowds as has Elitch's during the past two weeks of Blanche Walsh's engagement. It has been practically impossible to secure a seat any night after the curtain has risen, while standing room has been at a premium and unattainable at every performance.[10-4]

In *Under Two Flags,* Blanche Walsh played the role of "Cigarette," a spunky woman accompanying a French regiment to sell provisions and liquor to the soldiers, one of whom (Bertie Cecil) she loved. She was a splendid character from many points of view - always true, always brave, crude, loyal, vivacious, and able to swear like a soldier. She was willing to do anything to defend her country and her man. Needless to say, it was a difficult, demanding and challenging role for any actress. Blanche Walsh's interest in the role was reflected in a review of the play.

> Blanche Walsh played "Cigarette" last week with vast impetuosity. She was never quiet a moment. She filled the part from the time she entered the stage in the second act until she died to the thrilling music of the Marseillaise in the arms of the French soldiers. It was a wild, vivid, picturesque performance, full of vitality and dominated by the strong, turbulent personality of the player.[12-3]

The Resignation of Hobart Bosworth

Although Blanche Walsh was initially at Elitch for a four-week engagement, she agreed to remain for the rest of the summer as the permanent star of the stock company. Her engagement as a stock star led to the resignation of Hobart Bosworth, leading man of the company. Earlier in the season, Bosworth did not like it when cast member John T. Sullivan was given the title role in *The Little Minister,* but as Bosworth was not a small man, he had to surrender the role. When Blanche Walsh later became a permanent fixture with the company, he withdrew, as "he believed he had been engaged as leading man of a stock company, not to support a star." Robert Lowe, who had been Miss Walsh's leading man in the past, cut short his summer vacation and headed west to assume the leading man role at Elitch.[12-4]

Rose Coghlan

Mary Elitch engaged Rose Coghlan to be featured in three of the final four plays of the season, namely, *Peg Woffington,* Oscar Wilde's *A Woman of No Importance* and the world premiere of *Fortune's Bridge* by Charles Coghlan, her brother.*

While Miss Coghlan affirmed that one of her favorite stage plays is *Peg Woffington,* she admitted that "my particular reason for coming to Denver was to produce my brother's play - the one he finished just before his death. It is called *Fortune's Bridge,* but he didn't give it the name. Rather odd, by the way, the accident that gave the play that name."

> My brother Charles had left it in manuscript form, but it needed to be typewritten. It was sent to a typewriter. At the end was my brother's signature and his Canadian address: "Charles Coghlan, Fortune's Bridge." The typewriter girl put the address at the head of the first page so that it read "Fortune's Bridge, by Charles Coghlan." And the name seemed to fit the play so well I allowed it to stand.[12-5]

The play was written by Charles Coghlan especially for his sister Rose. He was an exceptionally gifted writer and actor and "was universally acknowledged (as) the most cultured leading man of his time."[12-6]

Preacher Warns to Prepare for the World's End

Not far from Elitch Gardens, its amusement rides and theatrical presentations, Rev. C. H. Bates delivered a sermon on July 17, 1901, warning that he expected the world to end at any hour. He believed that members of his sect would be housed in a home in a city on earth, "with streets of gold, gates of pearl, and all the splendor described by St. John." He was unable to identify the location of the city, but its dimensions would be 375 miles square and "the population will never vary, as there will be no marrying nor dying, and no additions to the elect." He concluded his sermon by reminding those present that should the world still exist on August 25th, the sect would hold its annual camp-meeting.[12-7]

Mary Elitch and Thomas Long Circle the Globe

After the 1901 season's end, in September, Mary Elitch and Thomas Long decided to circle the globe. Following a three-week stay in New York City, they returned to Denver for a few days before traveling to the Pacific Coast to commence their six-month tour around the world, starting with a steamer to Honolulu, then on to Tokyo, Canton, Hong Kong, Singapore, Ceylon, Calcutta, Bombay, Egypt, Rome, and through the Mediterranean to Gibraltar, just to name a few of the stops along the way. She was entertained by celebrities of the theater in London, Paris, Vienna

* Rose Coghlan, one of the featured actresses of the season was the wife of John T. Sullivan, also a member of the cast. *Denver Post,* July 23, 1901, p. 3. However, it appears that the two were in the midst of marital difficulties. See *Denver Post,* July 21, 1901, p. 17.

and Berlin. At a dinner given in her honor in Paris, a distinguished Frenchman introduced her, and surprised her by his first comment: "Madam has the most beautiful garden in America." They sailed home from London to New York City and then to Denver, arriving in April of 1902 in time to complete arrangements for the following season at the Gardens. The long ocean voyage had been recommended by Mrs. Long's physicians, as she suffered more or less from a nervous condition for several years, more than likely connected to her grief over the death of John.[14]

Notwithstanding the pyramids of Egypt, the elephant ride in India and climbing a crater to the center of Vesuvius, Mary Elitch stated upon her return, "I must say, the most delightful scenery we saw in our trip was the shore of Staten Island as we sailed into New York harbor ... It was a most enjoyable trip, but I am glad to be at home where I can feed the bears and lions and hear my own Colorado birds sing."[15-1]

The 1902 Season

Improvements to the Theatre

By the start of the 1902 season every building about the resort had been freshly painted and renovated. The Theatre evinced significant changes and improvements to such an extent that it was scarcely recognizable, even to its oldest patrons. Aisle steps had been entirely abolished and replaced by slanting aisles. The stage had been widened. The foyer which surrounded the auditorium was removed, the space being given to the auditorium proper. Seats were added. The number of exits was increased to nine on the first floor and to four in the balcony, thereby assuring a quick and safe exit for the audience. The number of exits allowed for a "complete emptying of the house in two minutes from the time of curtain fall, which is promised for this summer at 10:30 p.m. promptly."[16]

Elitch Theatre was examined for safety and the result was favorable and noted in the *Denver Times.*

> As a result of the visit of the building inspectors to the Theatre at Elitch Gardens the verdict has been given that it is the best constructed and safest structure of its kind in the United States.
>
> The Theatre, which has been remodeled, has 175 seats added to its former seating capacity. Three more aisles have been made and an exit is placed at each aisle. The Theatre is in fine condition.[17-1]

The Plays and Players of the Season

By this season Elitch Theatre patrons anticipated and expected the best in plays. Mary Elitch Long wanted no less than such expectations. In addition to the Bellows stock company, she adhered to her successful policy of bringing to the Gardens from time to time noteworthy stars of the theatrical world for featured roles in plays supported by the regular stock company. Among those special guests appearing in featured roles were Herbert Kelcey and Effie Shannon, Jessie Bartlett Davis, Marie Wainwright, Edmund Lyons and Maude Fealy.

Herbert Kelcey and Effie Shannon

Effie Shannon (1867-1954) was born in Cambridge, Massachusetts, and first appeared on stage as a child extra in a play in Boston in the early 1870s. Her career in theater was to span seventy-years. Herbert Kelcey (1856-1917), was born in England and after two years of performing there he came to America where he made his debut in 1882. Stardom came to each of them when they appeared opposite each other in 1898 in *The Moth and the Flame.*[7-2]

The play *Her Lord and Master* was written by Martha Morton especially for Kelcey and Shannon and was an instant and remarkable success when presented in New York for a ten-week engagement earlier in the year. Denver audiences were thrilled that it was among the selection of plays for the Elitch season.

> *Her Lord and Master* is not alone a powerful play, but it is an absolute novelty to the larger portion of Denver audiences, and, at ordinary times and in the regular season, local theatergoers would pay five or six times as much as the Elitch tariff and would in all probability witness a cast and staging which would suffer by comparison with the Garden's standard.[17-2]

My Lady Dainty was the second play that featured Kelcey and Shannon and it was also well received. The drama critic noted:

> As a whole, *My Lady Dainty* is one of the best presentations of the summer theatrical season, and a most commendable feature was the evenness of last night's performance. The company has had but one week's rehearsal, and yet not a line, not a situation was marred by the least degree of unfamiliarity. The fact that the entire cast was so admirably adapted to the parts and was so thoroughly conversant with the general atmosphere of the play gave the production a tone worthy of a metropolitan presentation.[17-3]

Not to be overlooked, however, was another significant factor that most likely contributed to the "evenness" of the performances. Many of the members of the company had played with Kelcey and Shannon on previous occasions. Accordingly, they knew their methods and fit into their respective parts "with that nicety which insures the most delightful and harmonious of results."[17-2]

The Shakespearean Plays

Jessie Bartlett Davis (1861-1905) was recruited by Mary Elitch to be featured in Shakespeare's *A Midsummer Night's Dream.* The *Rocky Mountain News* applauded the choice.

> A characteristically clever stroke of business and a brilliant engagement upon the part of Mrs. Elitch Long is the securing of Jessie Bartlett Davis for the production of *A Midsummer Night's Dream* by the Bellows Stock company ... The combination is superlatively attractive. Jessie Bartlett Davis has no peer among American singers.[18]

Ms. Davis studied voice in Chicago, then spent several years with various opera companies before joining the famed "Boston Ideal Opera Company." In time the group became popularly known as the "Bostonians." Those who were members of the ensemble group were of such high quality that they were recognized as the foremost group of its kind.[7-3]

The regular season boasted another Shakespearean play, *Twelfth Night,* in which Marie Wainwright played the featured role. The audience enjoyed the two Shakespearean plays during the regular season. Their positive reaction resulted in the addition of Shakespeare's *The Merry Wives of Windsor* featuring Edmond Lyons to a supplementary season.

Maude Fealy

As the season progressed and actors left to fill other engagements, changes were inevitable. At this time, Maude Fealy joined the company. She had previously appeared at the Elitch Theatre as a young girl in her stage debut. In the meantime, her career had flourished. As a young girl making her debut many years before, "she was engaged for the Elitch Theatre at the tremendous salary of $10.00 a week. Now, returning as (the) leading lady, she received the summer salary of $750.00 a week. She had commanded in her one year on the London stage a salary exactly one-half that of the President of the United States ..."[2-5] Maude Fealy was featured at Elitch in *The Little Minister, Her Majesty* and *The Christian,* the final three plays of the season.*

The *Denver Republican* applauded her performances in those three season-ending plays.

> Maude Fealy's local fame and popularity have been successfully enhanced by her Babbie in *The Little Minister* and her Honoria in *Her Majesty.* Her Glory Quayle in *The Christian* forms the apex of a triumphant triangle of successes. So great has been the hit made at the Gardens by Miss Fealy, and so pronounced and spontaneous has been the public desire to see her, that Mrs. Elitch Long has decided to extend her season one more week. In none of her varied roles has Miss Fealy been awarded a higher meed of public and critical praise than in Hall Caine's powerful play, *The Christian.* Her conception and interpretation of the part is said

* Maude Fealy first appeared in *The Little Minister* at Elitch in 1902 and would present it for a third time during the 1903 season.

to combine the ingenuousness of girlhood with the finished art of the actress. Her Glory Quayle is a beauteous, breathing entity, radiant with youth and winsome in the purity of its feminine charm.[15-2]

Stage Designs

Between the period 1893 and 1899, the Elitch Theatre used generalized or "stock" sets for nearly all the dramatic productions. These were comprised primarily of wings and backdrops, an attempt at scenic reality which was in general use in the American stock company from 1850 to 1900.

By 1898, the Gardens had accumulated ten complete sets, including the following: a garden, a wooden house, a "modern" house, an ancient house, an office, a street, a kitchen scene, a dense wood, a castle, and one described merely as a "center-door setting."[19]

Walter Clarke Bellows, in addition to his directorial skills in guiding actors through their performances, also emphasized the importance of scenic stage designs. His leanings were toward the David Belasco school of realistic stage designs. The management financially supported the improvement of scenic stage designs for the plays. In 1902, it was estimated that an average of $1,000.00 was spent each week for the needed scenery.

Director Bellows always had a sense for realistic casting techniques. In the play *Shenandoah,* the battle scene of the third act called for a knowledge of military behavior. Rather than engaging various local actors, Bellows hired militiamen with military training from the Denver community. As a result, Bellows vividly produced on the Elitch stage all the "pomp and circumstance of glorious war" with "the splendid climax of the tide of battle and wavering rout stemmed by Sheridan and his devil-may-care riders." The big Elitch stage provided the amplest of opportunities for a magnificent alignment of the famous battle scene with platoons of infantry and squadrons of cavalry.* [12-8]

The Reputation of the Gardens

Further evidence that the reputation of Elitch Gardens was known all over the world was reflected in a news article.

In *Die Woche,* an illustrated periodical published in Berlin, Germany, there appeared last month a lengthy article upon the Gardens with two full-page pictures of Mrs. Elitch Long with her bear and other animal pets.[17-4]

* During the 1906 season, Bellows selected members of the Arion Club, a social group composed of German-speaking youths of Denver, to act as the German students in his production of *Old Heidelberg.* Newspaper reviewers praised the realistic touch and were generally impressed by the group's singing of German songs. *Denver Republican,* Jun 11, 1906, p. 3.

Denver Pubic Library Western History Collection - No. z-1951

Maude Fealy (1902)

Denver Pubic Library Western History Collection - No. MCC-1226

Patrons of Elitch Theatre circa 1900

Chapter Seven

(1903 - 1904)

Henrietta Crosman, Maude Fealy, Amelia Bingham, Edwin Arden, Antoinette Perry

The 1903 Season

Henrietta Crosman

Henrietta Crosman (1861-1944) returned to Elitch Theatre with her own company and appeared in several preseason plays, namely, *As You Like It, Sword of the King* and *Mistress Nell.* She had performed successfully in each of these plays on the New York stage. Miss Crosman and her company also appeared in theatrical presentations of *Nance Oldfield* and *Madeleine, or The Magic Kiss.*

She made her first stage appearance in 1883. By the turn of the century, she had performed for such theater greats as Augustin Daly, Daniel and Charles Frohman and A. M. Palmer. However, it was in the role of Nell Gwynne in *Mistress Nell* (1900) that she approached stardom. In *Sixty Years of Theater*, it is stated that Henrietta Crosman's Nell Gwynne "will long be remembered for its variety, its animation, its delightful deviltry and its general fascination."[1]

Henrietta Crosman, like Sarah Bernhardt, Minnie Maddern Fiske, Richard Mansfield, Joseph Jefferson and others, rebelled against the Theatrical Syndicate. Upon her arrival in Denver, she made it known that she was an "independent" star, stating that "I'm not in the Syndicate."[2-1]

The Season

In addition to the preseason plays with Henrietta Crosman, an additional fourteen plays were presented as part of the regular season, which included *In the Palace of the King, A Royal Family, The Little Minister* and *The Little Christians.*

The featured roles were shared among various players and were supported by a large resident company. Walter Clarke Bellows was the director for this season and for many other seasons to come.

Members of the cast were often attracted to the animals of Mary Elitch's zoo. Such was the case with cast member Theodore Roberts.

> Early morning found him at the edge of the (bear) pits tendering choice breakfast fruits to the willing creatures below ... His method of feeding was by way of a long fish-pole, with the prize attached. He would fish by the hour after this manner, and the bears became adept in the sport of removing the bait.
>
> While thus engaged Mr. Roberts one day realized the loss of a very

highly prized ring. It had been devoured, but the loss of this valued treasure did not dim the actor's enthusiasm for the bears. When the loss was reported, Mr. Bellows, the director said: "Well, now I suppose Theodore has enough of the bears and will report to rehearsal on time." Not so, Theodore only seemed to grow fonder of Sam, who worn his ring internally.

Mr. Roberts, for the sake of family peace, managed to make better time at rehearsals thereafter; natheless,* many hours were spent in silent contemplation of the rotund body wherein reposed the souvenir of his London triumph as Canby in *Arizona.*[2-2]

Maude Fealy - In the Palace of the King

Maude Fealy was named the "most beautiful woman in the world" in an international beauty contest in Paris, France, April 20, 1903.[3] That summer, she returned to Elitch Theatre and in July she appeared in F. Marion Crawford's *In The Palace of the King*, as dramatized by Lorimer Stoddard, the first of the four plays in which she was featured. The play shows up the weakness of kings, at least King Philip of Spain, about November of 1570. The cowardly king, having killed a cardinal, cries to his brother Don John, "You must save your king. You must take the blame for this murder."

> In those early days a king's word was about as near as law as we can get things.
>
> Don John, being a dutiful subject, takes the blame, and when he is about to be led away to execution, the woman he has loved (Dona Maria Dolores) since childhood comes to the front. In bold words she tells King Philip that she will expose the plot unless he frees the brother. She knew all about it, for she had been hiding behind a curtain when the king struck down the cardinal.[4-1]

Maude Fealy was chosen for the role of Dona Maria Dolores. Unfortunately, the drama critic felt it was a role not entirely well-suited to her talents, which occurs from time to time to the best of performers.

Another critic who witnessed her performance of Dolores in *In the Palace of the King*, and who called the play "a badly constructed drama," sharply criticized the talents of Maude Fealy, although he later remarked that "I may be wholly wrong in my conclusions."

> It may be a sort of blasphemy to give my impressions of Miss Fealy, but, frankly, I can see no worthy advance in that much coddled young person.

*The word "natheless" is the archaic expression for "nevertheless, notwithstanding."

She continues to be singularly artificial, to invariably recite her lines, never to breathe into them the breath of life. Always that same monotonous rising inflection, that clear, well-studied elocution, that parrot-like utterance, sometimes suggesting a whine ...

It is too bad, for fundamentally there is a great deal to Maude Fealy. She has been finely, patiently, tenderly trained. In phrasing, attitudinizing, vocalizing, hours and days, months and years have been spent on her. A mother's unquestioned skill, a mother's love, a mother's splendid hope has been hers. And the finished product does that good mother infinite credit.

There are voices Maude Fealy does not hear, colors she does not see, doors that should be opened to her, but which cannot be unlocked until the surging sentiments of life rush over her.

To be the youngest leading lady the wide world has ever known does not in its actuality mean that one can sit complaisantly in the temple of Minerva and hold the place. To wear short frocks and carry one's hair gracefully down the back after reaching and passing the voting period may intensify ability, but it does not carry conviction.

It is, I take it, simply an expression of a mother's soft and beautiful love for "her baby." A mother's dislike to lose the child in the woman and, as such, it is a condition to be respected, respected profoundly. Still is it not largely a mistake?

Someday a man will come along - God grant he may be a good man - who will break down the motherly barriers and gaily carry Maude Fealy away to the mountains of the moon. She will then know life, its yearnings, its sweetness, its passions, its sorrows and its joys.

Then will she be an actress; a player to stir, to thrill, to move her auditors. At present she does none of these things. She is merely the reflex of her maternity; she is dominated, controlled, managed by the worthiest of dragons. It seems to me the time has come for a change.[4-2]

Upon further reflection, the critic recognized that Maude Fealy "is today a commercial success. She drew more money last year, and the year before, and will again this summer, than any star at the Gardens. She appeals strongly to the crowd. She satisfies and interests." And then he learned that when the sale of seats opened for her forthcoming performance at Elitch in *A Royal Family*, within an hour 2,700 seats were sold, with the crowd still clamoring.

The sharply critical assessment of Maude Fealy by the drama critic must have caught her attention as she went on to become an *actress*, in the critic's sense of the word.

Clearly, no other profession must deal with rejection as much as that of an actor or actress, with audition after audition hoping to move toward the pinnacle of one's ambition, that moment of greasepaint and applause.

The 1904 Season

An article in an August edition of the *Chicago Sunday Tribune* commented on the season of plays at Elitch Theatre:

> While the rest of the country has been in the theatrical dumps, the city of Denver has been the bright spot on the map. Much of the best of the fare given during the winter and spring to the East and Middle West has been served to Denver theatergoers since June 1st. And served, too, under conditions nearly ideal from the popular standpoint.
>
> The approach to the Theatre and the medley of outdoor entertainments is between rows of cherry and apple trees, under boughs that interlink, and beside flowering beds of every color and fragrance.
>
> The Gardens ceased long ago to be merely an amusement park. Its function is more that of a public resort catering to all kinds of pleasure-loving people, and conducted with a rigorous standard of cleanliness ...
>
> The Theatre, however, is the magnet for grown people, whether they are residents of Denver or visitors from the East; and that East, from the standpoint of Denver, includes Chicago as well as New York.[2-3]

Walter Clarke Bellows continued as director. The resident company included Bruce McRae, Henry Woodruff, Helen Tracy, Frederick Perry, Edward Mackay, Theodore Roberts and others. Maude Fealy, Amelia Bingham, Edwin Arden and May Buckley were among the featured players in several plays. Ernest Truex appeared in a few plays.

Noisy Children

The Theatre programs for the 1904 season, for the first time, contained the following admonition:

> Children in arms positively not admitted to Theatre. Ladies having in charge children who become noisy will be expected to promptly remove them from the Theatre.[5]

Amelia Bingham [6-1]

Amelia Bingham (1869-1927) was born in Hicksville, Ohio, and was educated at Ohio Wesleyan. She pursued a career in theater notwithstanding her deeply religious family's opposition. After a successful stage career in New York, she became an actress-manager on Broadway.

Miss Bingham appeared at Elitch in *Olympe* by Pierre Decourcelle, a play taken from the Alexander Dumas novel *M'lle Olympe De Cleve*. There are seven scenes in the play that takes place in Avignon, Lyons and Paris in 1758 during the reign of Louis XV.

> Olympe is an actress and in the opening scene she goes to the cloisters of Avignon. There she meets Jacques Banniere, who is studying for the priesthood. The young man falls in love with the fair actress, follows her to the theater and later deserts the priesthood and becomes an actor. He gives up this profession in turn and becomes a soldier. An odd complication is brought about by the fact that an actor deserts the stage and takes the place of the young priest in the work of the church.

While *Olympe* is a romantic drama, it is also known as a costume play. In addition to her excellent performance skills, Miss Bingham brought to Elitch the original costumes used in the New York production. She had spent some two months in France creating the costumes for the play, and, as a result, they were historically correct. One gown alone cost Miss Bingham $1,000, which gives one an idea of their beauty.

A Denver theater patron who had seen the play in New York commented - "If there was nothing to *Olympe* but the gowns, I could go a score of times to see the beautiful creations of Amelia Bingham."

Maude Fealy

After Amelia Bingham's departure from Elitch, the popular Maude Fealy joined the stock company and was featured in the next three plays, *The Cavalier, Janice Meredith* and *When Knighthood Was in Flower*.

Several months earlier the Elitch management made an effort to secure *The Prince and the Paupe*r for Miss Fealy, but the details could not be arranged. After Miss Fealy had concluded in *When the Knighthood Was in Flower, The Prince and the Pauper* was offered to the Gardens. Following her performance in Denver, Miss Fealy was scheduled to leave for England to join Sir Henry Irving's company in rehearsal for the forthcoming season. After a number of telegrams were exchanged between Miss Fealy and Sir Henry Irving, a delay was secured for her to remain an extra week in Denver. Miss Fealy agreed to take the dual role of *The Prince and the Pauper* in a dramatization of Mark Twain's book of that name. The play opened for a week commencing on July 31, 1904. Immediately after, Miss Fealy left Denver and after two days in New York sailed for England in time to open her engagement with the English actor on September 2, 1904.[6-2]

Miss Fealy became the leading lady for Sir Henry Irving, an English actor who dominated the last thirty years of Queen Victoria's reign. He was the first actor to be knighted.

It is said that Sir Henry Irving first became attracted to Miss Fealy because of her kindness in caring for his pet cat when she was occupying his dressing room in a London theater while he was touring the provinces, furnishing the cat daily fresh cream and new neck ribbons. The thoughtfulness of the young actress led the gentleman to watch her stage progress. While Sir Henry was playing in Buffalo some months later he took advantage of an opportunity to attend a matinee at the theatre where Miss Fealy was playing. His pleasure over the performance of the young star resulted in the invitation to become his leading lady.[7]

Edwin Arden

Edwin Arden, who was to have played at the Elitch Theatre for at least two weeks, left suddenly after a single week's stay, after appearing in *Soldiers of Fortune*. Before coming to Denver, Arden appeared in the *Soldiers of Fortune* leading role of Robert Clay for two weeks in Washington where his success "was of a record-breaking order." It was natural that the Elitch management sought him out to perform the part in Denver.

That the piece was a "go" was proven by the advance sale of tickets. The management of Elitch announced that "no more reservations can be made by telephone, owing to the long line of people who are constantly buying tickets at the downtown office in Scholtz's drug store."[6-3]

The play was well-done, well-acted and well-patronized, which left theatergoers wondering why Edwin Arden left suddenly after a single week's stay. The next play to be presented was *The Prince and the Pauper*. Certainly, Arden was not a failure. Under these circumstances, rumors circulated. In an article in the *Denver Post*, Frank W. White, its drama editor, described the essence of what occurred. The matter was essentially commercial.

> It was just this way: Maude Fealy's three weeks' engagement was a great financial success. More money was made through her than with any other stock star during this or any other season, and when it was found that the management could have her for another week, if they tried, of course they tried.
>
> An arrangement was conditionally made whereby Miss Fealy should put in a fourth week, and at the same time put money in her own purse and that of the Gardens. The proposition was essentially commercial.
>
> But there was Mr. Arden to be dealt with.
>
> Therefore Manager Long went to Actor Arden on the second night of *Soldier of Fortune* and said something like this: "My dear fellow, you have been engaged for the Gardens for two weeks, with a possibility of three, and your salary is to be four hundred dollars per week. Now, we can make more money with a local star than with you, and I want to say that

if you are willing we will next Saturday pay you for two weeks (at the end of one week's engagement) the full eight hundred dollars and you can retire. There is no possible dissatisfaction with you. You have pleased and satisfied. There is more money, however, with Miss Fealy, and I feel sure you can so understand."

Mr. Arden saw the position at once, took the money and probably went off fishing, while the managerial acumen was demonstrated by the packed houses that greeted Miss Fealy in *The Prince and the Pauper.*[6-4]

Antoinette Perry

Antoinette Perry was born in Denver, Colorado in 1888. She first appeared at Elitch Theatre this 1904 season as the fifth actress in the play *Olympe.* She later appeared during the 1908 season with David Warfield, Marie Bates, William Elliot and others in the preseason special productions of *The Music Master* and David Belasco's *The Grand Army Man.*

After her marriage to Frank Wheatcroft Freuauff in 1909, she retired from the stage to raise a family. Her two daughters successfully pursued careers in the theater. In 1922, after the death of her husband, she returned to the stage and appeared in many plays, after which she was active as a director and producer. She helped organize the New York Stage Door Canteen, and she served as chairman of the board and secretary of the American Theatre Wing. She died in 1946 at the age of 58. In 1947, the American Theater Wing established the Antoinette Perry Awards in her memory, and they have been presented annually for distinguished achievement in theater. The awards are commonly known as the "Tony" awards. The Tony award consists of a medallion depicting the masks of comedy and tragedy on one side and the profile of Antoinette Perry on the other side mounted on a black base.* [8]

Brief Comments About Some Plays

A Japanese Nightingale had never been given by any stock company in the United States before the Elitch presentation. The play required 125 players. It took several weeks of hard work to orient the chorus and dancers, let alone the other members of the play. The costumes used in the play were those used in the New York production. However, the New York owners of the costumes refused to allow them to be used without security being established for their safe return, for which the Elitch management provided a $10,000 cash bond. Pending their use, the costumes were placed on exhibit in a window of a downtown department store. In all, there were 219 costumes.

To secure the play, the management had to pay the largest royalty fee ever given for a play by a stock company. The management also paid an express charge of

* For a complete listing of winners and nominees of the American Theatre Wing's Tony Award with a history of the American Theatre Wing, see Stevenson and Somlyo (editors), *The Tony Award* (Heinemann 2001).

$100 for delivery of the costumes. Notwithstanding the expenses of production, the Elitch management did not increase the price of admission to the play.[6-5] Every regularly scheduled performance brought a crowded house, with the result that many patrons did not get to see it. Accordingly, the management scheduled three extra performances.[6-6]

Denver Public Library Western History Collection

Amelia Bingham

Chapter Eight

(1905 - 1906)

A Week of Shakespeare
Ernest Truex, Cecil B. De Mille, Maude Fealy
Minnie Maddern Fiske
Sarah Bernhardt and Douglas Fairbanks

The 1905 Season

The Opening of the Gardens

So eager were the people of Denver for the opening of the Gardens in the spring of 1905 that more than twenty thousand passed through the gates on the opening day.[1-1]

A Special Free Attraction

The Elitch management announced that it would have a special free attraction each week during the season. The attraction for the first week was Dr. Carver, who gave an exhibition of his great prowess with a rifle. Also Dr. Carver entertained the crowds with his two diving horses, Powder Face and Cupid, who dove from a raised platform thirty-five feet high into a pool of water.[2]

The Season

The season of 1905 had May Buckley and Bruce McRae in the leading roles and numerous supporting cast members, including Cecil B. De Mille, Ernest Truex, Olive Oliver, Eleanor Cary, Theodore Roberts, Charles Dixon, Julia Stuart, Harry Willard, Edward Mackey and J. Henry Kolker. In addition, there were featured players such as Maude Fealy, Minnie Maddern Fiske, Tyrone Power and Edith Crane. In her memoirs, Mary Elitch recalled that:

> As the season progressed many new names were added to the roster of my company as some favorites departed to fill other engagements.
>
> With the departure of Miss Buckley, Miss (Maude) Fealy appeared after another successful winter in London. Tyrone Power and his wife, Edith Crane, followed Miss Fealy. It will be recalled that Power's portrayal of Judas Iscariot in *Mary of Magdala,* supporting Mrs. Fiske, was rated as the most striking and intense characterization seen in New York for many years. I shall never forget the beauty of his voice nor his first utterance as he entered the Gardens: "I am about to realize a great ambition, and that is to play in the Elitch Gardens Theatre."[1-2]

The regular season boasted of numerous plays that included Edwin M. Royle's *My Wife's Husbands* and Paul Kester's *Dorothy Vernon of Hadden Hall. In the Palace of the King*, which was among the plays of the 1903 Elitch season, was again selected for the 1905 season. Minnie Maddern Fiske appeared in a pre-season presentation of C. M. S. McClellan's *Leah Kleschna.*

A Week of Shakespeare [3-1]

In past seasons, Mary Elitch Long delighted in offering her theater patrons "a week of Shakespeare." For example, *As You Like It* during the 1900 season, *Romeo and Juliet* in 1901 and *Twelfth Night* in 1903. This season it was *The Taming of the Shrew.* The Shakespeare week was said to be "a rather startling departure from the beaten path for summer garden theaters, but Mrs. Long is ever introducing departures from old ruts at the Gardens."

As You Like It was presented earlier in the season for only part of a week. Some patrons had the impression that this was the Shakespeare "week." However, Mrs. Long explained that *As You Like It* was "put on for the purpose of presenting Miss (May) Buckley in a more serious role than she had been seen ... (it being) the first time she had ever played Shakespeare." The *real* Shakespeare week at Elitch was *The Taming of the Shrew*, which featured Tyrone Power and Edith Crane.

Ernest Truex

Ernest Truex appeared at Elitch as a member of the supporting cast in *Tess of the d'Urbervilles*, which featured Tyrone Power and Edith Crane. Truex was born in Rich Hill, Missouri in 1889, where he made his first appearance as a child prodigy in 1894.[4-1] He later lived in Denver and was among the supporting actors at the Elitch Theatre, appearing during the 1903, 1904, 1905, 1906 and 1907 seasons.

> Ernest Truex began his career of "walk-ons" at Elitch while he was still a student at East High School (where his classmates included Douglas Fairbanks, Paul Whiteman, Harold Lloyd and playwright Mann Page). In addition to children's roles, Truex was assigned a variety of parts which ranged from "pages to executioners."[5]

He made his New York debut in 1908, appearing in numerous plays throughout the years, such as *A Good Little Devil* in 1913 and *George Washington Slept Here* in 1940. He continued acting for another 25 years, including roles with the American Repertory Theatre in 1946. He died in 1973.[4-1]

Cecil B. De Mille

Cecil B. De Mille was born on August 12, 1881 in Ashfield, Massachusetts. He became interested in theater and enrolled in New York's American Academy of Dramatic Arts. He made his acting debut on Broadway in 1900. He was invited to become a member of the Elitch company of 1905. Although he appeared in eleven of the fifteen plays presented that season, he played minor roles.

Following his summer at Elitch, De Mille gained further experience as an actor and a playwright.* He appeared in two successful Broadway shows - *The Prince Chap* (1905) and *The Warrens of Virginia* (1907).[6-1] He co-authored several plays with his brother William, namely, *The Genius* (1906), *The Royal Mounted* (1908) and *After Five* (1913).[6-2] The plays were moderately successful but definitely not "best sellers."

Notwithstanding Cecil De Mille's study, interest, and experience in theater, and some dabbling in playwriting, he is best remembered for his work in motion pictures and is "generally acknowledged as the man who more than anyone else helped Hollywood become the world's greatest film center."[7]

In 1926, more than two decades after Cecil B. De Mille appeared with the cast at Elitch Theatre, he sent the often-quoted telegram to John M. Mulvihill and the Elitch Company.

> It is a long time since I spent a very pleasant summer in stock at the Elitch Gardens. Today in Hollywood I can hardly go anywhere without meeting one or more now rather famous people who either during that summer or at other times played in what all actors and actresses consider one of the greatest cradles of the drama in American history. As you start a new season, permit an old-time actor in Elitch's Gardens to wish you a continuance of that success which was so rightfully yours in the early days of the stage. With kindest regards. Cecil De Mille.[8]

Maude Fealy

Following Maude Fealy's season in England as leading lady with the Sir Henry Irving Company, she returned to Denver to appear in the Elitch 1905 season and cemented her friendship with the people of Denver, knowing that she called Denver "home."

At the opening night performance of *Mice and Men* the public from all sides of the city and from every station in life was there to cheer and applaud her and to "cause her to recognize the fact that she has a firm and lasting place in their hearts and that they are proud of her; proud of herself personally and proud of the fact that a Denver girl has reached the eminence in her chosen profession that she has attained."[3-2] Denver society was scheduled to receive her the following evening.

A special matinee performance was held on August 31st to display the talents of Miss Fealy in scenes presented from *Becket* and *Romeo and Juliet*. Mary Elitch Long designated the event as Maude Fealy day and turned over the proceeds of the day less expenses to Miss Fealy.

Among the plays that featured Maude Fealy this season was *Dorothy Vernon of*

* De Mille's father enjoyed success in writing plays that were professionally produced. In addition, his older brother, William De Mille, was also an established playwright.

Haddon Hall. She was cast in the play with a young Cecil B. De Mille, who assumed the role of the "heavy." The play involved a scene in which they had to fight a duel with broad swords and De Mille coached the young actress for the scene. They became lifelong friends. After De Mille made his mark in Hollywood as a producer-director, he cast her in nearly every one of his epic films, including a part for her in *The Ten Commandments*.[9] Maude Fealy was also a dramatic coach for De Mille for more than ten years, training such performers as Nanette Fabray and Lynn Overman.

Minnie Maddern Fiske

Minnie Maddern Fiske (1865-1932) was one of America's greatest actresses. She was born in 1865 in New Orleans to the manager of the St. Charles Theatre and of Lizzie Maddern, an actress. She began her theatrical career on stage at the age of three and was billed as "Little Minnie Maddern." She made her New York debut in *A Sheep in Wolf's Clothing* in 1870. In adolescence she toured across the country in melodramas and farces and performed in roles such as Little Eva in *Uncle Tom's Cabin*, Prince Arthur in *King John* and other youthful roles. She then returned to the New York stage where she excelled in several plays. She achieved stardom in the role of Stella in *In Spite of All* (1885).

In 1890, she married Harrison Grey Fiske, editor of the influential *New York Dramatic Mirror*, and announced her retirement from the stage. Four years later, she could no longer resist the lure of the stage and appeared as Nora in *A Doll's House*, which brought her recognition as a serious actress. Thereafter, she remained active in the theater until a few months before her death in 1932.[10]

Together with others such as Sarah Bernhardt and David Warfield, Mrs. Fiske and her husband opposed the monopolistic Theatrical Syndicate in the early years of the century. As a consequence, the Fiskes were unable to secure rights to those plays by writers who were represented by the Syndicate. As in the case of Sarah Bernhardt and others who opposed the Syndicate, the Fiskes were forced to play in undesirable venues and even in tents. Harrison Fiske exposed the business tactics of the Theatrical Syndicate in 1897, which led to "a protracted libel case and the Syndicate's banning of any productions featuring Fiske's wife ... Minnie Maddern Fiske."[11]

> Since her husband's opposition to the powerful Theatrical Syndicate prevented her from appearing in their theatres, the Fiskes rented the Manhattan (Theatre) in 1901. For six years, she played there with a splendid company, putting on a series of fine plays which were not equaled until the early years of the Theatre Guild.* [12]

* *But see* - In Bordman & Hischak at p. 230, it states that "Many of these (plays) were at the Manhattan Theatre, which the Fiskes owned. But the costs of maintaining the house were too much, and the Fiskes eventually lost it."

In 1904, Minnie Maddern Fiske appeared on Broadway at the Manhattan Theatre in C.M.S. McLellan's drama, *Leah Kleschna*, which Mary Elitch Long characterized as "one of the biggest successes of the decade." She invited Mrs. Fiske to appear with her Manhattan Company in 1905 for a one week presentation of *Leah Kleschna*, with George Arliss and John Mason as part of her cast. Mrs. Fiske agreed and came direct to Denver from a thirty-one-week season of the play at her New York theater.[1-3]

On the evening of May 25, 1905, *Leah Kleschna* was presented at Elitch. The audience was large and quite enthusiastic. A review commented on the "independent" management of Elitch Theatre:

> It is a matter for sincere congratulation that the Theatrical Syndicate, which is able to shut Mrs. Fiske from most of the leading cities of the continent, does not control Elitch Gardens. To have been able to witness this finished actress in *Leah Kleschna* is, indeed, a cause for thanks. A presentation so thoroughly adequate as that at the Gardens last night is calculated to intensify the growing feeling among theatergoers that independence, after all, can be relied upon to bring forth the best in the drama as in other arts... It is noteworthy that most of the standing successes of the recent years have been under what is termed the "independent" management. [13]

Frank W. White, drama editor of the *Denver Post*, extolled Mrs. Fiske's virtues as an actress, then commented on "that rare voice of hers," as follows:

> That rare voice of hers, beautifully modulated, is still jerky and spasmodic, but it is also "soft and low," like Cordelia's, carrying infinite expression and fine intensity.[3-3]

Frank L. Webster of the *Denver Times* commented as follows:

> Seldom has Denver seen so finished and evenly balanced a production of a play as the presentation of *Leah Kleschna* at Elitch Gardens last night by Mrs. Fiske and her Manhattan company.
>
> Just one thing mars the otherwise perfect performance. Particularly in scenes of excitement where the lines go rapidly, her enunciation is so indistinct, her words so run together that at times one can scarcely understand what she is saying.[3-4]

During her lifetime, some believed that much of the criticism directed toward Mrs. Fiske "is suspect, possibly written by critics susceptible to the Trust's bribes." * [4-2] To others, however, Mrs. Fiske was admired "for the vivacity and naturalness of her acting."[12] The drama critic, Ward Morehouse, known for his

* Theatrical Trust was another name for the Theatrical Syndicate.

column "Broadway After Dark" featured in the *New York Sun*, wrote of her.

> Mrs. Fiske never had beauty, but she had magnetism. She had with all of her nervous, jerky manner, subtlety and finesse, and she was as much at ease in light-handed drawing-room comedy as she was in the problem plays of Ibsen.[4-3]

In a brief biography of Mrs. Fiske in the International Dictionary of Theatre the following was noted:

> She was known for her nervous, cerebral style, her tendency to speak lines quickly, as if conversing rather than declaiming, and her insistence on a "naturalness" of acting that included turning her back to the audience when the action demanded it (something that would never have been tolerated in the 19th-century US theatre). Her reputation as a "modern" actress resulted from this brittle, almost neurotic, performance style as well as from her choice of plays and supervision of productions.[14]

In 1907, she returned to Elitch with her Manhattan Company for pre-season special performances of *The New York Idea*, and in 1908, she returned for a pre-season performance of Ibsen's *Romersholm*, which she had performed in New York in 1907. Bruce McRae and Mrs. Fiske's Company appeared with her in the play at Elitch.

Mary Elitch characterized her treasured friendship with Mrs. Fiske as follows:

> I have treasured the friendship of Mrs. Fiske through many years of our association, and I am sure there has never been a woman on the stage more loved and respected. Whenever she returns to Denver we share some happy hours, for she always dearly loved the trees and birds of my Gardens.
>
> I recall an incident indicative of her rare thoughtfulness of others. She was filling an engagement at the Broadway Theatre; while her company rested she slipped away and came to visit me. This was quite early one Saturday morning, but my company was already busy at rehearsal. At Mrs. Fiske's suggestion we tiptoed into a dark corner of my Theatre to watch. With her unfailing consideration of others she would not allow me to announce her presence for she realized that the young actors might feel embarrassed if aware that she was in the Theatre.[1-4]

The End of the Season - Where Do the Players Go?

Audience members often assume that actors and actresses they have enjoyed simply move on to another play, being unaware that the actor that entertained them during the summer season may soon be unemployed while hoping for the phone to ring for another play, or at least an audition. Fortunately, some of the members of the Elitch cast had future engagements.

The 1906 Season

When the citizens of Denver dreamed of summer, they dreamed of the opening of Elitch Gardens. In their minds, the two coincided. It was affirmed by the *Denver Post* in an article that greeted the new season.

> About nine out of ten people do not believe that summer is really here until Mrs. Mary Elitch Long announces the personnel of her stock company and also the date of the opening of the Gardens. When she makes these two statements then the people settle down to the round of summer pastimes and pleasures.[15-1]

There was a great love for the Gardens by its patrons and "every man and every woman and every child in town looks upon the Gardens as his or her special property."[15-1]

Each season, patrons of the Gardens anxiously awaited to see how Mary Elitch Long enhanced their beauty with her magic touch. The arrangement of floral designs, the flowers in the banks along the avenue and the apple trees made each summer special and beautiful. But there was something very different that caught their eyes this season. It was a new house for Mary. Her familiar cottage had grown old and dreary as a residence.

> In its place and upon its site has been reared a two-storied house of cream brick and mortar of the bungalow design. Beautiful indeed is it in the greenery of its surroundings. There is a grass terrace, the fence is there and there are the flowers, too. It is one of the most striking houses in the city and its design speaks of Mrs. Long. Nobody but Mrs. Long would have thought of the design and the beauty of the house for her home in the Gardens.[15-1]

The late seating of theater patrons was a continuing problem in theater management. In an article by the drama editor Frank W. White of the *Denver Post*, stringent enforcement was recommended.

> No one should be allowed to climb over a lot of people after the curtain rises. They should be compelled to stay in the rear until the end of the act. No end of irritation is caused by late comers in crowding through the narrow aisles, brushing expensive wraps and bonnets to the floor and causing many angry glances from indignant women and annoyed men anxious to see the play and keep in touch with the stage atmosphere. That is really the needed reform of the hour.[15-1]

It was not uncommon at Elitch to present a play that had previously been presented during an earlier season. For example, *A Japanese Nightingale* was presented for the third consecutive season, and *The Little Minister* had been presented previously in 1902 and 1903. The 1906 season was grounded in these and other plays, such as

Hubert Henry Davies' *Cousin Kate*, William Meyer Foster's *Old Heidelberg*, William Gillette's *Sherlock Holmes* and Justin Huntley McCarthy's *If I Were King*.

There were several guest stars who appeared in some plays in featured roles, and included among them were Jane Oaker and Maude Fealy. Jane Oaker, in addition to being a talented actress, was said to possess the most beautiful neck and shoulders of any actress on the American stage.

> Miss Oaker has the swanlike neck that artists rave over, and the shoulders - in Webster's great dictionary there are not sufficient words to group into an adequate description of the beauty of her shoulders... The fact of the matter is that, although Miss Oaker has been besought by photographers the country over, only upon one or two occasions has she consented to a photograph showing the neck and shoulders.[15-2]

Maude Fealy appeared at Elitch in *The Crisis* and *The Little Minister*. Plays in which Maude Fealy had been featured in the past at Elitch held the records for attendance. During her 1905 summer engagement "the S. R. O. sign was displayed at every performance, and the five weeks she was at the Gardens were the five largest weeks in the history of the Theatre."[15-3]

While the 1906 season was to be a prosperous one, it was to be remembered mostly because of the appearances of Sarah Bernhardt and Douglas Fairbanks.

Sarah Bernhardt

In 1906, when her booking was canceled in San Francisco because of the earthquake, Sarah Bernhardt was invited to appear instead at Elitch for a pre-season one-day performance.* [16]

She appeared in a matinee performance of *La Sorciere* by Victorien Sardou and an evening performance of *Le Dame aux Camelias (Camille)* by Alexander Dumas. Leading players of the Elitch Theatre company gladly took bit parts, so they later could say they had played with Sarah Bernhardt.

In a review of her evening performance, the following was written of her:

> It would be regarded as something of an impertinence to criticize her. She is unquestionably at the very pinnacle of her art. She makes you feel and fully recognize that fact.
>
> And when she spoke her voice was soft and low, singularly sweet and tremulous with the vibrant quality of young womanhood. It was one of the marvels of the night, for, through the whole play, that gentle, musical, velvety vocalism was an exquisite delight. There was not a strident tone from beginning to end, and when we think of the years that have passed

* Sarah Bernhardt made her American debut at Booth's Theatre in New York in 1880. Her first appearance in Denver was in 1887 at the Tabor Grand Opera House.

> for this gifted creature, does not her voice become a physical wonder?
>
> She gave a performance full of intellectual power, brilliant coloring and quiet eloquence.
>
> The assimilation of the intellectual and emotional was strikingly exemplified in last evening's performance. It is this quality that has always elevated Bernhardt's acting from mere imitation to the actual representation of life and its passions.[15-4]

At one point during her visit, Sarah Bernhardt approached the animal houses of Mary's Gardens. The actress pressed against the cage of a restless young lioness and began to stroke the animal's head. Mary Elitch was fascinated by the animal's complete surrender to the strange power of this marvelous woman, accepting her as a friend.

In describing what followed, Mary Elitch said:

> "Continuing to stroke the great head, Madame Bernhardt turned to me and asked, 'Her name ... her name ... what is it?' I replied she had not yet been given a name. 'Then I shall call her Sarah!'
>
> "(Then) looking fully in the lion's face she spoke distinctly: 'You are Sarah Bernhardt.' The lion accepted the bestowal of a famous name upon her as she had the gentle stroking and patting of a famous hand upon her head and face - gently and as a matter of course.
>
> "A backward look as we neared the door showed the animal standing exactly as we had left her, motionless - gazing after her friend and sponsor."[17-1]

Douglas Fairbanks

The renowned actor and film star, Douglas Fairbanks, first appeared as an actor at Elitch Theatre during the 1906 season as Reginald Lumley in *Cousin Kate*. He was 23 years of age. He was described as "a striking actor, with life and vim in his work."[15-1] But Douglas Fairbanks was no stranger to Denver or to the Elitch Theatre. He was born and raised in Denver, and it was there that he became inspired to pursue a career in theater.

Douglas Fairbanks was born Douglas Elton Ulman in Denver on May 23, 1883, the son of H. Charles Ulman and Ella Adelaide (Marsh) Ulman. The house where he was born was in a modest neighborhood in the middle-class residential section of Denver. The house is no longer there, and the number and street have been changed - to 1207 Bannock Street.[18-1] He was baptized a Roman Catholic by Bishop Joseph Machebeuf on October 4, 1883. His baptism is recorded in the records of the Cathedral of the Immaculate Conception. He attended East High School in Denver. However, according to family legend, Douglas "left" that school in 1899 for "unauthorized use of green paint and ribbons at the school on St. Patrick's Day."[19]

When Fairbanks was five, his father deserted the family.

> Charles Ulman was fifty-five when, after the final collapse of all his mining ventures, he accepted a position as Republican campaign speaker for Benjamin Harrison in the presidential elections of 1888, and he left for New York in the summer of that year. He never returned to the family.
>
> Douglas was five that year ... Though Douglas never forgot his love and admiration of his father, Ulman's desertion of his family was something Douglas was never able to explain to himself or to anyone else.[18-2]

Douglas' mother obtained a divorce on the grounds of desertion before he entered the first grade. His mother had previously been married to John Fairbanks, a New Orleans planter and socialite. Shortly after the birth of their son, John Jr. in 1873, John Fairbanks died of tuberculosis. Following her divorce from Charles Ulman, Douglas' mother resumed the name of Fairbanks. Douglas subsequently assumed the name of Fairbanks. John Fairbanks, Jr., Douglas' half-brother, was later to become general manager of the Douglas Fairbanks Motion Picture Company. John Jr. died in Hollywood in 1926 and was buried in Denver at Mount Olivet Cemetery.[19]

In an interview recorded in a 1932 memoir about her life, Mary Elitch Long described Douglas Fairbanks' introduction as a boy to Elitch Theatre.

> The little boy, I think he was about twelve, was a great admirer of Shakespeare, his mother, a student of the poet, having read all of the plays with him. On hearing that Shakespeare was to be given at our Theatre, and not having sufficient funds to purchase a ticket, Douglas appeared at the Theatre one morning and asked the janitor if there was any work he could do to earn one. On being told that there was not, the future star walked onto the stage, and after looking it over, suggested that a good scrubbing might help its appearance, and stated that he was perfectly willing to undertake the scrubbing if his price - a ticket to the next performance - would be forthcoming. The rough boards received their scrubbing and the enterprising little boy his ticket.
>
> Perhaps if the incident had been brought to my notice the stage would not have been scrubbed that hot summer day, but after all, those precious ambitions and longings of a child's brave and determined heart played their part in the ultimate and magnificent success of this Denver boy.[17-2]

In the summer of 1899, when Douglas was 16 years of age, Frederick B. Warde, a famous American actor, was appearing at the Elitch Theatre. By then, Douglas' ambition was to become an actor. One evening, Douglas gained entrance into the Theatre and the star's dressing room with the help of a fire escape and an open window. When Warde returned to his dressing room, Douglas was there to greet him, and launched into a speech eulogizing the actor. Notwithstanding his surprise and annoyance, Warde noted that:

> The boy's sincerity and admiration were too genuine to be hidden, and the great tragedian decided that Douglas had some likable qualities.
>
> While he removed his makeup and changed into his street clothes, they talked. At first it was a two-way conversation; then at the boy's enthusiastic prompting, the actor began to relate some of his experiences in the theater.[18-3]

Fairbanks was inspired by the conversation and mentioned his desire to become an actor, but stated that his family was not enthusiastic about his ambition. Warde replied:

> They always are. It's a tradition in the theater that actors either come from theatrical families and can't make an honest living any other way, or from nonprofessional families who don't think it's any way to make an honest living.[20]

Although Douglas' mother opposed acting as a career choice, she nevertheless enrolled him for lessons at Margaret Fealy's acting studio "to keep him occupied and out of mischief ... (and hoping) he would outgrow his desire to become an actor."[18-4]

> Though Douglas' sessions with Margaret (Fealy) were marked by her frequent attempts to curb his exuberance and the interpolations that resulted in overacting, most of the dramatic qualities he later developed were the result of her expert drilling.18-5

Burns Mantle, the future drama critic in Denver and later for the New York *Daily News*, lived next door to Douglas when Douglas was a drama student. Mantle recalled, that he "would recite you as fine and florid an Anthony's speech to the Romans as you ever heard. With gestures, too ... He was studying then, I think, with Margaret Fealy, who was Maude Fealy's mother, and at the head of a Denver dramatic school."[18-6]

Douglas Fairbanks made his stage debut in Richmond, Virginia in 1900 as Florio in *The Duke's Jester*. His New York debut occurred two years later in *Her Lord and Master*.[4-4] After his appearance at Elitch in 1906, Fairbanks continued with his stage career when, in 1915, he was attracted to Hollywood, where his swashbuckling and other films were well received. In 1919, efforts were made by some to form a forty-million-dollar merger of all producing motion picture companies and "sewing up every exhibitor in the United States with a five-year contract."[21] Fairbanks, with his wife Mary Pickford (known as "America's Sweetheart"), together with D. W. Griffith, Charles Chaplin and their lawyers, met at Pickfair (Pickford and Fairbanks' famous home) and executed the documents that formed the United

Artists corporation to distribute their future productions, thereby protecting their independence and combating the merger.

The world was saddened by the separation of Douglas and Mary in 1933 and by the Cinderella couple's divorce in January of 1936. In March, Douglas Fairbanks married ex-chorus girl Lady Sylvia Ashley. In 1937, Mary Pickford married her former costar Charles "Buddy" Rogers, who was eleven years her junior. In December of 1939, Douglas Fairbanks died in his sleep of a heart attack.[22] He is buried in the Hollywood Forever cemetery in Burbank, California.

More About Sarah Bernhardt

In 1915, Sarah Bernhardt suffered an accident which resulted in her having a leg amputated. At the time she was playing the title role in Sardou's play *La Tosca.* While convalescing, she received a cable from the director of the Pan-American exposition in San Francisco, offering her $100,000.00 if she permitted her leg to be exhibited. The actress wired back, asking, "Which leg?"[23]

Sarah Bernhardt is buried in Pere-Lachaise Cemetery in Paris, France, about 50 feet from the tomb of Oscar Wilde.

Main entrance to the Gardens

Douglas Fairbanks

Sarah Bernhardt, earlier years

Denver Public Library Western History Collection - No. Rh-136

Mary Pickford and Douglas Fairbanks, later years

Chapter Nine

(1907 - 1908)

Clyde Fitch and David Belasco
Maude Fealy Is Secretly Married
May Buckley and David Warfield

The 1907 Season

From time to time, during the early and closing weeks of the summer seasons, patrons sometimes complained that the Theatre was too cold, particularly on chilly, rainy nights. Prior to the commencement of the 1907 season, the management had a steam heating plant installed, after which the concern seemed to be satisfactorily resolved.[1]

The alluring sign in the advertisements on streetcars had as the admission cost to Elitch Gardens - "10 cents."

Among the plays presented during the season, Clyde Fitch had authored four of the plays - *The Girl With the Green Eyes, Her Green Match, The Woman in the Case* and *Her Own Way*. Three of the plays presented during the season were written by David Belasco. Those plays were *Sweet Kitty Bellairs, The Darling of the Gods* (co-authored with John Luther Long) and *The Heart of Maryland.*

Clyde Fitch

Clyde Fitch was born in Elmira, New York in 1865, the son of a Union Army officer and a Maryland belle. He sought a career in New York as an architect and interior decorator. He wrote a number of stories and short plays which were successful. He was urged by drama critics Edward Dithmar and William Winter to write *Beau Brumell* (1890) for the renowned actor Richard Mansfield. The play was successful and launched Fitch's career as a playwright.

> During the next nineteen years he wrote nearly sixty plays, thirty-three of them original, and the remainder translations of foreign plays or adaptations of novels ... Fitch is considered the finest American playwright at the turn of the 20th century. His range and variety are startling ... Some works are domestic melodramas, others social critiques, still others historical romances. Quite probably his most glaring fault by modern standards was his contrived happy endings.[2-1]

A review of *Her Own Way* (1903), considered by many critics to be Fitch's best work up to that time, ends with the following comments, "in the perfectly orthodox and good old-fashioned way, hero and heroine wed and live happily ever afterwards."[3-1]

Fitch died in 1909, two years after his plays were presented during the 1907 season at Elitch. Before he died in 1909 at the age of forty-three, Fitch had written thirty-three original plays and twenty-two adaptations and dramatizations. In the 1900-1901 season, Fitch had four plays appearing simultaneously on Broadway, and three in the autumn of the next season.[4]

David Belasco

In addition to being a playwright, David Belasco (1853-1931) was also a producer and director of plays. Belasco was obsessed by realism on stage. Realism in the theater "refers to what is recognizable from everyday life," from the dialogue in a play, to the costumes worn, and even down to the smallest detail, such as "an actress can actually cook a meal on the stove; the toaster makes toast, the water tap produces water, and the light in the refrigerator door goes on when the door opens."[5]

The drama critic commented on the ability of the Elitch company to appear both in Belasco's *Sweet Kitty Bellairs* and in Fitch's *The Women in the Case.*

> It would be difficult to find two masters of stagecraft more dissimilar in treatment and method than David Belasco and Clyde Fitch, and it is speaking volumes for the ability of the present Elitch company that they pass so directly from the interpretation of the comedy of the one to the powerful drama of the other.[3-2]

A Visit From Ethel Barrymore

Miss Ethel Barrymore, who was performing at the Broadway Theatre, came to Elitch to watch a rehearsal with Mary Elitch Long of the play *The Girl with the Green Eyes.*[6]

Consuelo Bailey [3-3]

Consuelo Bailey was one of the featured performers of the season. She was only seventeen years of age and one of the youngest stars on the American stage. At an early age, her tendency toward the stage was evident. She was educated both in the United States and Europe and had appeared in numerous productions during the prior two years.

Miss Bailey came to Denver during the summer to visit her uncle, J. H. Frank Smokey, a prominent mining man in the city. She desired to rest in anticipation of her appearance in September with an all-star company at the Savoy Theater in New York in the production of *The Silver Girl,* one of the most realistic of Western dramas that had been presented in recent years.

Having learned of her arrival and having a part at Elitch which very few were capable of playing, the Elitch management invited Consuelo to fill a week's engagement at the Gardens. Her desire to rest gave in to the call of her profession. She appeared as a featured player in *The Pretty Sister of Jose.*

Maude Fealy as Mary Tudor

During the week of August 18th, Maude Fealy was featured in the role of Mary Tudor, the princess of England during the stirring times of Henry VIII, in *When Knighthood Was in Flower*.

> Maude Fealy, Denver's own star ... is expected to add more laurels to those which she has won in this city and in other places in the various characters which she has assumed since she began her stage career at Elitch.[3-4]

At the time, however, there were more stirring times in Maude Fealy's life than those of Henry VIII, occasioned by her secret marriage the month before.

Maude Fealy Is Secretly Married

On July 15, 1907, Maude Fealy was secretly married by Judge Grant L. Hudson in the Denver County courtroom to Louis Hugo Sherwin, a young newspaper man and dramatic critic for the *Denver Republican*. Immediately following the wedding, Maude Fealy returned to her mother's home at 826 East Colfax Avenue, and her husband went to his bachelor apartment at 2124 East Seventeenth Avenue.

> So well did the two keep their secret, and so indifferent were they to each other in public after the event, that no one had even a suspicion of it until yesterday (July 26, 1907), when the story leaked out.[3-5]

Not even Maude's mother, Mrs. Rafaelo Cavallo, professionally known as Margaret Fealy, who conducted a drama school in Denver, knew about the marriage, and when she learned of it, she went into hysterics, crying and sobbing bitterly.[3-5] Unfortunately, the story made headline news, particularly the mother's reaction.

> Mrs. Cavallo denied the marriage outright. It is supposed she means to have it annulled, but this will not be possible. She insists her daughter has spoiled her career. Mrs. Sherwin's grandmother said yesterday that the alliance with Sherwin was a dreadful disgrace, as he was "worthless and hadn't any money." It is thought Mrs. Cavallo had in mind for Maude a millionaire or at least a duke.[3-6]

A copy of the marriage license was published in the newspaper, signed by the judge and two witnesses. The newspaper summarized the relationship between Maude Fealy and Sherwin, and that Sherwin had been known by her mother and stepfather.

> (Mr. Sherwin was) an Englishman of stage parentage and connections, and has been in Denver only a short time. During his stay here he has spent many of his days at the Cavallo home and Mrs. Cavallo grew fond of counting him among her guests.

After a while Miss Fealy came home for the summer, and she met Mr. Sherwin. At the first meeting there was a wee, tiny blush in her cheeks, suggesting that she had at last wakened, even though only a little, to the sting of Cupid's dart. Mr. Sherwin came again and again.

Soon she began to accompany him to the theater and aid him by giving pointed suggestions about particular charms of the actors and actresses whom he criticized ... Miss Fealy had purchased an auto, and soon the two were observed speeding about the city together.

Even though Mrs. Cavallo did not realize the circumstances, friends did long ago. A glimpse of the couple was convincing.[3-5]

It was suggested that Mrs. Cavallo's concern may have been attributed to having heard a story of Mr. Sherwin having been in love in England and his father opposing the marriage, and "having no money to marry without parental aid, he came to America to win his fortune and then go back to wed the girl of his choice." Clearly, however, when Sherwin met Miss Fealy he evidently forgot all about the other girl.[3-5] However, the bliss was to be short-lived. A year later, Maude Fealy and Sherwin separated and later divorced.[7]

In 1909, she married James Durkin, and they were divorced in 1917. She married a third time, to James E. Cort, but obtained an annulment in 1923.[8]

The 1908 Season

Theatergoers were informed that Elitch Theatre would be steam heated in the event of damp or disagreeable weather.[9]

In keeping with the family environment of Elitch management, the following was called to the attention of Theatre patrons, by a notice in the 1908 Theatre programs.

Patrons of the Theatre will confer a distinct favor upon its management by reporting personally or by letter any inattention or incivility on the part of its employees.* [9]

Additionally, an announcement appeared in the Elitch Theatre programs requesting that its patrons not leave the Theatre before the end of the play.

Spectators are respectfully requested to remain seated until the curtain falls on the last act. This consideration is asked in order that the enjoyment of the audience may not be impaired by isolated examples of thoughtless discourtesy, and for the further reason that the final moments are regarded as the most delicate of the play.[10]

* A similar notice was to appear from time to time in future Theatre programs. E.g., Elitch Theatre program, week beginning Sunday, Jun 19, 1938, p. 4.

In her memoirs, Mary Elitch recalled - "How happy my 1908 company seemed, gathered for rehearsal under the blooming fruit trees on that lovely May day."[11-1] The resident company had 14 actors and actresses. In addition, guest stars May Buckley, Henry Woodruff and Doris Keane were engaged to play leading roles, supported by members of the resident cast.

After the regular season of plays, David Warfield and his company appeared in *The Music Master* by playwright Charles Klein and *A Grand Army Man* by David Belasco, Pauline Phelps and Marion Short. Each play was presented for a week. Warfield's company included Antoinette Perry. The plays were well-received. The company remained another week for eight additional performances of *The Music Master,* commencing on August 31, 1908.

May Buckley

A news article announcing the opening of the 1908 season of plays at Elitch stated:

> It will be glad news to every theatergoer in the city that Miss May Buckley comes to Elitch as its leading woman. During the past season, Miss Buckley has been co-starring with Theodore Roberts and Guy Standing in Sir Gilbert Parker's powerful drama *The Right of Way,* under the direction of Klaw & Erlanger, but Elitch wanted Miss Buckley, and Miss Buckley wanted to come to Elitch; so on Friday evening, May 29, she will appear in the role made famous by Blanche Bates in David Belasco's famous play, *The Girl of the Golden West.*[12-1]

May Buckley was one of the most popular leading ladies to appear at Elitch Theatre. This was her fourth appearance at Elitch, the earlier seasons being 1904, 1905 and 1906. In the first play, *The Girl of the Golden West* by David Belasco, she was favorably compared with Blanche Bates, who created the role of Minnie Falconer, the frontier tavern owner, in the original Broadway production at the Belasco Theater.[12-2]

After appearing in the first four plays, Miss Buckley announced her impending marriage, which was a surprise to Mr. Bellows and to the cast, and perhaps to Miss Buckley as well. The prior winter, when creating the role of Rosalie in *The Right of Way,* May Buckley met Martin Sabine, an English actor who was a member of the company. "It was a case of love at first sight," Miss Buckley assured a friend to whom she opened her heart and announced that Mr. Sabine was coming to Denver to claim her in marriage. There was to be a honeymoon of two weeks in the mountains, then a visit to San Francisco and back to New York.[12-3] The announcement resulted in concerns to the Elitch management as to the impact it would have on the future plays of the season in which she was to appear.

When Mr. Bellows organized the stock company for the Gardens and secured the services of May Buckley as leading lady, he imagined it was for at least a greater part of the summer. There wasn't a hint of anything like love having possession of the actress; not a single person had been taken into her confidence concerning the momentous question until yesterday, when she simply had to tell someone and chose a woman in the company to whom she opened her heart and revealed her plans.

> As a consequence this is May Buckley's last week at the Gardens, where for three seasons she has had half of Denver at her feet and the other half just ready to bend the knee at a moment's notice.[12-3]

A replacement was needed and, fortunately, Doris Keane, a talented and promising actress, was secured to take Miss Buckley's place.

Mary Elitch recalled in her memoirs the following:

> The selfishness on our part soon faded into happiness for our lovely May, and pleasurable preparation for her wedding, which occurred at midnight on June 27th. Walter Bellows led the beautiful bride to the altar of roses on the porch of my bungalow, where waited Mr. Walter Sabine, an English actor, the man of her choice. A supper was served in my home to the company and some of the bride's closest Denver friends, after which they left for the Pacific Coast. While at the table, someone remarked that the bride, who was seated in a veritable bower of blossoms, looked like a flower herself. The actress then told us for the first time the story of her introduction to the theater. It was at the age of nine - in a play called *May Blossoms*.[11-2]

About the time the news broke as to Miss Buckley's marriage, Doris Keane happened to be among the guests at a theater party held inside the Elitch Theatre and hosted by Samuel Newhouse. Impressed with the artistic Theatre, the actress said, "I'd just love to play out here."[12-4] She was looked upon as the most promising of the Charles Frohman stars.

After she had appeared in the next two plays, *The Rose of the Rancho* and *The County Chairman*, Charles Frohman suddenly called Miss Keane back to New York to rehearse for a one-act play to be produced in London. The *Denver Post* drama section commented on Charles Frohman's decision as follows:

> If Charles Frohman were within reach of Denver his ears would fairly tingle with the unkind things said about him for suddenly calling Doris Keane back to New York. The only thing that reconciles Denver theatergoers to Miss Keane's departure is that Miss May Buckley comes back to her own tonight. During her short stay Miss Keane added luster to her fame, and afforded most intense delight to the patrons of the Gardens. However, to the Denver public there is but one May Buckley,

> and Mrs. Elitch-Long is to be congratulated upon her success in having Miss Buckley forego her honeymoon and come back and take up her engagement.* [12-5]

Miss Buckley's return to Elitch was lightened by her appearance as Zuki in *A Japanese Nightingale,*** one of her favorite roles, for which she was first cast when the play was originally presented in New York.[11-3] She was praised for her "daintiness," her "pert and pretty little manners" and her "thready and piping voice" which gave realism and atmosphere to the role. A reviewer reported that "there is witchery in her folded fingers, her almond eyes, her coquettish ways."[13]

Following *A Japanese Nightingale,* Miss Buckley and Henry Woodruff performed the leading roles in the remaining four plays of the regular season. Woodruff was represented to be "one of the best-liked leading men at present upon the American stage."[12-1] Their performances were praised.

David Warfield

David Warfield was born on November 28, 1866 in San Francisco and began his theatrical career as an usher in the city's Bush Street Theatre. At the time of his death on June 27, 1951 in New York City, he was one of the world's richest entertainers. Although he appeared in many productions, his fortune and success in theater centered on his playing four major roles over a 25-year period: Simon Levi in *The Auctioneer* (1901), Anton von Barwig in *The Music Master* (1904), Wes Bigelow in *A Grand Army Man* (1907) and the title role in *The Return of Peter Grimm* (1911).

Prior to appearing at Elitch, David Warfield had played in *The Music Master* on Broadway from 1904 to 1907, appearing in more than 1,000 performances, followed by his appearance in *A Grand Army Man,* which opened at the Stuyvesant Theatre in New York on October 16, 1907 for 149 performances, his leading lady being Denver's Antoinette Perry.*** [14] The *Denver Post* announced the arrival of David Warfield and his company to the Elitch Theatre.

> Mrs. Elitch Long makes a splendid finish to her summer season by bringing in David Warfield for its two final weeks ... Were it not for her magnificent enterprise, Denver would be forced to forego seeing this truly great American actor. He is essentially American, and that his art is true is attested by his marvelous popularity everywhere with all classes.

* In 1913, Doris Keane was cast as Madama Cavallini in Edward Sheldon's *Romance* which opened in New York, and which later established a London run of 1,128 performances. Mantle and Sherwood (eds), *Best Plays of 1909-1919* (New York: Dodd, Mead and Co. 1943) at p. 18. Miss Keane made almost an entire career out of the Sheldon play, performing the leading part off and on (including a motion picture version) until 1927. Daniel Blum (ed.), *Great Stars of the American Stage* (New York, Greenberg Publisher, 1952) at p. 67.

** *A Japanese Nightingale* was said to be "the first play ever done in America written by a Japanese author." *Denver Post* (Magazine Section), Jul 12, 1908, p. 6.

*** Antoinette Perry also appeared in the Elitch presentation of *The Music Master* with David Warfield and was his leading lady. Dier at p. 107.

> Mr. Belasco sends Mr. Warfield and his New York company direct to Denver from his home theater, the Stuyvesant. He sends intact and complete *The Music Master* and *A Grand Army Man* productions.
>
> Of course, Mr. Warfield plays nowhere else in Colorado, and his Elitch engagement will doubtless be eagerly taken advantage of by many from all points in the state.[12-6]

A reporter for the *Dramatic Mirror* commented that "all Denver is Warfield mad! Never has an actor achieved so signal a triumph."[15-1] August 30th was declared "Warfield Day" and large theater parties arrived in the city from Colorado Springs, Pueblo, Greeley and Fort Collins, as well as Cheyenne, Wyoming, to attend the Saturday matinee and evening performances of *A Grand Army Man*.[11-4]

Warfield decided to retire at the height of his fame in 1922. However, he was bent on playing one last role, that of Shylock in David Belasco's production that year of *The Merchant of Venice*. Perhaps it was one play too many in his career. It was reported that "critics were divided, and though he toured with the work for two seasons it was one of his rare commercial failures."[2-2]

End of the Season Reflection

Upon the close of the season, Mary Elitch reflected in her memoirs upon the season as follows:

> With the Theatre silent, the gates closed, and finding myself left to a reminiscent peace, it was a satisfaction to read in the Sunday edition of a great newspaper, these words by a valued and just critic:
>
> "There can be no question that the plays presented by Mary Elitch Long this summer at the Gardens are not only the best Denver has ever seen during a summer season, but (also) in point of newness, reputation, excellence of cast and production ..."[11-5]

Notwithstanding Mary Elitch's reflections, the box office receipts for the summer were less than those of previous years, more than likely occasioned by repeating shows that had previously appeared at Elitch in earlier seasons.[15-2] For example, *A Japanese Nightingale* had been presented during the 1904, 1905 and 1906 seasons.

Municipal Auditorium

To promote Denver as a convention city, Mayor Robert W. Speer successfully spearheaded a drive to have a $500,000 Municipal Auditorium constructed, an auditorium which was to be the largest in America except for Madison Square Garden in New York. Construction commenced in 1906 and was completed in time to host the Democratic National Convention in 1908, at which William Jennings Bryan was nominated for President for the third time.

Thereafter, during the seasons of 1909 to 1911, the Shuberts presented twenty traveling productions at the auditorium under city auspices and supervision.

> (Through the years), many different types of productions - dramatic and operatic, professional and amateur, music festivals, dances, and exhibitions have been presented in this auditorium.[15-3]

In 2004, the auditorium was gutted, renovated, and renamed The Ellie Caulkins Opera House. The Opera House opened as Opera Colorado's new home on September 10, 2005, with a gala benefit for the Opera Colorado Foundation, featuring some of the best performers from the world of opera. Opera Colorado's first season in the new opera house opened on November 3, 2005 with a production of *Carmen* starring the internationally known Denyce Graves in the title role.[16]

The National Democratic Convention was held in Denver in the early part of July of 1908. The National Democratic Convention would again be hosted by Denver, but not until August 2008.

Denver Public Library Western History Collection

Mr. and Mrs. David Warfield arriving in Denver
for his engagement at Elitch (1908)

Denver Public Library Western History Collection

David Warfield in his dressing room at Elitch (1908)

Chapter Ten

(1908)

Lakeside Amusement Park
A Rival Amusement Park and Theatre
A Brief History

The town of Lakeside was founded in 1908 and has been described as the Liechtenstein of Jefferson County, the metropolitan area's tiniest incorporated town. It occupies about one square mile.[1]

In 1907, the Lakeside Realty and Amusement Company was formed for the specific purpose of developing another Denver area amusement park. Adolph Zang, founder of a Denver brewery, helped found the Company and became its President.[2] It was to be the last big amusement park to be built in or near Denver.

On Memorial Day 1908, Lakeside Park opened its gates to Denver and the vicinity.

> A crowd of 50,000, most traveling by trolley car, but some arriving in buggies or automobiles, paraded through the gates on opening day. While thousands waited in the park, Mayor Robert W. Speer, from his offices at City Hall, pushed a button that sent current flowing across the city to illuminate the thousands of electric bulbs in the park.
>
> The showpiece of the place was a 150-foot Tower of Jewels (still standing) which was illuminated with thousands of small light bulbs. As soon as the lights flashed on, Gertrude Zang, Adolph Zang's daughter, cracked a bottle of champagne against the tower, and White City officially was open.[2]

The investors called the Park "White City" since nearly everything in the park was white - the rides, the colonnades, the Tower of Jewels. Even the uniforms and gloves worn by the waiters in the elegant Porch Cafe were white. Gradually, the name "White City" faded, and the park took on the name of Lakeside.[2]

Other attractions in the Park included gambling in the $125,000 casino adjoining the Tower. Shetland ponies provided rides for the customers. There was a two-mile miniature train excursion circling the lake. There were amusement rides (including a Ferris wheel and carousel), a ballroom and a swimming pool. German specialties and beer were served in a rathskeller beside the Tower of Jewels.[2]

In 1910 at a cost of approximately $45,000, the casino was remodeled into a theater building that was to become known as the Casino Theatre.[3] The building was described as "a beautiful theater, graceful in design, artistic in coloring and comfortable to a degree." The theater introduced "girl ushers wearing natty gray uniforms and mortarboard caps."[4-1]

On May 28th, the theater opened with *The Promoters*, the first of several musical comedy productions by the Casino stock company. The *Denver Post* alerted theater followers of the opening production.

> Lew Kelley, Lottie Kendall, and the new Casino theater stock company will be the attraction at the theater. *The Promoters*, by Ward and Vokes, will be the first comedy given. This play promises to be an auspicious beginning for the comfortable new playhouse. There will be fifty-two people in the cast of this first production. This will include the chorus of forty girls and boys. New music and popular songs of the whistling kind run through the comedy, with scenic splendor never before attempted in Denver.* [4-2]

The plays were followed by light opera. The opening bill was *The Mikado*, which the management dedicated as a "week in old Japan."[4-3]

> Everything at Lakeside is to contribute to the atmosphere which is to make the White City a bit of Japan itself.
>
> Japanese tea girls will be the ushers in the theater, and the doorkeeper will be a huge Japanese. The lights in the White City are to be Japanese lanterns and the flower pots are to bloom with the flowers of Nippon. The week's fun will be as a romp in the land of Kimona san and Fushiama. Even Don Philippini, the sensational director, entering into the plot, will play the native airs of Japan with his famous band.[4-3]

The Mikado was followed by *La Mascotte*, by Audrien, one of the prettiest of the old English comic operas. The *Denver Post* reported the following:

> *La Mascotte* has the distinction of having been produced more times in America and England than any opera or other theatrical attraction ever written. More than 50,000 times has the curtain risen upon its characters, and just that many times has it captivated its audiences with its jingly music, its inimitable situations and the daintiness of its presentation ... The Casino company will find it one of its happiest mediums of entertainment, and it bids fair to be as popular with the Denver public as it always has been, and will draw as many interested theatergoers to the Casino as did *The Mikado* last week.[4-4]

After several weeks of light opera, vaudeville and concerts were presented until the end of the Labor Day week.[5]

* The drama critic who attended the opening performance noted that "Lew Kelley was seen at his best, and Lottie Kendall was not seen enough of." *Denver Post* (Section Two), May 29, 1910, p. 7.

The Fealy-Durkin stock company was engaged for the 1912 and 1913 seasons and was successful.

> The Fealy-Durkin company opened last evening at the Casino Theater, Lakeside, with every indication pointing toward a successful (1913) season.
>
> The company is good. James Durkin upon his first appearance on the stage was given a right royal reception. It was plainly demonstrated that the audience, and it was a good-sized, good-looking audience, were more than glad to welcome him back to Lakeside.* [6]

During the next several years, there were theater offerings of plays by various stock companies. In 1917, the offerings were by a musical comedy organization known as "The Lakeside Musical Comedy Company." **

In 1918, Lakeside's theater policy changed by offering dining and dancing, with a bill of vaudeville entertainers on the stage. Theater seats were removed to accommodate a dance floor installed with "ringside" tables, cabaret style. During the 1920 season, the theater initially presented six acts of vaudeville followed by "Emmet Vogan's 1920 Musical Review," a "chorus of twelve singing, dancing girls" presented in the "New Fountain Room" in the Casino.[7-1] In August, due to the inconvenience of a tramway strike, crowds were decidedly smaller at Lakeside and the theater closed about mid-August.*** [7-2] Thereafter, the advertising by the Lakeside management stressed its outdoor attractions, and "Casino Theater" was changed to "Casino Cabaret."[8] Traditional theatrical presentations of plays were no longer featured.

In 1915, when a number of economic factors resulted in placing Elitch Gardens into receivership, some claimed that the Gardens became less attractive because Mary Elitch's ideals were too high. She continued to bar intoxicants, while Lakeside was making money selling liquor. Notwithstanding, she persisted in continuing to operate the resort along absolutely clean lines, a place fit for families and children, "and anyone exhibiting the slightest evidence of unfitness was promptly ejected and told to keep away from Elitch Gardens."[9] In January 1919, the 18th Amendment, forbidding the manufacture and sale of intoxicants for beverage purposes, was ratified.

* For the convenience of those patrons who did not care to get their seats at the Lakeside theater, seats were made available to be purchased at the Denver Dry Goods store and at Baur's. *Denver Republican*, Jun 16, 1913, p. 10.

** For example, the Comedy presented *A Stubborn Cinderella*, advertised as being with "Sparkling Music - Great Cast - Lots of Pretty Girls - Company of Forty Clever Singers and Dancers," see *Denver Post* (Section One), Jun 17, 1917, p. 11, and later *Step Lively*, *Denver Post* (Section One), Aug 12, 1917, p. 9.

*** For the remainder of the season, patrons were offered "dancing, boating, bathing, cafe, rides, etc." *Denver Post* (Amusement Section), Aug 15, 1920, p. 9.

By 1933 the Depression had taken its toll on amusement parks, and Lakeside suffered. Benjamin Krasner, who started at the park as a food concessionaire in 1917, purchased the park in 1936. Krasner died in 1965, and the ownership and operation of the park was taken over by his daughter, Rhoda Krasner, and her uncle, Martie Ruttner. The man-made lake at the park, Lake Rhoda, was named for her. After Ruttner's death four years later, Rhoda Krasner continued as general manager. The Park was then placed in the name of a small closed corporation.[10]

Lakeside still exists. The main entrance is still painted white; however, its appearance has lost its luster. The entrance appears unattended and worn. The Casino Theatre sign, a memory of the past, is now whitewashed over.

The Lakeside Amusement Park survived for decades, especially as a bargain-priced alternative to the better-known Elitch Gardens. However, by the time Lakeside had opened its gates in 1908, Elitch Gardens had become a household name, was nationally known, and was embraced by a dedicated audience of citizens. If Lakeside had a clear advantage over Elitch Gardens, it was by its sale of liquor. Lakeside had control over its liquor laws, and allowed "Denver brewer Adolph Zang, to sell beer across the street from a then-dry Denver."[1]

The Park was developed on 160 acres, but has since shrunk from 160 acres to 40 acres of land and 40 acres of lake. The Park was considerably downsized when the Shetland pony grazing pasture was sold in the 1950s to Gerri Von Frellick for development of the Lakeside Shopping Center. The Park was and still is located at 4601 Sheridan Boulevard, a place now slightly south of Interstate Highway 70.

Denver Public Library Western History Collections - No. 73544

Lakeside Amusement Park

Chapter Eleven

(1909 - 1910)

The Call to Realism!
William Collier

The 1909 Season

In 1909, everyone in Denver knew that summer was upon them when Elitch Gardens opened in early June. This season brought changes in the Gardens, among them being the following:

> No one can afford to miss a first glimpse at that big classic entrance with the Greek portals and bas-reliefs symbolical of art and music.
>
> It's the same old Elitch which everyone loves, but it's better than ever with its impressive entrance, the handsomest feature of all the new improvements - an entrance with inner balconies with Greek columns between which palms and ferns and flowers are banked.
>
> The thousands of electric lights dotting the Grecian gateway flanked on one side by the greenhouse displays will make a new attraction at the Gardens.
>
> Flowers, flowers everywhere, that is the charm of Elitch; 60,000 plants, 30,000 more than last year, and in addition to the exquisite floating Gardens there are two other new features of similar effect. There is the Floral Merry Go-Round in a sort of sunken garden, which carries only masses of flowers ... (and) the floral electric auto gardens - beautiful masses of electric lights and flowers, whose revolving course may be regulated according to desire.
>
> (And) the Trocadero has a brand new floor and has been made one-third bigger in size.[1-1]

And amid all of this beauty stood the Elitch Theatre, once again prepared to bring a season of theatrical entertainment to its loyal theatergoers. The Elitch-Long Stock Company was prepared to maintain the excellence in performance for which the Theatre had achieved its fame and reputation.

Each season, in selecting plays to be performed at Elitch, Mary Elitch Long strongly considered plays that had been presented on Broadway, as well as the Broadway actors and actresses. Each of the plays performed at Elitch during this season had originally appeared in New York between 1903 and 1907 except for *The Regeneration*, which opened on September 1, 1908 for only 39 performances. Among the plays presented were *The Warrens of Virginia* and *The Man on the Box*.

The Warrens of Virginia

The *Warrens of Virginia* was written by William C. De Mille, brother of Cecil B. De Mille. The play had been presented at the Belasco Theatre on Broadway in 1907 for 190 performances, and thereafter the play had enjoyed a triumphal tour of the United States in which Christine Norman, Elitch's leading lady, had starred. The play has a romantic theme within the setting of the Civil War. This was the play's first production in Denver.

The Man on the Box [1-2]

In anticipation of the opening performance of *The Man on the Box*, the *Denver Post* drama critic alerted theatergoers that "Elitch will give Denver tonight one of the finest summer bills ever presented in the theater. It will be a comedy performance of the most laughable and enjoyable nature." The 1905 play by playwright Grace Livingston Furniss completed a successful Broadway run at the Madison Square Theatre.

> The story ... is that of a retired army man, Lieutenant Worburton by name, who falls desperately in love with a beautiful young lady whom he has seen while abroad only a short time before.

After returning from a long tour of duty, Lt. Worburton decides to surprise his sister by usurping the coachman's seat on her carriage when she leaves the embassy ball. Mistakenly, he picks up a carriage with a person other than his sister.

> (Lt. Worburton) drives her in a reckless and exciting pace all over the city, then leaping from the box he seizes what he imagines to be his sister and presses a kiss upon her lips. His astonishment and perplexity know no bounds when to his utter amazement he discovers that instead of his sister he has kissed the object of his love.
>
> He retains his disguise, is promptly arrested, but later his fine is paid by the young lady whom he has so rudely intruded upon, who engages him as her butler.

As in most plays, however, and after pages of humorous dialogue and events, all paths finally lead to love and understanding and a joyous ending. Lieutenant Worburton's disguise is at last penetrated and the young lady falls in love with him. As promised, the play was indeed a comedy "of the most laughable and enjoyable nature," that remained a nostalgic memory for Denverites for years to come.

The Call to Realism!

The drama editor of the *Denver Post* related an amusing conversation between the manager of a play and an actor, with regard to theatrical realism.

> To hire a blacksmith to play a blacksmith, a carpenter to play a carpenter, was the modern manager's triumphant response to the call of realism.

> A very capable actor, long out of employment, finally secured an opportunity. The contract was about to be signed, when the manager suddenly asked, "Excuse me, but is your father living?"
>
> "Yes," came the surprised answer.
>
> "Too bad (tearing up contract). The father of the man in the play is dead."[1-3]

The 1910 Season

During the summer of 1910, there were 215,000 inhabitants of Denver.

There were eleven theaters - the Auditorium, Broadway, Tabor Grand Opera House, Majestic, Orpheum, Curtis, Pantages, the Royal Theater at 243 Broadway, and a theater within Elitch Gardens, Lakeside and Luna Park, the latter three being summer amusement parks. The average seating capacity of the theaters was 1,500, with the Auditorium alone having a capacity of 3,330. Additionally, under construction were a big vaudeville theater at 1618 Curtis Street and the Morris Theater on Champa Street between Fourteenth and Fifteenth Streets.

Of greater concern to theater owners was the presence of twenty-five motion picture establishments located within the Denver area.

To the theatrical profession, Denver had become known as one of the best "show" towns in the United States, in that its appreciation of what may be generally termed "amusements" was of a very high order.[2-1]

Although there was competition among theater and motion picture managers, the reputation of Elitch Gardens as the place to see, continued to attract visitors to the Gardens and loyal patrons to its Theatre.

In addition to the excellent drama offered by the Elitch-Long Stock Company, the patrons of the Gardens enjoyed the summer symphonies.

> The summer symphonies at Elitch are decidedly the most artistic entertainment offered in Denver this season. At any time a ramble among the trees, shrubs and flowers of the beautiful resort is pleasant, but when the Cavallo orchestra interprets the splendid creations of the world's most famous composers midst such environment it is really enchanting.[2-1]

The Elitch Gardens management arranged for special Elitch automobiles to transport theater patrons from downtown Denver to the Theatre and for their return following the performance. Reservations for seats in the Elitch autos could be made at the Denver Omnibus and Cab Company's office. The round trip ticket cost was 50 cents. The ad read:

> Special Elitch Automobiles will leave the Oxford hotel at 7:30 p.m. and the Albany hotel at 7:35 p.m. each day, reaching the Gardens after a most delightful ride in ample time for the Theatre, returning direct to the hotels within ten minutes after the last curtain.[2-2]

The highlight of the season at Elitch was the appearance of William Collier as a guest star featured in the last four plays of the season, the plays being William Collier and Grant Stewart's *Caught in the Rain*, J. Hartley Manners and William Collier's *The Patriot*, H. A. Dusouchet's *The Man From Mexico* and Richard Harding Davis' *The Dictator*. Other plays included Booth Tarkington and Margaret Turnbull's *Cameo Kirby*, George Middleton's *The House of a Thousand Candles* and Eugene W. Presbrey's *The Barrier*.

Caught in the Rain is a farce, whose principal character is Dick Crawford, a Colorado mining man, but somewhat of a grumpy woman-hater.

> Caught in a downpour, (Crawford) finds himself shoulder to shoulder with a beautiful girl who quickly captures his affections, but she disappears before he can learn her name. About the same time he recklessly promises a friend, Mr. Mason, to marry his daughter to help him out of a financial problem. No sooner has he made his promise than he recalls the unknown girl and tries to back out. Even when he discovers that Mr. Mason's daughter, Muriel, and the mysterious beauty are one and the same, his problems are not solved, for Muriel is upset by his fickleness. Of course, all ends happily.* [3-1]

The final play of the season was *The Dictator*, a farce by Richard Harding Davis. The story of the play is propelled from a mistaken belief by Brooks Travers, a rich New Yorker, that he has fatally struck a cab driver in a fight over a fare. To avoid possible jail, Travers takes the first boat to Porto Banyos in South America, where revolutions are weekly events. After participating in and surviving several revolutions, Travers learns that the cab driver was not seriously hurt, and decides to take the next ship back, "preferring obnoxious taxi men to Latin instability."[3-2] Brooks Travers was played on Broadway by William Collier, who recreated the role at Elitch.

William Collier

Theatergoers anxiously awaited the "Collier season" at the Elitch Theatre.

William Collier had a stellar reputation in theater, a career which began as a juvenile in *H. M. S. Pinafore* in 1879. He left home over the objection of his actor parents to his pursuing a career in theater. He developed a flair for comedy, and his name became synonymous with laughter. In Peter Hay's book of *Broadway Anecdotes*, he shares the following:

* *Pitter Patter*, a 1920 musical, was based on the play.

> William Collier (1866-1944), actor and wit, once opened *The Patriot,* one of his own plays, on December 30. On January 2 he advertised with some degree of truthfulness: "Second Year in New York."[4]

His appearance at Elitch was a theatrical treat for the people of Denver. Other managers of stock companies had tried many times to have him appear, but he never would. The question was asked: Why Denver? Was there was a reason to believe why he chose Denver beyond the salary paid him, which was the highest ever paid by Elitch to a summer stock actor?[2-3]

Paula Marr frequently performed with Collier as his leading lady. She had a son from a prior relationship. Miss Marr won the heart of Collier and they married. Collier not only became devoted to her, but to her child as well.

Collier and Paula had been engaged to appear at the Broadway Theater in Denver, late in the spring of the 1910 season. The child was taken sick on the first night of their performance.

> He was stricken with scarlet fever and rushed to Steele hospital, while an inexorable fate, that had put their names to a theatrical contract, compelled the parents to appear at the uptown theater, laugh and joke and spring their quips and indulge in repartee, even as the tears stood in their eyes and the gloom of a tragedy gnawed at their hearts.[2-4]
>
> The battle against the disease was begun. The scarlet fever passed. The boy began to grow strong again. However, before the time came when he could be sent to his parents - before the danger of contagion was over - he fell a victim of typhoid.
>
> And once more the fight went on.
>
> His parents, called by engagements, went on and completed their season. They continued to make people laugh - just as they advertised to do. They did their weeping in private.
>
> The boy began to again improve. He had won the second fight.[2-3]

A short time later, the boy was released from the hospital into the Denver sunshine. He was strong and well. On August 14th, he joined his parents on stage in the performance of *The Patriot* at Elitch, appearing in the role of Kid Sugar. The child was given a new name, William Collier Jr., and it appeared for the first time in the Elitch Theatre program. The elder Collier did not wish to be called "stepfather," or "adopted father," or anything but just plain "daddy."

> (And) that's what the little fellow calls the elder one, whose name he has taken, and calls it with the love light shining from his eyes. And the elder refers to the child as "my boy," with the love of parentage in his voice.[2-4]

William Collier took the child into his company, "to teach him, to coach him, to raise him in the ways of the stage and the art of amusing people."[2-4]

Keeping in mind the events that impacted William Collier, a drama critic offered to answer the previously asked question - Why Denver?

> Whatever the reason this time - whether it be that (William Collier) was in Denver with a month on his hands, or whether his boy had been lying ill in a Denver hospital, and could not be taken on a long trip east without a rest, and there was chance for a fat pay envelope while he waited - anyway, he goes on tonight in *Caught in the Rain*, one of his past successes.[2-5]

Denver Public Library Western History Collection

Members of the 1910 cast at Elitch

Chapter Twelve

(1911 - 1913)

The Loyalty of Service
The Death of David Belasco's Daughter
Theatrical Realism
Favorable Economics
The Skills of Excellence
On Being a Stage Actress - A Point of View

The Loyalty of Service

While theater patrons continued to enjoy the plays and actors that were drawn each year to the historic Theatre, behind the scenes were the loyalties of many who silently went about their long service and devoted attention to the interests of their employer. Frank W. White, drama editor of the *Denver Post,* called attention to their service.

> They say that in no walk of life are the changes so frequent as they are in the theatrical business. Managers, agents, actors are all the time moving hither and thither. No one remains long in the same place. It seems to be an immutable law. And yet here in this city is the very exception which perhaps proves the rule.
>
> For instance, old Captain Shirley, who took tickets at the gate until his death this spring, was with the Elitches and later the Longs for over eighteen years. He was a fixture. His job was understood to be a life one. Mr. Alexander, who looks after the stage and Theatre, has been there twenty-two years, and his father eighteen years, or until he died. Signor Cavallo has been the musician at the Gardens for fifteen years, and it is hoped he will be there for fifteen more. Mr. Houck has been treasurer for a dozen years. Messrs. Earl Johnstone and Thomas Mohr have had charge of the box offices for nine years.[1-1]

These and others, together with their loyalty, brought comfort to Mary Elitch Long, who knew that should she be called away on business, or if time was taken for some vacation, the Theatre's interest would be carefully looked after as though she were present.

The 1911 Season

As in every season, citizens of Denver knew that summer had arrived when Elitch Gardens was opened to the public, as they looked forward to another wholesome season of theater, symphonies and family entertainment. And in their service to the people of Denver, local newspapers customarily joined in announcing the opening of the Gardens, as for example, in this season.

> There is an undying sentiment in this community for the Gardens, which will find expression when the Theatre opens tonight with what promises to be an excellent dramatic company, and again on Friday afternoon, when the summer symphonies commence. The refining atmosphere of the Gardens is its charm.[1-2]

Each of the plays presented had previously appeared on Broadway, among them being Israel Zangwill's *The Melting Pot,* James Forbes' *The Chorus Lady,* Frances Hodgson Burnett's *The Dawn of* a *Tomorrow,* Leo Ditrichstein's *Before and After* and Kellett Chambers' *An American Widow.* On June 29th, a special matinee was held of the premiere performance of *The Man Who Lied to Himself* by Mann Page, a prominent Denverite.

Bruce McRae, one of the biggest favorites among Denver audiences, returned to Elitch as the leading man after an absence of five years. He had just completed an entire season run with Blanche Bates in *Nobody's Widow* in New York's Hudson Theater. The leading woman was Jane Grey. Miss Grey was an Anglo-Australian actress whom Charles Frohman brought to the United States and who had just completed a ten-month run in the New York engagement of David Belasco's play, *The Concert*. Robert Morris was the director for the season.

The Broadway production of *The Dawn of a Tomorrow* "was inspired by the growing popularity of Mary Baker Eddy's Christian Science movement." The play is about the interaction of four characters, a terminally ill person with thoughts of killing himself, his ne'er-do-well son, a poor young girl, and a person falsely accused of a crime. By the play's end, "the four walk away confident that their futures are bright."[2-1] A drama critic summarized his thoughts of the play:

> (The play) proves that this isn't a bad old world after all. It proves that there is a something that rules this universe for the best, that all comes out right in the end, and that to "Laugh and the world laughs with you, weep and you weep alone" ... is true in the main.
>
> Anything that makes the fountain of hope spring anew for the butcher, the baker, or any of the candlestick makers can't help being acceptable to the American or English theatergoer. *The Dawn of a Tomorrow* drives care away. It teaches us there is always a better tomorrow, and that things are never so bad as they appear at first look."[3-1]

Three members of the Elitch cast, Julia Blanc, Suzanne Perry and George LaGuere, were members of the original company of *The Dawn of a Tomorrow.*[3-2]

An American Widow was a successful comedy that garnered "big laughs" at Elitch.

Mrs. Elizabeth Killigrew, the rich American widow, becomes enamored of young Lord Dexminster, or rather she wants to wear a coronet, and his seems procurable. The cautious late Mr. Killigrew, however, had appended a refrigerating note to his will transferring all his property to a nephew in case his widow married a second time anyone except a native born American.

A brilliant thought occurs to my lady (that wants to be): "It is only my second marriage that he safeguards against. I'll marry an American, divorce him and then get my title. What's the good of his money if I can't buy what I want with it?"

Mrs. Killigrew proposes to and is accepted by an American composer, Joseph Mallory. There are some pretty scenes between these two, before they both realize that neither of them wants that divorce."[3-3]

The drama critic wrote that "Mr. McRae is perhaps not at his best this week, except in his love scenes. As a lover he is always convincing."[3-3]

The Last Children's Day of the Season

Over 4,000 children of Denver enjoyed the hospitality of Mary Elitch Long on the last Children's Day of the season. Upon entering the gate they were given fruit and a souvenir. Never in the history of the Gardens were there so many children present.[3-4]

The Death of David Belasco's Daughter

On June 5, 1911, Augusta Elliott, the daughter of David Belasco, the famous theatrical manager, playwright and author, died in Colorado Springs from tuberculosis. She had become ill six or seven months earlier and on the advice of her physician was taken to various health resorts in the South. She failed to improve and was then brought to Colorado Springs from North Carolina in the hope of saving her life; however, it was too late in her illness, and she died three weeks later.[1-3]

Augusta Elliott was the wife of William Elliot, a well-known actor who was a member of the resident company of the Elitch Theatre in the 1908 season.

The 1912 Season

Mary Elitch inaugurated a special Dramatic Festival for the last five plays of the season, selecting some of the best plays obtainable in America, among them being Charles Klein's *The Third Degree*, Edward Shelton's *Salvation Nell* and A. E. Thomas' *Her Husband's Wife*. Helen Ware and Bruce McRae were selected as featured performers of the plays, joining the cast for the festival. Robert Morris, the director, worked diligently in preparing the plays for the festival.

Morris was one of New York's best known producers. He was a native of Denver and received his first stage training at Elitch. He was present when the resort first opened in 1890 and, as a boy, frequented the stage door, seeking training from the famous actors of that day. He came into prominence in New York with the companies of Charles Frohman. After a number of seasons with Frohman, Robert Morris joined the staff of Oliver Morosco, producing most of the biggest Morosco successes, including *The Bird of Paradise* and *Peg O' My Heart*.

Among the other plays presented were Edith Ellis' *Seven Sisters* and Augustus Thomas' *The Witching Hour*.

Seven Sisters

A great deal of publicity was given to the play *Seven Sisters* by the *Denver Post*, "which announced a Theatre box party for all families in Colorado having seven daughters. Nineteen Denver homes boasted such wealth, and the *Post* played host to one hundred and thirty-three young ladies during the week. Needless to say the Theatre was crowded for each performance."[4-1]

Seven Sisters is a farce built around an old Hungarian custom that prevents a younger girl of a family from being married until her older sisters have found husbands. The play centers around Mici, the fourth child of the family, who falls in love with a handsome and wealthy lieutenant who wishes to marry her.

> As the older girls are so unattractive that there is little immediate chance of their marrying, Mici encounters much trouble. Her mother puts her into short dresses to suppress her chances, and in every way treats her as a child. However, the girl is quick-witted and energetic, and she and her lieutenant sweetheart scheme to find husbands for the older sisters. The carrying out of their plan is very amusing ... so that the action never flags for a moment.[5-1]

Theatrical Realism

The City was the last play written by Clyde Fitch and was presented on Broadway in 1909 after his death. The opening night was described as "one of the most sensational in history, with near pandemonium reportedly breaking out" when Hancock (played by Tully Marshall) is told that he is an illegitimate child and his wife is in fact his sister. Hancock screams to his informer, "You're a God damn liar!" It was the first time "God damn" was used in a play in New York. "Damn" had been said before, but never the complete expletive.[2-2] Lucille Watson, who appeared in the Broadway production, stated that "when Tully Marshall yelled 'God damn liar' it was a terrific shock to the audience. We could feel that shock backstage."[6]

When the play was presented at Elitch, some reviewers were critical of the extreme realism of the play. The drama critic of the *Denver Post* noted that it was a "horrible story ... an abnormal form of pleasure-seeking, to say the least."[7-1]

> Realism, which may be accounted a modified form of naturalism, sought, at the end of nineteenth century, to substitute for the well-made play and the traditional declamatory acting of the period, dramas which should approximate in speech and situation to the social and domestic problems of every day, played by actors who rejected all artifice and spoke and moved naturally against scenery which reproduced with fidelity the usual surroundings of the people they represented.
>
> The movement began with Ibsen and spread rapidly across Europe, upsetting the established theater and demanding the evolution of a new type of actor to interpret the new playwrights.[8]

The play *Salvation Nell* presented at Elitch was another "realistic work." The lead role, that of a scrubwoman at Sid McGovern's seedy bar on Tenth Avenue, was played on Broadway by Minnie Maddern Fiske.

> Salvation Nell is a girl of New York's slums, who has reached the dregs of life. Her sweetheart, Jim Platt, is sent to prison for murder. During his absence Nell gets religion and becomes a Salvation Army worker. Platt serves out his sentence and returns to the girl. His first thought is to relapse into his old criminal life and drag the girl back with him. Patiently she sets out to save him and herself, and in the accomplishment of this struggle unfolds a beautiful and moving love story.[5-2]

Frank W. White, the *Denver Post* drama critic, wrote that while the play may be excellently performed, "one prefers, I think, being amused in August, rather than ... (be) troubled with dark slums of the wicked moderns."[5-2] A damning response was elicited in White's review of the play.

> *Salvation Nell* is the apotheosis of the brutish. As presented at the Gardens last night it was one of the most degraded entertainments ever given in Denver. It had few redeeming features. It was simply viciously unpleasant. I would certainly no more permit my daughter, or young son, to visit the drama at the Gardens this week than I would take them on a pleasure tour through the dens of Market Street, or introduce them to the degraded inmates of the county jail.
>
> Last night, nothing was left to the imagination. The opening act ... represents a low saloon on the extreme west side of New York. It is frequented by bullies, thieves, drunkards, prostitutes - the very scum of the earth ... Realism here reached its offensive point. The quarrelsome drunkards frequently indulged in loud profanity. Beer and whiskey flowed freely. The bartender swore at his customers; the flashy men leered and pawed the overdressed courtesans.
>
> "True to life," one would say. Precisely. But why present it for public

view? Why make a great display of moral, mental and physical filthiness? No, the picture at the Gardens this week is little less than shameful. It is so out of keeping with the tone and character of the lovely resort that I, who am no purist, grieve at the spectacle.

It will, however, attract the morbid, and may commercially prosper. In the interest of good taste, it might be as well if it didn't.[7-2]

By comparison, in the *Theatre Magazine,* the following was written:

"Salvation Nell" is from the heart of the times ... The intent is not to entertain us with the disagreeable or to make us acquainted with vice for our amusement. It is all incidental to the pity and sympathy which it should evoke.[2-3]

It is suggested by one writer that "inasmuch as *The City* and *Salvation Nell* were presented at the Gardens at a time when gate receipts were seriously declining, it is believed that they were selected as a rather desperate attempt to increase attendance." He also noted that the "clean and wholesome" management policy of the Gardens "was relaxed, at least temporarily, during the season of 1912."[9]

The Third Degree

The Third Degree was the first of the five plays in which Helen Ware was featured. In this play, its author, Charles Klein, set out to dramatize the public resentment of methods used by the police in extracting confessions from those who have been prejudged as guilty. The show was a Broadway success, with Helen Ware playing Annie, the wife of the one accused of murder. She is the only one convinced of his innocence and ultimately secures his release. Her performance raised her to a stellar position on the New York stage. The performance was replicated on the Elitch stage.

Geoffrey Stein's Resignation

It is a rare occasion when there is any dissent among members of a cast of players selected for the resident company of the Elitch Theatre. To the contrary, members of a company have usually worked well together. However, this season experienced some friction with a cast member, Geoffrey Stein, who finally resigned. Although Stein was primarily engaged for his remarkable work in *The City*, his presence was desired for the rest of the season.

The parts assigned him after the Clyde Fitch week *(The City)* did not please him, and he rebelled. The affair culminated when he was given the part of the elder son in *Mother.* It is the lead, but was declined, as I understand it, by Mr. McRae. It was then given Mr. Stein who, to be frank, played it very badly. Feeling that he was being discriminated against, he resigned peremptorily Monday night and will have nothing further to do with the Gardens. Actors are supersensitive, you know, and Mr. Stein, with all his cleverness, is of a nervous temperament. Some of the company sympathize with him, others do not.[5-3]

Favorable Economics

Although the season was still young, a prosperous season was anticipated among the amusement circles of Denver. In other parts of the country, three stock companies were reported to have failed, the backers refusing to continue to fund them. These were in Richmond, Virginia, Milwaukee, Wisconsin and Atlanta, Georgia.

Later reports affirmed the anticipations. It was reported in late July that despite the cool and gloomy week, Elitch did "fairly well."[5-4] At the end of the season, an article stated, "I hear the resorts have made a little money this season, the Gardens doubtless leading" and "the Gardens has had a week of great prosperity and will close in a wave of success."[5-3]

The 1913 Season

The Skills of Excellence

It has been estimated that the number of words a leading man or woman has to commit to memory and properly speak for a week's performance is over 7,000.

In a resident company, while a play is being performed, the actors are handed their parts for the next week's play, to begin memorizing their lines.

> (Actors) are at work from dawn until nearly midnight. If they are not good at memorizing, or worry over their tasks, the work must be enormously hard, the strain on their systems something tremendous.
>
> For you see the actors must absorb the atmosphere of the characters given them; must be ingenious in the matter of little bits of stage business; must think carefully of their dress, their exits and their entrances, and must do so many things to offer a perfect presentation that the memorizing is really but a minor part.[10-1]

The leading man was Lewis Stone. Chrystal Herne, one of the most promising and charming young actresses in the country, was the leading woman. She was the daughter of playwright James A. Herne. The director was Robert Morris. Among the plays for the season were George Bernard Shaw's *Man and Superman*, James A. Herne's *Shore Acres*, W. Somerset Maugham's *Smith* and William C. De Mille's *The Woman*.

Lewis Stone

Lewis Stone was considered by the critics to be the most popular leading man in stock in America at that time. For eight years, he held the role as leading man with the Oliver Morosco Stock Company in Los Angeles.

An amusing incident occurred while Stone was performing in a matinee at Elitch, at which his two young daughters were in attendance and seated in a box. Upon his entrance on stage, and above the applause of the audience, two happy voices could be heard excitedly calling "Papa ... Papa ... there's Papa!"[4-2]

Mary Elitch recalled in her memoir a charitable act by Lewis Stone.

> Hearing of the death of a man who ran a small concession in the Gardens, and the extreme need of his young wife and small children living in a little house some blocks from our grounds, Mr. Stone went to a neighborhood grocery and, placing $25.00 on the counter, told the storekeeper to see to it that the bereaved little family wanted for nothing; and to let him know when more money was needed and to *say nothing about it.* The groceryman kept his word until after Mr. Stone had left. I think the little family never knew who their kind benefactor was.[4-3]

In an effort to describe a "real good actor" the talent of Lewis Stone was chosen by example in an article that appeared in the *Denver Post.*

> A real good actor is known by his attention to detail ... Take leading man Stone at the Gardens. In the second act of the comedy he is supposed to go to the piano and play a delightful little Schumann melody. He sits at the piano facing the audience, which sees his face, his shoulders, and the movement of his upper arms. His expression denotes rapture, his body sways to the musical movement, his eyes wander over the keys; his work is the work of an earnest musician. Everybody in the audience instinctively remarks, "How well he plays." But it is make-believe; he is not playing, yet carries out the illusion perfectly. At another piano, close by, in the wings, Mrs. Worrell is playing the Schumann number.[10-2]

Man and Superman

George Bernard Shaw's *Man and Superman* had never been presented in Denver until this season at Elitch. It had been scheduled to have played at Denver's Broadway Theater, seven years earlier. The play was being presented at San Francisco when the earthquake struck, a fortnight before its scheduled appearance at the Broadway Theater. The earthquake so upset matters that all theater companies in San Francisco hurried back East as fast as trains would travel, canceling all engagements.[10-3] The success of the play at Elitch was unprecedented. It was a banner week in point of attendance.

The Woman

The Woman, a play by William C. De Mille, had a lengthy run on Broadway. The play is about Jim Blake, a corrupt politician anxious to push through a bill allowing railroads to inflate their stocks. He desires to smear the reputation of his idealistic opponent, Matthew Standish, by disclosing that Standish has been unfaithful to his wife. To learn of the identity of the woman with whom Standish is involved, Blake attempts to bribe a telephone operator to provide him with telephone numbers she learns from Standish in order for Blake to learn the identity of the woman. Unbeknown to Blake, the woman is his own daughter.[2-4]

> A telephone operator (played by Helen Ware) is pushed by a powerful syndicate of capitalists and corporation heads to reveal certain messages that she has heard over the wires. To do so involves the reputation of another woman. The plucky little operator refuses to betray her trust, although she is threatened with a year in jail.[11]

The operator finds a means to keep anyone from being hurt and wins the affection of Blake's son in the process.

On Being a Stage Actress - A Point of View

A Denver actress who had been on stage for several years, and who was in Denver with her company, was asked what advice she would give to a young lady with a good voice who wanted to pursue a stage career. She offered her point of view.

> I should tell her to go home and mend her stockings, do anything but go on the stage. There is no happiness in stage life. It is a life of continual worriment. The stage is no place for a woman who is not absolutely wedded to her art. The artist should not think of marrying. While she is on stage she is not fit to be the wife of any man. There is always a divided heart, and no man wants that.[10-2]

Denham Theater

In 1913, the Denham Theater was built at the corner of California and Eighteenth Street. On November 8th, C. D. Woodward, a stock manager from Kansas City, opened the theater with a resident company and the winter season of plays was successful. In 1933, the theater programs were abandoned in favor of motion pictures.

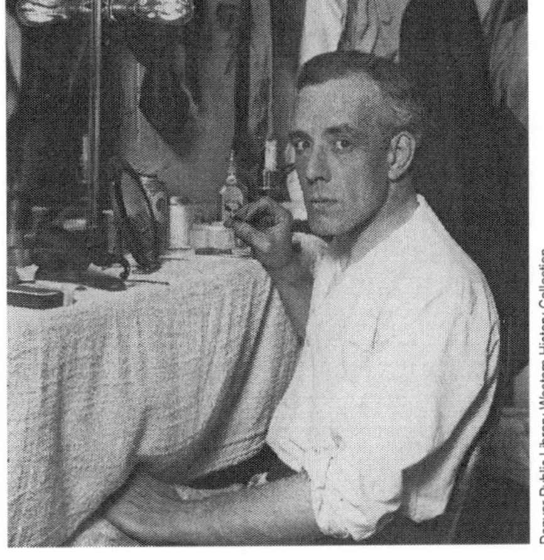

Denver Public Library Western History Collection

Lewis Stone in his dressing room at Elitch (1913)

Denver Public Library Western History Collection

Ben Johnson and Jean Shelby rehearsing (1913)

Denver Public Library Western History Collection

Mary Elitch and Members of 1913 Cast

Chapter Thirteen

(1914)

The Silver Jubilee Celebration
Thais Magrane, Bruce McRae and Eva Lang
A Darker Side of the World

The Silver Jubilee Celebration

The season of 1914 was a milestone in the history of Elitch Gardens. The 25th anniversary of the Gardens and its Theatre warranted public recognition and a celebration.

The *Denver Post* prepared the way for the celebration by its letter to Mrs. Mary Elitch Long dated May 18th inviting her to write her reminiscences of the quarter of a century just passed for publication in the *Post*. On May 20th, Mrs. Elitch Long responded favorably, stating: "I will do what you request with pleasure: that is, I will do the best I can, and endeavor to give you those personal experiences which are green in my memory, and which are of interest to me, at least, and which I trust may prove so to the great *Post* family."[1] The *Denver Post* thereafter received three lengthy, interesting and well-written installments from Mrs. Elitch Long that appeared in editions of the *Post* dated May 31st, June 2nd and June 14th. It provided the background for Denverites to better savor the history of the Gardens and to enjoy the silver jubilee celebration.[2]

Mary Elitch Long invited all those residents of Denver who witnessed the first performance in the Theatre at Elitch Gardens on May 1, 1890, to be guests of hers at the silver jubilee performance.

The silver jubilee celebration was held on June 6, 1914. Mayor J. M. Perkins officially opened the Theatre at Elitch Gardens for its 25th season. The speech that Mayor Wolfe Londoner made on the occasion of the opening of the Gardens twenty-five years earlier was read from the stage by Mayor Perkins, followed by a few felicitous remarks before the first theatrical performance of the season, Porter Emerson's *The Spendthrift*, was presented. City and state officials were present as well as an unusually fashionable audience.

A delightful jubilee banquet was scheduled and held following the performance. Mrs. Elitch Long related some of her experiences with the management of the Gardens. At the celebration she encountered many old friends who were present at the opening 25 years before, including Mrs. Wolfe Londoner, Adolph Meyer, Father William O'Brien and Peter McCourt and his wife.[3]

The Season

Among the plays selected for the season were those by such notable playwrights as W. Somerset Maugham, George Bernard Shaw and Arthur Conan Doyle. Each of the plays had its share of Broadway, with Rida Johnson Young's *The Lottery Man* having enjoyed a 200 performance run at the Bijou Theater.[4-1]

The members of the cast fulfilled the promise by Mary Elitch Long to celebrate the twenty-fifth consecutive year of her Gardens by securing the best, most highly seasoned actors for the season. As was apparent, the promise was redundant because that was always her goal.

The leading lady was Thais Magrane, a star of the notable producer Henry W. Savage. Bruce McRae, whose popularity was firmly established with Denver audiences in prior seasons, was the leading man. Eva Lang was invited as a special guest to close the season with her performance in the final play of the season.

Among the other cast members was Spring Byington, a Colorado native, who later became a popular film star. Robert Morris returned as director.

Thais Magrane

Thais Magrane was unquestionably a fine actress. In George Bernard Shaw's *You Never Can Tell,* it was said that Miss Magrane "has proved herself a finished actress, reliable, talented, carefully conscientious in her work, and high up in the technique and art of her profession."[5-1]

But audiences and critics began to notice other things about Miss Magrane that proved bothersome in the local and intimate setting that was Denver.

> Lacking nothing in intellectual comprehension, she is, however, quite without personality. She is like a thoroughly good clergyman, who, while being the icicle of sect, is wanting in the flame of a faith.
>
> Miss Magrane, while a rich dresser at times, is not a good dresser, and her hair, as generally worn, is an abomination.
>
> But for all this, this very accomplished woman is one the very best actresses that has been in Denver during any summer season.[5-1]

Unfortunately, Miss Magrane had to leave the cast before the season's end to fill another engagement. As a result, cast member Mary Edgett Baker appeared in the lead role of *The Speckled Band*. In a review of the play, a final farewell to Miss Magrane was written.

> Miss Magrane's departure, I am sorry to say, was not generally regretted. She is a good actress, a reliable, earnest worker. If she had gone after a stay of a month, her absence would have been deplored.
>
> In *The Spendthrift, Mrs. Dot* and *Years of Discretion,* the opening plays, she won approval. But after that Miss Magrane's popularity began to wane. She was not a good dresser, and, besides being frumpy, she

lacked personality, those qualities which women demand. As it is, women who support the Theatre, called for a change, and when that was not forthcoming, (there was) a dwindling of attendance. But no one can question the ability, the histrionic earnestness of Miss Magrane. In a traveling company, in a suitable part, she would shine most decidedly.[5-2]

Bruce McRae

Lewis Stone was to again be the leading man for the season. However, his youngest daughter became dangerously ill in Boston and he had to cancel his engagement. Mary Elitch recalled the urgency of the moment in her memoirs. She wired Mr. McRae with an urgent plea for him to come to her rescue.

> My message was received the day before he expected to sail for a much needed vacation in Europe. I received his answer at once: "Of course I will come. There is no other spot on earth that would lure me from my vacation in Europe. I consider it a privilege to play at the Gardens because I love the place, and all actors feel as I do."[6]

McRae was born in India, a nephew of the famed British star Charles Wyndham. He came to America with the intent of becoming a rancher; however, he soon turned to acting and made his debut in 1891 in *Thermidor*.* He appeared in numerous plays as Ethel Barrymore's leading man, among them being *Cousin Kate* and *A Doll's House*.[4-2] McRae had forsaken pleasantly anticipated vacation days in England and France for the opportunity to work at Elitch, to renew old friendships and to make new ones. McRae considered it a privilege to play and perform at the Gardens. He had previously performed at Elitch in 1904, 1905, 1908, 1911 and 1912.

Spring Byington

Spring Byington was a member of the cast and appeared in *The Spendthrift* and *Elevating a Husband*. She was born in Colorado Springs on October 17, 1893. She was orphaned at an early age. She made her acting debut at the age of 14 with the Elitch Gardens Stock Company. She later made numerous appearances with touring companies before making her Broadway debut in 1924. In 1933, she entered the world of film and played supporting roles in more than 100 films.[7]

Eva Lang

For several years, Mary Elitch Long brought a famous and popular theatrical star to Elitch late in the summer season to give distinction to the closing theatrical performances, such as Helen Ware, who was brought to Elitch from New York during the past two seasons.

* The *Denver Post* reported that McRae made his debut in New York in 1892 in Bronson Howard's *Aristocracy*. *Denver Post* (Section Two), Jul 21, 1914, p. 6.

> In planning a similar move this year, Mrs. Long looked over the whole theatrical field with a view to finding the actress most suited to her requirements. The matter of expense did not for a moment enter into her choice. But when she had considered the matter from every angle, only one name presented itself as being strong enough to fill the bill. That was Denver's favorite actress - Miss Eva Lang.
>
> Miss Lang had arranged to go to New York to star in a new piece that is being prepared for her; but when Mrs. Long mentioned the Elitch engagement to her, the young lady readily consented to postpone her departure and play during the closing week at the Gardens.[8]

Eva Lang appeared in the closing performance of the season, the comedy success, *Elevating a Husband*. She remained at Elitch for nine days, the closing week, and two additional days of performances on the following Sunday and Labor Day.

Years of Discretion

The season had a basketful of excellent plays to present, among them being the comedy *Years of Discretion*. The play tells of a Massachusetts widow, Ellie, living in the suburbs of Boston - rich, prim, and conventional - who all her life has been suppressed by New England proprieties. She now hates the learned societies, the mothers' club, and the high-brow gatherings, and she longs for "life" and all its frivolity.

> She rebels. She breaks away. At 48 she goes to New York to visit a fashionable friend. She declares she will, from that instant, dispense with her dowdy attire, and become a gay, dashing, elegantly dressed woman of the period, with a French maid, splendid costumes, and be on the lookout for "trouble."
>
> She carries out her plan. The transformation is astonishing. From a woman of about fifty - and looking it - she is changed by art, and her maid's skill, to look not a day over thirty.
>
> Three men fall desperately in love with her. They are all over fifty.
>
> In the end she marries Dallas, and when they are ready to start on a honeymoon around the world, she is conscience-stricken and feels she must confess to her husband the lie she has been living.
>
> She tells him that she is really an old woman; that she is a sham; that the things that won him are false.[5-3]

After Ellie confesses her age and shortcomings, Dallas comes forth and tenderly shares his confession.

> Ellie, do you think you are the only one who has feared and struggled? ... I am afraid that before many weeks I would have had to say what

> you were brave enough to confess first - I, too, am growing old. Yes, Ellie, I can't pretend any longer. I haven't paints and powder, Ellie, but I have rheumatism, and a great inclination to doze after dinner. I puff when I go upstairs, and I pant when I come down, and I am very fussy. YOU old! Why, Ellie, I have crossed the half-century mark. And I've been frightened to death, dearie, wondering how I was going to tell you!
>
> After this mutual confession the new wife goes indoors, returning in her former prim but comfortable costume. "Dal" lets out some notches in his belt, puts on his glasses. They settle down comfortably in natural peace, and as the curtain falls he observes to his wife, contentedly, "all the joys are not for youth alone."[5-3]

On opening night the play started late and ran late. It was nearly midnight when the curtain fell, yet no one was bored for even a moment, as the audience also came to the realization that "all the joys are not for youth alone."

A Darker Side of the World

While Denver enjoyed the success of the silver jubilee celebration at the Gardens, it was burdened by events that occurred in a darker side of the world. On June 28, 1914, the Austrian Archduke Francis Ferdinand and his wife were assassinated at Sarajevo, Bosnia by a Serbian fanatic.[5-4] Little more than a month later, World War I erupted.

Denver Public Library Western History Collection

Bruce McRae (1914)

Chapter Fourteen

(1915 - 1920)

The War Years
Hope Diminished
The Foreclosure Sale
The Sale of the Gardens to John M. Mulvihill
The Elitch Theatre - Welcome Home
The Death of Thomas D. Long

The 1915 Season

The 1915 season at Elitch Gardens followed its silver jubilee year. The leading players and the cast appeared to have been carefully selected, as well as the plays. All the plays had previously appeared on Broadway. There was hope that it would be a good year.

The delicate and lovely Edith Taliaferro, who had made her mark on the stage when in her early teens, was to appear as a "guest star" in the final four plays of the season. In the final scheduled play, she was cast in the role of Rebecca Rowena Randell in *Rebecca of Sunnybrook Farm,* which role she had performed in the play's original Broadway presentation at the Republican Theater in 1910.

George M. Cohan

Two of the plays presented in the 1915 Elitch season were written by George M. Cohan: *Seven Keys to Baldpate* and *The Miracle Man.* While most theatergoers associate George M. Cohan with the "Yankee Doodle Boy," he was a thoroughbred in the theater, with talents that included actor, composer, librettist, lyricist and producer. He was born into a family of vaudeville performers in Providence, Rhode Island in 1878.

Two of the greatest acting accomplishments of his career were in plays written by others. In 1933 he performed the role of Nat Miller in Eugene O'Neill's *Ah Wilderness!,* and in 1937 he played President Roosevelt in Rogers and Hart's *I'd Rather Be Right.*

Among the many song hits he had written for musicals were *Forty-Five Minutes From Broadway, Give My Regards to Broadway* and *Nellie Kelly, I Love You.*

Cohan died in 1942. In 1968, many of his songs were presented in the Broadway biography musical *George M.*

Ladies' Hats

In an effort to eliminate an annoyance to theater audiences, particularly during the jubilee year, the Elitch Theatre program contained an admonition to the ladies regarding their hats. It read as follows:

> The management insists that ladies will not wear their hats in any part of the Theatre. This includes the boxes. This is in justice to all patrons.[1-1]

For theater owners, ladies' hats had been a continuing issue.* At times, a divergent view was offered, as when the drama editor of the *Denver Post* defended women whose seating could not obstruct the view of others.

> For the life of me I cannot see, when a party purchases a box, why the women should not be permitted to wear hats if they so choose. Or, if they sit in the loges and cannot interfere with the observation of others, no one being behind them, why this privilege of feminine adornment is not granted.
>
> Some women look very pretty in the new headgear and, as vanity is our besetting sin, why not let them wear their pretty lids if they are willing to pay the price.[2]

Hope Diminished

The hope for a good year soon diminished. Concern over World War I had a negative impact on attendance at theaters throughout the country, including the Elitch Theatre. During Broadway's 1914-15 season, the immediate effect of the war resulted in a significant plunge in theater attendance. On May 7, 1915, the *Lusitania* was sunk by a German torpedo. Broadway producer Charles Frohman and playwright Charles Klein were aboard and among the dead.[3] The uncertainty of the future caused patrons of the theater and others to be focused on the war news rather than on the box office.[4-1]

Beginning in 1912, other factors began to surface that signaled a gradual decline in ticket sales at Elitch.

> Rival summer stock companies, such as Lakeside Amusement Park, the City Auditorium, and the new Denham Theater, provided almost overwhelming competition for the company at Elitch.
>
> Economically, this was a period of rising costs. Businesses that were able to meet rising costs with increased volume or value of sales, or both, coped with the situation successfully. But the theater, generally, was faced with declining volume of sales, and theatergoers did not react favorably to higher admission prices.
>
> The popularity of the automobile served as an additional distraction from the success of the road theaters in general and Elitch Gardens in particular. In Denver, the automobile increased the inducement for people

* This admonition against ladies wearing hats in any part of the Theatre appeared in earlier Elitch Theatre programs, e.g., Elitch Theatre program, Aug 24, 1908, p. 4.

> to stay out of the playhouse and to enjoy rides to the nearby mountain parks, which were now easily accessible.
>
> (And) the growing popularity of motion pictures seriously affected legitimate theater activity in Denver as well as in the rest of the United States.[5-1]

In addition to these causes, the month of May 1915 was the coldest since 1888. Also, the city experienced an unusually heavy amount of rainfall.* To use the vernacular, "the weather was 'rotten' and the audience, in consequence, dwindled."[6-1]

Efforts were made to increase ticket sales at Elitch. Frank W. White, the drama editor of the *Denver Post,* began a newspaper campaign designed to attract the public to the Theatre.

> At a time when summer resorts all over the land were dropping away in popularity (and) when the great public was driving automobiles or taking in the movies ... the (Elitch) company keeps on, and I want to say it is a good company, worthy of support. The three plays to be given this month are new and clever, and if there is a bit of sentiment in the Denver public, it should go out to the Gardens this week and next and give Mrs. Elitch Long the practical sympathy she ought to have. Being "sorry" is nothing. A pair of paid-for seats at the play is much more to the purpose.[6-2]

Another factor that contributed to the season's downfall was that the opening plays at Elitch were not new. Elitch always had the very best, and its patrons had been educated to expect something wonderful there. A fine performance of *The Thief,* the opening play of the season, "did only fairly well."[6-3] Aware of the distractions of automobiles and movies, people in the know had told the managers or directors "at the outset that the only hope lay in an extraordinary company, or some luminous star, or gay light opera."[6-2]

An effort was made to better the conditions by engaging the well-known star, Billie Burke, as a "guest star" to bolster box-office receipts. Billie Burke, who was later to play "The Good Fairy" in 1939 in the film, *The Wizard of Oz,* had completed her engagement at the Tabor Grand Opera House in early July; however, she declined the invitation to play at Elitch as she was keen to rejoin her "friend husband" Flo Ziegfeld in New York.[6-2]

To help address the financial needs of the Gardens, five Denver businessmen (including J. K. Mullen), loyal and close friends of Mary Elitch Long, each contributed five hundred dollars to that end.[6-4]

* "The weather had much to do with sparse audiences. The resorts need sizzling heat to draw the multitude out of town." *Denver Post,* Jun 13, 1915. p. 8.

There was also an issue with the lead players selected for the season. The drama critic noted:

> No one not in the business has an idea of the value of the leading man or leading woman in a stock company. It is personal popularity that counts, as much as artistic merit. This year Miss (Mary) Hall was chosen for leading woman, one of the best actresses in her line in the country. But she failed to attract, not on account of her personality, which, I am told, is charming, but for other reasons. One, perhaps, was that the leading man was much younger than the leading woman, making the conditions incongruous and a trifle unnatural.[6-2]

To make matters worse, Miss Hall retired from the stock company on July 10th, as did David M. Hartford, the director, and some others. Fortunately, their places were able to be filled with other performers.

A play new to Denver, Arthur Schnitzler's *The Affairs of Anatol*, was brought in toward the end of July. It stimulated business somewhat, but the change came too late. In an effort to make the season a success for Mary Elitch Long, John F. Harley, a local theater manager, assumed the managerial role and the financial burdens and control of the Theatre when Mr. Hartford left. He terminated his association with Elitch on July 31st after putting on three shows and sustaining a financial loss of $1,083.00.[6-5]

The Theatre was closed on August 14, 1915, and the final three plays with Edith Taliaferro were not presented. On September 23rd, the Gardens were placed into receivership.

The 1916 Season

The Foreclosure Sale

Mary Elitch Long struggled to keep the Gardens going. Throughout her financial crisis, she refused to admit how desperate the circumstances were. As of May 1915, Oscar L. Malo, son-in-law, lawyer and business manager of John K. Mullen, held a $20,000.00 mortgage lien on the Gardens. On April 18, 1916, the property was sold at the foreclosure sale to Malo for $26,911.07, a sum representing the amount of the mortgage, interest, money paid for taxes, and court costs.*

Public Benefit Honoring Mary Elitch Long

As the summer season of 1916 approached, to many of the citizens of Denver, the future of the Gardens and the Theatre and that of Mary Elitch Long were in doubt. News circulated that the Gardens and the Theatre would remain closed for the summer, and perhaps forever. On May 8, 1916, a public benefit honoring Mary Elitch Long was held in the city auditorium.

* *Denver Times*, Apr 18, 1916, p. 1.

Malo and Deputy Sheriff Schaefer were the only persons present at the sale. Levy at p. 71.

Four thousand Denver residents were in attendance to pay their respect and love to Mary Elitch Long and to let her know that while the Gardens may become a thing of the past, she and the Gardens would be held forever in the pleasant places of their memories. And they made it known that they would miss the inspiration of the finer and cleaner and more artistic stagecraft which the Elitch Theatre provided.

From the beginning, the event was well-organized. Signor Rafaelo Cavallo secured an orchestra of fifty concert musicians. The musicians' union passed a resolution in favor of their members playing for the benefit gratuitously. Margaret Fealy arranged and directed the stage presentations, which lived up to her promise that the program would be "the best that the Theatre's hard work and intelligence can make it." Among the program presentations was its magnificent concluding feature from the trial scene of Shakespeare's *Merchant of Venice*, done amid gorgeous settings.[7-1]

The *Denver Post* reported that the net result of the benefit "will doubtless be $5,000, perhaps a little more," and that the money will be placed in the hands of Godfrey Schirmer, president of the German-American bank, to be trustee of the fund. It went on to state that:

> (The money) will be carefully safeguarded for Mrs. Long's best interest. No one but the lady herself will receive a dollar. It will be outside the pale of creditors. A committee ... will meet Mrs. Long, get her views, and will decide then how the money shall be invested or used to bring all possible happiness in the future to the admired beneficiary.[7-2]

The article went on to state that "the books are not yet closed. Anyone who wishes can send in, this week, an offering to the fund, and thus add to the happiness of the good woman of the Gardens."

Mary Elitch Long was an old family friend of John K. Mullen. Oscar L. Malo arranged for the purchase of the Gardens for the benefit of Mullen, his father-in-law. Desirous of protecting her interest in the Gardens, Mullen purchased the resort for the $26,911.07 Malo paid at the foreclosure sale.*

The Sale of the Gardens to John M. Mulvihill

On June 20, 1916, about two months after acquiring the Gardens, Mullen sold the Gardens to John M. Mulvihill for $35,000 in notes, but with certain stipulations as part of the contract: first, that Mrs. Elitch would be allowed to live in her bungalow home on the grounds of the resort rent-free as long as she desired; second, that the resort would pay for all utilities concerned with the operation of the bungalow; and, finally, that the resort would pay Mrs. Elitch fifty dollars each month as long

* In the book dealing with "The Life of Colorado's Premiere Irish Patron, John Kernan Mullen," it states that "Malo arranged the purchase of Mary Elitch's Gardens for Mullen ..." Convery, *Pride of the Rockies* (University Press of Colorado 2005), p. 146.

as she lived. Mulvihill honored the notes and retired them early.[8]

The admiration and appreciation of the achievements of Mary Elitch Long were not overlooked by the Mulvihill family. In addition to adhering to the above stipulations, they continued to permit her to be associated with the Gardens and retained for her the special box reserved for her at the Elitch Theatre.

In the years ahead John Mulvihill would build Mary Elitch Long a new home in the Gardens to replace her bungalow home. It was to be a beautiful two-story brick home installed with the first gas and electric stove in all of North Denver.[9] Mary was to live in that house until her death in 1936. John M. Mulvihill, was born in Dudley, Pennsylvania on April 20, 1869, was schooled in Pennsylvania, taught school for a few years, had a position in the office of the State Reformatory, and in 1895 he was employed in the executive offices of the Carnegie Steel Mills at Pittsburgh. Because of a condition that threatened his lungs, he moved to Denver in 1900, having been advised to seek a higher altitude. The bracing air of Colorado served him well.

Robert W. Speer (Mayor of Denver from 1904 to 1912 and 1916 to 1918) was a lifelong friend of John Mulvihill. Speer was also born in Pennsylvania and worked for the Pennsylvania Railroad until 1878 when he moved to Colorado in an effort to recover from tuberculosis. Speer introduced Mulvihill to the officers of the Denver Gas and Electric Company, and Mulvihill was at once hired to assume charge of credits and collections.

It was apparent that John Mulvihill's background was not one that lent support to the skills and interest needed to manage a summer amusement park and theater, particularly one in crisis.

> (In 1916) Elitch Gardens as an amusement enterprise was threatening to fail. Its Theatre lost much of its patronage and its former glory. Its outdoor dance pavilion was drawing only a few patrons. The amusement devices were virtually idle.[10]

The Theatre Remained Closed for the 1916 Season

At the time that Mulvihill took over the park, it was too late in the season to select performers for a resident stock company. Accordingly, in 1916, the Theatre at Elitch Gardens did not open for the first time in twenty-six seasons.

The Gardens were open to the public, and the concession stands and rides were operating during the summer of 1916; however, Elitch Theatre remained closed for the season. While many were disappointed, Frank W. White reminded citizens of Denver that the Theatre was "a business."

> The theatrical business - for it is a business - is the quickest of all enterprises to feel the effects of economic disturbances. Hot weather, elections, depressions, war scares, almost anything that affects the public,

> has its immediate reflex on the attendance at the playhouse. Thus last week, with weather a trifle unseasonable, with an election progressing and Mexican excitements interesting the people, the theaters suffered. The attendance at all the places of amusement fell below normal. It is always so. The playhouse is a perfect barometer of conditions. If things are running quietly then the theatrical game prospers. But let any outside influence come along to excite or unduly interest the people and the box office suffers.[7-2]

Mulvihill began to consult others who were knowledgeable in the entertainment industry for guidance regarding policies of management until he gained the practical experience and confidence to make his own decisions.

Mulvihill began to spend a great deal of money on the Gardens. He was reported to have brought to the resort the Midas touch. The dance hall was lavishly and artistically decorated. It wasn't long before the turnstiles of the Gardens again began to click.

The 1917 Season

America's Declaration of War on Germany

> On 1 May 1915 the American tanker *Gulflight* was torpedoed and sunk without warning. Germany offered to make reparation for this "unfortunate accident" but refused to abandon submarine warfare. Six days later a U-boat torpedoed and sank Cunard liner *Lusitania* off the coast of Ireland, with the loss of over 1100 civilians, including 128 American citizens, some of them women.[11-1]

Other incidents of unrestricted German submarine warfare occurred. Finally, President Woodrow Wilson recognized that a position of neutrality was no longer feasible or desirable when the peace of the world was involved. On April 6, 1917, Good Friday, America declared war on Germany.[11-2]

The Elitch Theatre - The Struggle of the Season

In 1917, John Mulvihill had yet to develop the confidence to manage the Theatre himself. Accordingly, he decided to lease the Theatre to Joseph D. Glass, an experienced director of a stock company in El Paso, Texas, to install a resident stock company at Elitch to open its season on June 17th.[12-1]

After several postponements, the opening of the season took place on June 24th with the play *Jerry*, a comedy made popular in New York by Billie Burke. Glass announced that youth would be the dominant factor in the personnel of his stock company. Audra Alden, a 21-year-old, was selected to play the lead role in *Jerry*, as she "has been successful in Billy Burke roles."[12-2] While the play received satisfactory press, poor attendance raised a concern that the Theatre might be forced to close prematurely.[5-2]

It was suggested that the small attendance numbers at the performances were largely impacted by two factors. The cast of the resident company did not contain "name" players, and the plays scheduled for the first three weeks of the season had been performed in downtown Denver theaters during the two preceding seasons.[5-2]

As a result, Mulvihill called for a complete reorganization of the company on July 6, 1917, replacing Glass with O. D. Woodward, the successful manager of the Denham Stock Company in Denver. The popular Maude Fealy was engaged as the company's leading lady. She appeared in *Her Own Money*, *The Bachelor*, *Sauce for the Goose* and other comedies. Although the change was beneficial, the attendance at the Elitch Theatre did not reach a level that was financially successful.[5-3]

The War - It's Effect on Broadway

During the 1917-18 New York season, the war had a serious impact on Broadway.

> A number of actors and authors enlisted and temporarily or, in a few cases, permanently disappeared from the theatrical scene. Those left behind found themselves working overtime, not merely doing their accustomed theatrical chores but heading recruitment and war bond rallies, busily knitting for the troops, or rushing to nearby army camps to entertain trainees.
>
> Producers howled when Congress imposed a war tax that added another 10 percent to prices. Broadway was sure it discerned a playgoer rebellion when a number of shows closed almost immediately after they opened, and by January show after show was cutting its ticket prices. William A. Brady, always an alarmist, complained: "We are on the edge of a still panic, and in these circumstances it is only natural that the theater as a luxury should be among the first to suffer ... Business, if anything, will become worse as the war continues and taxes increase."[4-2]

The Lure of the Movies

In addition to war having an impact on the theatrical world, the temptations tendered by the motion picture industry to stars of the legitimate stage was likewise a matter of concern. Actors and actresses gradually succumbed to the attractive movie contract offers. For example, George M. Cohan had his tryout on the screen, and Fannie Ward was said to be away from the stage for good.

The 1918 and 1919 Seasons

The Elitch Theatre closed during the 1918 and 1919 seasons.

The World War ended by the signing of the armistice on November 11, 1918. A period of peacetime reconstruction and stabilization was to follow for America.

The disappointing attendance in 1917 and the mounting world affairs contributed to Mulvihill's decision not to open the Theatre during the 1918 and 1919 seasons, although the Gardens otherwise remained in operation as a popular "family" resort.

The question of what to do with the Theatre building was a matter of great concern to Mulvihill. He considered other possible options, such as utilizing it as a dance hall. Meanwhile, having been deprived of the opportunity to see good theater during the summer months for a period of nearly three years, theatergoers in Denver were hungry to resurrect the joys of the past. At least they besieged Mr. Mulvihill for an opportunity. The automobile was no longer a novelty, and motion pictures had not progressed enough to replace "live" theater. Notwithstanding some misgivings, Mr. Mulvihill decided to make a final attempt to revive the Elitch Theatre and made plans to reopen it for the 1920 season.[13] It was one of the most critical decisions in the entire history of Elitch Gardens.

The 1920 Season

The Elitch Theatre - Welcome Home

After two seasons without theater, John Mulvihill made the decision to reopen the Theatre for the 1920 season. It was a decision that the citizens of Denver awaited, as did the rest of the theatrical world. The *Denver Post* drama editor welcomed the challenge in an article that appeared on the eve of opening night.

> It is good to know that Elitch is to make an attempt to return to the theatrical field. Word has come to me from New York that there is quite as much excitement about the Lambs and Greenroom clubs over the opening of Elitch in Denver as there has been over any theatrical event in months. Many of the prominent stars of Broadway look back with happy memories to the days when they spent their summers playing to bright and jolly crowds in Elitch and send "the best of luck" to the new company which will attempt Monday night to bring the Gardens back to their old glory. It will, indeed, be like old times to go out to the Gardens and see a play. I presume Mrs. Mary Elitch Long will be there with all the sweetness, charm and lovableness of character that is really a part of the memories of old Elitch.[14-1]

In 1920, the government census bureau in Washington released figures showing an estimated increase in population in Colorado to 1,012,394 from 799,024 in 1910, and in Denver to 256,369 from 213,381.[14-2]

The season opened on June 28, 1920, with a performance of *Polly With a Past,* a comedy by playwrights George Middleton and Guy Bolton. The play was well-received, and "there was not left a vestige of doubt that the traditions of the best days of Elitch was the standard of quality for which the management was striving and it had achieved its aim ... (Indeed), Elitch has come back, beyond a doubt and its first play is a joy."[14-3]

In planning for the season, John Mulvihill had consulted Mary Elitch Long as to the selection of a new resident company. As she had done in the past, she recommended that he become familiar with the theater situation in New York. In the early spring of 1920, Mr. Mulvihill went to New York, observed several Broadway productions, and interviewed candidates for the position of director. Representatives of Actors' Equity offered guidance to Mr. Mulvihill. Mulvihill chose Rollo Lloyd for the position. Lloyd began his career in theater as an actor and stage manager in the company of Leo Ditrichstein and had experience with the Provincetown Players.* Lloyd was authorized by Mulvihill to select the company members as well as the plays for the season. Following the success of *Polly With a Past*, his talent and commitment were publicly noted.

> Too great credit cannot be given Rollo Lloyd, the director. He had the task of starting absolutely at the beginning. There was a vacant theater - a theater that had practically been dismantled; there was no aid left over from the past - nothing but a living memory of fine things that had been done and the expectation that any audiences would be skeptical and inclined to draw unjust comparison between whatever he gave them and the hallowed days of years ago. He went at his work and came off triumphant.[14-3]

Lloyd assembled an excellent and talented cast. As the leading woman, he selected Ann Mason, an actress with a delightful gift for comedy who could change in a fleeting moment to seriousness that could reach great depths. Charles Trowbridge, an actor who had a wide reputation on Broadway, having recently played the lead with Ruth Chatterton in *Moonlight and Honeysuckle* and having appeared with other stars in other plays, was the season's leading man. The talents of these leading performers were recognized in a review of the second play of the season, George M. Cohan's *A Prince There Was*.

> Ann Mason is as winsome, as pretty, as sweet-voiced and alluring this week in a story-book sort of role as she was last week as the vivacious Polly.
>
> Charles Trowbridge does excellent work in the role of the rich young man sick of the weariness of the world till he gets out and mixes into affairs - "bumps the bumps" as he puts it. He has a delightful, manly, virile personality ... and has firmly established himself as a favorite.[14-4]

* In an excellent history of the Provincetown Players, *The Provincetown: A Story of a Theatre* (1931), it is stated that "The Provincetown was more a laboratory than a theater ... To it belonged the task of developing playwrights, of taking risks with unknown actors and designers." See Bordman & Hischak, *The Oxford Companion to American Theatre* (Oxford University Press 2004), p. 513.

Because of the financial difficulties of the summer of 1917, Mulvihill limited the season to eight weeks, opening on June 28th and closing August 22nd. The wide variety of plays selected for the season by Rollo Lloyd assisted Mulvihill in knowing what appealed to Elitch audiences.

Mulvihill was satisfied and considered fortunate to have Lloyd aboard as resident director. He rehired him for the 1921 through 1924 seasons. In 1925, Lloyd was succeeded by Melville Burke, who successfully directed the remaining seasons under Mulvihill's leadership, which ended in 1929.

The admiration and appreciation by the Mulvihill family for the theatrical accomplishments of Mary Elitch Long were not overlooked and resulted in the retaining for her of the special lower right front box that had always been reserved for her at the Theatre.

Mulvihill - A Letter of Appreciation

Clearly, Mulvihill's decision to restart the Theatre proved successful. This was acknowledged by John Mulvihill in a letter to the patrons of the Theatre appearing in the August 16, 1920 Theatre program.

> When the Elitch Gardens Company decided upon opening the Theatre this summer, it was with a conviction that it was a duty that was owing to its former patrons and others to present only such plays and such a company as had in former years made Elitch famous the country over. It was fully realized that it was going to be a more or less difficult task, with a possibility that we were in error in thinking that the Denver people would approve of the venture. From the very first performance of the 1920 season we were agreeably convinced, however, that there was a large public willing and eager to applaud and uphold our efforts.
>
> We therefore desire to take this opportunity to thank them for their liberal and enthusiastic support and take this particular pleasure in assuring them at this time that for next summer and many other summers after, we hope, we will endeavor to be equally as worthy of their approval.[1-2]

The Comeback of Elitch Theatre - Some Final Comments

While the comeback of Elitch Theatre proved successful, it was not with great confidence that an effort to resurrect the Theatre would prove successful. In addition to the war years, there were lean years that factored into the decision to close the Theatre. The road back to the future was summarized in an article in the *Denver Post* by Frank W. White, as the 1920 season approached its final performance.

> On Sunday night the summer season at the Theatre at Elitch Gardens will come to a close.

The one outstanding fact about the Gardens this summer is that it has (as far as the Theatre goes) come back. Before the advent of the movies and before the automobile had brought the mountains to our very doors, the Gardens was a most thriving and prosperous place.

Then there came the lean years when its glory faded like a flower in the autumn. It seemed that the time had passed when prosperity would ever again smile on the famous resort. The beauties of the park and the widespread enthusiasm for dancing had kept the grounds animated, but the Theatre stood for years as a sepulchre of the drama.

When the management of the place was taken over by the present company, headed by J. M. Mulvihill, the question of what to do with the Theatre building was a most annoying one. Several schemes were advanced and considered. One was to utilize the Theatre as a dance hall. Another was to install an ice-skating plant. Another plan was to raze the building and use the space for a baseball grounds or an automobile parking place.

A bit of sentiment prevented any of these plans being executed immediately. It seemed such a pity to admit irrevocably that the Theatre could not flourish in the Gardens. Something of a compromise was reached. Mr. Mulvihill decided that he would try a season of drama, just once, and if it did not prove a success, then summer stock at Elitch was to be a thing of the past.

He went to New York, gathered a company together, selected a number of plays and brought them out. The result is now history.

It may be safely said that there has never been a more brilliant season at the Elitch Theatre than that of 1920. The response from the theater-going public was enthusiastic from the first ... The success of the venture has been due to a number of causes, the principal one being that theater-goers were hungry for it. They wanted to repeat the pleasures of the past. All they asked was an opportunity.[14-5]

The End of the Season - Actors Leave

During a season at Elitch, the actors were challenged, the city welcomed them, the company gelled into an excellent acting group, the applause of the theatergoers was warm and personal, and leaving was almost always accompanied with sadness and regret. It was no different this season. For performers, the end of the run meant a sad goodbye.

Albert Brown, a member of the company, returned to Broadway to play a role in *The Purple Mask* being presented by Leo Ditrichstein. Nevertheless, he was heard to say, "I'd rather stay here, though I understand it's quite impossible. You know, this place grips a fellow - makes him feel like himself - like he'd like to stay on."

Other members of the cast had future commitments for the winter season, while others began their search for another role, answering in the meantime, "I don't know what I'll do this season 'till it's done."[14-5]

The Death of Thomas D. Long

Thomas D. Long, husband of Mary Elitch Long, died on September 13, 1920, as a result of an automobile accident on a steep hill three miles north of Colorado Springs. The automobile went out of his control, crashed through a wooden rail and plunged down a thirty-foot embankment. In the car with Mr. Long was Mrs. Frank F. Crump, owner of a Colorado Springs greenhouse of which Mr. Long was manager. They were returning from the Woodman sanitarium, where they had been putting in an ornamental flower bed. Mrs. Crump incurred only a few minor injuries. Long had been business manager of Elitch Gardens for several years. Mary Elitch Long was notified of the accident soon after it happened. Mr. Long was 58 years of age.[15]

Mary Elitch and Thomas Long had encountered some difficulties at some point in their marriage and separated from each other but did not divorce. [16] In the obituary of Mary Elitch Long in the *Denver Post* on July 17, 1936, the following is stated:

> Looking back upon the halcyon days when Mary Elitch Long presided like a queen in her realm, it is not difficult to realize the pricelessness of personality and character.
>
> Over her, as over others, clouds of misfortune gathered. In her marriage to the late Thomas Long she had looked for companionship which in a large measure for a number of years was hers.
>
> She had hoped for his comradeship when the twilight should darken at life's end, and this she missed through misunderstandings preceding his death.[17]

John M. Mulvihill - Purchased Elitch Gardens in 1916

Chapter Fifteen

(1921 - 1924)

John Mulvihill - A Duty to the Citizens of Denver
Helen Menken and Edward G. Robinson
From Broadway to Denver/Denver to Broadway

The 1921 Season

John Mulvihill - A Duty to the Citizens of Denver

After assuming ownership of Elitch Gardens, John Mulvihill continued working at the Denver Gas & Electric Company. With the success of the Theatre's reopening in 1920, the summer Theatre became a center of special interest to Mulvihill, and he was committed to its continued success. In 1921, Mulvihill left his employment at the Denver Gas & Electric Company and devoted all of his energy to the Gardens.[1] In a lengthy statement to the people of Denver appearing in the *Denver Post*, John Mulvihill, as president and on behalf of Elitch Gardens and its Theatre, stated that "we have a responsibility - a duty to the citizens of Denver."

> In the past Elitch Gardens has been noted the country over for the brilliant companies of players that came summer after summer to the Theatre. Last year we opened the Theatre after several years of idleness and put in a group of Broadway actors who jumped into instant favor with Denver theatergoers ... we need the Theatre to give Elitch the atmosphere we are so jealous of and are willing to pay for it.
>
> In the conducting of Elitch grounds and Theatre we feel that we are performing a duty to Denver and ask our fellow citizens that they point out to us wherein we are remiss.[2-1]

The reputation of the Theatre grew, and so did that of John M. Mulvihill. He brought theatrical headliners to the stock company shows. In New York, wherever those of the stage gathered, Mulvihill of Denver was a familiar and esteemed figure. Actors and actresses knew what it meant to boast some day that they once played Elitch Gardens Theatre of Denver.[1]

> Mr. Mulvihill knew his theatrical talent. Not only that, but he always chose stage directors and assistants who knew it, too, and who could help him in choosing plays and casts for Elitch Gardens.[1]

Among the plays selected for the 1921 season was *The Lady of the Lamp* by Earl Carroll, who would soon become famous for his girlie shows, a series of revues commencing with *Earl Carroll Vanities of 1923*. Among the other plays were Guy Bolton and George Middleton's *The Cave Girl* and *Polly With a Past*. Paul Gordon and Ann Mason were selected to play lead roles. Among the cast members were Edward G. Robinson, Albert Brown, C. W. Secrest and Edith King. Robinson had played various minor roles on Broadway during the 1920 season, and was invited by director Rollo Lloyd to assume character roles during the 1921 Elitch season. Robinson's theatrical ability enabled him to assume various character roles, all in a convincing manner.

The reviews by the drama critics centered more on the talent of the performers than on the substance of the plays. A comment or two skirted the essence of the plays, but the details of the reviews belonged to the performers.

Paul Gordon - The Unexpected

Paul Gordon was receiving reviews that favorably endorsed his abilities as an actor. He looked forward to his role in *Polly With a Past*, a play that was described as "one of the most skillfully built comedies that has been seen in Denver for years." Actors are always concerned about the unexpected last minute occurrences that derail their appearance, such as a sore throat or, in Gordon's case, an ulcerated tooth. Gordon's condition had become so painful that it was not possible for him to speak the lines.

Some directors direct but do not act. Rollo Lloyd had, from time to time, appeared in the plays he directed. Upon learning of Gordon's condition, Lloyd quickly got up for the part and appeared in Gordon's place. During the performances of *Polly With A Past*, Lloyd also began rehearsing Gordon's scheduled role in *Toby's Bow*, the last play of the season, in which Rollo did, in fact, appear.[2-2]

The 1922 Season

Most of the plays presented at Elitch had experienced a lengthy run on Broadway, as for example, Jules Eckert Goodman's *The Man Who Came Back* (457 performances), Winchell Smith and Victor Mapes' *The Boomerang* (522), Austin Strong's *Three Wise Fools* (316) and Gilda Varesi and Dolly Byrne's *Enter Madame* (350).

Rollo Lloyd returned to Elitch for his third season as its director. Ernest Glendenning and Helen Menkin played the lead roles. The cast included Edward G. Robinson.

Ernest Glendenning was born and educated in England. He appeared on stage in 1903 with John Drew. His father, John Glendenning, was a successful stage actor. Helen Menken was born in 1901, and attended school at the convent of Manhattanville and later went to the Sacred Heart convent in Brighton, England. She made her theatrical debut at the age of five as a fairy in a 1906 production of Shakespeare's comedy, *A Midsummer Night's Dream*. Prior to appearing at Elitch in the 1922 summer season, she had attained major recognition on Broadway for her role as Miss Fairchild in *Three Wise Fools* (1918), then won further acclaim as the poor waif Diane in *Seventh Heaven* (1922).[3]

Denver critics lauded her acting skills, praising her "winsomeness, grace and charm."[2-3] Comments had been made as to the expressive use of gestures in her acting. Most likely, this was fostered by her knowledge of sign language necessitated by the fact that her parents were deaf mutes.[2-4] In the play *Everyday*, the drama critic said of her that what is "particularly good is her pantomime. One knows the very thoughts of the girl without waiting for her to speak them."[2-5] She was to return to Elitch as the leading lady of the 1926 season.

Helen was to become one of Humphrey Bogart's four wives, the last being Lauren Bacall, with whom he fell in love during the making of *To Have and Have Not*.[4]

Edward G. Robinson had returned to Broadway following the 1921 season at Elitch and had become of a member of the Theatre Guild that had been organized in 1919, and which became renowned as an exciting and responsible producing organization of the 1920s and 1930s.* Robinson continued to develop his talent as a character actor. Upon his return to Elitch, it is said that John Mulvihill repeatedly reprimanded Robinson for his sloppy appearance, perhaps resulting from his assortment of character roles. He was again singled out for his skillful ability to perform numerous roles in plays.

In 1958, Edward G. Robinson appeared in Denver with the touring company of Paddy Chayefsky's *Middle of the Night* (and later in the movie), playing the role of the elderly widower who marries a young bride. Of this time, Whitfield Connor recalled that in 1958 "Robinson returned (to Elitch Theatre) ... as a visitor, sat out front to look at the stage than went backstage and wrote on Connor's dressing room mirror, 'Good luck to the leading man. Eddie Robinson.'" [5]

Edward G. Robinson was born in Bucharest in 1893. He gave up plans to be a rabbi or a lawyer in favor of acting during his studies at the City College of New York.**

The Elitch Gardener Magazine

The Elitch Gardener magazine was a weekly publication which first appeared in 1922 and was published by the management of the Gardens with irregularity through the 1929 season. It contained information about the activities of the Gardens and the actors performing at the Elitch Theatre. For example, a column entitled "The Question Box" listed questions and answers pertaining to members of the resident company.

* The Theatre Guild produced many successful Broadway plays, including *The Philadelphia Story* (1939) and *Sunrise at Campobello* (1958), as well as several other hits. "By the 1970s the Guild existed only on paper, its productions so infrequent that most thought the group was gone ... In its heyday the Guild was the principal producer of such playwrights as George Bernard Shaw, Eugene O'Neill, Maxwell Anderson, and Robert Sherwood and greatly advanced the careers of such players as Lunt and Fontanne." Bordman & Hischak at p. 609.

** This author proudly claims the City College of New York as his own alma mater.

The 1923 Season

Improving the Comfort of the Audience

Before the opening of the 1923 season, a row of mezzanine boxes and a few seats in the balcony were removed. This allowed more room between the aisles as well as between the rows of seats. On the lower floor, an inner wall was built between the lobby and the foyer, cutting off the noise from the outside amusement concessions and rides. The audiences welcomed the improved comfort that the changes provided.[6-1] The *Rocky Mountain News* applauded the changes, stating that "one of the most pleasing features of the Gardens this summer is the Theatre, which has been altered so that it is vastly improved."[7-1]

The Season

The opening play of the season was Booth Tarkington's *Rose Briar*. Among the other plays presented were Mary Roberts Rinehart and Avery Hopwood's *Spanish Love*, Thomas F. Fallon's *The Wasp* and William Archer's *The Green Goddess*. The director was Rollo Lloyd, and the cast was known as the Elitch Garden Players. Violet Heming was the leading lady of whom it was said that "aside from her deftness as an actress, she is captivating because of her faultless beauty and her superb taste in clothes."[6-2] Unfortunately, she had to leave before the end of the season to star in a play scheduled to open in Boston on Labor Day. She was succeeded by Lily Cahill, whose first appearance was in *Spanish Love*.[7-2] Ernest Glendenning returned again as leading man, of whom it was said that "it is doubtful if any actor has ever given such complete satisfaction in such a wide variety of parts as Ernest Glendenning has this summer and last."[7-3]

This was the second season that John Mulvihill engaged G. Bradford Ashworth as the scenic director for Elitch Theatre. He would continue in that role for Mulvihill through the 1927 season. After the death of John Mulvihill in January 1930, Ashworth would continue to serve as scenic director under the leadership of Arnold Gurtler for the seasons from 1930 through 1935. His artistic skills enhanced the productions at Elitch, as would those of other scenic designers for the Theatre, offering the best theater possible for its patrons.

The play *Spanish Love* was one of the biggest hits on Broadway, but could not easily be sent on tour because of necessary stage alterations.* The Elitch Theatre accepted the challenge.

> You will never recognize Elitch Theatre this week. A very novel, picturesque and passionate piece, *Spanish Love*, has completely

* Difficult stage alterations sometimes made touring with a show impractical. For instance, the successful 1952 musical *Wish You Were Here* with Jack Cassidy ran for 598 performances on Broadway, but made a touring company impractical because a swimming pool had to be built into the stage as part of the play's Camp Kare-Free vacation site in the Berkshires.

> transformed the place. It is one of those intimate plays, the stage extended down into the theater, and the players saunter in from all parts of the house and stage while the audience feels as though they are participating in the action or have accidentally happened into a Spanish colony and are privileged to witness a very dramatic episode. The production is the most unusual presented in Denver in a long time and exquisitely achieved by the Elitch players.[7-4]

The 1924 Season

The Amusement Tax of 1924

The Internal Revenue Code of 1924 dealt with a modification of the admission tax on theater tickets. Under the new law, no tax was to be imposed on admissions of 50 cents or less, but the tax of 1 cent for each ten cents or a fraction thereof was to be continued on all admissions in excess of 50 cents. However, there was not a general exemption of 50 cents on each admission. Thus, on an admission charge of 60 cents, a tax of 6 cents was to be collected.[6-3]

The Season

The program again listed Rollo Lloyd as director. The leads were June Walker and Norval Keedwell. Among the plays presented was Winchell Smith and Tom Cushing's *Thank You,* a story about an underpaid Reverend who cannot get along on his meager salary and relies on donations from his parishioners. His orphaned niece wages a campaign to get him a decent stipend and to regain his self-respect. After leaving New York, the piece played four years on the road, where it was "hailed by ministers and teachers as a powerful argument for underpaid educators and as the best friend the clergy ever had."[8]

The Return of Helen Menken

Helen Menken first appeared at Elitch during the summer of 1922. Following the season, she was cast in the Broadway long-running play, *Seventh Heaven*. John Mulvihill had contacted her prior to the 1924 season and had invited her back to perform in some of the plays. She was not certain, as she had plans to travel to Europe during the summer for a period of time to rest before returning to her role in *Seventh Heaven.*

June Walker, Elitch's leading lady, was invited to try out two new plays with producers of her last two New York engagements. Her scheduled departure after her fourth play at Elitch created the necessity for a new leading lady to replace her. John Mulvihill again contacted Helen Menken and invited her to return to Elitch to star in the final seven plays of the season. Simply stated, the choice was whether to go to Europe for a rest or return to Denver for seven weeks of hard work in summer stock. The following were her comments:

> After *Seventh Heaven* closed, I thought I would like to do absolutely

> nothing for months. I arranged to go to Europe, and had made arrangements for quite a long stay in Italy. Then I got a wire from Mr. Mulvihill, asking me if I could come for a longer time than we had considered when we talked about Elitch in New York last winter.
>
> The desire for work grew very strong. I had almost been thrown out of John Golden's office (her manager) after having gone in four times to ask how soon *Seventh Heaven* was going to open again. But I went back when I heard from Elitch, and asked his advice. He told me that playing at Elitch under Rollo Lloyd was just the thing for me to do. Then I wired Mr. (David) Belasco. He wired back the same advice - said it would be the wisest thing I could do and that he wished me well and hoped he and I might do big things together in the near future.
>
> That settled it, and I wired Mr. Mulvihill that I would come out right away.[6-4]

Upon her arrival by train in Denver, Ms. Menken was met by John Mulvihill. As she hopped from the steps of the train into his arms, she stated, "I am as excited and as happy as a child at coming back." Mulvihill admitted he was glad to see her.[6-4]

The opening play for Miss Menken at Elitch was *Drifting*, in which she had scored a notable hit in the role of Cassie Cook in the play's successful New York run, making her a star overnight. The play was originally cast on Broadway with Alice Brady, daughter of producer William A. Brady playing the lead role. However, she became ill and a substitute was needed. "Helen Menken was called in. She studied hard, had a rehearsal or two and opened. After the first performance Brady had Helen Menken's name put in the electric sign over the theater and she played the season out. Critics went to see the play with the new star, and then predictions of a great future were made in the press."[6-4]

In a review of Helen Menken's performance in the role in the Elitch presentation, the drama critic wrote:

> We who have watched her for a summer at the Gardens have thought we knew all about her acting, but Sunday night she turned loose things that are beyond anything she ever showed before and much that was superior to her best work in the plays two years ago.[6-3]

From Broadway to Denver/Denver to Broadway

It has often been the case that Elitch management had engaged actors and actresses for summer stock who had appeared on the Broadway stage. As previously stated, in this season, Helen Menken had returned to Elitch having previously appeared on Broadway in *Seventh Heaven* and *Drifting*. And George Farren appeared at Elitch this season in the role he had created in New York in *Gypsy Jim*.

Likewise, players who spent the summer at Elitch Theatre were sometimes selected to appear in stage successes on Broadway. Helen Menken was an example, having been cast in *Seventh Heaven* following her 1922 appearance at Elitch. The prior summer, Violet Heming left Elitch Gardens to rehearse for *Spring Cleaning*, which proved to be one of the big hits of the season in Chicago and New York. Three years earlier, Ann Mason left for New York, after having been received with favor at Elitch, and assumed the leading feminine role in *The Last Warning*. Playing opposite Ann Mason in the big city was Charles Trowbridge, who had been a leading man at Elitch's historic playhouse.[6-5]

Two Fellows and a Girl - The Final Play of the Season

The play *Two Fellows and a Girl* was written first by Vincent Lawrence. Then George M. Cohan fixed it up to suit his requirements and produced it successfully in New York. The critics wrote that Cohan had put more charm and delightful humor into this play than any he had done for years.

Briefly, the play is a tale "of the eternal triangle but, instead of there being a serious problem with a lot of messy sobs, as you expect in most triangle stories, this one is the sort of stuff you expect from George M. Cohan - a lot of wise cracks and laughs enough to last you for quite a while." The play "avoids every angle that might in any way be off-color."

It was an appropriate play with which to close the season, "for it fulfills the dictum of the famous Cohanism always to 'leave them laughing when they say goodbye.'"[6-6]

History Colorado - # 10038232

Helen Menkin and Ernest Glendenning (1922)

History Colorado - # 10039858

Edward G. Robinson (1922)

Chapter Sixteen

(1925 - 1926)

Anna Christie
The Pulitzer Prize for Drama
Cardboard Fans to Keep Cool
Fredric March and Florence Eldridge

The 1925 Season

The play that was the highlight of the season was Eugene O'Neill's Pulitzer Prize play *Anna Christie*. Others included Frederick Lonsdale's *Aren't We All* and Lewis Beach's *The Goose Hangs High*. Sutten Vane's *Outward Bound* was also presented and was also to be among the play selections at Elitch during the 1940 and 1943 seasons.

The leads were Florence Eldridge and Tom Powers. Florence Eldridge was born in Brooklyn in 1901 and made her professional debut in the chorus of a 1918 musical. In 1922, she won theatrical acclaim for her portrayal of the terrified heroine Annabelle West in *The Cat and the Canary* and the stepdaughter role in *Six Characters in Search of an Author*.[1-1]

Beulah Bondi was another member of the cast. She was born in Chicago in 1892. She appeared in many years of stock productions before becoming a part of the resident company at Elitch in 1925. That same year she made her Broadway debut on December 21, 1925 in *One of the Family*. She returned to play the 1926 season at Elitch. After six years and several more stage productions on Broadway, she began a film career, appearing in *Street Scene* and *Arrowsmith*.[2]

Melville Burke succeeded Rollo Lloyd as director in 1925 and was to continue in that role through the 1929 season. Burke had extensive experience with stock companies and had acquired the ability to rehearse a cast and prepare a play to be performed within the limited time frames of stock theater.

In a 1927 edition of *The Elitch Gardener*, after recognizing "the fine quality of the performances" at the Theatre and "the remarkable smoothness of the productions," tribute was paid to the skills of Melville Burke, noting that "he has the viewpoint of the actor because he formerly was an actor himself" and that he was called by a writer in the Theatre Arts Monthly "one of the few creative directors in the American theatre."[3-1]

The final play of the season, *Anna Christie*, was the dominant play, a drama, and a sharp contrast to some of the light and delightful comedies that easily and otherwise satisfied the mood of a summer audience.

For example, *The Goose Hangs High* was a play

> ... that should give comfort to every distracted parent throughout the country. Mothers and fathers who are worried about what they believe college life is doing to their children, transforming them from well-mannered, guileless boys and girls into fresh, fox-trotting cake-eaters and bobbed-hair, cigarette-smoking flappers, will find their fears quite groundless, because when the emergency arises the dear children know how to put aside their nonsense and turn up to be the best of trumps.[4-1]

Anna Christie [4-2]

Anna Christie, the 1921 Pulitzer Prize-winning play by Eugene O'Neill, was hailed as "the most widely popular American play ever written." John Mulvihill was persistent in his efforts to acquire the right to present the play at Elitch and, in doing so, he paid the highest royalty he had ever paid to date for such a right.

> It may seem strange that an Irishman, such as Eugene O'Neill, should have conceived this colossal drama of an old Swedish captain and his daughter, who becomes a victim to his fear of the sea - which he makes an excuse for evading parental responsibility - and of an Irish stoker who falls in love with the girl and comes into conflict with the old squarehead, who is frantically determined that his girl never shall marry a sailor.
>
> But O'Neill is an international artist. He has sailed the seven seas on tramp boats and rubbed elbows with the scum of the world in its greatest ports. His deep knowledge and understanding of the people about whom he writes and the conditions under which they struggle is the reason why *Anna Christie* contains so much dramatic dynamite that it sends crinkles down the blasé spines of New York and London audiences with its frank realities and uncompromising truths.

Florence Eldridge said that playing the part of Anna Christie was the greatest opportunity she ever had for, by common consent, it is "the finest role ever written in the history of the stage for an actress."

> No more poignant heroine of fiction or drama has been presented on the stage of any country than this tragic waif of the Northwest, who is redeemed from the depths of evil by the influence of the sea and a great love.

A *Denver Post* headline stated that the "Original 'Anna Christie' is Discovered, Living in Denver." The article noted, without identifying the person by name:

> The woman who gave Eugene O'Neill the idea for one of the most gripping dramas ever presented upon the American stage - once a queen in the New York night world - now lives alone and forgotten in the

section of the city (Denver) where red lights once flickered and painted women beckoned from gaily-trimmed windows.[4-3]

The Pulitzer Prize for Drama [5]

The Pulitzer Prize was established in 1917 by Joseph Pulitzer, an American journalist and newspaper publisher. Prizes were awarded as an incentive to excellence in many areas, including journalism, literature, music and drama.

The Prize for drama is the most prestigious of all drama awards, and was created to honor "the original American play presented in New York which shall best represent the educational value and power of the stage in raising the standards of good morals and good manners." The Pulitzer is a playwright's award, given to a script and not a production.[1-2]

The awards committee consisting of one academic and four critics recommends the recipient for the prize; however, the committee's recommendation may be overruled by the advisory board, consisting of the trustees of Columbia University. This happened in 1963 when the committee's recommendation of Edward Albee for his play *Who's Afraid of Virginia Wolf?* was overruled by the board because of the play's then controversial use of profanity and sexual themes.

The first Pulitzer Prize for drama was awarded in 1918 for *Why Marry?* by Jesse Lynch Williams. The second Pulitzer was awarded in 1920 to Eugene O'Neill for *Beyond the Horizon*. O'Neill went on to win three other Pulitzer awards: *Anna Christie* (1922), *Strange Interlude* (1928) and *Long Day's Journey into Night* (1957). The Pulitzer may be withheld if it is determined that the plays that year are deemed not worthy of the award.

In establishing the award, Pulitzer made provisions that enable the advisory board to make changes in the system of awards. The advisory board has been renamed the Pulitzer Prize Board. The Board has increased the number of awards and introduced poetry and photography as subjects, while adhering to the spirit of the founder's intent.

The eligibility period for the drama award originally ran from March 2 to March 1, to reflect the Broadway "season," rather than using the calendar year, as with awards in other areas. This was changed in 2007, when the drama prize was based on works staged during the calendar year.

The first Pulitzer Prize for a musical was awarded in 1932 for *Of Thee I Sing*. The musical award is usually extended to the composer, the lyricist and the story author.

The End of the Season

After an intense summer of preparing and presenting plays to captivated audiences, it was time for the members of the company to say goodbye to Elitch, to Denver, to the audiences and to the Theatre management and personnel. Such goodbyes were burdened with sadness but lifted by the hope of someday returning to Elitch for another summer.

Tom Powers planned to spend a month in France resting before opening in a Chinese theatrical piece on Broadway with Florence Eldridge, who planned to rest on Long Island for several weeks before beginning rehearsals. All other members of the company had roles in Broadway productions and were scheduled to begin rehearsals early in September.[4-2]

The 1926 Season

There was an important change by the Elitch management in its handling of congratulatory telegrams they received each year upon the season opening. *The Elitch Gardener* weekly publication described the change.

> For years the Elitch Gardens management and the members of the Elitch Theatre Company have received congratulatory telegrams from famous actors and playwrights on the opening night of the summer stock season. These wires always have been kept in the office of the management or in the dressing rooms of the players. This year, prompted by the thought that the Theatre patrons might enjoy reading these telegrams, some of the messages were pinned up on a board in front of the Theatre on the opening night of *The Swan*.

Among the many telegrams received was the often quoted one from Cecil B. De Mille in which he described the Elitch Theatre as "one of the greatest cradles of the drama in American history." Among the many others who sent best wishes were Bruce McRae, Helen Menkin, May Buckley, Lynn Fontaine and Alfred Lunt.

May Buckley, a favorite leading woman at Elitch in past seasons, wired from a one-night stand at Madison, Wisconsin, the following:

> The happiest memories of my life are connected with those glorious gardens and dear Mrs. Elitch Long. A happy, glorious season to you all.[6-1]

Members of resident stock companies at Elitch became well known to Denver audiences because of their relatively long stay in Denver during summer months. Audiences indicated their approval of certain "favorites" by enthusiastic applause which greeted an actor's first appearance on the stage. There were numerous occasions when service clubs entertained the entire company at special functions in downtown Denver. For example, the Kiwanis Club always allotted one of its weekly luncheon meetings for a reception for members of the Elitch company.[6-2] Performers sometimes appeared in advertisements approving a product.*

* See, *e.g.*, Elitch Theatre program, Jun 22 - 28, 1913, p. 8, in which Lewis S. Stone, Elitch's leading man, agreed in an ad that the Queen City Dye Works was "Denver's leading Dye Works." In the Jun 15 - 21, 1913, program at p. 12, the same ad appeared, but with leading lady Chyrstal Herne and not Lewis S. Stone.

Three of the plays selected for the season had been awarded the Pulitzer Prize for Drama: *Icebound* (1923), *Hell-Bent for Heaven* (1924) and *Craig's Wife* (1926). However, controversy surrounded the selection of *Hell-Bent for Heaven*. The drama jury had actually selected George Kelly's *The Show-Off* for the award but was overruled by the award's advisory board. It resulted in one juror's resignation and another issuing a letter of protest.[1-3]

Prices for evening performances ranged from 50 cents to $1.25, and for matinees, from 50 to 75 cents.

Cardboard Fans to Keep Cool

The Elitch Theatre lacked air-conditioning. This summer must have been unusually warm. Patrons of the Theatre were given a cardboard fan to cool themselves. The fan contained the name of the play, the actors and their roles, and a synopsis of the play on one side of the fan, together with informative notes and a statement as to the next week's performance. The front of the fan contained a photograph of a member of the cast.

Fredric March and Florence Eldridge

Fredric March and Florence Eldridge were the lead actors for the season. In a book entitled *The Elitch Garden Story (Memories of Jack Gurtler)*, by Jack Gurtler and Corinne Hunt, and published in 1982, the following story is told about Fredric March and Florence Eldridge. John Mulvihill (Gurtler's grandfather), had a policy that no leading man would be married to his leading lady because he believed that "people would not pay money to watch a man make love to his own wife on stage." During the run, Fredric March informed John Mulvihill that he was in love with Florence Eldridge and that they wanted to get married. Mulvihill alerted March to his policy. March may not have taken him seriously, for he and Florence Eldridge drove to Colorado Springs and got married. Mulvihill confronted March, saying "I understand that you are now man and wife," to which March replied, "That's right, J.M.! I love this girl too much to take the chance of losing her by waiting till the season's over." Mulvihill fired Florence Eldridge. Mulvihill had already engaged another to play her part during the season.[7]

The story is at variance with interviews that Edwin Levy, head of the theater department at the University of Denver, had with Fredric March and Melville Burke in 1952 and 1953, respectively. The interviews revealed the following:

> Miss Eldridge met Mr. March at the home of a mutual friend in New York before the summer of 1926. After the Elitch season, they were married in Mexico. Manager Mulvihill, making plans for the season of 1927, believed audiences would not be interested in seeing a leading man play love scenes with his own wife on stage and decided not to rehire Miss Eldridge for the summer of 1927.[8]

Loyal Alumnus - Fredric March Balks at Role

The Poor Nut is a hilarious play about college life. John Miller is the play's main character, a role assigned to Fredric March, the season's leading man.

> (Briefly, John Miller is) a serious-minded student who is working his way through the University of Ohio, and who is suffering from an inferiority complex and love-letter writing. In his letters he has claimed to be an athletic hero and when the object of his pen and heart comes to town he is forced to be the hero he asserted that he was. Compelled to join the track team and separated from the girl he really loves, John wins the track meet against Wisconsin University and becomes hero of the hour.* [9-1]

Upon rehearsal of the race scene, March walked off stage and refused to play the title role. The reason was March's sympathy to the University of Wisconsin from which he graduated in 1920 at which time he was president of his class, the football manager for two years, and a member of Alpha Delta Phi fraternity. March said:

> While I realize this is only a play, I do not feel I would be loyal to my university to appear in the role of a student of Ohio State who defeats his Wisconsin opponent, even in a stage presentation.[9-2]

March requested management to wire Elliott Nugent, one of the authors of the comedy, to change the play so Wisconsin would not be defeated. The author refused the requested change, wiring back:

> Sorry unable to oblige Fredric March, but it is impossible to change the action of *The Poor Nut* so as to let Wisconsin win the race. It would upset the plot, upset me and they never beat Ohio State anyhow. At least we don't admit to it.[9-3]

March understood his professional commitment to management, undertook the role, stating that "despite my feeling for any college, I intend to make John Miller run as fast as he can to win for Ohio."[9-2] As was expected, the presentation of the play was a success.

The Swan

The Swan is one of the most popular of Ferenc Molnar's plays. It is said that much of Molnar's play was written on scraps of paper in a Budapest cafe.

> The Hungarian playwrights have the pleasing habit of gathering in some large cafe for luncheon and remaining there all day in conversation or writing. According to rumor the idea of writing a satirical comedy

* The relay race, with an actual reproduction of a college track meet, required more than sixty people on the stage.

> about royalty came to Molnar while seated at a cafe table and he hastily jotted down the idea on the back of the menu. Thus the continental dramatist reverses the habit of the American author who, if he has something to write, usually secludes himself in a mountain cabin or goes into retreat in the Maine woods.[3-2]

The Swan ran on Broadway for almost a year with Eva Le Gallienne as the princess and Basil Rathbone as the tutor. It later became the subject of several movies, the first being with Francis Howard in 1925, then Lillian Gish in 1930, and the more recent and most popular with Grace Kelly in 1956. The latter film is said to have given "Princess Grace Kelly ample time to act in reel life what she shortly became in real life."[10]

Actor-Audience Relationship [11]

Both theater and film essentially present the same material. Yet, "no matter how closely a film follows the story of a play, no matter how involved we are with the people on the screen, we are always in the presence of an image, never a person." The presence of an audience is important to a performer in a theater, and of no consequence to actors on the screen.

Drama critic Walter Kerr elaborated on what it means for the audience and the actors to be together.

> It doesn't just mean that we (the audience) are in the personal presence of performers. It means that they are in *our* presence, conscious of us, speaking to us, working for and with us until a circuit that is not mechanical becomes established between us, a circuit that is fluid, unpredictable, ever-changing in its impulses, crackling, intimate. *Our* presence, the way we respond, flows back to the performer and alters what he does, to some degree and sometimes astonishingly so, every single night. We are contenders, making the play and the evening and the emotion together. We are playmates, building a structure.

Kerr then compares the role of the audience as it relates to film.

> (What happens in the theater) never happens at (the showing of) a film because the film is already built, finished, sealed, incapable of responding to us in any way. The actors can't hear us or feel our presence; nothing *we* do, in our liveness, counts. We could be dead and the film would purr out its appointed course, flawlessly, indifferently.

For these reasons, film stars frequently seek out opportunities to appear on stage to experience the challenge of theatrical performances.

History Colorado - # 10039859

Florence Eldridge

History Colorado - # 10039830

Melville Burke

Chapter Seventeen

(1927 - 1928)

Lea Penman - A Denver Girl
The Death of Bruce McRae
The Death of John Drew
The Jazz Singer
Sylvia Sidney
The Command to Love - Naughty But Nice?

The 1927 Season

Among the twelve plays selected for the season were Arnold Ridley's *The Ghost Train,* Frederick Lonsdale's *The Last of Mrs. Cheyney,* Lula Vollmer's *The Shame Woman,* Willard Mack's *The Dove,* Russell Medcraft and Norma Mitchell's *The Cradle Snatchers,* Anne Morrison and Patterson McNutt's *Pigs* and the never-to-be-forgotten *Gentlemen Prefer Blondes* by Anita Loos and John Emerson.

Melville Burke was again the director. The leads were Flora Sheffield and Fredric March. March's career was an example of combining hard work with extraordinary talent.

> After being graduated from the University of Wisconsin, he endeavored to follow his family's desires and become a banker. After a few months' work in New York he decided that banking was not his forte, and he turned to the stage.[1-1]

He finally received a small part in a David Belasco production and then went into stock, playing with the Mabel Brownell company and others. In 1925, March appeared in New York as the leading man in *The Half Caste*. He was seen by Melville Burke, the director at Elitch Theatre, who was so impressed with his performance that he engaged him as the leading man at Elitch for the 1926 season. In reflecting upon his acting career, and his three seasons as a lead actor at Elitch Theatre, Fredric March, in an interview in 1952, stated:

> I felt exceedingly fortunate to be selected as leading man in 1926. It was the tradition of the place. At that time it was known all over the East and it was considered a feather in the cap of an actor to have played a season at Elitch. Anyone who was successful there had an excellent chance of getting better parts when he returned to New York.[2]

Florence Rittenhouse, noted Broadway actress, joined the Elitch Gardens players to appear in the final three plays of the season, giving the Elitch company two leading ladies.[1-2]

Lea Penman - A Denver Girl

Lea Penman, a member of the Elitch cast, was a Denver girl who had attended the University of Denver. It was there that she had appeared in her first hit as Rosalind in *As You Like It*. She enhanced her career and gained a professional reputation as a member of stock companies.

After the Wednesday matinee of her play, *The Dove,* Miss Penman sponsored a tea at the Orchard Cafe for her "Pi Beta Phi" sisters from the University of Denver and the University of Colorado. A cake was prepared by the chef of the Cafe as a surprise to Miss Penman. It was a long cake iced with "Lea" in the center and ""Pi Beta Phi" traced in icing on it as well as a model of a dove, in compliment for her performance as Dolores in *The Dove.*[1-3]

The Denver Dry Goods Company's Annual Affair

The Denver Dry Goods company hosted its annual affair of honoring the Elitch Gardens players and promoting the season of plays. On a Tuesday afternoon in July, the public was invited to enjoy a cup of tea in its large tearoom and to watch members of the Elitch cast in street costume, present a scene from *Gentlemen Prefer Blondes.* Carlton Miles, the publicity director of the Gardens, gave a short talk on the plays of the season, and a group of songs were presented by Rex Mayne, tenor soloist with the Tommy Watkins' Paramount orchestra. Autographs were secured from Flora Sheffield and Fredric March prior to tea being served.[1-3]

The Ghost Train

Every summer the Elitch players tried to stage one mystery play, if an appropriate one was available. This season the selection was *The Ghost Train,* a mystery comedy by Arnold Ridley that takes place on a branch line of an English railroad.

> (The play) is the story of a band of travelers who find themselves marooned in a little station on a lonely branch line. The aged station master tells them the story of (a wreck several years prior and of) a phantom train that appears at the station every night at midnight, bringing death to anyone who sees it. The fear that this causes among the travelers and the efforts to unravel the mystery make up the thrill as well as the comedy of the three acts.[1-4]

Fredric March led the cast as Teddie Deakin, a supposedly brainless Englishman, who, in reality, is a Scotland Yard detective.

The exceptional skills of set designer G. Bradford Ashworth were at work to reproduce the very realistic offstage effect of the phantom train thundering past the station.[1-5]

The Shame Woman

The Shame Woman by Lula Vollmer was one of the finest dramas ever to be presented on the Elitch stage. New York critics had unanimously praised the play. The following is a brief summary of its story line:

> For twenty years, ever since she was seduced by Craig Anson, Lize Burns has been shunned by her North Carolina hillbilly neighbors as a "shame woman." She has lived in an isolated cabin with only her adopted daughter, Lily, for company. Lonely and heartsick, she has never had the courage to tell Lily of her past or to warn her not to wander carelessly among the hills.
>
> However, learning that Lily has been meeting a man at night, Lize finally forces herself to tell Lily her history, which causes Lily to run from the room and kill herself. When Anson calls at the cabin, Lize finds out that he was Lily's seducer. She kills him with a potato knife to prevent him from boasting of his latest conquest and from disclosing that Lily, too, had become a "shame woman."[3]

Florence Rittenhouse appeared in *The Shame Woman*, in which she was featured in the role of Lize Burns in the Broadway production, a role she considered to be one of the finest in modern dramatic literature. Offers of good parts in Broadway productions came to her but she refused them because "I want to play Lize."[4]

Pigs - A Visit from a Father [5]

For a play to have been running for three years, one on Broadway and two on tour, "and for the father of one of the authors to see it for the first time at the Elitch Gardens was a pleasant incident connected with the production of *Pigs*."

J. P. Hawkins of 619 Pine Street in Boulder, Colorado, the father of Anne Morrison, who wrote the comedy *Pigs* in collaboration with Patterson McNutt, attended a matinee presentation of the play and afterward went backstage and introduced himself to Melville Burke, the director. He also met members of the company, including May Buckley, who was in the original cast of the play.

Mr. Hawkins later wrote a letter of appreciation to Mr. Burke, stating:

> Will you please pardon me for taking a few moments of your valuable time to tell you how much I appreciated the wonderful reception you ... and the capable cast of performers gave me ... I feel that my daughter's play is in capable hands and is produced with the proper spirit as daughter would wish it. I shall always remember you all and wish you the greatest success and happiness.

The Death of Bruce McRae

Bruce McRae (1867-1927) was among the cast members at Elitch for five seasons - 1904, 1905, 1911, 1912 and 1914 - and was usually assigned the role of leading man. He was an accomplished actor and well-liked by Denver audiences. Bruce McRae died at the age of sixty in 1927.

Bruce McRae was born in India, a nephew of the renowned British comic actor, Charles Wyndham. Prior to his first appearance at Elitch in 1904, McRae had played significant roles on Broadway. For example, in 1899, he was the original Dr. Watson in *Sherlock Holmes* and later portrayed Charles Brandon in *When Knighthood Was in Flower*. He was particularly honored to be selected by Mary Elitch to be the leading man for the 1914 Silver Jubilee.

In the lengthy obituary that appeared in *The Elitch Gardener*, the following comments were included:

> The Elitch Gardens mourns the death of Bruce McRae, leading man here for several seasons and one of the most beloved actors who ever played at the Gardens.
>
> A fine actor, a man who numbered his friends by the hundreds, McRae's death, which occurred in May after several months of illness, will be felt almost more than that of any player on the American stage ... He had a great affection for the Elitch Gardens and no matter where he was playing never failed to send a wire of congratulation on the opening night. Last summer J. M. Mulvihill received the following message from McRae: "My heartiest greetings and all best wishes to dear Mrs. Long, to Mr. Burke, to all the members of the company and to the technical staff of the Elitch Gardens Theatre and may this be the happiest and most successful season of the most famous of all summer stock companies."[6]

The Death of John Drew

In July of 1927, the theatrical world watched and mourned as the last curtain descended on the life of John Drew (1853-1927), noted American actor, dean of American legitimate stage stars and the beloved uncle of Ethel, John and Lionel Barrymore. He was 73 years of age.

Mr. Drew's leanings toward the theater followed those of his parents, both of whom were players of note. His father, also named John Drew (1827-1862), was born in Dublin and came to America with his parents at the age of ten. He excelled in roles that depicted Irish characters. Drew's mother, Louisa Lane Drew (1820-1897), a versatile actress on the American stage, became manager of the famous Arch Street Theater in Philadelphia. Her daughter, Georgiana Drew married Maurice Barrymore, and the union produced Ethel, John and Lionel Barrymore.

Young John made his debut at his mother's Arch Street Theater in 1873, performing there for two seasons, until Augustin Daly, director, actor and playwright, saw him and invited him for a role in a Broadway play. His career was launched and his climb was rapid, continuing as an actor until his death. In the latter part of May 1927, he arrived in San Francisco to play an engagement in *Trelawny of the*

Wells, when he became ill and was hospitalized until his death. John Drew had one daughter, Louise Drew, who achieved success as a stage actress.[1-6]

John Drew was once asked when his daughter wanted to go on stage whether he should object to her seeking a career in theater. His response was clear and quick.

> Why should I object to anyone's going on the stage? I know it is a traditional objection for an actor to have, but it is very different with our family. We are spared a great many of the humiliations and drawbacks. You see, we have been on the stage for over a hundred years, and we have been brought up in the atmosphere of it. We know nothing else. It is our family metier, just as there is one family all physicians, another all lawyers. We know just what to expect when we go on the stage. We realize its hardships, we know the hard work it means. We don't expect anything else. We are spared the heartburnings that come from jealousies, from disappointments when someone else gets the part we think we ought to have, because we know those things are bound to happen. We know, too, that we can't reach the top at one bound. We don't expect it for ourselves or for others.[1-7]

Many from the theatrical world expressed their condolences at Drew's passing. Burns Mantle, renowned drama critic, summed up his passing with the following words.

> Many fine things have been written, many glowing biographies will yet be written of John Drew. I am content to say farewell to him with these words. He was born a gentleman, he was a good actor, he lived and died a gentleman. The profession he adorned is richer for his having lived, and poorer now that he is dead.[1-7]

Denver theater audiences were familiar with John Drew, his having played in ten productions for them. His appearances were not in summer stock, such as at Elitch, but in the regular seasons in other theaters in Denver. His initial appearance was at the old Tabor Grand Opera House in 1889, in the role of the dashing Lt. Howell Everett in *The Railroad of Love*. He appeared seven years later at the Broadway Theater during the week of September 28, 1896, as Christopher Colt Jr., in *Christopher Junior*, with Ethel Barrymore and Maude Adams in the supporting cast. He appeared again at the Tabor Grand during its opening performance on September 9, 1897. His later appearances in Denver were between 1901 to as recently as five or six years before his death.[1-6]

The Jazz Singer[7]

On December 27, 1927, *The Jazz Singer*, the first feature sound film, starring the popular Al Jolson, premiered. The film was based on a play by the same name that had been showing on Broadway for three years, starring George Jessel. The play was based on a story called *Day of Atonement*, written by a student at Champaign, Illinois. It was about a Jewish cantor who couldn't persuade his child to give up the theater.

Warner Brothers studio was in financial straits and Darryl F. Zanuck, a new young executive, persuaded the studio to produce a full-length sound film. The studio decided on filming *The Jazz Singer*.

> Jessel was the obvious choice to star in the picture. But with a new invention like talkies to worry about and with the unknown effect it was likely to have on his career, a man like him wanted insurance - to the tune of $100,000.
>
> Warners said "No." Eddie Cantor was approached - and he, too, said he was too worried about the effects of talking pictures on his career to contemplate the idea.

Al Jolson was approached to play the part and to invest money in the picture and draw stock from its earnings. Jolson, known for his renowned love of a gamble, agreed to the arrangement. The film was to make $3,500,000 net profit and before long Jolson's own stock in Warner Brothers was to be worth $4,000,000.

> The talking picture took its toll of show business much quicker than anyone could have guessed. It not only killed the silent picture, it assassinated vaudeville.
>
> The Keith-Orpheum circuit, which controlled and ruled a vaudeville empire that stretched from one end of the United States to the other, wound up their theater interests and joined with the Radio Corporation to form a new film studio - RKO.

As far as film actors were concerned, "careers were smashed as studios realized that faces which had previously sent millions of women into swoons belonged to voices which would now transport them into hysterical laughter."

The 1928 Season

Sylvia Sidney

Among the twelve plays of the season were Fritz Gottwald's *The Command to Love*, which sparked some controversy among the theatergoers, and Arthur Wing Pinero's *The Second Mrs. Tanqueray*, which was first performed on May 27, 1893 at the St. James Theater in London.

The leads for the season were Isabel Elsom and Fredric March. It was the third consecutive season in which Fredric March was the leading actor. His popularity with the audience continued. Sylvia Sydney was the ingenue of the season. The cast celebrated her 18th birthday on August 18th with a big party. After the season of stock, she went on to stage and screen stardom. In 1931, she starred in *Dead End*, the film in which the Dead End Kids first appeared. She returned to Elitch Theatre decades later and celebrated her 66th birthday while starring in *Sabrina Fair*.[8]

The Command to Love - Naughty But Nice?

The Command to Love was promoted as a "hot" show that "is going to be one of the most talked-about things ever presented in the Elitch Gardens Theatre."[9-1] Fredric March played the role of Gaston, a young military attaché of the French ambassador stationed in Madrid. Isobel Elsom was cast as Manuela, wife of the Spanish war minister.

> Gaston ... is called upon to engineer an affair of the boudoir with Manuela, wife of the Spanish war minister, in order that she will influence her husband to vote for a certain treaty highly desired by France. But, being already engaged in a love affair with the wife of his superior, the French ambassador, Gaston finds it difficult to turn his attentions to Manuela - particularly since his ambassador's wife possesses certain incriminating letters from Gaston.
>
> How (Gaston) finally is persuaded to renounce his vow to Mrs. Ambassador; how he arranges matters with Manuela and her war minister husband; how Gaston's incriminating letters come into the hands of his superior officer, only to be regained by Gaston just as he is about to be disgraced - these are things that make *The Command to Love* the unusual bit of stagecraft it is.[9-2]

The spicy dialogue of the play "wavers between sparkling wit and clever acting throughout the three scenes." In the second act, there is a love scene between Gaston and the wife of the war minister, interrupted half a dozen times, which was described as "the laughing high spot of the whole play."[9-3]

The play sparked comments to the drama editor. The following letter by a theater patron, critical of the play, was published in the *Denver Post*.

> I have just returned from seeing *The Command to Love* at the Elitch Gardens Theatre, and I am so boiling mad at having had to sit through such a suggestive play that I cannot refrain from asking you to warn others who may contemplate going to Elitch during the rest of the week. Really, I never have seen anything quite so "raw" in all my days of theatergoing, and it was embarrassing for me to remain in the Theatre throughout the show.
>
> I used the word "suggestive" in my first paragraph of this letter, but that word actually doesn't apply to *The Command to Love*. The play is NOT merely suggestive - it leaves absolutely nothing to the imagination.
>
> The idea of asking the public to watch a play in which the leading man

> is having a sordid affair with a married woman! It's positively shocking and disgraceful. And the dialogue! Why, people would be arrested and sent to jail if they talked that way on the streets!
>
> *The Command to Love,* in my estimation, is a show that nobody would want to see and hear, and if half the audiences do not get up and walk out during every performance of it, then I have the wrong impression of Denver theater patrons.[10]

However, another letter from a theater patron applauded the play.

> I saw the show Sunday night and I do not hesitate to say publicly that it absolutely is the smartest, cleverest, most interesting play I ever have seen in Denver at any theater.
>
> The lines and situations are the cleverest I have heard and seen, and while some of them are risqué, they are so brilliant and pointed that they cannot give offense, and the way the players carry their parts is a real delight.
>
> I, for one, hope Mr. Mulvihill will give us many more plays as sparkling and scintillating as *The Command to Love*, and I am sure if he does his theater will be filled to capacity at every performance.[9-4]

The drama critic, in a review of the play, can be said to have had a more authoritative and better word.

> There are both lines and scenes that are boldly risqué, but one loses sight of them as the utter cleverness of the farcical play overshadows what otherwise might be objectionable.[9-2]

The Second Mrs. Tanqueray

After more than thirty years, a play is usually not able to withstand the passage of time without suffering by comparison with the work of more modern writers. *The Second Mrs. Tanqueray* was an exception. The play was first performed on May 27, 1893, at the St. James Theater in London.

The playwright, Arthur Wing Pinero, was born in London in 1855. He was first trained in law and worked in his father's law office until he was nineteen years of age, when he was drawn to the theater and became an actor. While an actor, he wrote several plays, one being *Daisy's Escape*. The success of the play and his belief that he was not destined to become a great actor caused Pinero to abandon his acting efforts and to devote himself entirely to writing plays. For his achievements as a dramatist, Pinero was bestowed the honor of knighthood in 1909.[11]

His fame as a playwright was strongly supported by the public acclaim he received for *The Second Mrs. Tanqueray*. The play has been heralded as one of the most perfectly written dramas of all time.[9-5] It recounts the failure of the marriage of a "woman with a past" arising out of the double standards of morality applied unequally and hypocritically by Victorian men and women of the time.

> The plot deals with the complications which arise when Aubrey Tanqueray, a widower with a 19-year-old daughter (Ellean) who has determined to pursue the career of a nun, marries a socially-outcast woman (Paula) whose station in life is decidedly below his own, just as the daughter suddenly changes her mind about the nunnery and decides to come home. Tanqueray, prepared to be rebuffed by his friends because of the marriage, is not prepared for the problem presented by the return of his daughter at this inopportune moment ...[9-5]

Notwithstanding the efforts of Mrs. Tanqueray to straighten out the tangled skeins of their lives, the play moves forward toward its tragic ending.

> The situation (at the Tanqueray home) is tense. The neighbors, although old friends of Aubrey's, have conspicuously refrained from calling. Ellean, too, senses something in Paula that repels her, while Paula is jealously anxious to win Ellean's confidence and friendship.
>
> (As the play progresses, Ellean asks) her father's permission for her engagement to a Captain Ardale. Paula feels impelled to confess to Aubrey that the man who now wants to marry his daughter had been her lover. Ellean with uncanny instinct divines the situation and taunts Paula with the sort of "past" that she has already condoned in Ardale. In a final realization that for a woman with a "past" there can be no future, Paula kills herself.
>
> "Yes," wails Ellean, "Yes, so everybody will say. But I know -- I helped kill her. If I'd only been merciful."[12]

John Mulvihill and the Broadway Theater

Peter McCourt was president of the McCourt Amusement & Investment Company of Denver, the lessee of the Broadway Theater for more than thirty years. His poor health for more than a year prior to his death in April of 1929 caused McCourt to give up his business activities.[13] More and more the theater and amusement business became John Mulvihill's life, and in 1928 he became the president and general manager of the McCourt Company, and thereby controlled the Broadway Theater of Denver.

> This move placed Mr. Mulvihill in a position to provide amusement for the Denver public the year round. In the winter the road shows played at the Broadway and when they ceased in the spring, the Elitch Gardens Theatre began its regular summer schedule.[14]

The Lights of New York

The Jazz Singer sound film released in 1927 was essentially a silent picture with musical accompaniment and four talking and singing sequences. Its success caused Warner Brothers to release *The Lights of New York* in July 1928, a quickly-produced, first full-length, all-talking picture.[15] This first all-talking picture was presented at the Aladdin movie theater in Denver in July of 1928. The film depicts the drama in the lives of those who inhabited "that colorful section of New York City known as the 'Roaring Forties,' and especially of two small-town lovers who are caught in the maelstrom of crime. Each character speaks every line in the entire seven reels."[9-6]

History Colorado - # 10039855

Helen Gahagan, Fredric March and Flora Sheffield (1927)

Chapter Eighteen

(1929 - 1930)

The Talkies
Isobel Elsom and Actors' Equity
Backstage Superstitions
The Stock Market Tumble and Depression Years
The Death of John M. Mulvihill

The 1929 Season

Some Events in 1929

The first passenger airline flight between New York and Los Angeles took off. Penicillin was discovered. Elmer Rice received a Pulitzer Prize in Drama for *Street Scene*. Martin Luther King, Jr., Audrey Hepburn, Arnold Palmer and Grace Kelly were born.

The Talkies

Following the success of Warner Brothers with talkies in 1927 and 1928, other major studios began to convert to sound as quickly as possible.

> At the end of 1928, of the 20,500 theaters in the United States, only 1,300 had sound installations. By the end of 1929, there were over 9,000 theaters equipped to handle the new medium.
>
> The public's enthusiasm for sound was so strong that attendance leaped from 60,000,000 paid admissions per week in 1927 to 110,000,000 in 1929.[1-1]

Denver newspapers during the 1929 season advertised theaters that offered talkies, films such as *The Gamblers*, a "Warner Bros Vitaphone All Talker," and *Behind That Curtain*, a "Fox Movietone All Talker."[2-1]

The advent of sound movies had its impact on the theater, playwrights and stage performers.

> Script writers who had trained themselves to think in terms of pictures gave way to playwrights who thought in terms of stage dialogue.
>
> Many a popular star - especially the European importees - suddenly found himself unemployed; while the Broadway stage was again swept clean to replace those actors whose foreign accents, faulty diction or bad voices the temperamental microphone rejected.
>
> To fill the need for dialogue at all costs, plays - good, bad and indifferent - were brought up and rushed before the cameras.[1-2]

An article in the *Denver Post* noted that Broadway stage stars were flocking to Hollywood "and furthermore, they're making good." Gertrude Lawrence, star of the English stage, signed a long-term contract with Paramount, her first film to be *The Gay Lady*. Marilyn Miller was to be paid $100,000 for her appearance in *Sally* for First National studios.[2-2] However, Jack L. Warner vigorously defended screen stars as the backbone of the film industry. In an article by Louella Parsons that appeared in the *Denver Post* on July 7, 1929, she wrote of Warner's comments:

> Three years ago, he says, when the talkies first threatened the bulwark of the film citadel, he said very few screen players would be affected by the talkies.
>
> "You may quote me as saying," he declares, "that fully eighty per cent of the screen stars have microphone voices. And certainly with their pantomimic ability and the personalities that first attracted the public to them they are more valuable than actors who must be trained to meet the camera".

The reality of the situation was that talkies had resulted in a boon to legitimate theater. As Hollywood had welcomed stage stars in its films, theatergoers welcomed film stars to appear on the stage for an up close look at their movie favorites.*

This was the background of the entertainment world of film and screen in 1929 which was to continue to develop through the years. In the meantime, the Elitch Theatre honored its commitment to fine theater with an excellent selection of plays and cast for its thirty-eighth season.

The Season

William Harrigan and Isobel Elsom were the leads. The cast also included Alan Campbell, George Brent, Donald Dillaway, Madge Evans, C. Henry Gordon and Lea Penman, among others.** Melville Burke directed. Victor Jory appeared as a "guest star" in the role of the Assistant District Attorney in *The Racket*. The play had originally been produced at the Ambassador Theater in New York on November 22, 1927 with Edward G. Robinson and ran for 119 performances.

The season's opening play was Philip Barry's *Paris Bound*. Among the others that followed were George M. Cohan's *Whispering Friends*, Bartlett Cormack's *The Racket*, J. M. Barrie's *What Every Woman Knows* and James Forbes' *Precious*.

* When television made film stars more accessible and familiar to audiences, Elitch Theatre established the "star package" system of plays for its seasons, in which movie stars frequently headed the cast of its various plays.

** Following the close of the Elitch season, Dillaway returned to New York to appear in a new drama entitled, *A Lady at the Bar*, with Claudette Colbert in the cast. He refused an offer to play in two talking pictures, preferring to return to Broadway. *The Elitch Gardener*, Aug 11, 1929, p. 8.

The Death of Peter McCourt

On April 5, 1929, one of the most widely known members of the theatrical business in the United States died at his apartment in the Park Lane hotel in Denver after a prolonged illness. Peter McCourt was born in Oshkosh, Wisconsin, in 1859, and came to Denver in August 1883, to assume the position of assistant manager of the Tabor Grand Opera House which had been erected about two years before by the late United States Senator H. A. W. Tabor, whose second wife ("Baby Doe" Tabor) was a sister of Mr. McCourt. McCourt later came into full management of the Tabor Grand as lessee and in 1896 became lessee of the Broadway Theater as well.[2-3]

> Almost, it might be said, from his early manhood to the day of his death, the life history of Mr. McCourt was the history of the stage in Denver. His operations extended beyond Denver through the booking of practically every theater in Colorado and Wyoming that was open to road dramatic and operatic companies.*

Some months prior to his death, McCourt selected John Mulvihill to become president and general manager of the McCourt Amusement & Investment Company of Denver, which controlled the Broadway Theater in Denver as its lessee. In 1929, John Mulvihill established a stock company at the Broadway Theater and moved it to Elitch Theatre for the summer.[3]

Isobel Elsom and Actors' Equity

Isobel Elsom appeared as the leading lady for the Elitch season of 1928. At Elitch, she appeared in the role she created in the play *The Outsider* earlier that year on Broadway. A reviewer of the play wrote:

> If there is anybody in this man's town who doubts that Isobel Elsom, leading woman at the Elitch Gardens Theatre, is an actress of the highest rank, let that doubting Thomas see her work in *The Outsider* ... She not only is scoring a brilliant personal triumph, but is demonstrating to local playgoers exactly why she was one of the most popular actresses London ever knew![4]

In 1929, Miss Elsom was signed for a second summer at Elitch, again as the leading lady.

In 1928, after an American actress, Alden Gay, was barred from a British production, Actors' Equity placed limitations upon the membership of foreign

* *Denver Post*, Apr 5, 1929, pp. 1, 3.

As the railroads and the miners traveled west to Colorado, in the late 19th century, McCourt became the booking agent for theaters throughout the front range. See generally, Barrett and Barrett, *High Drama* (Western Reflections Publishing Company 2005), pp. 14-17.

actors. Equity passed a regulation requiring alien actors "to either absent themselves from this country for a period of six months following each production engagement or, if they preferred, to remain in idleness in America for that duration of time. This decree applied to all foreign actors who had not played a total of one hundred weeks on this side (in America)." At the time the ruling was put into effect by Actors' Equity, Miss Elsom, an English actress, had played only fifty weeks in America. In compliance with the Equity ruling, Miss Elsom returned to England in September after the 1928 season at Elitch and remained there until shortly before the opening of the Broadway Theater season in Denver during the Spring of 1929.[5-1] She appeared at the Broadway Theater in the production of *The Trial of Mary Dugan*, which opened March 31, 1929.[2-4] After the close of that engagement, Miss Elsom appeared during the first half of the Elitch season when the objection came from Equity which necessitated her departure from the company in the 1929 season.* Isabel Elsom left the Elitch cast after completing her appearance in *The Silver Cord*, a performance that was thoroughly appreciated by Denver audiences, "attested (to) by the frequent storms of applause that greeted her."[2-5]

The actress Jessie Royce Landis substituted as leading woman for the roles Isobel Elsom was to play in the final six plays of the season, beginning with *The Second Man*. Miss Landis had not appeared in any earlier plays of the season. She was asked to come to Denver suddenly from Evanston, Illinois, where she had intended to spend the summer season. In the review of the play *What Every Woman Knows*, it was stated:

> It is fortunate that the play had not been produced before the arrival of Jessie Royce Landis. Because Miss Landis is simply perfect in the role of Maggie Wylie.
>
> The audience witnessing the initial performance was the largest Sunday night crowd we have seen there this season ... No previous production has inspired as lusty a round of applause when the curtain dropped on the first act.[6]

Miss Landis had previously appeared on Broadway with Otis Skinner in *The Honor of the Family* and later in two plays with Laurette Taylor, one of which was *The Furies*, and a more recent engagement as the leading woman for Henry Hull in *Young Alexander*.[2-6]

* It was suggested that a challenge to the Equity ruling, which, as far as was known, was the first instance of Equity applying its ruling to a stock player, had an excellent chance of securing a verdict in her favor. However, inasmuch as such action would mean considerable expense and inconvenience, Ms. Elsom chose instead to comply with the Equity demand. *The Elitch Gardener*, Jul 7, 1929, p. 6.

William Harrigan

Elitch's leading man, William Harrigan (1894-1966), was the son of Edward Harrigan of the famous team of Harrigan and Hart. He made his stage debut at age five in his father's musical *Reilly and the Four Hundred,* a vehicle in which his father scored one of his greatest successes.

William Harrigan was considered in theatrical circles as "a reliable, general, all-purpose actor on stage and screen who never became a star but remained a familiar face for decades ... By 1920, he was playing adult characters on Broadway, and he continued to play supporting roles or solid leading men for the next thirty-five years. Perhaps his most notable role was the dictatorial Captain Morton in *Mister Roberts* (1956)."[7]

Backstage Superstitions

Preoccupied with the rumor that stage people are superstitious, the Facts and Fallacies editor of *The Elitch Gardener* weekly publication sought out members of the cast for its backstage beliefs. Some of the responses included the following:

> (a) Harm will befall anyone even remotely connected with the theater who permits a broom to fall upon the floor of a stage.
>
> (b) Never throw a hat on a bedspread or a dressing gown on a table.
>
> (c) Don't whistle in a dressing room.

There was no dissenting vote that lighting three cigarettes from one match is disastrous.[5-2]

Some examples among those in the film industry were noted.[8]

> Loretta Young feels swearing on the set is very bad luck which can only be overcome when the offender makes a contribution to her favorite charity. She recently got a record collection during "It Happens Every Thursday," when the crew proved more profane than usual.
>
> John Ford won't direct a picture without his shabby old coat and hat which he used in making his first smash hit. Visitors to the set often wonder why one of the highest salaried men in the business looks like a tramp.
>
> English director Alfred Hitchcock says his lucky trademark is his appearance in a scene of each picture he makes. Since he is a bulky individual this isn't easy. Once he appeared in a photograph in a newspaper used as a prop - a wanted criminal with a number on his chest. Another time he was a dead body floating in the water at the scene of a shipwreck.

Ethel Barrymore and Ruth Elder Visit Elitch Theatre

During the summer of 1929, Ethel Barrymore was performing at the Broadway Theater in Denver in *The Kingdom of God,* and she took advantage of a free afternoon to attend a matinee performance at the Elitch Theatre of *The Silver Cord*. The evening performance of the play was attended by the pioneer aviatrix, Ruth Elder, as a guest of George Brent. In addition to enjoying the Theatre, Miss Elder was intrigued by the sky-rocket coaster in the amusement park and made the thrilling ride eighteen times during the course of the evening.[2-7]

The Stock Market and Broadway

The advent of sound films in 1927 impacted both the movie and theater industry. On October 29, 1929, known as Black Friday, live theater was again to be impacted by the stock market crash and the onset of a nationwide depression. Nearly seventy, or approximately half of the new plays of the 1929-1930 Broadway season, ran for three weeks or less. Twenty-five of those plays closed in the same week they opened.[9]

The 1930 Season

The Stock Market Tumble and Depression Years

In 1929, the stock market tumbled, as did the dreams and hopes of Americans. The crash impacted the nation, tossing it into a Depression, which gradually found its way to Denver, although it was not as critical as in many other places in the country, where industrial centers were paralyzed and the unemployment ranks rapidly swelled.* The unemployed, who were attracted to Denver from these industrial centers, did not arrive with pockets full of money to spend on theater attendance. Notwithstanding this national economic downturn, Elitch Theatre presented plays for Denver audiences throughout the Depression period and beyond.[10]

Amid the widespread financial depression in the country, during which "140 other theatrical stock companies, including five major organizations, have taken the air,"[11-1] as of mid-season in 1930, Elitch Theatre was "already 10,000 paid admissions ahead of the same period last year."[11-2]

The Death of John M. Mulvihill

After several weeks of illness, his heart weakened from bronchitis, John Mulvihill died on January 14, 1930, in his home in Denver at 4209 W. 38th Avenue. He was born on April 20, 1870. The newspapers paid him tribute. The following appeared in the *Rocky Mountain News*:

* *Rocky Mountain News*, May 3, 1932, p. 18. The article noted that Denverites owned 25.3 automobiles and 14.1 radios for every 100 residents, while the national average was only 18.4 automobiles and 9.8 radios for every 100 people. However, in other news, the Trustees of the University of Colorado announced that teachers would have to give up their sabbatical leaves for an indefinite period until the Depression passed. *Rocky Mountain News*, Jan 16, 1932, p. 1.

> His passing removes from Denver and Colorado a man of unusual personality - one whose talents shone in widely contrasted activities.
>
> Not only will Denver and the state feel the loss of John M. Mulvihill. They'll miss him, too, on Broadway, New York.
>
> There, if anything, they knew him better than he was known by the general public of Denver. Here tens of thousands depended on him for years to supply them with varied entertainment, but only a relative handful knew Mr. Mulvihill on sight.
>
> But in New York, in the theatrical booking headquarters, in the offices of the big theater impresarios, or wherever those of the stage gathered, John M. Mulvihill of Denver was a familiar and esteemed figure.
>
> They liked him for his seeming brusqueness, his instinct to pick out that which was best suited for the tastes of the Denver public, and his shrewd business ability to drive a bargain.
>
> Actors and actresses, whose names glitter in Broadway in the "electrics," sought out John M. Mulvihill. They knew it "meant something" to boast some day that they once played in the famous Elitch Gardens Theatre of Denver.[12]

In the *Denver Post* "A Tribute of Appreciation" was presented in his honor, excerpts of which follow:

> In middle life he found courage to step away from a secure job and strike out for himself by assuming responsibility to drag Elitch Gardens out of the financial slough into which the property, regarded as a shrine, had fallen.
>
> He knew Elitch Gardens had won an unusual place by being the cleanest, happiest amusement resort in the world. He made up his mind always to keep its name and fame clean.
>
> Nothing but the best was good enough for Elitch Gardens or Denver, according to the Mulvihill rule. A play might be ever so successful in New York but if there was about it the semblance of immorality or dirt, down went the Mulvihill thumb even when agents protested.[11-3]

Among the many who wired their sympathy to the Mulvihill family were scores of theatrical luminaries who knew him through contacts formed in New York City and lasting friendships formed during the periods they played under his auspices at the Elitch Theatre.[11-4]

A requiem high mass was held at the Cathedral of the Immaculate Conception in Denver. Father Mark W. Lappen, pastor of the Holy Family Catholic Church where Mr. Mulvihill was a parishioner for years, delivered the final comments, emphasizing, among other things, Mulvihill's faith in God. The Church was packed with friends, well-wishers and dignitaries paying their final respects to a man they loved. Among the many notables in the crowd were Frederick G. Bonfils, Oscar Malo, Benjamin Stapleton, Philip Hornbein and Frank White.[11-4] The sermon was brief and telling.

> I speak not in eulogy, but rather in appreciation of John M. Mulvihill.
>
> And if I were to eulogize him, I'd use no words. But I would point to this host of friends that are gathered here this morning to honor him in death.
>
> I would point to his straightforwardness in all his business dealings, to the great love his friends held for him and to that outburst of sympathy and feeling extended to his family at the end.
>
> All these speak more in eulogy of the man than anything I can say.
>
> You who are here this morning knew him as a business man. But I and the priests who knew him saw John Mulvihill in a different light - as a man with a simple, childlike faith in God.
>
> As an example of his simple faith, he cherished an old rosary that someone had given him years ago.
>
> He said that there was not enough money in the world to buy that rosary from him.
>
> And today it is being buried with him.[13]

Following the requiem high mass, John Mulvihill was buried at Mount Olivet Cemetery at the outskirts of Denver.

Arnold B. Gurtler

Upon the death of John Mulvihill, the man who succeeded him in the management of Elitch Gardens and the Theatre was his son-in-law, Arnold B. Gurtler.

Arnold Gurtler's parents were married in Central City, Colorado. Arnold was born on January 17, 1896 in Leadville, Colorado, a mining town in the Colorado Rockies that was located two miles above sea level. He received his education in Leadville and in the Denver Public Schools. In 1912, upon completion of his education, Gurtler obtained a position as the chief window dresser in the display department of the prestigious Daniels and Fisher Department store in downtown Denver, where he was employed for eleven years. In 1916, he married Marie Mulvihill, daughter of John Mulvihill. In 1923, he became manager of the Trocadero Ballroom at the amusement park. His management of the Trocadero was so successful that Mulvihill named him secretary of the amusement park corporation in 1927, an executive position he retained until the death of Mulvihill three years later.

Mr. Gurtler's experience in the theatrical atmosphere of Elitch Gardens made him the appropriate successor to manage the responsibilities of the Elitch Gardens and Theatre. During his management of the Gardens, he made many changes. Among the changes, one of the first was to remove the wooden fence surrounding the park and replace it with a wire fence through which the public could see the joyful happenings inside the park. The John Elitch baseball field at the southwest corner of the Park was enlarged, and a grandstand was built to accommodate the fans. The greatest change was his elaborate decoration of the Trocadero Ballroom, expressing a different theme each season. It became "The Summer Home of the Big Band Sound." The most popular bands of the era were engaged to play at the Trocadero.[14]

The Theatre programs provided to audiences during Mulvihill's management consisted almost entirely of advertising except for an occasional joke or two that sometimes appeared, contrary to the programs during Gurtler's administration which had stories, photographs and summaries of resident companies. His advertising tempted the Denver public to "Come to Elitch Gardens where a quarter can buy a day of dreams!"

Jack and Budd Gurtler, sons of Arnold B. Gurtler, got their first jobs as ushers at the Theatre, and they often escorted Mary Elitch to her box seat. This season, Jack Gurtler appeared in *Those We Love* in the role of "a young son," which he played with "an air of real professionalism."[11-5]

The Season

In 1930, the resident cast of twelve included Donn Cook (later and more commonly known by his full name, Donald Cook) and Selena Royle as leads. G. Bradford Ashworth returned to Elitch to serve as scenic director under Arnold Gurtler and would continue in that role through the 1935 season. The first director selected by Gurtler was John Hayden, who had extensive experience with stock companies and in directing Broadway plays.

> Hayden staged a total of thirty-six plays at the Gardens in three years and was asked to return for a fourth season in 1933, but illness prevented his accepting Mr. Gurtler's offer.[15]

Twelve plays were presented in 1930, among them being Donald Ogden Stewart's *Rebound*, Edward Childs Carpenter's *The Bachelor Father*, Avery Hopwood's *Let's Misbehave* and Herbert Ashton, Jr.'s *The Brothers.*

Opening Night Without John Mulvihill

The first play of the season was Philip Barry's comedy *Holiday,* which took New York by storm in 1928. The drama critic asserted that "the play is beautifully constructed ... and is generally one of the most satisfying comedies ever to have been presented locally."

The best of times, however, could not erase the fact that John Mulvihill was not present at the Theatre that he loved so much. Placed in the center of the review in the *Denver Post* were comments framed in black, among them being the following:

> How John M. Mulvihill would have enjoyed Saturday night at the Elitch Gardens! Perfect weather for the Theatre opening - the first time in many seasons; a play that was clicking right down the line; a company that had completely won over its audience before half of the first act was through ... (close friends) knew the Theatre was John Mulvihill's pet and the apple of his eye; they knew that his joy would have been boundless because of the brilliant opening - and their own pleasure was diminished because John Mulvihill was not there to witness and feel the warmth of that first audience![11-6]

Donald Cook - Theatre Romance, Hollywood and Thereafter

Donald Cook made his Broadway debut in 1926 as Donn Cook, and was billed as Donn Cook at Elitch during this season. During the 1930 engagement at Elitch, Cook met and fell in love with Frances Beranger, another member of the company. "We were in love, and she urged me to go to Hollywood," Cook said. "I did, and we were married when she returned to the coast from Denver." The marriage lasted six months. However, "the prestige of my Elitch engagement helped me get my first Hollywood contract - with Warner Brothers." His break came in the film *Public Enemy*, the gangster film that made James Cagney a star. Film buffs will recall Cook's role as the good brother, and the dramatic end of the film when Cook opens the door to the house and the wrapped body of the murdered Cagney topples on to the floor.[16] He continued to appear in films from time to time playing leads and second leads in mostly B pictures, his last film appearance being in 1950 in *Our Very Own*.[17]

Cook fared much better in theatrical performances, including memorable Broadway stage appearances. In 1939, he appeared in *Skylark* with Gertrude Lawrence. In 1940, he was invited to Elitch as the leading man. In 1941, he appeared on Broadway in the romantic comedy *Claudia*, which ran for three years and made a star of Dorothy McGuire. He played opposite Tallulah Bankhead in the 1948 revival of *Private Lives*. In 1951, he appeared with Barry Nelson and Barbara Bel Geddes in *The Moon is Blue*, which ran for three years. In 1954, he played the cartoonist Larry Larkin in the comedy *King of Hearts*.

In 1958, he returned to Elitch for a third time, appearing in lead roles.

Donald Cook was born in Portland, Oregon in 1900. The former bank clerk became a formidable actor. He died in 1961.

Theatre Season Extended Two Weeks

During the week of August 10th, Arnold B. Gurtler announced that the Theatre season would be extended by two weeks. This was the first time in the history of Elitch Gardens that there was an extension of the regular Theatre season. In making the announcement, Mr. Gurtler stated:

> We literally have been deluged with letters and personal requests for a longer Theatre season, and since our policy always has been to give our patrons what they want, there was but one thing to do - give them two more weeks of drama. We have prevailed upon members of the cast to remain in Denver for the additional period and have selected plays which we feel certain will appeal to the local theatergoing public.[11-5]

Stage Stars Take the Lead in Films

A survey of players under contract to ten major Hollywood studios revealed that 141 players who were drafted into talkies were from the stage, while 135 were identified with pictures alone. At Fox, stage players predominated by nearly 3 to 1, and both at Warner Brothers and Pathe there were twice as many stage recruits as film people.[11-7]

The Broadway Theater [10]

John Mulvihill was the manager of the Broadway Theater in Denver at the beginning of the 1929-1930 winter season. The season opened on September 10, 1929, with Thomas Mitchell appearing in *The Little Accident,* a comedy written by Mitchell with Floyd Dell, which had recently played in New York.

After John Mulvihill died on January 14, 1930, Arnold B. Gurtler took Mulvihill's place as manager of the Broadway Theater, in addition to Gurtler's management of the Elitch Theatre. However, at the end of the 1929-1930 season, Gurtler gave up the management of the Broadway Theater. On September 25, 1930, Arthur M. Oberfelder signed a three-year lease on the Broadway Theater, announcing that "he was forming a stock company which would open on October 11 and present a full season of stage fare, including current drama and some new plays."

Isobel Elsom

Upon the death of John Mulvihill in January of 1930, his son-in-law, Arnold B. Gurtler, succeeded him in management of the Gardens and Theatre.

Chapter Nineteen

(1931 - 1933)

Dark Times on Broadway
Whistler - The World Premiere
Happy Birthday to Mary Elitch Long
Elitch Theatre Prices Offset Tax
A Tribute to Selena Royle
The Death of Frederick G. Bonfils
The Scarcity of Broadway Stage Stars - Some Points of View

The 1931 Season

A Tribute to Elitch Theatre

Carlton Miles, a former drama editor of the Minneapolis Journal who, a few seasons earlier, had served as a press agent at Elitch Gardens, wrote a tribute for the then current issue of *Equity* in commemoration of Elitch's fortieth birthday. The following are among his comments:

> In the center of a Denver amusement park, a low, gray-painted wooden building preserves the atmosphere that we like to term tradition or feeling of theater as strongly as any playhouse I have seen. About it clings that indefinable association you sense in only a few theaters. The Empire in New York is one, the Walnut Street in Philadelphia is another, Ford's in Baltimore, a third. Yet nowhere is the tradition more strongly marked than in the Theatre of the Elitch Gardens, where theatrical performances have been a summer event for the last forty years.
>
> Some time ago in the early morning I stood looking for the first time at the building that now perhaps houses the oldest stock company in the United States. Arriving in the city almost at dawn, no time was lost in reaching the playhouse. The park was deserted. At the end of a short walk I came suddenly to the building, fronted by a lobby in which there were rows of framed photographs of former stage celebrities ... a heterogeneous collection of pictures of various decades.
>
> Since the passing of the A. M. Palmer Union Square company, the Daly and Frohman organizations and the Boston Museum, there has been nothing to parallel this institution. It is doubtful if any company has had more notable names connected with it.[1-1]

Dark Times on Broadway

In May of 1931, while Elitch Theatre was looking forward to another successful season, half of the Broadway theaters were empty. Equity received numerous complaints from many casts about lack of payment. Nationwide unemployment was between four and five million people.[2]

The Season

The opening play of the season was Walter Ferris' *Death Takes a Holiday*. The season ended with Vincent Lawrence's *In Love With Love*. In between, there were some one word titles, such as *Paris* by Martin Brown, *Whistler* by Pauline Hopkins and Sarah J. Curry, *Skidding* by Aurania Rouverol and *Gambling* by George M. Cohan. Katherine Alexander and Harvey Stephens were the leads.

Katherine Alexander

Katherine Alexander received many praises for her performances during the 1931 season.* Her first interest, however, was not the stage at all. She loved music and soon became known as a child prodigy of the violin and the piano. At one of a number of recitals arranged for her in New York, Jessie Bonstelle, one of the few female theatrical producers in America, was present and saw possibilities for Miss Alexander in the world of theater. Miss Alexander was invited to appear at Bonstelle's Detroit theater. She accepted the invitation and looked upon the offer as a mere novelty for her, a break from her rigorous and continual practice of music.

> But the novelty turned into a tremendous success. Not since the days of Katherine Cornell on that very stage had any actress made such great strides. She was soon featured and then New York producers grabbed for her. She was given the lead in *The Awful Mrs. Eaton*, a play about the Mrs. Ganns of President Jackson's days. "Awful" was a good name for the play, but Katherine Alexander stood out so prominently that the aristocratic Theater Guild sought her for Shaw's *Arms and the Man*. From that day on the violin merely became a hobby to play in private. Her success was assured and she was in continual demand.[1-2]

Opening Night of the Season

In selecting a play to open a season, Arnold Gurtler preferred a play in which every member of the company had the opportunity to perform in a role, allowing the Denver audience to be immediately acquainted with what to expect for the season. *Death Takes a Holiday* served that purpose. While it is difficult to imagine that a play about death could be the subject of comedy, Denverites who witnessed the opening performance would have vouched that death "can be as charming as a prince of royal blood."

* The other actors in the company were also praised for their acting ability. For example, J. Arthur Young in *Ladies of the Jury* "turns in his usual performance that is without a flaw," *Denver Post*, Jul 20, 1931, p. 21; Flobelle Fairbanks in *On the Spot* "is a versatile young woman who can make good with any role that is handed her," *Denver Post*, Aug 3, 1931, p. 12; and Arthur Pierson in *Skidding* "as usual, turning in a smooth well-studied performance," *Denver Post*, Aug 17, 1931, p. 13.

The play advances the startling premise that Death, tired of his labors, takes a three-day vacation as a harmless guest in the castle of Duke Lambert, there to ascertain why mortal men fear to meet him. Traveling incognito, as it were, under the name of Prince Sirki, Death meets and jests with various members of the duke's household, learns the ways of men, finds romance and takes as his willing bride, Grazia, the only member of the party who recognizes him for what he is, and fears him not.[1-3]

Skidding

The *Denver Post* referred to the play *Skidding* as a comedy built around homey events and homey people, "and as it meanders through the various phases of political intrigue, romance, lovers' quarrels, the kid brother's first date with a girl and all the other things that happen - or might happen - in an average family, an evening of wholesome entertainment, intermixed with homeopathic doses of sound logic and good advice, is provided for those who see it."[1-4]

Essentially, Judge Hardy is up for renomination and is opposed by crooked political cronies because he has been more attuned to justice than politics. His law-student daughter, Marion Hardy, decides to break off her engagement with the man she loves and begin her political career by helping her father in his campaign. Judge Hardy's campaign is successful. So is Judge Hardy when he makes his daughter realize she will be equally successful and happy in marriage.

Does the name "Hardy" in a homey family plot sound familiar? It should! The play served as a basis for Hollywood's popular Andy Hardy movies. Mickey Rooney was cast as Andy Hardy, the son of a small-town judge.[3]

Whistler - The World Premiere

Whistler began its world premiere engagement at the Elitch Theatre prior to its production in New York. The play deals with certain sensational incidents in the life of America's most unconventional artist, James McNeil Whistler, during a period around 1883 in the Chelsea district of old London, concerning the romance between Whistler and the Irish model, Jo, who sat for many of his paintings, including "The Little White Girl."

Out-of-town engagements for a new play are designed to objectively examine the script to assess its potential for success. In the process, depending on the playwright, the director of the play sometimes recommends appropriate changes. While most playwrights feel that for anyone to make even the slightest alteration in their work is sacrilegious, such was not the case with the authors of *Whistler*.

Director John Hayden of the Elitch Theatre worked with playwright Pauline Hopkins in getting the play in shape for the public. After he read the play, changes he believed essential were sent by telegraph to Mrs. Hopkins, and she acquiesced.

> (Hayden recalled that) "there were more changes - perhaps a scene originally written into the first act really belonged in the last. More telegrams. Certain dialog looked wonderful on paper, but when read or spoken lost its force. The telegraph office served again."
>
> "It probably is the first time in history," Hayden believes, "that a play was 'doctored' by telegraph. If the public likes it - and I believe it will - *Whistler* will owe much of its success to the fact that we had a playwright who did not for one instant interfere with the tearing down and rebuilding of her brainchild."[1-5]

The 1932 Season

Happy Birthday to Mary Elitch Long

Mary Elitch Long was preparing to leave for a lengthy visit to California. On March 5, 1932, the Denver Woman's Press Club decided to celebrate her May 10th birthday early at a reception attended by a multitude of friends. At the same time, it gave friends an opportunity to say farewell.

> The beautiful studio of the club was crowded to capacity. Tables were laden with gifts, felicitations for present and future happiness were offered and, as a souvenir of her devotion and loyalty, Mrs. Long presented a life-sized portrait of herself to the organization.[4-1]

For more than forty years, Mary Elitch Long had held a place in the hearts of the people of Denver as "The Lady of the Gardens," although for eighteen of those years she had been playing a watching part. So loved was she that her life was neither lonely nor friendless. Editors, artists, politicians, leaders in business, and religious and educational professionals were proud to call her friend and to accept the hospitality of her home.

The Death of Philip Golding

On March 19, 1932, the *Denver Post* reported the death of Philip Golding, the last owner of the restaurant that had been acquired from John Elitch, and whose name was changed from the Elitch Palace Dining Room to Tortoni Dining Parlors, or "Tortoni" for short. The restaurant had dining rooms upstairs where men of wealth often met and consummated deals involving millions of dollars. Political campaigns were planned there in private, behind locked doors. After the restaurant's closing in 1916, Golding continued to live at his home at 2704 Curtis Street until his demise. He died at the age of 94. He was laid to rest at Mount Olivet Cemetery after services at Sacred Heart church.[4-2]

The Season

Selena Royle was the leading woman and Roger Pryor the leading man. G. Bradford Ashworth returned to handle the scenic end of the productions. The director for the season was again John Hayden.

Selena Royle, a favorite New York actress, was heartily welcomed by Denver audiences upon her return to Elitch after successful performances in the 1930 season.

Among the plays presented were H. M. Harwood's English comedy *The Man in Possession*, Philip Barry's *The Animal Kingdom*, John Van Druten's *There's Always Juliet*, Benn W. Levy's *The Devil Passes* and Floyd Dell and Thomas Mitchell's *Cloudy With Showers.*

The Man in Possession was described as a "broad English comedy served in American fashion." The story centers on an old English custom in which a sheriff's officer, otherwise known as "the man in possession," is placed as an occupant of the home or apartment of any party or parties unable to pay their debts. The "man in possession" is to stay on the debtor's premises until the debt is paid in full.[4-3]

> When the debtor is a pretty young woman and the officer, a handsome young man (and an incorrigible optimist), some amusing situations are certain to arise.
>
> With Selena Royle as the pretty debtor, it's equally certain that the sheriff's officer can't be expected to merely stand around until the creditors are satisfied.[4-4]

Elitch Theatre Prices Offset Tax

The new federal tax on amusements was not felt by Elitch Theatre patrons, for the management announced lower admission charges to offset the tax. Under the revised schedule, regular $1.25 seats were $1.13 plus 12 cents tax; regular $1 seats were 90 cents, plus 10 cents tax; and 75-cent seats were 68 cents, plus 7 cents tax.

The new price reduction, in addition to the fact that many seats throughout the Theatre were lowered in price at the beginning of the season, amounted to a 23 percent reduction from the prior season's prices.[4-5]

A Tribute to Selena Royle [4-6]

Selena Royle was paid a tribute that expressed the appreciation of the theatrical profession for her Dinner Club in New York, which helped to provide free meals for hundreds of unemployed actors. The tribute was in the form of a poem by C. C. Fellows that was published in the magazine of Actors' Equity.

To Selena Royle

You saw the need, you spoke the word
Of understanding that was heard
By others, who knew what it meant,
This dread, this stark predicament.

You followed word with glowing deed
And so superbly have you freed
Your harassed fellows there are none
But what give thanks for what you've done.

You and all your shining "crew"
Who saw the need and saw it thru
For all the human hearts of you
Our thanks - our thanks made glad and true.

The 1933 Season

The Death of Frederick G. Bonfils

Frederick G. Bonfils, founder, editor and publisher of the *Denver Post*, father of Helen Bonfils, died on February 2, 1933, after a brief illness. Services were held in his home at 1500 East Tenth Avenue, where Rev. Hugh L. McMenamin, pastor of the Cathedral of the Immaculate Conception, and the Rev. Henry Ford, associate pastor of the Church of the Holy Ghost, administered the blessing to the dead.[5-1]

Messages of sympathy poured in from around the country. Arthur Brisbane, world's greatest editorial writer, acclaimed Mr. Bonfils as one of the three greatest editors in the country. Arthur B. Gurtler of Elitch Gardens conveyed his sympathy as well, saying:

> I was deeply shocked and grieved to learn of the untimely death of our beloved friend. The entire community shares in the sorrow. Mr. Bonfils leaves an imperishable record of achievement as a civic leader, as a humanitarian, as a man. We mourn his passing greatly, as a friend, a citizen and a benefactor. We have all lost a friend who cannot be replaced.[5-1]

Helen Bonfils, still unmarried, was forty-three when her father died. She took over his office at the *Denver Post*. Now that her controlling father was gone, she was "free to date anyone she wished - if only she knew someone to date. But then she discovered the most precious freedom of all: she was free to pursue an acting career!"[6] She was to play a dominant role in the future of Elitch Theatre.

The Theater World Awaits the New Season [5-2]

The world of theater and its nationally famous stars who were associated and vitally interested in Elitch Theatre awaited the first news of the opening of its forty-first regular season.

> New York, which has sent some of its best talent to Denver, will be keenly interested in the dramatic season opening here. Broadway audiences who have enjoyed Margalo Gillmore in many outstanding Theater Guild successes will be anxious to hear of her important engagement in the West. Washington, D.C., whose famous National theater sent Donald Woods to Denver, will take pride in the appearance of one of its most popular leading men on a Denver stage.
>
> Hollywood and its famous movie colony, which has sent three members of Elitch's new company, will be looking toward the mile-high city and the gala opening of Elitch Theatre.
>
> As the resident company at Elitch prepared for the opening of the season, there was a spirited and contagious feeling among its members, "and the very air seems charged with the idea that this is going to be an extraordinary season."

The Season

The regular season at Elitch Theatre was to open with the play *Forsaking All Others*. However, the season began earlier than scheduled with another play. A road show production of the comedy *Her Majesty the Widow*, starring Pauline Frederick and her excellent company, was originally scheduled to open at the Broadway Theater in Denver for a week. Arthur M. Oberfelder, with whom the actress was under contract, sensed the cool surroundings of Elitch Gardens would be a better site for the production. Miss Frederick's reaction to the change was a happy one as she held the Elitch Theatre in high esteem. Arrangements were made with Arnold B. Gurtler to accommodate the play and it was presented for five nights from June 19th through June 23rd. When the change in venue was announced, it resulted in a deluge of mail orders for seats.[7] Pauline Frederick was described as "one of the most distinguished stars of stage and screen ... (and) of the very few to win worldwide fame in both fields."[8]

The leads of the resident company were Donald Woods and Margalo Gillmore. Miss Gillmore was born in London into an acting family. While still a child she was brought to America, where she studied at the American Academy of Dramatic Arts. Her father, Frank Gillmore, was president of Actors' Equity. She appeared in numerous Broadway plays and was much admired for her beauty and fine talent.[9] G. Bradford Ashworth returned as scenic designer. Addison Pitt was new to Elitch as a director; however, in 1903 he had appeared at Elitch as the juvenile with the

Henrietta Crosman Company. Pitt had been associated with Charles Frohman, David Belasco, Sam and Lee Shubert and others on Broadway and had directed Peggy Wood, June Walker, Henrietta Crosman, Otto Kruger and Pauline Lord, to name a few. He remained as director at Elitch through the 1935 season.

Among the other plays that graced the Elitch stage in 1933 was Raymond Van Sickle's *Best Years. Best Years* is a play that presents a story that happens in real life in many a home. Briefly stated, "in facing the best years of (her) life, Cora Davis must decide between marriage or devoting her life solely to her mother, for her mother's selfish devotion will have no compromise."[5-3]

The Scarcity of Broadway Stage Stars - Some Points of View [5-4]

Veteran producers of Broadway shows had complained of their inability to cast plays calling for a star because lucrative film salaries had attracted them to Hollywood. Others had pointed out that promising actors had opted for film rather than to go through years of the repertory training necessary to reach stardom as a stage actor. However, others had said that the stage no longer attracts performers of the Barrymore and Mansfield caliber because "the days of individual stardom are waning; that audiences are more interested in group acting; (and) that Shakespeare was right when he said, 'The play's the thing.'"

Denver Public Library Western History Collection - No. X-27366

The brick home built by John Mulvihill on the grounds for Mary Elitch

Chapter Twenty

(1934 - 1935)

Helen Bonfils
George Somnes
An Old Stage Belief - An Actor Must Have "Lived"
Behind the Scenes of Success
The Federal Theatre Project

The 1934 Season

The season opened with the A. E. Thomas comedy *No More Ladies*, a Lee Shubert production that closed for the summer at the Morosco Theater in New York, to be resumed there in the early fall. Shubert carefully guarded the rights to the play.

> Arthur B. Gurtler sought the play for Denver and its loyal clientele. As a result the Shuberts released it for this city alone, and, unless signs change, Denver is the only city that will witness the play until it has finally ended its run in New York when a touring company will carry it to the key cities of America.[1-1]

Among the plays that followed were Sidney Kingsley's Pulitzer Prize play *Men in White*, Claire Kummer's *Her Master's Voice* and Lawrence Langner and Armine Marshall's *The Pursuit of Happiness*.

Lora Baxter was selected to be leading lady and Donald Woods to be the male lead. Lora Baxter was the wife of William Rose Benet, the distinguished author and editor of the *Saturday Review of Literature*.[2-1] She won favorable attention on Broadway in 1932 with her performance opposite Leslie Howard in the Philip Barry comedy *The Animal Kingdom*. Ms. Baxter had played at Elitch as the ingenue of the 1924 company.[1-2] Helen Bonfils and Glenn Langan, Denver actors, made their first appearances at Elitch in *Men in White*, playing minor roles.

Alan Campbell was a member of the Elitch company. He was also a writer whose articles appeared regularly in the *New Yorker* magazine. His wife was Dorothy Parker, famous short story writer and satirical poet.[2-2]

As a drama critic, Dorothy Parker became famous for her caustic dismissal of plays and performers, once accusing Katherine Hepburn of running the gamut of emotions "from A to B."[3-1] When Campbell was cast for the summer season at the Elitch Theatre, he and Parker left their Manhattan East Side apartment for Denver and took up residence in a rental unit on Meade Street, a long way from The Cort or The Biltmore in New York. Alan was described as "outstanding in his small but important role" in the play *Men in White*.[2-3] He appeared in nine of the ten plays presented that summer.

In Peter Hay's book of *Broadway Anecdotes,* he shares the following amusing anecdote about Dorothy Parker.

> Frank Case, the famous proprietor of the Algonquin Hotel (in New York), once called Dorothy Parker's room and asked her whether she had violated one of the hotel's rules: "Do you have a gentlemen in your room?"
>
> "Just a minute" said the incorrigible Miss Parker, "I'll ask him."[4]

As usual, the opening night of a season was a special event at Elitch, marked by excitement and attended by a capacity crowd of first-nighters.

> Autograph hunters came to seek out the celebrities with which the cast is studded this season. Drama lovers came to hear some of the most sparkling lines ever spoken from behind the storied footlights of the Elitch stage. The governor and the mayor contributed a few words. Society turned out for a brilliant first night.[2-4]

From time to time, things unexpectedly happen on an opening night. During this opening night, Alan Campbell inadvertently broke off the back of a chair while leaning over to talk to Lora Baxter; however, because of his expert handling of the matter, the audience wasn't sure "the occurrence wasn't called for in the stage directions."[2-4]

Helen Bonfils

Helen Bonfils made her first appearance at Elitch Theatre this season in a bit part in Sydney King's Pulitzer Prize play *Men in White.* She was born on November 26, 1889, in Peekskill, New York, the youngest daughter of Frederick Bonfils. The Bonfils family came to Denver when Helen was six years old and established itself in a brick home at 939 Corona Street. Frederick Bonfils was a shrewd businessman and became one of the founders of the *Denver Post.* Helen attended St. Mary's Academy and Denver's Wolcott School for girls, where all the best families of Denver sent their daughters.* Helen then attended the Brownell School, a finishing school in New York.[5-1]

From an early age, Helen Bonfils' great love was the theater. She often attended matinee performances with her grandmother and mother at the Tabor Grand and at Elitch Theatre. She appeared in many amateur productions with the Denver Civic Theatre Company. As her acting skills matured, she wondered whether she could act within the professional ranks of the theater. However, since her father

* The well-known Wolcott School was advertised as "The West's Leading School for Girls ... Accredited with the best Eastern Colleges for Women (and having) High Grade Equipment and Expert Teachers." The school boasted of having "all departments from Kindergarten through High School and College Preparatory" and urged that "Your girl should be with us." See, *e.g.*, Elitch Theatre program, Jul 5-11, 1914, p. 27.

was opposed to Helen's desire to become a professional actress, she did not begin her work in the theater until after his death in 1933. In 1934, she set off to audition at Elitch Theatre. To her delight, director Addison Pitt selected her from among a dozen hopefuls to perform for the season.

> She wasn't young, she wasn't gorgeous, but Pitt obviously thought he saw in her the talent of a character actress. When he referred to her as "Miss Barton," Helen corrected him. She was actually Helen Bonfils, she explained. She had used her mother's maiden name to audition because she didn't intend to fail as a Bonfils.
>
> Helen was forty-three when she made her first appearance on stage that summer in the part of an Italian woman in *Men in White*.* She wasn't bad, as it turned out. Much later, her friend Edwin Levy of the drama department of the University of Denver (and sometimes-director of the Denver Civic Theatre) claimed that Helen was one of the most popular actors to appear at the summer theater over a period of fifteen years. He praised her performances and wrote that she had a "spectacular, versatile flair for bringing vivid characterization" to the secondary parts she played, such as Addie in *The Little Foxes*.[5-2]

She played "walk-on" roles during the 1934 and 1935 seasons before becoming a regular member of the company in 1936. Although she usually played various relatively minor roles,** she also appeared, on occasion, in a major role, such as Adeline in *Whiteoaks* (1939) and Fanny Cavendish in *The Royal Family* (1941).

George Somnes [6]

George Somnes had long been associated with show business and was considered an artist of the broadest culture, a professional of the highest value in his chosen work and, most of all, a lovable human being. He was born in Massachusetts, reared in Boston and educated in Europe.

Somnes was a formidable actor who made his first Broadway appearance in *An Old New Yorker*, a play produced by William A. Brady. He went to England in 1914 and became the first American to gain prominence in the famous Old Vic Repertory Theater, to a high degree for his portrayal of King Claudius in *Hamlet*. In 1917, when the United States entered World War I, Somnes left England and went into the Army, emerging in 1919 as a top sergeant in the field artillery. After the armistice, Somnes returned to the American stage as an understudy to John Barrymore in *Peter Ibbetson*. After many years of acting, Somnes moved on to his true love -

* Having been born in Nov. 1889, Helen Bonfils would have been forty-four rather than forty-three in this first appearance at Elitch.

** *E.g.*, gangster's moll in *Night of January 16* (1936), a maid in *No Time for Comedy* (1940), and the old-time stripper in *Burlesque* (1940).

directing. He organized the Indianapolis Civic Theater and the Cape Playhouse in Dennis, Massachusetts, before answering a call from Hollywood. Somnes was a motion picture director in California from 1929 to 1934 and directed films starring Sylvia Sydney, Claudette Colbert, Gary Cooper, George Raft and others. In 1934, Somnes lowered the curtain on his California interlude and went back to the life of the theater.

The 1934 season was significant in the lives of Helen Bonfils and George Somnes. It was during this season that Somnes was introduced to Miss Helen Bonfils. Somnes bore a striking resemblance to Helen's father, and she felt an instant attraction to him. Helen and George Somnes were to marry in 1936. Both would play significant roles in the future of the Elitch Theatre.

Men in White

Sidney Kinglsey's Pulitzer Prize-winning play, *Men in White*, required a cast of thirty persons. To fill that number of performers, director Addison Pitt called upon a number of actors from the Denver community to lend support to the regular Elitch company. Because of the number of cast members needed, the play had been presented by few stock companies, "and it is doubtful if the play has been as effectively staged anywhere as at Elitch."

> (The story) concerns the choice a brilliant young interne must make between furthering his career by advanced study or marrying a wealthy girl who offers him a life of ease and a regular practice. The matter becomes more complicated when the interne is involved in an affair with a student nurse at the large hospital where he is studying. In simpler words, it's a choice between love and duty, and, later, between duty and the "right thing."[1-3]

In preparing to play the lead role, Donald Woods arranged through hospital authorities to watch a delicate thyroid operation at Colorado General Hospital. The experience accorded Woods a more real "atmosphere" for his role in the play, as well as a greater appreciation for the medical profession.

> "I have never realized until now, and I am sure that most people unacquainted with the medical profession do not know, what infinite skill is required to perform such delicate work," Woods said afterward. "I deeply appreciate, more than ever, the sacrifices, the arduous years of training that a man must serve to become a doctor. My hat is off, literally, to the medical profession."[1-4]

An Old Stage Belief - An Actor Must Have "Lived"

Must a girl have been in love before she can play Juliet? There is an old stage tradition that actors and actresses must "have lived" before they can aspire to greatness. "Living" is said to be "necessary to give the actor a profound understanding of human nature, and a firm grasp of character."[7]

> "The smallest of tragedies," Cecil B. De Mille believes, "leave their scars on the souls of artists. Poverty and youthful struggles, disappointments and moments of despair have effects nearly as marked as those made by deaths and by the abiding feeling of futility that is so common among true artists.
>
> "But the great thing is life itself. Life will form the artist, given time enough, if his soul is sufficiently malleable to shape and sensitive enough to take impression."[1-5]

The 1935 Season

Roy Roberts and Nancy Sheridan were the leads. More comedies were presented this year at Elitch because the company selected was especially suited for comedies, although their many years of experience allowed them to also take on heavier and more dramatic roles that might have been required by a script.

In *Accent on Youth*, the opening play of the season, Roy Roberts, Elitch's relatively young leading man, was cast as the 47-year-old playwright involved in a romance with a girl in her twenties. This was noted by the drama editor.

> Roberts, the leading man, is a bit unfortunate in having to make his initial appearance before Denver theatergoers in a part that calls for him to enact a character some twenty years older than himself, but Roberts' performance in the part gave promise of a summer characterized by a practically flawless leading man.[1-6]

The play *Ah, Wilderness!* was the only comedy written by Eugene O'Neill. It was a Theatre Guild production in 1933, running for 289 performances on Broadway, and was described as "the tenderest and most amusing comedy of boyhood in the American Drama." George M. Cohan appeared as Nat Miller, the father, and was praised for his fine-tuned performance.[8] The play had never been presented in stock until permission was granted to Elitch Theatre, an honor paid to America's well-recognized Theatre.[1-7]

Eugene O'Neill, like many playwrights, strongly objected to cutting any parts of his plays. When a director asked him to shorten the script of *Ah, Wilderness!*, O'Neill phoned him the following day and informed him that he had cut 15 minutes. When asked about what was cut, O'Neill replied, "we have been playing this thing in four acts. I've decided to cut out the third intermission."[9]

Ceiling Zero required a large cast which made it necessary to augment the Elitch company to double its regular size, using local performers to assist, including Jack

Gurtler, son of Arnold B. Gurtler.[1-8]

Behind The Scenes of Success

While Denver theatergoers were enjoying another summer season of success, and while actors were fortunate to be engaged by the Elitch management, behind the scenes in America were theaters and actors without work, still impacted by the Great Depression. This layer of unemployment was not to be neglected by the new administration and its New Deal. The Federal Theatre Project was to become a vital part of America's theatrical world. The following section provides a brief history of the Federal Theatre Project.

The Federal Theatre Project

A Brief History (1935-1939)

The Federal Theatre Project (FTP) was a part of the New Deal Administration Program to fund theater and other live artistic performances in the United States during the Great Depression. It was sponsored by the Works Projects Administration (WPA). Its purpose was to create jobs for theatrical professionals idled by the Depression. The circulation of public funds through the project was also felt to strengthen the economy.

The Project was established by legislation on August 27, 1935, with Hallie Flanagan Davis, a theater professor at Vassar University, selected to lead the project. She was "not only an extraordinary theater visionary but an individual of unusual character, integrity, and drive - qualities that in combination made her one of the greatest leaders in the history of American theater."[10-1] She was promised by the administration a theatre that was "free, adult, (and) uncensored."[10-2]

More than ten thousand professionals were employed in all facets of the theater, which included actors, writers, designers, theater musicians, dancers, stage hands, box office staff, and others necessary to carry out the enterprise. More than nine out of ten employed came from relief roles. About 1,000 productions were presented in four years in 40 states, at comparatively low prices, and often for free.[11]

Productions ranged from imaginative revivals of old classics through new plays, children's plays, African-American productions, plays in foreign languages, marionette shows and evenings of dance.[3-2]

The federal project made theater available to many who had never seen theater before. In *Federal Theatre Magazine* this voice was heard.

> We're a hundred thousand kids who never saw a play before. We're students in colleges, housewives in the Bronx, lumberjacks in Oregon, sharecroppers in Georgia. We're rich and poor, old and young, sick and well. We're America and this is our theatre.[12]

Hallie Flanagan Davis "was never opposed to using the theater for propaganda purposes, if that meant exposing political corruption or unjust social conditions. Although she was often accused of promoting Communism and even of being a Communist herself, she never consciously allowed the Federal Theatre to be used for the purpose of endorsing political parties or advancing political aims. Indeed, she did not hesitate to cancel plays that seemed overtly partisan to her."[10-2]

It wasn't difficult to be called a Communist during such times. For example,

> ... within Equity there were very few black actors. There was a conservative, reactionary body within Equity, and it was a solid unit, keeping blacks out of Equity or keeping them in only certain theaters, trying not to mix. If you would accept them, greet them at a union meeting, you were clearly the other side. You were clearly a Communist.[10-3]

Notwithstanding the assertions of Hallie Flanagan Davis, many of the productions were perceived as left-wing propaganda pieces, and opposition to the project grew, especially among conservatives.[3-2]

> Eventually, the House Un-American Activities Committee, under the chairmanship of the notorious Martin Dies of Texas, saw the political controversy engulfing the Federal Theatre as an excellent opportunity to attack the Roosevelt administration.[10-4]

After heated debate in Congress, the Federal Theatre Project came to an end on June 30, 1939, when its funding was terminated.[13]

Much has since been written in defense of the Federal Theatre Project, lauding its contributions and acknowledging its legacy of a new generation of theater artists whose careers began with the Project, such as Orson Welles, John Houseman, Arthur Miller, Elia Kazan, Jules Dassin, Katherine Dunham and Canada Lee.[14]

The Federal Theatre Project also helped to launch the career of Mary Coyle Chase as a playwright. Mary Chase was born in Denver in 1907, and had a long career there as a journalist before writing her first play, which was titled *Me Third* and presented by the Federal Theatre Project. *Me Third* was then produced in New York during the 1936-37 season under the title *Now You've Done It*, but closed after a run of three weeks.[15] Miss Chase later wrote the Pulitzer Prize-winning play *Harvey* (1944), and after its success, she wrote *The Next Half Hour* (1945), *Mrs. McThing* (1952), *Bernadine* (1952) and *Midgie Purvis* (1961).[3-3]

Denver was one of the cities chosen to take part in the Federal Theatre Project. Twenty-five to thirty unemployed actors in the Denver area benefited from the program at a salary scale from $55.00 to $90.00 a month.[16-1] The plays that were initially produced were presented at public schools, hospitals, churches and those buildings that had an auditorium. In August 1936, the project moved into the old Baker Theater at 1447 Lawrence Street. The playhouse was cleaned, repainted, and renovated and became known as the Baker Federal Theatre. It opened with its first production in October.

> When it opened on October 20, 1936, the theatre was rather unique; but it was representative of similar activities in other American cities of the time, since it also housed art exhibits from Federal Art Projects, a weekly concert by the Federal Music Project, and fashion shows staged by women on various sewing projects, as well as plays staged by the Federal Theatre Project.[17]

Regular programs were presented for a nominal entrance fee of forty cents.[16-2] The opening play of the season was Mary Coyle Chase's *Me Third,* described as "a farce with a political background." It was deemed fitting that the opening play of the season be by a Denver writer, who had earlier been a staff writer for the *Rocky Mountain News*.[18] Among the other plays presented was the dramatization of Sinclair Lewis's controversial *It Can't Happen Here,* an antifascist work that was accused by some of being "pro-Roosevelt New Deal, communist, fascist, and 'PROPAGANDA - naked and unconcealed.'"[19]

As in the case of other theaters, the Baker Federal Theatre had its periods of darkness. The Theatre closed on June 25, 1939.

Denver Public Library Western History Collection

Nancy Sheridan - Leading Lady (1935)

Helen Bonfils - Her first appearance at Elitch (1934)

George Somnes - Director (1934)

Chapter Twenty-One

(1936 - 1940)

The Death of Mary Elitch Long
Marriage of George Somnes and Helen Bonfils
The Orchard Cafe
Appeal for the Actors' Fund of America
Leather Upholstered Seats
Federal Tax on Theater Tickets / Taxes on Theaters

The 1936 Season

The Death of Mary Elitch Long

On July 15, 1936, Mary Elitch Long suffered a heart attack at the home of her sister-in-law, Jeannette Arnold, at 4567 West 38th Avenue, where she had lived for four years. She moved there from her home across the way in the Gardens where she had lived for forty years. Her home in the Gardens was a gathering place for the great from the world of the theater.

She was reported to be unconscious throughout the evening. On the following day, July 16, 1936, she sank into a coma. Monsignor William F. O'Ryan, her longtime friend, administered the last rites of the Catholic Church to her at her bedside. She died at 10:02 p.m. without regaining consciousness. She was 80 years of age.[1]

Funeral services were conducted in the Cathedral of the Immaculate Conception in Denver. Monsignor O'Ryan preached the sermon and sang the solemn mass of requiem. Hundreds of friends from every walk of life attended the funeral.

The *Denver Post* reported that:

> For one who had lived all of her adult life in the glare of spotlights that shine upon a place of public entertainment, like Elitch Gardens ... the funeral of Mary Elitch Long was marked by extreme simplicity and complete lack of pomp and circumstance.[2-1]

She was eulogized as one of the most beloved women in Denver's history. In speaking of her, Monsignor O'Ryan said:

> Her standards of morality were firmly fixed and that is why she created a monument out of a public playground that has always stood for what is clean, right, good before the world.[2-1]

On July 17, 1936, the following appeared in the *Denver Post*:

> The better part of her life story will not be found in rigid biographies or histories of Who's Who in Colorado or in America, but in the hearts and memories of those who, entering the gates of the Gardens she created

> and owned for so many years, came into contact with a personality whose quick sympathy, understanding, joyousness, gentleness and rare good humor enriched the experience of each.[2-2]

The life of the Theatre continued, even in mourning, but curtain time was appropriately described as follows:

> It was curtain time at the nationally-famed Elitch Gardens Theatre in Denver, Colorado, a July evening in 1936. Few programs rustled; even fewer eyes sought the footlights spraying the forty-five-year old hand-painted curtain. Instead they rested on the lower right front box, empty and draped in black. Mary Elitch, patroness-founder of Elitch Theatre, would enter her personal box that evening in spirit only.[3]

Mary Elitch Long was buried on July 21, 1936 in Fairmount Cemetery beside John Elitch. No person is presently in charge of their graves. They are kept and maintained by the management personnel of the cemetery. Their grave sites are Lot 63, Block 5.

A Place in History

The name of Mary Elitch is associated with those pioneer women theater-owners in America, including Laura Keene and Mrs. John (Louisa) Drew.

> It was Mary Elitch's success with (Elitch Theatre) ... that inspired the formation of other stock companies through the West. And it was the standards of decency and respectability that she has maintained and guaranteed for 30 years that have set so definite a mark for all other amusement park proprietors to shoot at.[4]

In 1855, Laura Keene opened up her own playhouse in New York on Broadway just below Beeker Street. She managed her own company and starred in her own productions.

> The onset of the Civil War presented financial problems for her, which she met initially by offering elaborate musical spectacles. When these finally palled, she abandoned her theater and took to the road. She was playing *Our American Cousin* at Ford's Theatre in Washington when Lincoln was assassinated there. While she had no part in the assassination, her career never recovered from her association with the incident.[5-1]

Laura Keene died in 1873.

In 1861, Louisa Drew became manager of the Arch Street Theatre in Philadelphia, which she ran until 1892. She installed her own stock company in addition to booking touring attractions. Under her rule, the theater "was generally considered to offer the finest company and the finest productions outside of New York." Mrs. Drew was the grandmother of John, Ethel and Lionel Barrymore. Mrs. Drew died in 1897.[5-2]

Opening Day at the Gardens

The largest opening day crowd in the 46-year history of Elitch Gardens - 14,931 paid admissions - filled the 26-acre amusement park and acclaimed it to be "more beautiful and spectacular than ever."[6-1]

The plays selected for the season included Jay Mallory's *Sweet Aloes*, Edward Wooll's *Libel!*, Robert E. Sherwood's *The Petrified Forest* and Ayn Rand's *The Night of January 16*.

The leads for the season were Irene Purcell and Kenneth MacKenna. George Somnes was selected by Arnold Gurtler to direct the season of plays. He remained as director for Elitch Theatre from 1936 through 1947 and later from 1951 through 1954. In addition to directing the plays, having had a background as an actor, Somnes occasionally performed in his own productions. Among such roles were those of counsel for the defendant in *Libel* (1936), Sherman Whiteside in *The Man Who Came to Dinner* (1941), Sandor Turai in *The Play's The Thing* (1942) and the title role in *Uncle Harry* (1943).

In tribute to Mary Elitch Long, the box she habitually occupied at the Elitch Theatre was draped and empty upon her death and remained so until after her funeral service.[2-2]

Opening Night for the Actors of a New Company

Opening night to an actor is different from any other performance of the season. Facing a capacity audience for the first time, with drama critics in place to notice every move and hear every word, the anticipation of the performer is immeasurable.

> Opening night at the theater is always a time of tenseness, high-strung emotions, anxiety, eager anticipation and swift responses.
>
> Kenneth MacKenna and Irene Purcell, leads in the 1936 company, are seasoned troupers, but they felt the electric forces that hover in the wings as the footlights flash on and the curtain starts upward.
>
> The Elitch Gardens Theatre is a playhouse of national reputation. It is big-time - as famous in the summertime amusement world as are the time-honored theaters of New York's winter Broadway. The whole nation knows it. The impressions scored by a new company there on opening night make theatrical news from coast to coast, and every member of the cast knows it.
>
> That knowledge keys them all to a performance backed by their best efforts - and Denver's first night audience knows and appreciates that.[2-3]

Perfect Acting

Lucien Self, the stage manager for *Libel*, also played the role of a seriously injured German soldier known only as No. 15, who can neither move, speak nor understand.

> (He) remains in full view of the audience for fully 20 minutes without blinking his eyes or moving a single muscle. Only by watching the rise and fall of his chest does one realize that he is a living man and not a mummy.
>
> So perfectly does he play the part ... that one is apt to overlook his part entirely. That, indeed, is perfection in acting.[6-2]

The Night of January 16th

Most readers associate Ayn Rand (1905-1982), the Russian-born author who came to America in 1926, with advocating the rights of the individual with her novels, such as *The Fountainhead* and *Atlas Shrugged*. Yet, she was also the author of the Elitch Theatre presentation of *The Night of January 16th* (1935), a murder mystery, which ran for 232 performances on Broadway. Her only other play to reach Broadway was *The Unconquered* (1940).[5-3]

Marriage of George Somnes and Helen Bonfils

In the fall of 1936, George Somnes and Helen Bonfils were married in the rose garden of the Gurtler home at 4209 W. 38th Avenue. Helen was 46 years of age. In addition to the home they maintained in Denver, the couple also leased and eventually purchased a luxurious apartment in New York, which was along the East River and had a gorgeous view.

Together they formed the Bonfils and Somnes Producing Company and backed a number of plays on Broadway, including *Sun-Kissed* in 1937 and *The Brown Danube* and *Pastoral* in 1939, all of which were later included among the plays presented at Elitch. Helen also performed in Broadway shows under the stage name of Gertrude Barton, having appeared in *The Greatest Show on Earth* in 1938 and *Topaz* in 1947. Their marriage was characterized by love and the glamour of the theater.

The 1937 Season

Elitch Theatre's Continuing Popularity

An article in the *Rocky Mountain News* referenced comments made in *Time* magazine that expressed the continuing popularity of Elitch Theatre throughout the country.

> Denver is becoming more and more important in the nation's scientific, literary and cultural life. Evidence of this pops up daily. In mind at the moment is (the) July 5 issue of *Time*. Out of seven columns devoted to

theater, Denver's own Elitch Gardens gets the biggest slice. Says the magazine:

"Elitch Gardens is the great-grandfather of all U.S. summer stock companies ... (since the opening) the place has been a repository of big names ever since ... nearly every personage in U.S. show business, from General and Mrs. Tom Thumb to Douglas Fairbanks, has at one time or another played Elitch."[6-3]

The Season

Kenneth MacKenna returned for the second successive season as the leading man. Barbara Robbins was the leading lady. A note in the Elitch program states, "Kenneth MacKenna, Barbara Robbins and others of the company hurry up Lookout Mountain practically every evening after the show ... They never tire of the view of Denver as seen from Wildcat point ..."[7]

George Somnes was director for the season, and Brad Hatton was the stage manager. Victor Paganuzzi, an artist new to Denver, was the scenic designer. He remained at the Gardens for nine successive seasons through 1945.

The play selection included George Kelley's *Reflected Glory,* Bella and Samuel Spewack's *Boy Meets Girl,* and two plays by Maxwell Anderson, *Both Your Houses* and *Winterset.*

James Spottswood

James Spottswood, a member of the cast, was educated in Washington D.C. and received a law degree from Georgetown University. He was a direct descendant of Alexander Spottswood, first colonial governor of Virginia in 1710. During his last year in law school, he studied dramatic art to hone his skills for courtroom appearances. A stock company in Washington sent out a call for extra players, and James responded and was cast in a speaking role. That ended his pursuit of the legal profession in favor of acting. He achieved success in theater, including performances on Broadway and in film at Paramount and Warner Brothers Studios in Hollywood.[8]

Bradford Hatton

Bradford Hatton was educated in the public schools of Denver and, as a boy, made his first contact with the Elitch Theatre as an usher. He completed two years of college at Boulder before pursuing his interest in the stage, an interest he inherited from his parents. As an infant, Hatton came to Denver in the traditional theatrical trunk. His parents, Adele Bradford and Clare Hatton, were members of O.D. Woodward's original Denham Stock Company in Denver.[2-4]

The Man the Audience Never Sees on Stage

While theatergoers usually measure the success of a season on the quality of performance by the actors, one of the most important members of a theater company upon whom the success of a season depends, is never seen by the audience. There is evidence of his presence in every performance, but he is not to be seen on the stage.

This season, as in many others, that person was George Somnes, the director. Upon his judgment, a great deal depended.

> It is up to director Somnes to see that the players know their lines; then, knowing the lines, to deliver them as they should be delivered. He must see that laugh-producing lines are "timed" correctly. It is his job to be certain that the proper inflection is given to each speech by each player. He must see that the costumes are right, that stage settings are atmospheric of the play, that the lighting is effective. For the director is the Atlas of the show business - the fellow upon whose shoulders rests the weight of the show world![2-5]

Winterset

The play *Winterset* (1935) has been hailed as Maxwell Anderson's masterpiece. It was Anderson's second attempt to dramatize the Sacco-Vanzetti story. His earlier collaboration with Harold Hickerson, *Gods of the Lightning* (1928), had failed.* [5-4] The trial of Sacco-Vanzetti and their execution on August 23, 1927 were the subject of essays attempting to exonerate them due to a trial that was distorted by the bias and weight of public hysteria. In 1977, their names were "cleared" when Governor Michael Dukakis of Massachusetts signed an official proclamation to that effect.

Excursion

Excursion was the last play of the season and the resident company was augmented by dozens of extras into a cast of 45 "passengers" on the S.S. Happiness, a ferry boat that had been plying its way between New York and Coney Island for many years. The captain is informed to make one last trip to Coney Island and then to retire his beloved old boat to the junk yard. Having never given in to his youthful ambition to be a deep sea sailorman, the captain decides, with the consent of his passengers, to alter his course in the middle of the run to the open seas and a fabled tropical island somewhere near Trinidad,

> ... where they can found a new society in which there will be no department stores, no stinking markets, no jealous husbands, no screaming children, no necessity for changing your name if it happens to be Fitchell.[6-4]

* In a comment on the play *Gods of the Lightning*, it was stated that "The *Times* hailed the play as a 'strong, harrowing drama.' Perhaps tired of the whole Sacco-Vanzetti affair, theatergoers would not buy the play." Bordman, American Theatre: A Chronicle of Comedy and Drama, 1914-1930 (Oxford University Press 1995), pp. 364-365.

At this point of the play, the passengers (and the audience) must have been substituting the words "Shangri-La" and "Utopia" for the fabled tropical island somewhere near Trinidad.

> (And the passengers begin to realize) that anything out there on the water that might await them would be better than what they would have to go back to in New York.
>
> And yet - when the little dream is over and the Coast Guard puts a shot across the bow of the Happiness, not a soul on board is really sorry to be going back home.[6-5]

The play was the most expensive production of the season.[6-6] It was described as a "personal feather in the cap" of its director, George Somnes, for the manner in which he handled "large groups of people with genuine dexterity, bringing intimate scenes into focus against a kaleidoscopic background."[6-5]

Death of Catherine N. Mulvihill [2-6]

On November 13, 1937, the wife of John M. Mulvihill, Catherine N. Mulvihill, a woman who devoted her life to her home and to the church and charitable organizations, died at her home in Denver at 4209 W. 38th Avenue following a long illness. She was 65 years of age. She was born on June 14, 1872. She was a member of St. Vincent's Aid, the Queen of Heaven Aid, the Tabernacle Society, the Catholic Women's Press Club, the Altar and Rosary Society of Holy Family Church and the Board of Loretto Heights College. A requiem mass was held at Holy Family Church, followed by her interment in the family plot at Mount Olivet Cemetery.

Don Wilson [2-7]

During the summer season of 1937, Don Wilson, the noted announcer of the Jack Benny program, was selected to appear in his first Universal film entitled *Behind the Mike*. After graduating from North Denver high school, Wilson attended the University of Colorado at Boulder where he was a member of the Sigma Chi fraternity and on the football team for two years under head coach Myron Witham. The film was associated with another former Denverite, its producer, Lou Brock, whose father is said to have owned and opened the first motion picture theater in Denver in 1905.

Wilson's mother, Mrs. Lincoln Wilson, resided in Denver at 3841 Wolff Street. His father, who had died about a year earlier, was widely known in the wholesale drug business and had served a number of terms in the Colorado legislature.*

* Lincoln Wilson was owner of the Alcott Pharmacy at 3973 Tennyson Street in Denver. Johnson, *Denver's Old Theater Row* (A Gem Publication 1970), p. 5.

The 1938 Season

Once again, telegrams from theatrical and motion picture notables from all over the country poured in to Arnold B. Gurtler expressing wishes for an exceptional season of the Theatre. Among the well-wishers were Mary Pickford, Donald Woods, Bing Crosby, Gary Cooper, George Raft, Fredric March and Florence Eldridge.

A wide variety of plays were selected for the season.

Jacques Deval's "Tovarich"
Robert E. Sherwood's "Idiot's Delight"
John Murray and Allen Boretz's "Room Service"
Zoe Akin's "The Old Maid"
Matt Taylor and Sam Taylor's "Stop-Over"
Noel Coward's "Tonight at 8:30"
Katherine Dayton and George S. Kaufman's "First Lady"
Mark Reed's "Yes, My Darling Daughter"
Elsie Schauffler's "Parnell"
Frederick Lonsdale's "Once is Enough"

The leading lady for the season was Rose Hobart, and the leading man was Kent Smith. This season, the cast welcomed two members whose roots were in Colorado. Leona Powers was born in Salida, Colorado and attended school in Denver for four years before playing stock from coast to coast. As a child, she played with such stars as Maude Adams, Richard Mansfield, the three Barrymores and John Drew. She played in many New York productions and the audience welcomed her return to Denver.[9] Bradford Hatton had extensive experience in stock and had been with George Somnes in New York for the past three seasons before returning for this season as stage manager.*

The Orchard Cafe

The Orchard Cafe, one of the original buildings at the opening of Elitch Gardens, encouraged and regularly made reservations to seat theater parties for dinner prior to the theater performance.[10-1]

In announcing the opening play of the season, *Tovarich*, the *Denver Post* noted:

> Other Elitch Gardens attractions came in for their share of popularity during the Theatre opening. The Orchard Cafe, filled to capacity, was the scene of many theater parties and dancers anxious to test the creations of the new chef before moving on to *Tovarich*, and to the Trocadero, where Louis Panico and his Chicago College Inn band are offering compelling dance rhythms and entertainment.[10-2]

* In 1953, Bradford Hatton became the business manager for the Bonfils Memorial Theater, a position he held for some time.

Intermission Note

The program cautioned theatergoers to promptly return to their seats following intermission. It read as follows:

> The bell at the Coaster, at the Trocadero and in front of the Theatre will ring five minutes before the rise of the curtain.
>
> The second bell will ring three minutes later.
>
> The curtain will rise promptly two minutes after the second bell, and no one will be seated after the rise of the curtain on the second and following acts.[11]

A Season of Plays and Performers - Some Observations

Stop-Over is a fast-moving play of back-to-back comic scenes. Bartley Langthorne, the principal character in the play, decides to forsake the bright lights of his city dwelling in exchange for the peace and comfort of his country home. Unfortunately he chooses Halloween day for his day of solitude. The comic situations arise from a sign placed over the gate of his country home that reads "Tourists Accommodated," put there as a Halloween prank by mischievous boys. People traveling on the road take the sign seriously.

> (The result is that) before morning the Langthorne household had served as hostelry for a pair of elopers, a World War veteran, his wife and three children; had witnessed a shooting and the nervous breakdown of the housekeeper; the near reformation of a desperate criminal, the near resumption of romance between the war veteran's wife and the village doctor and the temptation for a priest to turn playwright.[10-3]

The Old Maid is set in New York in the 1830s and its theme embraces the drama of mother love. New York critics were divided as to the play's merit. Notwithstanding, the play was awarded the Pulitzer Prize for drama in 1935. In the following season, after the Pulitzer had bypassed *Winterset* and because of the dissatisfaction with the 1935 selection, the New York Drama Critics Circle was established with its own award.[5-5]

Members of the cast were challenged by the opportunity to play various roles throughout the season, as demanded by the plays. For example, *Room Service* had 14 roles to perform, *The Old Maid* had 16 roles, and *Idiot's Delight* had 27 roles. The drama critic of the *Denver Post* noted:

> The test of any stock company is the versatility of its members and their ability to get strictly into character each week instead of automatically portraying the same character week after week throughout the season. The Elitchers have withstood this test - and that's why Denver likes them.[10-4]

The 1939 Season

The lead roles were played by Jane Wyatt and Donald Woods. The plays for the season included Thorton Wilder's *Our Town*, Mazo de la Roche's *Whiteoaks*, Jeffrey Dell's *Payment Deferred* and Benn W. Levy's *Springtime for Henry*.

Jane Wyatt

Jane Wyatt had considerable stage and film experience when she was engaged to appear at Elitch. She was the feminine star of the spectacular film *Lost Horizon* and also appeared in the stage version of the film. She appeared in the films *One More River* and *Great Expectations* at Universal Studios and in *We're Only Human* at R.K.O. She was on the New York stage in *The Bishop Misbehaves*. Notwithstanding these and other credits, she considered her engagement at Elitch a highlight in her career and she met it with great anxiety, expressing herself accordingly:

> I could almost feel the presence of the famous stage people who have trod the boards (of that marvelous playhouse) ... and I know I'm going to love it!
>
> I'm the luckiest girl in the world to draw this assignment, and if the people of Denver like me as much as I know I'm going to like them - well, it's going to be a great season![12-1]

A Successful Season

Denver audiences were treated to a variety of plays that made for a successful season. The plays ranged from comedy to romance to melodrama to a murder thriller. And then there was Thorton Wilder's Pulitzer Prize winner, *Our Town*, which the drama critic said is not a comedy, nor a drama, and "is not strictly a play."

> For as the audience enters the theater it is confronted by an empty stage, with the curtain up. Actor Donald Woods enters the stage, tells briefly what the proceedings are about, and as he gives his talk, various members of the cast pantomime the atmosphere of the setting without benefit of the usual stage props. Then, as the explanations proceed, the players portray the action depicting the quiet, unobtrusive life in the small town of Grover's Corners, N.H., from 1901 to 1915, with its marriages and births and deaths and the other small events which distinguish the little community from the hustle and bustle of city life.[12-2]

Director George Somnes successfully enjoyed the unique task of transforming the historic Gardens playhouse into the atmosphere of Grover's Corners.[12-3]

Payment Deferred is the thriller that introduced Charles Laughton to the American stage in 1931. At Elitch, his role as the bank clerk was flawlessly played by Donald Woods.

(The play deals) with an English bank clerk who is so beset by his debts that he executes the "perfect murder" in order to replenish his depleted funds.

Many suspenseful moments are created for the audience which constantly expects further violence by the harassed bank clerk seeking to hide his crime.

In an ironical twist of the plot which is unsuspected by the audience until the story takes that sudden turn, the banker is convicted of a crime he did not commit, while his original misdeed remains undiscovered.* [12-4]

Appeal for the Actors' Fund of America

The Elitch Theatre program published an appeal by Daniel Frohman, President of the Actors' Fund of America, as follows:

The Actors' Fund of America is a theatrical charity organized in 1882 by the great men in the theatrical profession for the purpose of taking care of the impoverished aged and infirm members of the theatrical profession.

The profession of Acting is the most precarious of all professions. An actor's income entirely depends upon the degree of success attained by the play in which his services are employed and may be terminated in two weeks or even less.

The actor's fame is temporary and fleeting, no matter how great. The painter, the sculptor, the writer, leave evidence of their artistic accomplishments behind them; but the actor "struts and frets his hour upon the stage, and then is heard no more."

So let's be kind and helpful to him while he lives.[13]

The 1940 Season

Leather Upholstered Seats

Theatergoers were treated this season to a new feature of the Theatre - comfortable leather upholstered seats.[14]

4,320th Performance

The opening play of the season, S. N. Behrman's *No Time for Comedy*, was the 4,320th performance in the Elitch Theatre.[15-1]

* The 1946 film titled *The Postman Always Rings Twice*, with John Garfield and Lana Turner, and based on James M. Cain's celebrated novel, has a similar theme, namely, justice "achieved" by the conviction of a crime that was not committed.

The Season

In addition to *No Time for Comedy*, the plays presented included Elizabeth Ginty's *Missouri Legend,* Sutton Vane's *Outward Bound,* Paul Osborn's *Morning's at Seven* and *The Vinegar Tree.*

The Theatre company had the following among its array of players: Sylvia Field, Michael Whalen, David Wayne, Helen Trenholme, Francis Compton, Donald Cook, Ruth Lee, Millard Mitchell, Helen Bonfils, Viola Roache, Brandon Peters and Robert Stewart. George Somnes was again director, and Victor Paganuzzi was the scenic designer.

Sylvia Field and Michael Whalen were the leading players. Prior to appearing at Elitch, Field had been in the movies and on radio and appeared in most of the "straw-hat" houses of the East. She had been in plays with two members of the cast - Millard Mitchell and Francis Compton. The *Denver Post* described her as the "youthful veteran of theater."[15-2] In *Missouri Legend,* Donald Cook replaced Michael Whalen in the lead,* and Helen Trenholme replaced Sylvia Field as leading lady in *A Slight Case of Murder.*

In the opening play of the season *No Time for Comedy,* after praising the leads for their performances, the reviewer stated:

> The show-stopping lines are those of Helen Bonfils, who, playing one of her favorite characters - a darky maid - sent the initial audience into paroxysms of laughter with almost every line she uttered.
>
> (Francis) Compton, who likewise knows his comedy, added plenty of it to the play with just the proper gestures - or lack of gestures - at the proper time.
>
> Ruth Lee was a charming "other woman," Brandon Peters a properly polished "other man" to bring the story to a swift climax ...[15-3]

Playwright Paul Osborn

Paul Osborn (1901-1988) was born in Evansville, Indiana, the son of a minister, and was educated at the University of Michigan and at Yale. He taught at both schools before seeing his first plays produced. He scored his first Broadway success when his efforts turned to comedy with *The Vinegar Tree* (1930). His domestic comedy *Morning's at Seven* (1939) won a place in Burns Mantle's list of the ten best Broadway productions of the 1939-40 period, and became Osborn's most produced play.[16] Both of these plays were selected for presentation during the Elitch season. The *Denver Post* drama critic wrote:

> In some ways *Morning's at Seven* and *The Vinegar Tree* have much in

* The reason for Mr. Whalen's departure was vague, "but was understood to have resulted from unforeseen commitments." *Rocky Mountain News,* Jul 2, 1940, p. 5.

> common. Both have one single objective - to make people laugh. And *The Vinegar Tree,* like *Morning's at Seven,* shows the same quaint habit of the author to give his plays names which have no bearing whatever upon the subject matter.[15-4]

Elitch theatergoers were delighted with the nonsensical satire of *Morning's at Seven,* "the most ideal theatrical fare imaginable at a time when the world in general needs the tonic of good, hearty laughter."[15-5]

> It is sufficient to say that (the play) deals with a group of oldsters, most of them with one-track minds, who are viewing their too-brief future and the fleeting present with full and frank discussion of themselves and their associates. It is silly, nonsensical, asinine - and it is one long laugh from beginning to end as the playwright laughs at and with the frailties of human nature.[15-5]

The Vinegar Tree, the final play of the season, was characterized by "a verbal barrage, bountifully acrimonious between two women ... as they take conversational potshots at each other over (the man who is) the object of their mutual affection," and "while their bickerings are distasteful to him, they are a joy to audiences."[15-4]

Osborn's later works were successful adaptations of novels, such as *A Bell for Adano* (1944), *Point of No Return* (1951) and *The World of Suzie Wong* (1958).

Missouri Legend

Missouri Legend is "an idealistic biographical comedy of the later days of Jesse James."

> (It is replete) with dry humor, the keynote of which comes in the first act with Jesse James, just home from church services, discussing with his men plans for their next train robbery and talking calmly of murder and morals in the same breath ...[15-6]

Jesse James was played by Donald Cook, who learned his lines for the play as he traveled from New York to Denver. Cook arrived in Denver on Saturday and had time for just two rehearsals with the company before appearing in the Sunday opening performance. Notwithstanding, the drama critic noted that Cook "has a good part and carries it off well." The critic also praised Sylvia Field, who "turns in a second-to-none performance as the Ozark hill woman who is saved from the foreclosure of her little farm by the soft-hearted desperado."[15-6]

Federal Tax on Theater Tickets/Taxes on Theaters [15-1]

Starting on July 1, 1940, a federal tax of 10% was assessed on all theater and other entertainment tickets costing 21 cents or more. This tax formerly did not apply to low-priced tickets but began with those costing 40 cents or more. Increasing the scope of the tax to catch the 21-cent or more ticket was part of the tax program to pay for the New Deal's armament projects.* [15-7] The drama editor of the *Denver Post* put the tax increase into greater perspective, stating that "the public will pay more for the privilege of going to the movies (and theater) to forget its troubles - such as the war for which the New Deal is preparing."

While Congress was increasing the tax on ticket prices, theater owners were facing additional operating costs and higher income taxes.

> It is more expensive to operate theaters today than it was during the era of national sanity before it became popular to toss public money about in bales like hay. Not the least of these increased operating costs is represented by higher taxes, the theater men assert, and the end is not in sight. For theaters, as well as theatergoers, are to have their income taxes raised.

All of this resulted in a strongly worded caveat to theatergoers as follows:

> So, Mr. and Mrs. Theatergoer, when you start paying taxes on tickets which hitherto have been exempt; when your theater ticket begins to cost more money than it does now, don't blame the theater or the theater owner. Put the blame where it belongs - on the shoulders of the spendthrift zealots who have been preaching the gospel of "spend your way into prosperity" since 1933, and who did not recognize until 1940 that there was any need for national defense.

Denver Public Library Western History Collection - No. Rh-1241

The Marriage of Helen Bonfils and George Somnes (1936)

* The tax also applied to dances, sporting events and other forms of entertainment to which an admission fee was charged. *Denver Post*, Jun 29, 1940, p. 9

Chapter Twenty-Two

(1941 - 1945)

The Golden Jubilee
The Shadow of War
The War Years
John Chapman and Burns Mantle - The Changing of the Guard
The Fire at Elitch Gardens
Hope for a Peaceful Future

The 1941 Season

The Golden Jubilee

The drama editor of the *Rocky Mountain News* detailed the events of the 50th anniversary season at Elitch Gardens in an article bearing the headline, "Capacity Crowd Marks Elitch's Jubilee Opening."[1]

> The Golden Jubilee got under way a half hour before the scheduled radio broadcast from the stage, with Mrs. A. B. Gurtler breaking through a paper barricade across the lobby of the theater for benefit of camera.

A crowd of well-wishers had already assembled and the Theatre was filled to capacity with an audience ready to celebrate the occasion. Bide Dudley, New York drama critic and formerly a Denver newspaper reporter, officiated as master of ceremonies during the radio broadcast carrying the celebration throughout the country. In attendance were Governor Ralph L. Carr, Mayor Benjamin Stapleton, other state and local officials and representatives of society, business, the professions, arts and sciences and the military service. Emcee Dudley introduced Governor Carr, who told of his first thrill at Elitch's - riding a Shetland pony. Mayor Stapleton praised the Theatre and added that he'd been coming to see stage plays for some thirty years. Cornelia Otis Skinner, the great actress, came from Evergreen, Colorado to add her loveliness to the celebration and brushed away a tear when she recalled that her father, Otis Skinner, appeared at Elitch Theatre 30 years prior.* Producer-Director George Somnes proposed a toast to Mary Elitch, founder of the Theatre, and to John Mulvihill, who carried on its tradition. Arnold Gurtler was the final speaker before the Theatre darkened for the first performance of the 50th season - Samson Raphaelson's comedy, *Skylark*. The history and traditions of the oldest stock company in America were shared. Patrons of the Theatre were given an Elitch Gardens Golden Anniversary Souvenir Program (1891-1941) commemorating

* Although Cornelia Otis Skinner choked a bit and brushed away a tear in recalling her father's appearance at Elitch Theatre, the fact is that her father never appeared at Elitch. He had appeared many times, however, at the Broadway and Denham Theaters in Denver. Levy at p. 363.

the event.[2] Among its contents was a letter from Mayor Benjamin F. Stapleton to A. B. Gurtler with the following remarks:

> Elitch Gardens Theatre is a part of Denver and a very fine and important part. The Theatre has provided Denver with the highest class of entertainment and many of America's most famous artists of today started their careers at Elitch Gardens.
>
> Our citizens look forward each season to the opening of Elitch Gardens Theatre with unusual interest and our people are a unit in declaring "There Must Always Be An Elitch Gardens Theatre."

And with the preliminaries out of the way, the curtain rose on the sophisticated comedy, *Skylark*. Thus ended the Elitch Gardens Theatre celebration of the fiftieth anniversary opening night, an evening that would have stirred the hearts of Mary and John Elitch and John Mulvihill.

The Fashion Parade

In addition to the dignitaries that appeared for the golden anniversary festivities, the traditional Monday night theater audience that for many years was the important social gathering of every week resumed for the opening summer season and for the golden jubilee celebration. For example, Mrs. Lawrence C. Phipps attended with her husband, Senator Phipps, and wore a soft green wool costume and a pink flower hat. Miss Eleanore Weckbaugh wore a flame-colored, snug fitting crepe gown.

The Season

The season ran for eleven weeks, one week longer than the usual Elitch season. Donald Woods was the leading man and Ruth Matteson the leading woman. The Golden Jubilee Theatre Program stated of Donald Woods:

> It's natural that Mr. Woods should have a sincere affection for the old stage of the famous Theatre, as it was here, in 1933, while playing in *The Pursuit of Happiness* that he was discovered by a motion picture scout and given a Hollywood contract. He skyrocketed to fame immediately and is known everywhere today as one of the screen's most popular leading men.

Ruth Matteson played the leading feminine roles of the season that had been performed by well-known actresses in the Broadway productions of *Skylark* (Gertrude Lawrence), *The Philadelphia Story* (Katherine Hepburn), *The Little Foxes* (Tallulah Bankhead) and *Ladies in Retirement* (Flora Robson). The newspaper reviews favorably embraced each of her performances. For example, she was described as "exuberant, dynamic, a bit of a beauty and an excellent actress," [3] "whose enthusiasm makes one believe everything she says and does."[4]

After being honored to be selected as the leading lady for the golden jubilee season, Ruth Matteson would again return to Elitch as the lead in 1942, 1948, and 1949. Among her qualities for the role of a successful leading woman in summer stock were the following:

> She was a "fast study," with the ability to learn and retain a leading role in a minimum of time; she also possessed patience, a rare "spirit of cooperation," and a dependability which made her fellow-workers uncommonly secure. According to director George Somnes, Miss Matteson, even in rehearsals, never "walked through a role," a phrase describing a listless, routine interpretation. During the first three days of rehearsal, she spent as much time as possible perfecting the mechanics of memorization, and during the final three days of rehearsal, the actress worked for the refining qualities of timing, coordination, and "sharpening the listening aspects." It was the latter quality, according to Somnes, which made her equally appealing to audiences and to fellow actors.[5]

It is difficult to imagine a better selection of plays to honor the golden jubilee season. Audiences would long remember *Golden Boy* (1937), the story of an American-born Italian boy who is torn between two life interests - becoming a violinist or fighting his way out of the slums as a prizefighter. The play was made into a film of the same name in 1939 starring William Holden in his breakthrough role and also served as the basis for a 1964 musical. Likewise, *The Philadelphia Story* (1939) would long remain a favorite. It played on Broadway for 417 performances with Katherine Hepburn in the principal role of Tracy Lord. Playwright Philip Barry wrote the comedy with Katherine Hepburn in mind. It was made into a successful film in 1940, starring Hepburn, James Stewart, and Cary Grant. It was successfully revived on Broadway in 1980.

These and other plays, such as *The Man Who Came to Dinner* by George S. Kaufman and Moss Hart, *The Little Foxes* by Lillian Hellman, *The Show Off* by George Kelly and *Private Lives* by Noel Coward, contributed to making this golden jubilee season one to be remembered.

The Shadow of War

During the 1941 season, America was living under the shadow of war, with Germany engaged in a fierce battle in Russia and Pearl Harbor only a few months away. Americans were subject to the draft and engaged in other ways to aid the national defense drive.

In Denver, Bob Marinaro, a Denverite who graduated from North High School and who had been an usher at Elitch, was engaged as an extra during the season in bit parts at Elitch. He got caught in the draft and by early September was to be in khaki, which cut him from Preston Sturges' plan to give him a "meaty role" in his comedy, *Unfaithfully Yours,* due to open in Hollywood early in November.[6-1] The Victory Theater in Denver gave away "V" for Victory buttons to each of its patrons, to make the public "V for Victory" conscious.[7] And in Hollywood, H. B. Clifford, a 40-year-old Hollywood restaurant owner, brought in 335 pieces of aluminum and won first prize in the "Pots and Pans Derby" sponsored by Paramount Pictures to aid in the national defense drive. The first prize was a 45-second kiss with Hollywood film star, Paulette Goddard.[6-2]

The 1942 Season

War was not limited to the battle between armed forces in the field. Those at home were expected to do their part to support the war. The activities of those at the "home front" were extensive. Families were encouraged to plant "victory gardens" to grow food for their families so that the major agricultural output of the nation could be used to feed soldiers fighting abroad. Citizens became volunteers for organizations like the Red Cross or took jobs in defense industries.

Actors, actresses and theatrical and film organizations did their part as well. In Hollywood and elsewhere, actors and actresses made promotional movies, or public appearances, urging Americans to buy U.S. War Bonds to help the government finance the war. The American Theatre Wing opened the New York Stage Door Canteen on March 2, 1942 in the 44th Street Theatre for the benefit of soldiers on leave. Food, drink, and entertainment were provided, and theatrical and film notables volunteered their time and talent, which included cleaning off tables, washing pots and pans, and mixing and dancing with the soldiers. Katherine Cornell, Marlene Dietrich, Selena Royle, Alfred Lunt and lyricist Dorothy Fields, were among many from the theater and film world that appeared at the Canteen. Stage Door Canteens were opened in other cities in the United States, such as in Philadelphia, Hollywood and San Francisco, as well as in Paris and London.

In 1942, a musical revue entitled *This is the Army* was staged with an all-soldier cast and songs by Irving Berlin with the proceeds donated to service charities. Among the songs were *I Left My Heart at The Stage Door Canteen, Oh, How I Hate to Get Up in the Morning, The Army Made a Man Out of Me* and *This is the Army, Mr. Jones.*

Alan Ladd and the Cuffless Pants

The War Production Board controlled the output of industry. Civilian consumption of clothing had to be curtailed to assure that supplies of cotton and wool would be sufficient for military needs. The Board mandated changes in style to conserve raw material. A "Victory Suit" was promoted with cuffless trousers and narrower lapels. The reductions in the amount of cloth to be used resulted in shorter, pleatless skirts and two-piece bathing suits for women.

An article in the *Denver Post* bore the following headline: "Alan Ladd First to

Wear Cuffless Pants in Movies." The article stated:

> A careful checkup reveals that other masculine stars still are wearing cuffs on their pants. Maybe they all had a lot of preregulation suits to use up.
>
> In any case, Ladd leads the Hollywood field in the new order of male apparel. He plays a dressy gangster in the first part of his current film, "Lucky Jordan." Later he dons a uniform after being drafted into the army. In the early scenes, though, Ladd is impeccably tailored. And his trousers have neither pleats nor cuffs.[8-1]

The Season

With the opening of the Elitch season, the *Denver Post* noted that, "as a smile of high courage and a toast to victory, Elitch's opens its fifty-first theater season in war as in peace to give Denver playgoers welcome relaxation and a glorious summer of grand entertainment."[8-2] The plays selected for the season included Lillian Hellman's *Watch on the Rhine*, a drama centered about the Germany of World War II. Most of the other plays were devoted to comedy, offering theater patrons some moments of laughter in a troubled world.

On Sunday, August 30, 1942, all officers and men in the uniform of the armed forces in or near Denver were guests of Elitch management at a free noon-to-curfew party at the Gardens. The invitation included soldiers, sailors, marines and members of the coast guard.

A letter to "Elitch Patrons" from A.B. Gurtler, President of Elitch Gardens Company, appeared in the final Elitch Theatre program of the season, and contained the following:

> Elitch's is one shining 1942 example of the truth of that well-worn Shakespearean quip, "The Play's the Thing." Yes, the play and some of the enduring pleasures of civilized man have managed to carry on, Herr Schickelgruber notwithstanding. We hope that you found pleasure, relaxation, and some rare moments of keen enjoyment in the famed old Elitch Playhouse this summer. May another year see the lifting of the clouds of war, and full attainment of every principle for which we, as a nation, are striving.

The 1943 Season

Edith Atwater, one of Broadway's most famous leading ladies, was chosen to be the leading lady for the Elitch season. Her many Broadway successes included *Springtime for Henry* with Henry Hull, *Brittle Heaven* with Dorothy Gish, *The Country Wife* with Ruth Gordon and *Susan and God* with Gertrude Lawrence. Lawrence Fletcher, who won wide favor with Denver audiences at Elitch during the past two seasons, returned as the season's leading man.

George Somnes, the director, occasionally played leading roles in plays he directed, such as *Design For Living* this season.

Against a backdrop of the headlines of war, the Elitch management engaged and satisfied Denver audiences with a good mixture of plays sandwiched between the wisely chosen opening and closing plays, *Without Love* and *The Command to Love*. The play *Theater* caused some confusion at the box office. Josh Billings at the Elitch box office reported that calls were coming in wanting to know what's next at the Elitch playhouse. He said "Theater" and they invariably popped back with, "Yes, that's right. What's next in the theater?"[9-1]

The Command to Love - Then and Now

The comedy *The Command to Love* was wisely chosen to end the season. The comedy was first presented to Denver audiences at Elitch during the 1928 season. John Mulvihill was induced to present the play in 1928 by director Melville Burke and drama editor, A. DeBernardi, Jr., notwithstanding Mulvihill's vigorous and vehement objections.

> "All right, (conceded Mulvihill grudgingly) if you birds say so, I'll let it go on. But the customers won't like it! Why, this thing's so full of candid situations and spicy lines that I can already see people walking out of the Theatre right in the middle of some of this risqué dialog! I've got to admit it's funny, and clever, too, but we've never done a play like this. Our clientele simply won't stand for it!"[9-2]

The play was presented with Fredric March and Isobel Elsom as the torrid leads. Briefly, the play is about Gaston, a philandering military attaché who is ordered by his superior officer to make love to Manuela, the wife of the Spanish war minister, in the hope, through her influence as a result of being compromised, of effecting a desired treaty which her husband controls. Gaston willingly agrees to this command to love "in the line of duty," but the situation is complicated because he is already engaged in a love affair with the wife of his superior, the French ambassador.[9-3]

> (The result in 1928 was that Mulvihill) was right. But only partly right. His patrons never before had seen such a show in his Theatre. Some of them walked right out on it. But every time one walked out, there were a half a dozen others waiting to battle for his vacated seat. And those who remained laughed until they were sore from head to foot, beat blisters upon their hands applauding the play and the players, and went out into the highways and byways telling everyone about the side-splitting comedy they had seen. When the week ended, Mulvihill found that *The Command to Love* had shattered every existing attendance record at the Elitch Gardens Theatre![9-2]

For the 1943 season, Director George Somnes added new lines and eliminated some old ones, to bring the comedy up to the minute and make it thoroughly modern without losing so much as a whiff of the spicy gaiety of the original. And once again, the results were favorable.

John Chapman and Burns Mantle - The Changing of the Guard

John Chapman and Burns Mantle were two of the foremost and most well-known drama critics. Both had connections with Denver.

Burns Mantle (1873-1948) was a close friend of Mary Elitch. He had been the best man at the wedding of Mary and Thomas Long. Although he was born in Watertown, New York, he became a drama critic in 1898, serving on Denver and Chicago newspapers before going to New York as critic for the *Evening Mail*. In 1922, he joined the staff of the *Daily News*, where he remained until 1944. Among his many writings, "he is best remembered as the originator and editor of the *Best Plays* series, an annual anthology of plays and statistics, which he continued to edit from 1920 until shortly before his death. His writings were warm and reasonable without any of the ostentation of some his fellow critics."[10-1]

John Chapman (1900-1972) was born in Denver, the son of journalists. He studied at the University of Colorado and at Columbia University. Chapman began his newspaper career in 1917 on the *Denver Times* and joined the *New York Daily News* in 1920, becoming its drama editor in 1929. He also served as Burns Mantle's assistant on the *Best Plays* series.

On August 28, 1943, toward the close of the Elitch season, it became known to the theater world that Burns Mantle was retiring from his post as drama critic at the *Daily News* and that John Chapman was chosen to succeed him.

The letter from Burns Mantle to John Chapman congratulating him as his successor was published in the *Denver Post*, and contained the following:

> Dear John: ... I have decided to quit being a professional reviewer of plays. I shall retire to those calmer precincts where there are no deadlines, and where a man can write what he wants to write when he wants to write it. The glory of dying in harness appealed strongly to me until the harness began to chafe.
>
> You are to succeed me ... That pleases me greatly. It means, in a way, a continuation of our work together which started when you were practically a child in plus fours and I was a gay young man about the Empire Theatre and environs.
>
> Of course, you understand, I am not leaving the theater - just the hard work of the theater. I shall go on editing that sturdy annual "Ten Best Plays," of which, it appalls me to observe, there are now twenty-four volumes in print...

> Good luck to you, young fellow, my lad. Broadway is your oyster. Open it. Season it with a dash of salt and a lot of pep - but go easy with the Tabasco. Yours, Burns.[9-4]

Thus, John Chapman became drama critic for the *New York Daily News* in 1943, a post he held until his retirement. A year before Mantle's death in 1948, John Chapman began to edit the *Best Plays* series, continuing to do so from 1947 until 1952.

More Wartime Restrictions - Clothing

To conserve materials, the War Production Board ordered all knitted outer garments standardized during the duration of the war.

> (The order) bans double-breasted sweaters, eliminates embroidery, spangles, appliqués and "exaggerated" sleeves, provides for "plain, unadorned" knitted gloves and mittens, forbids side stripes and belt loops on swimming trunks and limits the length of knit mufflers to fifty-two inches.
>
> Women's sweaters are restricted to seven basic models with six color arrangements for a season.[9-5]

The 1944 Season

Three of the eleven plays selected for the season were related to wartime themes. They were *Tomorrow the World* by James Gow and Arnaud d'Usseau, *The Doughgirls* by Joseph Fields and *Janie* by Josephine Bentham and Herschel Williams.

Raymond Burr was the leading man. He had extensive theatrical experience before making his debut at Elitch. He made his New York debut in the musical *Crazy With the Heat* in 1941. He appeared with Marlene Dietrich, Martha Raye and other leading stars in over 300 camp shows for the men in the armed forces. He is best remembered for his television role as Perry Mason that would come later in his career.

Martha Sleeper was the leading lady and made her debut at Elitch in the 1944 season in Frederick Lonsdale's *Another Love Story*. She was encouraged to begin an acting career by Cecil B. De Mille. At the age of 13 Martha was consumed with the desire to become a film actress. Her parents were acquainted with Cecil B. De Mille and sent her to him in hopes that he would dissuade her from her childish ambition. But De Mille was impressed with the youngster's enthusiasm and believed she possessed talent.

De Mille encouraged her to pursue work in Mack Sennett or Hal Roach comedies, "which he considered the best school for beginners to learn timing and the ground work for a higher dramatic career." Aware of the pie-throwing antics of the Sennett studio, Martha chose to settle for a part with the Hal Roach comedy shorts. Not many years passed before she played lead roles opposite Noel Coward, Otto Kruger, Richard Dix and other famous names in Hollywood and on Broadway.

After retiring from the screen in 1937 for a successful career on the Broadway stage, Martha Sleeper returned to film only once to play a supporting role in *The Bells of St. Mary* in 1945. She gave up acting altogether in 1946 to start a thriving costume design business.

The "Wartime" Plays

Tomorrow the World was described as "one of the war's more literate propaganda pieces." It is the story of a 12-year old boy whose American mother died in his infancy and whose liberal German father was killed in a concentration camp. The young boy, raised in Germany and indoctrinated into the Nazi philosophy, is brought to the United States by his uncle, a university professor. The young boy "spews hatred, tries naively to spy for the Germans, and in a particularly vicious moment slashes an old family portrait." In the end, an American playmate leads the troubled youngster into the paths of right thinking and righteous understanding.[11]

The play appeared on Broadway in 1943 and ran for 500 performances. Skippy Homeier played the young Nazi, and in 1944, at the age of 14, replicated the role for the film of the same name.

The play *The Doughgirls* was hailed as a "mad salute to wartime Washington."[10-2]

> Based on the strange alliances brought about by crowded living conditions in Washington, D.C., in wartime, *The Doughgirls* takes sly digs at the curtailment of hotel service, twenty-minute generals, the ups and downs of federal bureaucrats, and civilian ignorance of military affairs as it tells its tale of three feminine war workers, their boyfriends and near-husbands, and a Russian "lady sniper" (who had killed 397 Nazis and deserted the Soviet embassy) who moves in on them.[12]

Janie is a 1942 comedy by Josephine Bentham and Herschel Williams. Janie Colburn is a 17-year-old high school girl who forgets her high school boyfriend, Scooper Nolan, once she meets Pvt. Dick Lawrence, the son of her mother's old friend.

> And when her parents and their friends go out for the night, Janie has Dick invite all his army buddies to a hastily got-up party at the Colburn house. The older Colburns return to find the house overrun. Dick must go off to war, so Janie realizes she will have to make up with Scooper.[10-3]

The play exemplified "the recourse playwrights had to youngsters and old folks as principals when so many draft-age men and women had joined the war effort."[10-4]

The Fire at Elitch Gardens [13]

On July 16, 1944, Elitch Gardens experienced the second worst fire in the history of Denver. The earlier fire occurred in 1895 when the Gunrey Hotel blaze on Lawrence Street resulted in a full company of firemen being trapped in the flaming hotel after an explosion had rocked the building. Only one fireman escaped. Several hotel guests also perished.

The fire at Elitch occurred at the Old Mill, which contained a series of buildings housing the winding, scenic boat canal. The fire broke out in the canal tunnel, about three-quarters of the way through from the entrance. It was not clear what caused the fire, but officials of the resort suspected that a carelessly-thrown cigaret may have ignited some of the decorations in the tunnel. Within seconds, the tunnel began to fill with smoke as the flames leaped higher.

Six persons died in the fire, two of whom were attendants at the concession stands "who braved the blinding smoke and flames in a fruitless effort to save those trapped" in the tunnel. Top-ranking officials of the fire department who investigated the happening of the fire were unable to determine its cause. The *Rocky Mountain News* reported that -

> No clues as to the origin of the blaze were found, Chief Boyne (in charge of fire prevention) pointed out, among the debris since the damage virtually was total. Chief Boyne advanced the theory the blaze may have started either from a carelessly-thrown cigaret or from defective wiring. In either event, it would be almost impossible to develop evidence as to which was the cause.
>
> Chief Boyne said the premises were inspected by the department at intervals for elimination of fire hazards.

The 1945 Season

The War's End

On May 7, 1945, General Alfred Jodl of Germany signed an unconditional surrender at Allied Headquarters in Rheims, France, ending the war in Europe. And on September 2, 1945, the Japanese foreign minister signed the surrender documents on the deck of the battleship *Missouri*, ending the war in the Pacific.[14]

The stresses of war were gradually lifted in many ways, and families looked forward to being reunited and even to once again enjoy a relaxing Sunday stroll in the world famous Elitch Gardens and a visit to the summer playhouse.

The Season

John Archer was the leading man. He had appeared on Broadway in the deeply-moving drama *One-Man Show*. He replicated the role in the Elitch presentation in the final play of the season. Katherine Anderson, Elitch's leading lady, left the beginning of a successful writing career at MGM studios to pursue a career as an actress. She had appeared on Broadway and also performed on radio on the Ellery Queen show and a number of times on the Lux Radio Theatre and the Kate Smith Show.

The opening play of the season was the ever popular *Blithe Spirit* by Noel Coward, a play that audiences do not seem tired of seeing over and over again. The play is a difficult one to present. It is the story of an author who holds a séance to obtain material for a book and finds that he has unwittingly aroused the spirit of his first wife, Elvira.

Among the other plays selected for the season, some touched upon themes that were rooted in the war years, such as Lillian Phoebe and Henry Ephron's *Three's a Family,* Ruth Gordon's *Over 21* and Lillian Hellman's *The Searching Wind.* For example, *Three's a Family* is a comedy built around the troubles of wartime on the home front - families doubling up in living accommodations, aunts sleeping on sofas, hard-to-get and harder-to-keep maids, and babies all over the place. In wartime, life's happenings are often shared.

Over 21

Over 21 is a three-act comedy written in 1944 that concerns the humorous side of the lives of members of the army air force who enter officers' candidate school. Most theatergoers know Ruth Gordon as a formidable actress and not as a playwright. *Over 21* is the first of two plays she wrote. It was said of Gordon's effort in writing *Over 21* that she "displayed a competency and versatility rare among leading actresses."[10-5]

Hope For a Peaceful Future

After enjoying a season of plays, theatergoers had hope for a peaceful future after the surrender of Germany and the end of the war with Japan. During the Elitch season, the government commenced the process of relieving the nation of its wartime restrictions.

In July, butter became more available to consumers, and a wider range of dresses, suits, coats and hats were announced to be available for the fall selection. In August, the Office of Price Administration (OPA) announced the immediate termination of the rationing of gasoline, fuel oil and oil stoves, as well as all blue-point foods, which consisted of canned fruits and vegetables and such products as catsup and chili sauce. The wants and needs of a nation at peace were gradually being restored and met.

Ruth Matteson - Leading Lady (1941)

Donald Woods - Leading Man (1941)

Chapter Twenty-Three

(1946 - 1950)

Patricia Neal and Peter Cookson - Behind the Scenes
New Scripts - A Departure From Tradition
Whitfield Connor
Matinee Performances
American Premiere - A New Policy
Cecil B. De Mille - Memories of Denver
A Professional Actor
Poets Have Fewer Ulcers - Advice to Actors

The 1946 Season

This season marked the beginning of George Somnes' eleventh year at the directorial helm of the famous Elitch Theatre. The opening play of the season, *The Mermaids Singing*, was his 101st play as director. Regarding this, Somnes commented, "The first hundred plays are the hardest."[1-1]

To many directors and producers, the close of the New York season of plays means a relaxing summer on a Connecticut farm or other places of rest. But George Somnes loved his summers in the Rockies and thrived on the busy schedule and hard work at Elitch. For ten years, he had commuted between New York and Denver with his winters devoted to Broadway and his summers absorbed by Elitch.

Among the plays presented were *Angel Street, Dear Ruth* and *The Late George Apley*.

Angel Street

The tense drama of Patrick Hamilton's *Angel Street* is a familiar plot to most theater and film buffs. The spine-tingling career of the play began in London in 1939 under the title *Gaslight* and later ran for 1,295 performances on Broadway. It is the story of "a suave husband who under the guise of loving solicitude conveys to his wife that he fears she is becoming the victim of hereditary insanity."[1-2] The play was made into a Hollywood movie in 1944 and won Ingrid Bergman an Academy Award as the innocent young bride who, unfortunately, marries Charles Boyer who is trying to persuade her that she is going insane.

Dear Ruth

Norman Krasna's *Dear Ruth* is one of the most delightful wartime comedies. Elitch cast member Lenore Lonergan recreated the role of Miriam Wilkins for which she was cast in the 1944 Broadway production.[1-3] The plot of the comedy is as follows:

> Miriam Wilkins is almost sweet sixteen and determined to do her share for the war effort. She writes over sixty letters to a lonely American

soldier overseas, signing them all with the name of her elder sister, Ruth, and enclosing Ruth's picture. Home on leave, the soldier, Lt. William Seawright, appears at the Wilkins home without warning, on the very day that Ruth has accepted a proposal of marriage from Albert Krummer. Although Bill has only two days to spare, it is time enough for Ruth to fall in love with him and ditch Albert. Ruth's father, a judge, performs a hasty wedding ceremony, and the newlyweds rush off to a quick honeymoon. They are no sooner gone than the doorbell rings. It is a young sailor looking for Ruth.[2]

The Late George Apley

John Marquand, author of the Pulitzer Prize-winning novel, *The Late George Apley*, teamed up with George S. Kaufman to write the play of the same name based on the novel. The play is a satirical comedy on life in Boston, which echoes the verse of the poem attributed to various people:

And here's to good old Boston
The land of the bean and the cod
Where Lowells talk only to Cabots
And Cabots talk only to God.

George Apley is a Harvard-educated blue blood who considers Boston the center of all that is good in the world and where his son and daughter should remain and only associate with Bostonians. When his daughter falls in love with a Greenwich Village bohemian who is a Yale graduate, and his son falls in love with a Worcester girl, George Apley is faced with a reassessment of his values, which seem to be vanishing. The time frame of the play is circa 1912.

The 1947 Season

Arnold Gurtler chose Patricia Neal and Peter Cookson as the leads. Donald Woods was engaged to play the lead in the final play of the season, *The Two Mrs. Carrolls*, because of Peter Cookson's prior commitment to play a leading role in the play *Washington Square* in New York. Woods was a favorite with Elitch audiences, having been the leading man in 1933, 1934, 1939 and 1941.

Patricia Neal came to Elitch from playing a season on Broadway as Regina in Lillian Hellman's hit play, *Another Part of the Forest*. Her performance in that role earned her numerous awards. The New York drama critics selected her as one of the "most promising young actresses," and *Look Magazine* called her the year's "most promising newcomer." She was also awarded one of the Antoinette Perry Memorial Awards by the New York Theater Wing.[3-1] She was reported to have turned down a $50,000 movie contract to play at Elitch.[3-2]

Patricia Neal and Peter Cookson - Behind the Scenes [4]

Prior to her appearance at Elitch, Patricia Neal had fallen in love with the forty-five-year-old actor Victor Jory. She had met him at an actors' benefit where he had performed. They were attracted to one another. Notwithstanding his being married, they soon began dating.

At Elitch, her leading man was Peter Cookson. He had appeared on Broadway and was considered a promising young actor. He was thirty-four and strikingly handsome.

> Upon her first glimpse of Cookson, Patricia knew immediately that her affair with Victor Jory was over. Within days, Patricia contacted Jory in California and broke off their romance, her sights now firmly set on Cookson - who was married and had two children.
>
> Cookson's marriage was on the rocks. He and his wife, Maureen, had separated that spring, and that summer they were attempting a reconciliation, taking a house along with their two children in Denver. That effort was doomed once Cookson met his young and beautiful leading lady.

When Maureen learned about her husband's affair with Patricia Neal, she left him. In a biography of her life published in 2006, Patricia Neal recalled with shame the horrible scene when Maureen and the children left Denver, about midway through the summer season. She stated that "It was the only time in my life that I wrecked a marriage, but in those days I had no conscience."

Following the season at Elitch, Patricia and Cookson spent time together in New York and joined the Actors Studio, which trained actors in the style later to become known as "method" acting. Patricia later received a contract offer from Warner Brothers which she accepted and arranged to go to California to sign the contract and to prepare for work on her first film.

> Peter Cookson was committed to the run of a play and could not accompany her. Their affair had begun to wane already, as Cookson had grown melancholy over the separation from his children. Still, the farewell at Grand Central Station the second week of December 1947 was a tearful one.

In Hollywood, Patricia was invited to various functions around Hollywood and soon was surrounded by new friends.

> At the same time, Patricia and Peter Cookson's relationship was more than strained. It was only then when he notified her that he was divorcing his wife that Patricia knew she couldn't put off the inevitable. She wrote a letter telling him, "I am sorry, Peter, I really am, but it's not right and we're not right." He never responded.

In 1949, Cookson was appearing in *The Heiress.* When the play went on the road, Cookson met and married his leading lady, Beatrice Straight, thirty-four years of age and a member of the wealthy Whitney-Vanderbilt family. In 1953, Patricia married Roald Dahl, a gifted writer.

Joan of Lorraine [5]

Maxwell Anderson's *Joan of Lorraine* is a play within a play depicting the history of Joan of Arc.

> Anderson has made his play about the French girl-crusader a contemporary work by weaving the character of a saint into the part of the girl playing the heroine on the stage. The conflict between the leading lady and the director, arguing about the author's conception of Joan's attitude toward the world, brings the story up to 1947.

During the play's rehearsal of the play within the play, the backstage setting was made drab by the use of steam pipes and old furniture, with some cast members partially costumed and the others in street clothes. However, "realism is added when the director steps from the stage into the audience in order to work from a spectator's view."

Joel Marston - A Young Actor's Advice

Joel Marston was a member of the cast.* He had appeared at Elitch for several seasons and was popular with Denver audiences. He played a wide-variety of roles, always well. Joel's first Broadway leading role was in *Wallflower,* which played for seven months. He then appeared in *The Streets Are Guarded* and *Marriage is for Single People.* Betty Craig, drama editor of the *Denver Post* cornered him one afternoon at a table next to the Trocadero, reading a book, *Mr. Roberts.* Miss Craig asked him what advice he would give to stage-struck youngsters.

> "Well, the theater is a pretty tight profession right now," he said. "An actor going to New York to break into the live theater will find he's going to have a better chance if he has had experience in a reputable summer stock company first. And as long as you have asked for my advice, I might add, a term or two in drama at a good college or university certainly doesn't hurt."
>
> "One thing that can save the theater, to my way of thinking," the actor said, "is to take the theater away from New York and spread it around the country a little more. If there were a theater company like Elitch Gardens in every city, I think the theater wouldn't be as tight a profession as it is now. [6]

* During the season Joel Marston had a charming visitor - blond Marilyn Maxwell of movie fame, who was driving back to Hollywood where she was to make a picture with George Raft. *Denver Post,* Aug 10, 1947, p. 6B.

New Scripts - A Departure From Tradition

The traditional policy in selecting plays for a summer season at Elitch Theatre had been to produce only established plays fresh from Broadway successes. The Theatre management announced that a departure from that policy was to be considered, and the tryout of a new play would be produced at Elitch if and when a good script came up that warranted consideration.

The 1948 Season

The 57th season at Elitch's boasted an array of well-known playwrights and plays. A successful season was indicated as early as May by a record number of renewals from season ticket holders. In August, Arnold B. Gurtler, President of the Elitch Theatre Company, affirmed that 1948 was one of the most successful seasons in the Theatre's history. The leads in the cast were Ruth Matteson, returning for her third season at Elitch, and Donald Woods appearing in his fourth season.

The following comprised the season of plays:

Donald Ogden Stewart's "Rebound"
Forenc Molnar's "The Swan"
J.B. Priestley's "An Inspector Calls"
Elmer Rice's "Dream Girl"
Brandon Thomas' "Charley's Aunt"
Lillian Hellman's "Another Part of the Forest"
Arthur Miller's "All My Sons
George Bernard Shaw's "Pygmalion"
Maxwell Anderson's "Elizabeth the Queen"
Noel Coward's "Tonight at 8:30"

All My Sons

Arthur Miller's *All My Sons* (1947) ran for 328 performances on Broadway. The story of Joe Keller who sold defective airplane parts to the government during the Second World War, resulting in a number of young pilots losing their lives in plane crashes, is well-known to theatergoers. It was an appropriate and timely selection for presentation at Elitch Theatre.

Louis Kronenberger, who taught drama at Columbia and Harvard, felt that *All My Sons* allowed Arthur Miller "to stand easily first among our new generation of playwrights." Miller's fame as a playwright skyrocketed with the outstanding success of *Death of a Salesman* (1949), *The Crucible* (1953) and *A View From the Bridge* (1955). His 1987 autobiography *Timebends* is worth reading.[7]

Whitfield Connor

It was during this season that Whitfield Connor came to Denver as a member of the resident company, an association with the Theatre that was to last for the rest of his life. He became the leading man at Elitch in 1949 and remained so for each season through 1953, playing the lead roles in numerous plays. He later returned for two partial seasons, including three weeks in 1963 when he starred in *The Moon is Blue* and *Sabrina Fair*. The 1963 season was the last time he would appear at Elitch as an actor. In 1964 he became the executive director and general manager of the Theatre under producer Helen Bonfils. In 1972, after the death of Helen Bonfils, he became producer of plays for the Elitch Theatre Company with his wife, Haila Stoddard, and formed a corporation with him and Haila as stockholders. He continued to be active with the Theatre until it closed in 1987.

Whitfield Connor received his Bachelor of Arts degree from Wayne State University in 1940, and continued his education at the University of Michigan where he graduated with a Master of Arts degree. While a student he was a voice on the Lone Ranger radio show in 1940. During World War II, he served in the Pacific as a lieutenant in the Coast Guard.

In 1945, he made his Broadway debut in *Hamlet*. He had many more Broadway appearances. In 1948 he appeared in the role of Macduff in the production of *Macbeth* starring Michael Redgrave and Flora Robson. His film credits include *Tap Roots* in 1948 and *Butterfield 8* in 1960.

Elitch Plays Host to Fathers

The management of Elitch Gardens invited all fathers to be guests on Father's Day. All a father had to do to celebrate his day was to go to Elitch accompanied by a child or children, and he would be admitted free. There were "prizes, surprises, a smoke and a boutonniere for dad."[8-1]

The 1949 Season

The season opened with Whitfield Connor as the male lead. Ruth Matteson returned to play the female lead for the first part of the season, with Ruth Ford assuming the female lead the last four weeks of the season.

Matinee Performances

In 1893, when the Frank Norcross stock company appeared, there were four matinees (Tuesday, Thursday, Saturday and Sunday) each week, as well as seven nightly performances, making a total of eleven performances weekly. In 1896, this was changed to three matinees each week (Tuesday, Saturday and Sunday). In 1899, the Tuesday matinee was changed to Wednesday. In 1901, the matinee performances were reduced to Wednesday and Saturday. This continued until 1949, when the Actors' Equity Association limited theater companies to eight performances a week, and for this reason the Saturday matinee at Elitch was discontinued, leaving Elitch with seven nightly performances and a Wednesday matinee.[9] In 1960, however, Sunday night openings were abandoned by Elitch in favor of Monday night, and the Saturday matinee was eventually restored.

Ticket Prices

The Elitch Theatre was advertised as the "year's greatest entertainment at popular prices." Sunday nights and Wednesday matinees ranged from 60*c* to $1.30. Nightly, Monday through Saturday, cost 80*c* to $2. Tax was included. As formerly, there was a 10% discount for season reservations paid in advance.[10-1]

Some Plays at Elitch - Some Comments

Herman Wouk's *The Traitor* was a topical play containing a long dissertation on the pros and cons of the Red Menace. On opening night, a mistake in timing occurred backstage resulting in the spy being killed twice. Red flares and three gunshots sounded outside a window during what was supposed to be the quietest part of a scene. The same red flares and triple gunshots had to be repeated a few minutes later to kill off the spy.[10-2]

The Winslow Boy by Terence Rattigan (1911-1977) is a classic play that was based on the Archer-Shee case that shocked England in the days before World War I. The play was made into film, the earlier one in 1950 starring Robert Donat and Margaret Leighton, and the more recent 1999 film adapted from the play by screenwriter David Mamet, and starring Nigel Hawthorne, Rebecca Pidgeon (Mamet's wife) and Jeremy Northam.

> (The play) is the story of Ronnie Winslow, 14-year-old student in the Royal Naval Academy at Osborne, accused of stealing a five-shilling note (about $1.25) from a classmate's locker.
>
> Believing fully in his son's sworn innocence, young Winslow's father embarks on seemingly endless litigation to clear his son's name. The fact that his own health is broken, his daughter's romance shattered, and the entire family impoverished in the course of it does not deter him in his fight for a principle.[10-3]

In the Archer-Shee case, on which the play was based, the young boy was represented by Edward Carson, the prosecutor of Oscar Wilde.

American Premiere - A New Policy

The final play of the season, the British comedy *Clutterbuck* by Benn W. Levy, ran during the entire prior season in London and was widely acclaimed. The Elitch Theatre was selected for the first American showing of the comedy.

> (The) decision to present the first U.S. showing of the important play in Denver represents a new departure in American theater practice, and the opening is being watched closely by New York City theatrical circles.
>
> Normally, a new play is given a try-out in some large Eastern seaboard city and then its premiere showing on Broadway.

> In the case of *Clutterbuck,* Producer Irving L. Jacobs will introduce the comedy to American audiences in Denver and then take it to Broadway for an extended run.
>
> Jacobs explained yesterday that the prestige of the famed old Elitch Theatre in the world of theater was the reason Levy sent his bell-ringing play - a witty high comedy of premarital affairs - to Denver.
>
> Jacobs said he has been informed a large number of prominent figures from the New York theatrical world will come to Denver to view the play in its American opening.[10-4]

Arnold Gurtler stated that the premiere presentation initiated a new policy for the Elitch Theatre, and an opening was to be planned for each season in the future if the right plays came along to be tested.

Cecil B. De Mille - Memories of Denver [10-5]

Cecil B. De Mille, renowned producer-director, had completed for Paramount studios the three-million dollar film epic, *Samson and Delilah.* The question was: Where should the studio take the film for the crucial first test - or sneak preview? The executives were considering Pasadena, Santa Monica, possibly Long Beach or some other California community.

> At this point, De Mille, spoke. "Think we'll take it to Denver," he said quietly.
>
> The executives were aghast, Denver? "But, C.B., no Paramount picture has ever been tested in Denver. Why Denver?"

The answer was easy. De Mille had always had a soft spot in his heart for Denver. In 1902, he and Mrs. De Mille were married in New York and spent their honeymoon in Denver. A stage actor in his youth, De Mille had fond memories as a member of the Elitch Theatre cast of players in 1905. In a telegram to John M. Mulvihill in 1926, he recalled his pleasant summer in stock at the Elitch Theatre in what "all actors and actresses consider one of the greatest cradles of the drama in American history."

And so, De Mille responded to "Why Denver?" as follows:

> "I like Denver," said the man with the calm, scholarly manner. "It's a nice town. It's friendly. It's got all kinds - important people and little people. Maybe the folks around our state are too movie conscious, too movie wise. Maybe, too, there are too many critics here - too many artists. I want a typical American audience to see this picture, and I think I can get one in Denver."

The report on the sneak preview of *Samson and Delilah* went well, the *Rocky Mountain News* commenting as follows:

We can report now that Denver didn't let "C. B." down. I have just come from reading every one of the 750 audience cards on which the patrons wrote their comments right after the preview ...

You can understand De Mille's warm glow. The comments sound like studio blurbs, such as: "The greatest emotional experience of my life." "This picture will never be excelled."

Now can you blame De Mille for being a one-man chamber of commerce for Denver, with headquarters in Hollywood?

The 1950 Season

Of the ten plays presented during the season were Noel Coward's *Present Laughter*, Garson Kanin's *Born Yesterday*, Phillip King's *See How They Run* and Moss Hart's *Light Up the Sky*. The leads were played by Katherine Meskill and Whitfield Connor. Among the cast members were Mary Alice Moore and Phil Truex.

Walter N. Greaza, one of the most popular actors to have appeared at Elitch, returned as the season's director. In conversation among the members of the cast, Greaza remarked that his earliest ambition was to be a streetcar motorman, to which Katherine Meskill replied, "Well, Walter, that probably indicates your trend toward directing."[11-1]

A Professional Actor

Mary Alice Moore defined a professional actor as follows: "When one is making the rounds and can feel a dime through the sole of his shoe, then, by golly, he's a professional actor."[11-2]

Phil Truex

The dressing room assigned to Phil Truex at the Theatre was the same room his father, Ernest Truex, occupied forty-five years earlier when Phil was fourteen years of age. Carved on the wall of the room was the inscription: "Ernest Truex, Little Lord Fauntleroy, 1905."[11-3]

Attendance from Every State

John Gurtler reported that on July Fourth, "In the huge Elitch parking lot, every state in the country was represented by at least two cars, with 20 Texas license plates; 19 from Kansas; 19 from California; 18 from Wyoming; 16 from Nebraska and 13 from Illinois." [11-4]

Poets Have Fewer Ulcers - Advice to Actors

During a poetry workshop that Rolfe Humphries (1894-1969), outstanding poet and teacher, was conducting at the Rocky Mountain Writers' conference on the University of Colorado campus, he expressed his opinion that poets have fewer ulcers and are less neurotic than people in other creative professions. Humphries said that the reason is that the poet doesn't worry about whether he can make a living.

"He knows he cannot," said Humphries.[8-2]

Denver Public Library Western History Collection - *Rocky Mountain News Archives*

Patricia Neal - Leading Lady (1947)

Chapter Twenty-Four

(1951)

The Sixtieth Anniversary Season
A Visit from Harold Lloyd
Grace Kelly
Grace Kelly and Gene Lyons

The Sixtieth Anniversary Season

The sixtieth anniversary season once again brought an array of congratulatory telegrams that were on display in the Theatre lobby on the opening night of the season. Among the numerous stars of stage and screen that sent good luck messages were Tallulah Bankhead, Fredric March, Marlon Brando, Mary Martin, Gloria Swanson, Katherine Cornell, John Garfield, Lili Palmer, Dennis Morgan, Celeste Holm, Ray Milland, Shirley Booth, John Payne, Montgomery Clift, Ronald Reagan, Joan Bennett, Signe Hasso, Kay Francis, Maurice Evans, Basil Rathbone, Rex Harrison, Raymond Massey, Gregory Peck, Richard Widmark, Marlene Dietrich, Betty Field, Helen Hayes and Jane Wyman.

The leads were Nancy Coleman and Whitfield Connor. Other members of the cast included Grace Kelly and Gene Lyons. George Somnes directed and was cast in *The Man Who Came to Dinner*.

Belonging to a resident stock company offers a variety of experience to an actor and actress. For example, Gene Lyons played so many different character roles during the season that it was said that he would hardly know his own face when he looked in the mirror. Among his many faces were a half-wit boy who was part Boris Karloff and part Mickey Rooney, an old man (on two occasions), a slaphappy burglar and a goofy professor interested in cockroaches.[1-1]

Nancy Coleman was born in Everett, Washington and studied drama at the University of Washington. While she was touring the country with *Susan and God*, she received a telegram from David O. Selznick wanting her to quit her role in the play and to promptly proceed to Hollywood to test for the role of Scarlett O'Hara. She wired back that she was still under contract for several months and the test would have to wait. The Elitch Theatre program noted that she "now considers herself a member of the 'We Were Thought of for Scarlett O'Hara Club,' an organization of probably 10,000 young women."[2-1]

A Visit from Harold Lloyd

The famous screen comedian, Harold Lloyd, paid an unexpected visit to the Elitch Theatre. In a letter to friends of the Theatre, Arnold B. Gurtler wrote:

> Mr. Lloyd was simply keeping a date with his childhood dreams, with

an unforgettable experience in an unforgettable Theatre. He just wanted once again to walk on the stage where he had played as a boy.

Like the young actors who come to Elitch for the first time, Harold went on a sightseeing tour of the Theatre. He was filled with awe and reverence, and then, like Cecil De Mille and others who have returned to this beloved playhouse to catch up with old memories, was inspired to express his deep feeling for the tradition and historical significance of "the Theatre in a garden."[2-2]

Harold Lloyd was born in Burchard, Nebraska, on April 20, 1893. During Harold's early years, the Lloyd family lived at various times in Nebraska (Pawnee City, Humbolt, Beatrice and Omaha) and Colorado (Denver, Fort Collins and Durango) because of Lloyd senior's difficulty in keeping a job.[3] Two addresses identified as boyhood homes of Harold Lloyd in Denver are 1134 W. 13th Avenue and 64 S. Lincoln Street.[4] In 1909, Harold's father was forced to leave the family in Denver as he took a temporary job in Omaha. During this stay, Harold attended East High School.* In 1910, tired of this nomadic existence, Harold's mother obtained a divorce. In 1912, Harold's father received a monetary settlement arising out of an accident while working for the Singer Sewing Company in Omaha, after which he decided to move to San Diego, California. That year, Harold and his older brother Gaylord went to live with their father in San Diego. Harold completed his last year of high school in San Diego, as he had promised his mother he would.[5-1]

Harold Lloyd's interest in theater was spawned by his mother's passion for the theater. As a young lady she wanted to be an actress and thought of leaving her home in Toulon, Illinois, for the stage, a daring feat in the 1880s. On a trip to visit relatives in Nebraska, she met James Darsie Lloyd. Upon marrying him, she remained in Nebraska and they had two children. However, she never abandoned her love for the theater.

> She ... kept in touch with everything theatrical she could. She read all the plays she could get her hands on and even took a New York paper for a while for the reviews it gave. She would drive for miles through a snowstorm to see a ham troop in some barn opera house, and she read Shakespeare for amusement ...
>
> She also read Shakespeare to young Harold, who later recalled falling asleep in her lap, listening drowsily to a speech of Juliet's. At four or five, he began to put on his own solitary shows at home. He would collect old Halloween masks, cover them with sundry caps and hats and place the

* East High School was the first high school in Denver, opened in 1875 with a total enrollment of 108 students. The first graduating class was in 1877. Other notable attendees included Douglas Fairbanks, Sr., Antoinette Perry, Paul Whiteman and Hattie McDaniel. See www.easthighschool (Denver) - Wikipedia, the free encyclopedia.

results in position all over the living room ... Harold would begin to act out the plays he had made up himself.[5-2]

The Man Who Came to Dinner

The Man Who Came to Dinner was first presented at the Elitch Theatre in 1941. George Somnes directed the play and scored an unprecedented triumph in the role of ego-maniac Sheridan Whiteside. In planning to commemorate this sixtieth anniversary season, Elitch theatergoers were questioned as to which play of all the ones presented on the historic stage of America's oldest summer stock theater they would like to have presented again. The overwhelming choice was *The Man Who Came to Dinner*. For George Somnes, it was a command performance, both as the director of the play and, once again, its principal performer.[1-2]

Helen Bonfils, George Somnes' off-stage wife, also had a role in the play - that of his nurse. A special amusing moment in the play occurred when "he would call out to Bonfils - 'Oh. Miss Bed Pan!' - and an uproarious cheer would erupt from audiences unaccustomed to hearing the dignified owner of The (Denver) Post (newspaper) referred to in such a way."[6]

Gramercy Ghost - The Show Must Go On

Leading lady Nancy Coleman was scheduled to play the Nancy Willard lead role in the comedy *Gramercy Ghost;* however, a sudden illness disabled her the Saturday before the Sunday opening. George Somnes frantically phoned actresses who had been previously considered for Elitch, all of whom were out of town for the weekend. Coincidentally, Somnes recalled that *Gramercy Ghost* had just closed on Broadway and he knew the name of the leading lady, Ellen Fenwick.

Ellen Fenwick received a phone call at her home in Manhattan from George Somnes at 2:30 p.m. on Saturday, August 18, 1951. She had never met him. Somnes "greeted her with a request to come to Denver and play the Nancy Willard part in *Gramercy Ghost* the next evening, a part in which she was well-versed, having played it in New York." She left New York at 6 p.m., arrived in Denver at 10:45 p.m. and reported for a dress rehearsal on Sunday morning. On Sunday evening, "she was behind the footlights in the (Elitch) Theatre about which she had heard a great deal and in which she had long wished to work."[7] The reviewer of the play commented on her performance:

> From the minute Miss Fenwick made her first entrance, she radiated such a buoyant personality and played with such charming self-assurance that long before the first curtain the audience had taken her to their hearts.[1-3]

When Miss Fenwick was interviewed after the Sunday night performance, she confided that it was her third emergency appearance in a play, and that she was lucky to be "a quick study."

"I had five days to learn this part for New York as Martha Scott was to have played Nancy Willard."

When Susan Peters was taken ill in *Barretts of Wimpole Street,* Ellen played the role with the script in her hand the first performance and knew the part after that. She was standing by for both girls (Blanche and Stella) in New York when *A Streetcar Named Desire* was on tour and she flew to St. Louis to take over the Blanche role. And she played with the company in Toledo, which is her home town.[1-3]

In keeping with the tradition of the show business legend that "The show must go on," the young actress remained at Elitch to appear in the final play of the season, *The Glass Menagerie,* playing the role of the cloistered daughter.

Grace Kelly

Grace Kelly will always be remembered by Denverites as being a member of the resident stock company at the Elitch Theatre in the summer of 1951. Unbeknownst at the time, she was to become an Oscar-winnng movie star and later the Princess of Monaco.

Grace Kelly was born on November 12, 1928, the third of four children, into the well-to-do Kelly family in Philadelphia. She was raised in the Kelly household at 3901 Henry Avenue, which was clearly a comfortable and almost dreamlike environment. It was Grace's uncle, playwright George Kelly, who channeled her interest toward the theater and later, when she was 18, her enrollment in the Academy of Dramatic Arts in New York City.[8-1]

On graduation from the Academy, she had rejected out-of-hand a standard seven-year contract that major studios commonly offered beautiful young actresses on the gamble that one in a hundred of them could become a star. To Grace such an arrangement resembled indenture and implied self-betrayal. As she had no wish for a Hollywood career in any case, she told her agents, she would not consider a term contract.[8-2]

Kelly made her debut on Broadway in 1949 in the revival of *The Father* with Raymond Massey and Mady Christians.[9] In 1951, she received an invitation to become a member of the company at Elitch's well-known Theatre. Although she was not yet a seasoned actress, Whitfield Connor stated that she had "a cool beauty, breeding and intelligence" and was "well-liked by the company and the Elitch Theatre audience."[10-1] Ten days after she arrived in Denver, "her mother came to town, convinced that her daughter would end up stranded in dusty squalor before the season was over ... But her mother was captivated by the beauty of Elitch and stayed the entire summer with her daughter in a rented basement at 4020 Raleigh

Street. Kelly rode her bicycle to the Theatre each day.* [6]

She received favorable reviews during her stay at Elitch's. For example, in the opening play, *For Love or Money*, the *Denver Post* reviewer wrote:

> Grace Kelly has the brightest role in the play. Her handling of it was impressive. As the naive girl who judges people by the rules of Edgar A. Guest, her winning freshness and clear enunciation made a definite impression.[1-4]

In the weeks at Elitch Theatre, Grace Kelly gained a variety of theatrical experiences and her reputation as a stage actress was beginning to establish itself.** On August 10, 1951, she received a telegram from producer Stanley Kramer of Hollywood, offering her the role of Gary Cooper's wife in the classic Academy Award winning film, *High Noon,* and requesting her immediate arrival in Los Angeles to begin filming.[11-1]

Whitfield Connor, in a letter written on August 16, 1983 to a biographer of Grace Kelly, recalled the circumstances as follows:

> It is my recollection that Grace was in all but the last two (plays), and she would have been in those had it not been for a telegram that arrived from the Hollywood producer, Stanley Kramer.
>
> During the prior spring Mr. Kramer interviewed Grace in New York. They simply talked together for about half an hour. It was not an audition. I would say it was around August 10 or so that Kramer's telegram found her at the Theatre in Denver. I believe it came as a complete surprise to her. It was a firm offer: "Can you report Aug. 28, lead opposite Gary Cooper, tentative title HIGH NOON."
>
> She asked my advice and at first thought that she could not accept because her Elitch Theatre contract would not expire until around September 3rd. She was not aware that she could give the management a two week notice. I urged her to do this and to wire an immediate acceptance to Mr. Kramer. She left Denver two weeks later and was in plenty of time to meet Kramer's deadline.[10-1]

Summer stock was often referred to as the straw hat circuit, most likely because in early years plays were frequently presented in barns.

* "The actors (in the resident company) lived close to the Theatre in furnished rooms (private houses), apartments, etc. Proximity to the Theatre was important, since the company had to rehearse and perform in ten plays in eleven weeks, a rather grueling schedule." History Colorado, Denver, Elitch Theatre Collection 1364, Box 11, File Folder 923 (see letter by Whitfield Connor dated Aug 16, 1983).

** Kelly played the shoplifter in *Detective Story*. *Denver Post*, Jul 8, 1951, p. 4E. In the opening play of the season, *For Love or Money*, she had to make her entrance in 8 performances with her honey-colored tresses sopping wet. Following the closing of her hit performance, she stated, "Now I know how Mary Martin must feel. I'm goin' to wash that play right out of my hair!" Elitch Theatre program, 60th Year, Jul 8-14, 1951, p. 6.

Whitfield Connor, as President of the Council of Stock Theaters, Inc., was the guiding hand, along with George Barrie and Cary Grant, in establishing the annual presentation of straw hat awards, granted for top achievements in acting during summer theater seasons.

In 1971, Whitfield Connor wrote to Grace Kelly, then the Princess of Monaco, inviting her to receive the highest straw hat award - the life achievement award. The award is given to one who began a career in summer stock and went on to make an important contribution to the American Theater. She was unable to attend the ceremony, and the award was given to the next nominee, Henry Fonda.

The letter to Whitfield Connor from the Princess of Monaco was dated April 20, 1971 and read as follows:[10-2]

> Dear Whitfield:
>
> It was very nice to hear from you after all these years and I was most interested to learn of the newly originated Straw Hat Awards.
>
> Unfortunately I am not able to leave Monaco before the 10th of June as my schedule is very tight and I will go to Los Angeles by way of Philadelphia, arriving there only just in time for the Motion Picture Relief Fund benefit.
>
> I am very sorry that I am unable to change these dates in order to accept your very kind invitation for June 8th and it is with deep regret that I must refuse this wonderful award.
>
> I always think of my summer at Elitch Gardens with great pleasure, and I am delighted to know that you are still connected with the Theatre.
>
> With all best wishes.
>
> Sincerely,
>
> /s/ Grace

The rules of the Council of Stock Theatres, Inc. provided that in the event the first nominee is unable to attend the awards ceremony to receive the award, he or she would be invited for the award the subsequent year. Accordingly, on March 9, 1972, Grace Kelly was again invited to receive the award in 1972, in recognition of her dual career as an actress and humanitarian. Cary Grant was to present the award.

On March 20, 1972, in a warm and lovely communication to Whitfield Connor, Princess Grace expressed disappointment that she would be unable for a second time to be in the United States. The award was given to her good friend, the next nominee, Jimmy Stewart.[10-3] After the 1974 season, the awards were discontinued. By then, most summer stock theaters were merely presenting celebrity one-nighters.

Grace Kelly and Gene Lyons

In three biographies of Grace Kelly, reference is made to her relationship with Gene Lyons, whom she met when they were members of the 1951 cast of players at Elitch Theatre.[12]

Grace Kelly enjoyed the challenge of summer stock in Denver. The work was hard, as with any resident company, learning lines for a different play each week; nevertheless, she told a fellow actor that she would be happy to "stay here forever." In Grace's case, it was more than the fulfillment of her theatrical achievements, reflected in reviews of her performances. She had fallen in love with Gene Lyons, who was ten years her senior.

> Like Grace, he came from Pennsylvania and was of Irish descent. But while Grace had grown up in the comfort of Henry Avenue, Gene Lyons came from poverty in Pittsburgh, and was proud to label himself "shanty Irish." Lyons was handsome, complicated, unexpected, and very charming. "Mother," confided Grace, "I think I'm in love."
>
> (It seemed that) Lyons appealed to the bohemian side of Grace. He was a step back from the gilded salons of the Waldorf, toward the carpet dealers of Thirty-third Street, and he shared her passion to make it on the stage. (Grace's mother recalled that) "he not only knew how she felt, but he felt the same way. He kept telling her that they could be stars in the theater together, that they would stimulate each other to success and fame."[11-2]

Lyons was regarded within the New York acting community as one of the most promising actors of his generation.

Drama critics during the Elitch season affirmed his talent. For example, in *The Glass Menagerie*, the review stated that: "Gene Lyons as the gum-chewing extrovert (gentleman caller) gives a commendable performance,"[13] and in *Detective Story*, Gene Lyons was "outstanding ... as a four-time loser who's good for many laughs before his participation in the play's sudden dramatic ending,"[1-5] and in *The High Ground*, "there is a vigorous honesty in Gene Lyon's portrayal of Willy Pentridge."[1-6]

After filming *High Noon*, Grace resumed her relationship with Lyons in New York, where he had enrolled in the Actors Workshop. They appeared together in a television production *The Rich Boy* by Scott Fitzgerald. However, the relationship drifted apart, although she wrote Lyons a long letter so he would learn of her engagement to Prince Rainier III of Monaco before reading about it in the newspapers.[11-3]

Lyons appeared in the original Broadway cast of *Witness for the Prosecution* as the defendant and Broadway critics lauded him highly.[14] While Lyons achieved some success, he never fulfilled his promise as an actor, burdened by excessive drinking.

In his later years, he played a supporting role in the TV series *Ironside*. He died in 1974, comparatively young and reportedly, a hopeless alcoholic.[11-4]

History Colorado - # 10039862

Gene Lyons and Grace Kelly

Chapter Twenty-Five

(1952 - 1955)

Backstage Relaxation After Opening Night
World Famous Chef at Orchard Cafe
Haila Stoddard
The First Rehearsal - The Apple Orchard
The Glenn Miller Story
A Letter From Maude Fealy
The Task of Selecting Actors and Plays
Television and Theater
The New Backstage Area and Other Remodeling

The 1952 Season

Opening of the Season

> The opening of a new season of theater at Elitch Gardens is always an occasion for its patrons, many of whom are occupying seats to which they have subscribed - and their parents before them - for season after season.[1-1]

The excitement of opening night was evident as the audience witnessed the first play of the season, the comedy *Love and Let Love.*

> Applause greeted the famous asbestos curtain with its picture postcard scene of Anne Hathaway's cottage. Applause greeted the rise of the velvet curtain. Applause greeted the appearance of each player. And applause brought gratifying curtain calls after the play's end.[1-1]

Backstage Relaxation After Opening Night

The informal backstage party after opening night is tradition in America's oldest stock theater. When the curtain falls, the cast members gather on stage for some "shop talk" discussing the inevitable question, "How did it go?" In this case, director George Somnes assured the cast that it went very well, as the applause of repeated curtain calls rang in their ears. Then Jack Gurtler, manager of the historic playhouse came by with a handshake and praise for a good performance.[1-1]

The Season

The lead roles were played by Whitfield Connor and Margot Stevenson. The blond Miss Stevenson, in addition to being pleasant to gaze upon, was said to have a "captivating way with speech and faultless diction, which keeps the audience from missing a line or a meaning."[1-1]

Among the plays presented were Valerie Wyngate and P. G. Wodehouse's *Her Cardboard Lover*, Laszlo Bush-Fekete and Mary Helen Fay's *Faithfully Yours*, Edward Mabley's *Glad Tidings* and Lesley Storm's *Black Chiffon*.

Reginald Denham - Visiting Playwright

Reginald Denham, the British-born playwright and husband to Mary Orr, a member of the Elitch cast, visited Colorado and the Elitch Theatre for the first time. Mary Orr wrote the Cosmopolitan magazine serial which was the basis for the award-winning film *All About Eve*. While visiting the historic Elitch Theatre, Denham renewed a long-standing friendship with George Somnes. Denham was impressed with Elitch Theatre, stating, "This is the most truly unique theater I've ever been in and I've been in theaters on two continents."[1-2]

The Painting in "Black Chiffon"

The set in *Black Chiffon* called for a painting of the "Battersea Bridge" in London to be hung over the fireplace in the drawing room of the Christie house. Upon the very talented Harry Cummins' completion of the painting, with justifiable pride, he stood back to gaze upon his work. A member of the company mentioned that the traffic on the bridge was unfortunately on the wrong side of the street.

> Harry was about to agree, when he suddenly realized that in painting the picture from memory, he had, without giving it a second thought, placed the traffic on the wrong side of the street (to us) but the proper side for London vehicles, even though it had been many years since Harry has driven on London thoroughfares.[2]

It is appropriate to mention that Cummins began his career in Dublin, Ireland, where he was born, and in 1938 had been admitted to the Royal Academy of Dramatic Arts in London.

World-Famous Chef at Orchard Cafe

The Orchard Cafe at Elitch Gardens, the dining place for actors and theatergoers, engaged Henri Kechid, a man who had served as chef in cuisine capitals of the world. Henri brought thirty-three years of experience in the kitchen to Elitch. Taking pride in his profession, he boasted that the kitchen is "no place for amateurs."[1-3]

The 1953 Season

Welcoming the New Season

The congratulatory telegrams to welcome the new season once again included many notable theatrical names, such as Helen Hayes, Katherine Cornell, Marlon Brando and Maurice Evens.

The Plays and the Cast

Louis Verneuil's "The Affairs of State"
Vena Delmar's "Mid-Summer"
Allan Langdon Martin's "Smilin' Through"
John Van Druten's "Bell, Book and Candle"
Emlyn Williams' "Night Must Fall"
Paul Osborne's "Point of No Return"
Lawrence Riley's "Personal Appearance"
J. B. Priestley's "Dangerous Corner"
S. N. Behrman's "Biography"
Jan de Hartog's "The Fourposter"

Haila Stoddard

The leads for the season were Whitfield Connor and Haila Stoddard. In the years to come, Haila Stoddard was to play a significant role in the future of the Theatre.

Haila Stoddard was born on November 14, 1913 in Great Falls, Montana. She was a graduate of the University of Southern California. Her first part in New York was as the daughter in *Yes, My Darling Daughter*.[3-1] Shortly thereafter she appeared in a national tour of Jack Kirkland's successful play, *Tobacco Road*.

In 1947, at age 24 she married Jack Kirkland, age 36, and settled in Springtown, Pennsylvania, where they were supporters in the creation of the Bucks County Playhouse, where she often appeared in a variety of roles.[4] She also had many Broadway credits, which included Noel Coward's *Blithe Spirit* with Clifton Webb and Peggy Wood and *Who's Afraid of Virginia Wolfe*, following Uta Hagen in the starring role.

Stoddard and Kirkland had three children, one being Christopher Kirkland, who would later likewise play a significant role with her and Whitfield Connor in the management of the Elitch Theatre Company. The Haila Stoddard and Jack Kirkland marriage ended in divorce. She later married Whitfield Connor. Christopher Kirkland became the producing director for the Elitch Theatre Company in 1972 and held that position until the Theatre's closing in 1987.

Stoddard was a leading actress of the American stage, and during the 1952 season she developed a close relationship with Helen Bonfils. After the season, they started a New York production company called "Bonard Productions" (the "Bon" from Bonfils and the "ard" from Stoddard), which company produced numerous Broadway plays, including *The Birthday Party, Sail Away* and *A Thurber Carnival*.[5]

The First Rehearsal - The Apple Orchard

Upon the arrival of the cast members, the first rehearsal in preparation for the 63rd season of the historic Elitch Theatre was held in an apple orchard on the cool, pleasant grounds of the famous gardens.

> The choice of the apple orchard, where Mary Elitch Long used to spend the summer afternoons when the Gardens and Denver were both two generations younger, was a sentimental gesture to the glory of one of the nation's longest theatrical traditions.
>
> Nowadays, Director George Somnes regularly conducts rehearsals in an enclosed garden beside the Theatre stage door. But the apple orchard is the first of the series of work sessions which give the plays of the ten-week season the polish for which the Elitch Gardens Theatre has been noted through the years.[6-1]

Whitfield Connor and the Valley Drive-In Theater

Whitfield Connor took time out from his leading role assignment at Elitch Theatre to visit the Valley Drive-in Theater where he was appearing on screen in *City of Bad Men,* his latest motion picture. When Connor arrived, he discovered an old friend in Stan Bradford, manager of the drive-in. Connor had worked together with Bradford in the cast at Elitch during the 1949 season.[6-2]

The Fourposter - An Extra Week For the First Time

Arnold B. Gurtler informed the patrons of the Theatre that:

> For the first time in the sixty-two year history of the Elitch Theatre we are departing from the policy of one-week play engagements in order to allow every theatre-lover in the region the opportunity to see one of the greatest play hits of modern times.
>
> The decision to depart from this long-standing custom and to extend our season an extra week was made when we were accorded the high honor and privilege of being the first theatrical company in America, off-Broadway, to present *The Fourposter*.[3-2]

The *Denver Post* agreed with the extra week of performances, noting that it "seems mandatory in order to allow the maximum number of theater-lovers to witness one of the greatest plays on married life ever presented."[6-3] The two-character play surveys the marriage of Michael and Agnes for thirty-five years until they move from their home and leave their four-poster behind.

Playwright Jan de Hartog "carefully balanced his two characters so that they could be played by husband and wife - as they were by Hume Cronyn and Jessica Tandy on Broadway." Rex Harrison and his wife, Lili Palmer, starred in the 1952 film.[6-4] While Whitfield Connor and Haila Stoddard were not married when presenting the play at Elitch, they married a few years later.

A Play Scratched

The Elitch audience was to be the first in America to see *Here We Come Gathering,* a play that promised to be a hit on Broadway in the fall. It was co-authored by Phillip

King, who had won many laurels as a playwright. The play was described as "a rollicking new comedy of family life." An earlier play by King, *See How They Run,* had been presented at Elitch in 1950.[3-3]

On short notice, the scheduled play was scratched and *Bell, Book and Candle* was substituted. The management stated in its program, "Our apologies are due you, the audience, for not producing *Here We Come Gathering* as previously announced for this week. As we told you, this was a brand new play, and Elitch was to be privileged to present a pre-Broadway production. At the last minute, the author felt it best to recall the play for revision and script changes. In *Bell, Book and Candle,* however, a completely delightful play by John Van Druten, we feel you will be amply compensated for the change in program."[3-4]

The Glenn Miller Story

The Trocadero at Elitch Gardens was selected as the ideal place for Hollywood to shoot the ballroom scenes for *The Glenn Miller Story*. Jimmy Stewart and June Allyson, with a crew of 75 technicians and other actors along with the famous Air Force dance band, appeared on July 17, 1953 from 1:00 p.m. to 7:30 p.m. to shoot the scenes. Tickets were sold by Elitch for $1.50 each, with the proceeds going to the Children's Hospital drive fund. Bearers were entitled "to see a movie being produced, the chance to be in some of the scenes, an afternoon of dancing ... and of course, the chance to see Jimmy Stewart and June Allyson."[3-4]

The following week, a scene in the movie required the presence of a full colonel in the United States Air force. Universal International Studios was going to fly an actor in from Hollywood to handle the role when they learned of actor Donald McClelland of the cast at Elitch Theatre. McLelland received a temporary two-hour commission as a full colonel and the scene was shot with Jimmy Stewart at Lowry Air Force Base.[3-5]

"The Glenn Miller Story" was the first full-length motion picture ever filmed on location in Denver.[6-5]

The final film sequences shot in Colorado were at the University of Colorado campus at Boulder, where Glenn Miller attended school and where he met his wife, Miss Helen Burger of Boulder.[6-6]

> The nostalgic occasion was given added poignance through a second visit paid to the filming ... by Mrs. Mattie Lou Miller of Greeley, the 82-year-old mother of the bandleader who was killed in a World War II plane crash.
>
> (Jimmy) Stewart was also greeted by three former members of the Colorado University dance band in which Miller played from 1922 to 1924. They were Clifford Houston, dean of students at CU, J.H. Kingdom of Boulder and William A. Fairchild of Boulder.[6-6]

Before leaving for Hollywood, James Stewart and June Allyson were designated by the *Denver Post* to be members of its staff as "occasional correspondents" to cover the Hollywood scene and their own busy careers.[6-6]

Donald McClelland and His Sublease

Donald McClelland was among the cast members at Elitch. When he left New York for Denver, he subleased his apartment but neglected to have his phone listing discontinued. He later learned that his sub-lessee was thrilled to receive 9 offers of TV work, among them, "Westinghouse Summer Theatre," "You Are There," and a role in "Suspense." However, the sub-lessee, not being an actor, was not able to accept the offers.[3-6]

A Letter From Maude Fealy

Arnold B. Gurtler informed friends of Elitch Theatre in the initial program of the 1953 season of the letter from a well-known actress who appeared at Elitch many years before.

> The letter was from Maude Fealy, who made her debut at Elitch as a child star, and returned in 1902, hailed as the youngest American star, and the Gardens' leading lady for three seasons.
>
> Miss Fealy wrote that she had her eye on a young actress whom she thought would be excellent for our company. "I suggested Elitch Gardens for her debut, as the happiest days of my theatrical career were spent on the Elitch stage. The Denver public was always very good to me ... a glittering memory in my life."[3-1]

Maude Fealy was born into a theatrical family, her mother being the famous Margaret Fealy, who ran a dramatic school in Denver. Maude appeared at Elitch Theatre in lead roles during the summer seasons of 1899, 1901 through 1905, 1909 and 1917. Among the plays in which she was featured were *Little Lord Fauntleroy* in 1905, *Peter Pan* in 1909 and *Her Own Money* in 1917. She remained a celebrated star for more than twenty-five years before retiring to Hollywood where, like her mother, she hosted a dramatic school.[7]

The 1954 Season

The Task of Selecting Actors and Plays

The work of management in the selection of actors and plays for a summer season is not an easy task.

> (The theater management) can't just select any twelve pleasing actors and actresses at random for the Elitch company. The supporting characters must be chosen very carefully to compliment the leads, so decisions about the entire cast depend on acceptances from the leading

man and woman. Actually the cast must be fitted together like a jigsaw puzzle.

> (For actors) to appear successfully at Elitch, they must be able to learn roles in a matter of days, to accept intensive direction in rehearsing one role, while actually playing another on the stage. They must maintain the furious summer theatre pace for ten full weeks and at the same time bring freshness and charm to each new role after less than a week of rehearsal. To find actors and actresses of sufficient ability and stability to do this for ten successive weeks is a big job in itself.[8-1]

Fortunately, however, Denver had always been able to draw upon the best of talent for several reasons. The city is attractive for summer work because of its mile-high climate away from the humidity and congestion of larger cities. Also, Elitch Theatre had acquired a national reputation in which actors were proud to say, "It's great to have played Elitch." Laurence Hugo, a leading man at Elitch said that "on Broadway they say if you've played Elitch you've lived ... just as in vaudeville days ... 'you hadn't arrived 'till you played the Palace.'"[9-1] Robert Cass, a member of the 1954 summer cast at Elitch, stated, "Being with the Elitch Theatre gives me a big boost to the coveted place in the theater."[8-2] Not to be overlooked, however, was that Helen Bonfils and George Somnes were connected with the New York theater community as producers of Broadway plays.

The process of lining up ten current plays which were to be attractive offerings was sensitive and complicated, particularly when many playwrights had "a decidedly debonair attitude toward immorality and irregularities of conduct ... (that) would offend Elitch's family audiences."[8-1]

There are still other factors that may affect the selection of a play.

> Whether a play will close its Broadway run and be available in time for the Elitch season is one question. Sometimes a play that is wanted is found to be tied up by a group of actors who plan to tour summer theaters with it as a "package" deal.
>
> Since Elitch doesn't operate on a star system but depends on a resident company whose members play different roles every week, the choice of plays must depend on whether it can be produced with the available cast and that, in turn, depends on the versatility of the actors, something Somnes and Gurtler Sr. bear constantly in mind in selecting actors.[10]

With these guidelines in mind, each fall a member of the Gurtler family traveled to New York, saw every new Broadway play and made notes not only on the play itself, but on each of the actors and actresses, any one of whom might be considered at some future date for the Elitch cast. The notes were then transferred to a master file in Denver and kept current with information as to the plays, actors and actresses, as well as television productions and Hollywood films.

In the spring another trip to New York was made by the Gurtlers for casting interviews of applicants desirous of appearing at Elitch, who had been screened beforehand. Auditions were held and choices were then made as to which performers best fit into the plans of the company. In the year 1953, over 150 applicants were interviewed for the Elitch Company. Many of those interviewed were auditioned. Each audition usually lasted 15 minutes.[8-1]

The Season

The season opened with Samuel Taylor's *Sabrina Fair*. Among the other plays were Charles Morgan's *The Burning Glass*, Arthur Miller's *The Crucible* and Sam and Bella Spewack's *My Three Angels*. Margot Stevenson returned to Elitch as the leading lady, with Laurence Hugo as the leading man.

Helen Bonfils was again part of the resident cast and was acknowledged to have played in at least 78 plays at Elitch. The program noted that she is "a versatile and accomplished theatrical artist, who adds color and charm to every play she appears in - and who handles any role, from gay young things to doddering old ladies with consummate skill."[8-3]

In the second act of *The Burning Glass*, an absorbing adult drama, Margot Stevenson remarked to the prime minister, "Oh, there are some men outside." During a matinee performance, "two workmen making some repairs back stage, in search of a drink of water, walked right across the terrace of the set without realizing they were on stage ... just as Margot gave the previously mentioned line. It couldn't have been timed better if the workmen had been cued."[8-4]

The Crucible, the Arthur Miller play about the scandalous witchcraft trials in Salem, Massachusetts, is a page torn out of the past of America but which clearly had meaning for contemporary America. It opened on Broadway at the Martin Beck Theatre on January 22, 1953.

> (The play is) an absorbing and historically exact account of the Salem witch hunt, a day when an accusation was enough to prove guilt, when the "big lie" conquered truth, when guilt by association was a rule of law.[11-1]

The play is included in the publication *50 Best Plays of the American Theatre*. In John Gassner's introductory comments to the play, he writes:

> (Arthur Miller) wished to write a play that "would lift out of the morass of subjectivism the squirming, single defined process which would show that the sin of public terror is that it divests man of conscience, of himself."
>
> "It was not only the rise of 'McCarthyism' that moved me," (Miller)

declares, "but something which was much more weird and mysterious. It was the fact that a political, objective, knowledgeable campaign from the far Right was capable of creating not only a terror, but a new subjective reality, a veritable mystique which was gradually assuming even a holy resonance. That so interior and subjective an emotion could have been so manifestly created from without was a marvel to me. It underlies every word in *The Crucible*." To the author's contentions, in so far as they are intended to explain *The Crucible*, it is possible to object that while it is true that Salem had no witches, it is not true that contemporary America had no Communists. But it is true that Miller's concern was with a rather different matter - namely, the matter of conscience.[12]

My Three Angels is a comedy that playwrights Sam and Bella Spewack adapted from Albert Husson's French *La Cuisine des Anges*. During the fourth week of the season, this comedy depicting the escapades of three convicts provided Elitch audiences with such laughter and enjoyment that the management acknowledged the popular request to have the play return for another run during the eleventh week of the season. This was the first play in the history of Elitch Theatre that was repeated in the same season.[11-2]

Not to See Elitch is Not to See Denver

Advertising promotions of Elitch Gardens frequently contained the slogan "Not to see Elitch is not to see Denver." During a backstage interview after an opening night performance, Lawrence Hugo was asked how he liked Denver. Laurence smiled ruefully and stressed the painstaking hard work of an actor in summer stock.

"You know that saying, 'Not to see Elitch is not to see Denver'? Well, among actors we say 'To act at Elitch is NOT to see Denver.'" He went on to explain that with the very heavy rehearsal schedule, the many hours to be spent learning lines, and the constant play performances, the actor's eye view of the mile-high city consists mainly of the confines of Elitch, their own summer homes, and the route traversed between the two.[9-2]

Television and Theater

As part of a panel at a Rotarian luncheon, Laurence Hugo was asked if appearing on television was akin to performing on the stage. Laurence replied:

Television is frightening to an actor because it lacks the basic ingredient which helps an actor to get his role across ... a live audience. An actor's training constantly stresses the "audience value." The worst case of stage-fright is usually cured once an actor has delivered his opening lines and feels the warmth of the folks on the other side of the footlights. In television, however, where you're working in a crowded studio, with

> twenty or more technicians interested only in performing their jobs ... and not in how you're performing yours, it's difficult to get the feel of the role.[8-2]

The 1955 Season

The New Backstage Area and Other Remodeling

In the final weeks of December 1954, the Elitch management commenced its remodeling plans for the Theatre - that of building a new and larger backstage area. The project was completed before the commencement of the 1955 summer season.

The project was described in an article that appeared in the *Denver Post*.

> The entire backstage area of Elitch's famed summer theater was gone Thursday, leveled to make way for a remodeling and addition that will give Denver ... one of the largest and finest stages in the nation ... The new structure will be equipped to handle any kind of modern staging.
>
> The new backstage area will be a giant (cinder block, steel, and brick) building, 100 by 126 feet, rising 60 feet to the roof over the playing stage so that sets can be "flown" readily for quick changes between acts and scenes.
>
> On the playing stage and around it - for an area of 100 by 50 feet - there will be no structural posts or obstructions ... This will greatly simplify assembling and handling of sets ... Where the Elitch crews had to build the sets to fit between poles, and steer them carefully on and off over a pre-arranged path, in the future the sets can be brought in and removed from almost any direction.[11-3]

The new and attached structure would also house new dressing rooms, a new prop department and a new carpenter shop. Footlights were to be recessed to make more varied and elaborate lighting effects possible.[11-3] The extensive remodeling program also included winterizing the building and changing the Theatre's electrical layout and plumbing system and enlarging the stage.[11-4]

The Dressing Room Door

In an article that appeared in the *Denver Post* on June 29, 1980, Whitfield Connor recalled the tradition relating to the dressing room door at Elitch.

> Connor ... remembered a tradition dating back to the beginning of theatrical productions when famous actors and actresses customarily at the end of a play autographed a special dressing room door. When a large backstage building was added in the 1950s, the original part of the Theatre was refurbished and repainted. Unfortunately, a hapless or possibly near-sighted painter brushed fresh paint on the irreplaceable, invaluable door and the decades of autographs were forever lost. This

> was such a blow, that the management had toyed with the idea of sending a new door from coast to coast for autographing by Elitch's theatrical alumnae. But the idea never materialized.[13]

The Season

Among the plays selected for the season were Jean Kerr and Eleanor Brooke's *King of Hearts*, Frederick Knott's *Dial M For Murder*, Sylvia Regan's *The Fifth Season*, James S. Hagen's *One Sunday Afternoon* and William McCleery's *The Lady Chooses*.

Laurence Hugo returned to Elitch for his second consecutive season as leading man. Carole Matthews was the leading lady. Mary K. Wells was a member of the cast. Luther Kennett was the director. Harry Cummins was in his fifth season at Elitch and recognized among the country's top stage designers.

> The young designer got his first professional experience with Ireland's Abbey Theater, where he worked with Anne Yeats, daughter of the celebrated Irish poet (William Butler Yeats). During World War II, he did design work on military projects, then returned to set designing at London's famed Drury Lane theater.[14-1]

The Lady Chooses was the final play of the season prior to its Broadway opening in the fall. It was a new comedy about politics and home life. The response by Denver audiences to the play was so favorable that the play was held over for a second week, making choice seats ordinarily taken up by season ticket holders for the final regular performance of the season now available to the public at large.[14-1] The principal roles were played by Laurence Hugo, Mary K. Wells and Ward Costello. To prepare for the role, Mary Wells met with two widely known and highly successful politicians in Denver, Governor Ed Johnson and Mayor Will Nicholson, for advice on campaigning.[14-1] In the play, Mary Wells is called upon to choose whether or not she will run for the U.S. Senate, but also to decide as well between her husband and an admiring ex-governor, who is abetting her political career.[14-2]

The Rotarian Luncheon - About Acting [14-3]

As in the past, Arnold B. Gurtler again arranged a luncheon meeting for the actors to appear before the Denver Rotarians to discuss what acting was like on the stage, before television and movie cameras and in front of a radio microphone.

Carol Matthews, whose prior experience was mostly in motion pictures and television, said she was finding her new experience at Elitch, "entirely different - proving you can't specialize as an actress anymore." She added,

> The chance to learn timing, to build a part and perform it before a live audience and not the staring eye of a camera and bored grips and electricians can only be realized in the live theater.

Laurence Hugo, whose prior experience was mostly on the Broadway stage, including such long runs as 1,000 performances in *Born Yesterday* and more than 500 in *Stalag 17*, observed that a stock company such as Elitch's "draws better work out of me because I am called on to do a whole lot of different parts and there is no time to get bored with a performance."

Mary K. Wells, whose prior experience was mostly as a leading actress in radio soap operas and in television, admitted that the security of a long run radio show with its weekly pay checks had its advantages. She then added:

> But one can experience creativeness only in the theater where the performance has to come out of your soul. This can happen only before a live audience.
>
> I like radio but it is not self-satisfying. If you've played Elitch, you've lived.

The Orchard Cafe, one of the Gardens original buildings, encouraged and regularly made reservations to seat theater parties for dinner prior to the theater performance.

Chapter Twenty-Six

(1956 - 1959)

The Death of George Somnes
Advice to Latecomers
The Anniversary Waltz Party
The Marriage of Whitfield Connor and Haila Stoddard
Gurtler Management by John and Arnold B. Gurtler, Jr.
The Eleventh Play
Marriage of Helen Bonfils to "Tiger Mike"

The 1956 Season

The Death of George Somnes [1]

George Somnes died on February 8, 1956 at his home in Denver at 737 Washington Street. He had been in ill health for some time. He was frequently praised for his imaginative work in theater and for his cultural contributions to Denver. He was active in the affairs of the Central City Opera House Association. He and Helen Hayes organized the American National Theater and Academy, and he was still a director of the organization when he died. He had been a director of Elitch Gardens Theatre from 1936 to 1947 and 1951 to 1954, having staged at least 200 productions, which is most likely a record for stock companies throughout the country.

Among the contributions of George Somnes in Denver was his participation in the construction of the Bonfils Memorial Theater located at East Colfax Avenue and Elizabeth Street in Denver, which opened in October 1953. The Bonfils Memorial Theater was the first playhouse for live theater built in Denver in 40 years, one that critics praised and called "the finest of its kind in the nation." The theater was later gifted to the City of Denver by Miss Bonfils as a memorial to her parents. The theater has since ceased operating, and its space has been converted into The Tattered Cover bookstore.

On February 10, 1956, in the *Denver Post* George Somnes was described as follows:

> His long eminence in the dramatic arts, as actor, director and producer, was fashioned not just "of the stuff that dreams are made of," not merely of his gifted use of the magic, the music and the power of words. Underlying that was his perception - shared only by the best in his profession - that life provides all the elements of the play, and that, therefore, the play must be made of the elements of life.
>
> He was an artist of the broadest culture; he was a professional of the

> highest rank in his chosen work, and he was, most of all, a lovable human being. Of him it can be truly written, as Dryden wrote: "Whate'er he did was done with so much ease. In him alone, 'twas natural to please."[2-1]

A. B. Gurtler wrote a memorial about George Somnes in the Elitch Theatre program. He noted:

> In the distinguished annals of theatre history, occasionally a man appears who combines tremendous theatrical talent, expert managerial ability, and rare personal charm. When this happy blending occurs, the world acclaims a great director. Such a man was George Somnes.[3]

Walter Bellows, director for ten seasons in the early 1900s was second to George Somnes in the number of plays produced by a director at Elitch. Except for Somnes and Bellows, prior directors averaged a term of three or four years at the most.[4]

George Somnes is interred in the Bonfils family mausoleum in Fairmount Cemetery in Denver.

The Season

The leads at Elitch brought together two veteran performers with exceptionally wide backgrounds and experience, Anne Kimbell and Carl Betz. Kimbell was best known to Broadway at the time for her starring role in *The Seven Year Itch* with Eddie Bracken and her national tour in the same play. She was also cast in the leading role in *Arms and the Man* with Marlon Brando. Carl Betz had been featured on Broadway with Walter Abel in *The Long Watch*, played 15 weeks opposite Veronica Lake in *The Voice of the Turtle* and was featured as Alfred in *My Three Angels* with Walter Slezak. In addition to his Broadway accomplishments, he was characterized as a marathon performer, having played in 62 plays in 64 weeks of continuous stock in theaters up and down the eastern seaboard.[5]

Denver audiences were treated this season to a wide range of plays, from *The Seven Year Itch*, the familiar hilarious comedy about Richard Sherman, a man seven years married who finds himself involved with the girl upstairs while his wife and little boy are away on vacation,[2-2] to *The Desperate Hours*, a nerve-tingling story of an American family held prisoner in its own home by three desperate escaped convicts. In the original Broadway production of *The Desperate Hours*, Nancy Coleman, Elitch's leading lady of the 1961 season, played the role of the mother, while another Elitch actress, Mary Orr, was also in the Broadway company.[2-3]

Theatergoers responded to the programs offered by filling the seats of the theater and making the season a success.

Advice to Latecomers

The following announcement began to appear in the Theatre programs:

ATTENTION THEATRE PATRONS

The management of Elitch's Gardens, the Elitch Theatre cast and the crew of theatrical workers wish to express their deep appreciation to those considerate theatergoers who are always in their seats at curtain time. And in courtesy to those who are punctual and in deference to the actors,

WE REGRET THAT WE MUST MAKE IT A RULE NOT
TO SEAT ANYONE AFTER THE CURTAIN HAS
RISEN, UNTIL INTERMISSION.

A flurry of late seating detracts from the enjoyment of the audience, distracts the players on the stage and creates general confusion. We ask your cooperation in this, and your indulgence when we must refuse to seat you while the play is in progress.[6]

The Anniversary Waltz Party

The theater season opened with Jerome Chodorov and Joseph Field's comedy *Anniversary Waltz* on Sunday evening, June 17th. Prior to the performance, and during the afternoon hours from 2:30 p.m. to 5:30 p.m., the Elitch management, together with the *Denver Post*, celebrated the observance of the 65th anniversary of the famed amusement center by sponsoring "The Anniversary Waltz Party." The invitation was directed to any person celebrating an anniversary, such as a wedding or birthday or any other anniversary of significance. Such person and a guest were admitted free to the Elitch Trocadero Ballroom between the designated hours, during which Eddy Howard and his band entertained. A highlight of the party was a waltz contest with the winning couple over age 50 and the winning couple under age 50 each receiving a season pass to the Elitch Theatre. Additional gifts at the event were 150 copies of Howard's top Mercury recording of "Anniversary Waltz," and ten "Day-at-Elitch's" ticket strips for a free day in the Gardens, including gate admission, three rides, admission to the Trocadero Ballroom and a lunch in the park.[7]

The Marriage of Whitfield Connor and Haila Stoddard

Haila Stoddard and Whitfield Connor met in 1953 when Miss Stoddard came to Denver to be the leading lady at Elitch and Connor arrived for his fifth season as leading man. An Elitch Theatre summer romance that began in 1953 culminated in their marriage on January 26, 1956 in a ceremony in New York City.[2-4] They remained constant companions, and Haila Stoddard joyfully assisted Whitfield

Connor each summer in recreating theatrical romances at Elitch Theatre until its close.

On April 22, 1956, the *Denver Post*, in reporting their marriage in an article captioned "Elitch Romance," the following was stated:

> It is a theatrical truism that leading men and leading women cast opposite each other in 10 plays - one play a week for 10 weeks - either come to love or loathe each other.
>
> As they played opposite each other during a season which included such hits as *Summertime*, *Smiling Through*, and for the last two weeks of the season, the ecstatic married couple of *The Fourposter*, Miss Stoddard's and Connor's interest in each other grew.[2-4]

The 1957 Season

Frances Melrose, the drama editor for the *Rocky Mountain News* commented that Denver "has become the mecca of premieres this year." Two of the ten plays selected for the season, were premiere presentations - *Love Out of Town* and *The Gimmick*. The review for *Love Out of Town* was headlined "Drama Deserves Broadway," and for *The Gimmick* the headline was "New Elitch Play Should Go Places."[8]

Among the other plays presented were J. M. Barrie's *The Admirable Crichton*, Terence Rattigan's *The Sleeping Prince*, Alex Gottlieb's *Wake Up Darling* and Agatha Christie's *Witness for the Prosecution*.

The season brought together two outstanding performers as leads - Leora Dana and Carl Betz. Miss Dana, a graduate of Barnard College, appeared on Broadway as the wife in *Point of No Return* with Henry Fonda. She then replaced Margaret Sullavan in *Sabrina Fair*. Carl Betz started acting in high school and never stopped. He returned to Elitch following a successful season during the summer of 1956.

Gurtler Management by John and Arnold B. Gurtler, Jr.

Since the end of World War II, Arnold B. Gurtler had been gradually relegating the responsibilities of management to his two sons, John M. Gurtler (commonly known as "Jack") and Arnold B. Gurtler, Jr. (commonly known as "Budd"), although he still retained the nominal position of President and General Manager of the corporation and acted as an advisor whenever questions of management arose. Jack and Budd Gurtler got their first jobs as ushers at the Theatre and remember helping Mary Elitch to her reserved seat at the Theatre.

In 1957, Arnold B. Gurtler turned the management of the park over to his two sons. He informed the Theatre patrons of the change by an announcement that appeared in the Theatre program.

> This year, just as my father-in-law, John M. Mulvihill, handed the torch of the Theatre on to me, with the hope that my love and respect for the

> proud traditions of Elitch would inspire me to cherish the flame, so I am passing the torch on to my sons, John M. and Arnold B. Gurtler, Jr.
>
> Surrounded as they have been, from earliest childhood, with the atmosphere and associations of Elitch, and imbued with the deepest regard for the historic park, I am serenely confident that they, with their tremendous enthusiasm and younger vigor, will enhance the brilliance of the famous Theatre - so that its fire will blaze even brighter, in an ever-increasing circle throughout the entire theatrical world.[9]

The 1958 Season

Kathleen Maguire was the leading lady, and John Dutra was the leading man.

It is often said that stock companies are too demanding of actors, what with their need to perform in a play while, at the same time, rehearsing to perform in a new play the week following. This strenuous effort at times reflects itself in the performance of a play, as noted in the drama reviews of two plays in the season.

The review of *Anastasia* was favorable; yet, it contained the following comments.

> The Elitch rendition is a workmanlike production which should increase in effectiveness. The players appeared edgy in the first act of the Sunday night opening, but this is a condition not uncommon to stock companies. *Anastasia* is a drama more demanding than the usual run of summer fare. The cast should be at top form by mid-week.[10-1]

The Trial of Mary Dugan, a 1927 play by Bayard Veiller, had been recently and successfully revived on the London stage, and that inspired the Elitch management to include it in its summer program. The drama is about Mary Dugan, a chorus girl who is on trial for the fatal stabbing of her wealthy paramour. The drama critic noted in his review.

> The drama still stands up, but it wasn't benefited at Sunday night's opening by several slipshod performances and a general awkwardness. The result was that the play sagged when it should have been taut and suspenseful.
>
> The Elitch company is a generally able one, and things should be shipshape before long. *The Trial of Mary Dugan* demands a large cast - there are 28 roles - and is obviously a difficult one for a stock company to lick in five days of rehearsal.[10-2]

The Eleventh Play

A season at Elitch generally consisted of ten plays. From time to time, the regular theater season was extended by offering an eleventh play, as with this 67th season. The eleventh play was Noel Coward's *Nude With Violin*, which starred Donald Cook in the role he performed during the past Broadway season. The play was a satirical comedy about modern art and ran for two weeks.

The 1959 Season

Arthur Sircom was named director for the season. He had an extensive background in theater, having been associate professor at the Yale Drama School, head of the drama department at the McPhail College of Music and Drama, director at Cape Playhouse in Dennis, Massachusetts for 15 years and director of 32 Broadway productions.[11-1] The leading lady was Ludi Claire, and the leading man was Thomas Coley.

One of the plays presented was Howard Teichmann's *The Girls in 509,* a political satire. The play was inspired by an original story by Helen Worden Erskine, a writer in the slick-paper journals who got her start on a Denver Newspaper. Peggy Wood and Imogene Coca starred in the Broadway production.

> (The play is) about two devotedly Republican women, an aunt and her niece, who isolate themselves in a hotel room on the night of Franklin D. Roosevelt's election and promise not to emerge again until "the country has been saved from the Democrats." Twenty-seven years later they are still ensconced in their hotel suite, unaware that the GOP has been in Washington for seven years. Then the imminent conversion of the hotel to a clubhouse for Democratic women provokes a crisis. The ladies must be moved.[11-2]

Needless to say, the opening night audience was overrun with laughter.

The final play of the season was Thorton Wilder's 1938 Pulitzer Prize-winning play, *Our Town.*[12] The play is the story of the little community of Grover's Corners, New Hampshire, population 2,642. The story is mainly told through the lives of two families, the Gibbses and the Webbs, whose homes stand side by side.

> Wilder's gentle and compassionate drama is the evocation of theatrical magic. He is unconventional, both in his use of a bare stage, and in the structure of his drama. He uses a narrator, the Stage Manager, whose prose soon fills the stage with life, so that Grover's Corners materializes with only the simplest of stage props - a few chairs and tables.

Coincidentally, Elitch's director, Arthur Sircom, was the choice of Thorton Wilder to direct the first production of the play before its Broadway run.

The critical role of the Stage Manager in its Broadway run was Frank Craven, and in later revivals the role was played by Henry Fonda (1949), Spalding Gray (1988) and Paul Newman (2002). For the Elitch production, the management specially cast well-known actor Wendell Corey as the Stage Manager. Alice Wiley (Mrs. Wendell Corey) also joined the cast and performed the role of Mrs. Gibbs. Thomas Coley and Ludi Claire were excellent as the Webbs.

Marriage of Helen Bonfils to "Tiger Mike"

On April 2, 1959, Helen Bonfils married Edward Michael Davis, the man who had been the chauffeur of Helen and George Somnes for many years. After the marriage, he quit driving her and became an oil wildcatter, doing business as Tiger Oil Company. He liked to be called "Tiger Mike." At the time of the marriage, Helen was 69 years of age and "Tiger Mike" was 28 years of age.

The marriage was performed in upstate New York by a judge. When the news traveled west, all of Denver wondered why Helen married "Tiger Mike," who was to many a mysterious bridegroom.[13-1] She told a friend, that when she was with him, she felt so much younger. According to Haila Stoddard, when they were apart, Helen thought of him obsessively.[13-2]

> It didn't even matter that her eyes were almost level with the top of his prematurely balding head when she was wearing her customary stilt heels. Or that he was a grade-school dropout, smart and sassy and frequently crude and ungrammatical - so unlike the proper people who usually surrounded her.
>
> He was especially different from George (Somnes), dear urbane George, so suave with his pencil-line mustache, handsomely turned out in his dark, pinstriped suits and homburg.[13-3]

With Helen being at the helm of the *Denver Post*, her business advisors, predominantly Donald R. Seawell, rewrote her last will to protect the newspaper, and further, Helen gave all her *Denver Post* stock to the Helen G. Bonfils Foundation, which could dispose of it only to the Employees Stock Trust.[13-4] Predictably, the marriage was not a good one, and ended up in divorce in 1971.

When asked why she married Tiger Mike, she replied that "loneliness is a terrible thing."[14]

In 1957, Arnold B. Gurtler turned over the management of the Gardens to his two sons, John M. Gurtler (commonly known as "Jack") *on the left* and Arnold B. Gurtler Jr. (commonly known as "Budd") *on the right*.

Edward G. Robinson and Budd Gurtler during a nostalgic visit by Robinson to the Theatre (1958)

Chapter Twenty-Seven

(1960 - 1963)

The Death of Mrs. Arnold B. Gurtler
Opening Night - A Change
A Live Audience
"Harvey" Starring Joe E. Brown
The "In-Between" Boredom of an Actor's Life

The 1960 Season

The Death of Mrs. Arnold B. Gurtler [1]

Mrs. Arnold B. Gurtler died at the age of 64 on January 27, 1960 at St. Joseph's Hospital after a long illness. She was born Marie Mulvihill on February 12, 1895 in Pittsburgh, Pennsylvania and came to Denver with her parents, Mr. and Mrs. John M. Mulvihill, about 1900.

> Mrs. Gurtler's interest in the theater began when her father became owner of Elitch Gardens. She accompanied her father and later her husband on many annual trips to New York to choose plays and casts for the Elitch Gardens Theatre.

When John Mulvihill died on January 14, 1930, Mrs. Gurtler and her husband, Arnold B. Gurtler, took over the management of Elitch Gardens and the Theatre. At the time of her death, she was secretary of the Elitch Gardens Company. Mrs. Gurtler was a member of the Denver Club, the Denver Country Club, and the Twelfth Night Club of New York City, a theatrical association.

A requiem high mass was sung at the Holy Family Catholic Church at W. 44th Avenue and Utica Street, after which burial was at Mount Olivet cemetery.

The Plays and The Players

Jean Dalrymple and Charles Robinson's "The Feathered Fauna"
William Inge's "The Dark at the Top of the Stairs"
James M. Barrie's "What Every Woman Knows"
Jerome Lawrence and Robert E. Lee's "The Gang's All Here"
Lorenzo Semple, Jr.'s "Golden Fleecing"
Harry Kurnitz's "Reclining Figure"
Elmer Rice's "Dream Girl"
Robert E. Sherwood's "The Road to Rome"
Dore Schary's "Sunrise at Campobello"
Abe Burrows and Marion and Richard Bissell's "Say, Darling"

Arthur Hill was engaged for the first five plays as Elitch's leading man. Whitfield Connor finished the season as leading man in the final five plays. *Reclining Figure* was Connor's first appearance on the Elitch stage in seven years. He had appeared in numerous plays as the leading man at Elitch from 1949 to 1953.[2-1] Fayne Blackburn, an Oregonian, was the leading lady. Other actors included Joel Marston who returned for his fourth season, having been at Elitch in 1947, 1955 and 1957, and Lawrence Fletcher, who had performed in 31 Broadway productions and returned to Elitch after an absence of nearly two decades.

Joan Van Ark, a 17-year old Boulder High School girl was signed for a prominent role at Elitch in playwright William Inge's *The Dark at the Top of the Stairs*. It was the first time in many years that an ingénue from Colorado was signed to appear in Elitch productions. Among her credits were the leads in *The Diary of Anne Frank* for a local theater group known as the Nomads and in *Brigadoon* for the Boulder Civic Opera.[2-2]

Opening Night - A Change

Opening night was changed to Monday evenings in contrast to the traditional Sunday openings, with performances continued through Saturday evenings. A matinee was presented each Wednesday at 2:00 p.m. The Theatre remained dark on Sunday nights.[2-3] When Helen Bonfils took over the management of the Theatre in the 1964 season, she introduced two performances on Saturday - a twilight performance commencing at 5:30 p.m., followed by a performance at 9:00 p.m.* In the 1967 season the twilight performance was dropped in favor of a Saturday matinee commencing at 2:30 p.m.

Some Plays of the Season - Some Comments

The Feathered Fauna, a comedy by Jean Dalrymple and Charles Robinson, was selected to open the new season as a premiere pre-Broadway tryout. The Theatre was honored by the presence of the playwrights on opening night.[2-3] Miss Dalrymple was a Broadway producer and director of the New York City Center, while Robinson was a former carnival barker, actor, newspaperman (New York Herald Tribune), and co-author (with Kenyon Nicholson) of the 1930s Broadway hit, *Sailor Beware*. The successful presentation of *Sailor Beware* on Broadway was directed by Arthur Sircom, director of the 1960 season Elitch company.[2-4]

Unfortunately, the drama critic, while complimenting the cast of *The Feathered Fauna* for its performance, did not offer consoling remarks for the play's future goal.

> The comedy is certainly funnier than two other pre-Broadway tryouts which have played in Denver in the past season . . . but its Broadway

* In the 1966 season the Saturday twilight performance was changed to begin at 5:00 p.m.

> chances would seem to be minimal at best. Its girl-meets-boy, girl-chases-boy plotting may have sufficed a decade ago, but it lacks substance for the theater of today.[2-5]

Dore Schary's *Sunrise at Campobello* was one of a number of plays centering on the problems of the handicapped, in this case Franklin Delano Roosevelt's battle with polio.

> (The role of Roosevelt was) a particularly difficult part in that, except for the opening scene, Roosevelt is the victim of infantile paralysis and is paralyzed from the hips down. The actor must play most of the scenes in a wheelchair.[2-6]

Connor said that the role of Roosevelt "was perhaps my favorite dramatic role at Elitch." He continued, "That play was one in which the audience's emotional involvement with the characters portrayed was most important. It was written and produced at a time when the memory of FDR was still fresh. I remember one night when I slipped and fell to the floor as I attempted to get up on the crutches. A man gasped in the audience, and I knew that for him it was not the actor who had slipped and fallen but FDR himself."[3]

Elmer Rice's *Dream Girl* is one of his few ventures into light comedy. The play was a gift to the playwright's young wife, actress Betty Field, who gave a brilliant performance in the play on Broadway. Her role was one of the longest roles every written for a woman in the history of the theater. The role required her to be on stage for all but two minutes of the performance.[4] As much as *Dream Girl* is demanding of its title role, the show is a challenge in staging. The comedy is played in 28 scenes.

The musical *Say, Darling* was the first musical presented at Elitch Theatre in 40 years. Jack Haskell, the singing star of the Jack Paar Show, and for three years on Dave Garroway's "Today," was brought in specifically for the singing lead.[5-1] The play was written by Abe Burrows and Richard and Marion Bissell with the music and lyrics by Jules Styne, Betty Comden and Adolph Green.

> (The play is a musical) about the making of a musical. It is, in fact, a rather autobiographical account of the misadventures of a corn-fed mid-western novelist who comes to Broadway to adapt his best-selling book into a musical ...[2-7]

Coincidentally enough, playwright Richard Bissell, achieved this goal in real life. He, together with George Abbott, helped create the hit musical *Pajama Game* (1954), which was based on Bissel's novel of labor relations in a Davenport, Iowa pajama factory, *7 1/2 Cents*.[2-7]

Because of the enthusiastic demand for tickets for *Say, Darling*, a second week of performances was added by the Elitch management.[2-8]

The Stage Manager

John Holden was the stage manager for the 1960 season, having previously managed or directed over 250 productions, many with the biggest names in the theater. He also was production manager for five years with the late Lee Shubert.[5-2]

A stage manager is the director's right hand. The stage manager must know the play as well as the director, for when the director leaves, it is the stage manager who keeps the performances exactly as the director set them.

The stage manager oversees the entire show each time it is performed.

> He must be ready for all emergencies. Often doors stick, phone bells fail to operate, light bulbs blow out, dimmers burn up. Often actors forget to carry necessary articles used on stage. The stage manager must check with each actor to see that nothing is forgotten.
>
> Every article you see on the stage has been carefully checked and re-checked by the stage manager, who sees that each night everything is as the actors have been used to ... a chair or a table or a cigarette lighter an inch out of place will upset an actor. All doors and windows must be checked, either open or shut when each act begins.[5-3]

John Holden amusingly revealed an occasion when he allowed his six-year-old nephew to watch rehearsals of a mystery play he was doing. The nephew came to the first matinee of the show.

> The actors on the stage were searching for a hidden message. "Where is it? Where can it be?" the leading lady cried. My nephew's voice came from the audience. "Look in the vase on the mantel."[5-4]

The 1961 Season

The season began with Samuel Taylor and Cornelia Otis Skinner's *The Pleasure of His Company* and ended with *Little Mary Sunshine,* a musical by Rick Besoyan (book, music and lyrics). Other popular plays presented included Jean Giraudoux's *The Mad Woman of Chaillott*, Moss Hart's *Light Up the Sky* and Howard Lindsey and Russel Crouse's *State of the Union*. Members of the resident company included Joel Marston, Pat Sully, Lawrence Fletcher and David Whorf.

The Elitch management could not have selected a better play than *The Pleasure of His Company,* a comedy, to launch the 70th anniversary season of The Elitch Theatre. The play's single setting is the living room of a house high on a hill in San Francisco.

> (The principal character is) Pogo Poole, the global playboy who returns to San Francisco to attend the wedding of the daughter he has not seen for 15 years.

> The motivation of the prodigal parent ... (is to) disrupt his daughter's wedding - to take her away from a predictable future of a marriage to a wholesome young rancher and to sail the far waters to the fabled isles of Greece.
>
> The daughter, whose instincts respond to her father's call to undetermined adventure and to the romantic lure of the exotic lands, ... is sensible enough to realize that mother knows best and that her future lies in the stable marriage promised by her rancher fiancé.[6-1]

The musical *Little Mary Sunshine* is a warm and amusing spoof satirizing operettas of the 1920s such as *Rose Marie* and *Rio Rita*. Its setting is Colorado. The songs are in the tradition of operetta, such as "Colorado Love Call," a romantic duet, and Miss Mary's "Look For a Sky of Blue," but "they stand on their own as musical numbers and the (Elitch) audience went out humming and whistling them."[7]

Bonard Productions

Helen Bonfils and Haila Stoddard had previously consulted Helen's attorney, Donald R. Seawell, with a view toward producing Broadway plays. The corporation called Bonard Productions had been created in 1952. Bonard Productions, in association with Michael Davis, were co-producers of *A Thurber Carnival*, which had a long Broadway run and established a Central City record for attendance and box office gross during the summer of 1960 when the New York production was moved to Colorado for a month.[6-2] In 1961, the Bonfils-Stoddard team produced Noel Coward's musical comedy *Sail Away*, which opened in Boston en route to its Broadway opening at the Broadhurst Theater on October 3rd. The play is a satire on life and character aboard a cruise ship.

The 1962 Season

Mala Powers and Charles Braswell were the leads for the first five plays, and Gene Raymond and Jan Clayton were the leads for the last five plays.

Mala Powers was Roxanne opposite Jose Ferrer in the movie version of *Cyrano de Bergerac* and was making her debut in summer stock this season at Elitch. Charles Braswell was featured the past season as the purser in the Bonard Productions' presentation of Noel Coward's *Sail Away*, which ran more than 100 performances on Broadway. Jan Clayton was the original Julie Jordan in the Broadway cast of *Carousel*, and played the mother in the "Lassie" TV series. Gene Raymond was a known star of films and television.

Among the plays offered were two murder-mystery dramas, *The Unexpected Guest* and *Write Me a Murder*. A murder-mystery drama is a dramatic art form with many variations.

> There is the whodunit, the problem as to the murderer's identity which if the playwright is successful is fitted together like a completed jigsaw puzzle as the curtain falls. Then there is the will-he-catch-him in which the audience knows the identity of the killer and the problem is whether he will get away with his dastardly crime.[8-1]

The Unexpected Guest by Agatha Christie is an example of the former, in which "everyone on the Elitch roster gets into the act and each of them, with the exception of the police inspector, becomes a suspect at one time or another." The play is vintage Christie who keeps the audience at bay while leading them "up and down blind alleys which are strewn with false clues." Christie plays were usually well-received. *The Unexpected Guest* was no exception.[8-1]

Write Me a Murder, the other murder-mystery presented, was written by playwright Frederick Knott, author of *Dial M For Murder*. As in the case of *Dial M for Murder*, the play fell into the watch-him-do-it category. The drama critic's review of the play noted that "some of the ragged edges of the plot had not been honed down at the opening night performance" and that "a clue to murder was left inadvertently in plain view of (the) constable and audience." While the critic recognized that the performances were generally competent, the play was "difficult for a stock company to perfect in a week of rehearsals." He then added that "things should be shipshape in a night or so, however."[8-2]

Kiss Me Kate, rated one of the best musical comedy Broadway plays (1953) in many years, was the final attraction of the Elitch season. It was the third musical comedy presented at Elitch in its recent history, the others having been *Say Darling* and *Little Mary Sunshine*.

A Live Audience

In an interview with Larry Tajiri, the drama editor for the *Denver Post*, Mala Powers said, "I don't know when I've worked as hard, but I'm having a delightful time at Elitch. I've done radio, television and motion pictures, but the stage is my favorite medium. Nothing can substitute for a live audience." In comparing those mediums, Tajiri noted that, "there are scripts to hold and read on radio, idiot cards in television and short takes in films. The theater is the only one of the acting mediums which demands total knowledge of a script at one time."[8-3]

Understandably, many actors who have achieved success in film and television do not experience a sense of professional completeness unless they have successfully met the challenge of live theater.

The "Faithful Ones" [9]

The "Faithful Ones" was a special group of Elitch Theatre fans who regularly attended Wednesday matinee performances. This audience of fans is said to have been regularly in attendance for 50 years.

"Seldom do good seats become available," said an Elitch spokesman.

He cited one occasion where a woman willed her theater seat to her niece. And, another, where a fan phoned to say she saw someone's obituary in the paper and wanted to speak for the four seats the woman held in the eighth row.

Choice seats for the Wednesday shows seem to have become a sort of status symbol, he said.

Clearly, if the fans enjoy the Wednesday matinees, so must the actors. Said an actor, "Wednesdays are the highlights of our week. It's fun to play to an extremely appreciative audience - which these ladies are."

The 1963 Season

That Time of Year Again

It was that time of year again when one yearns for a leisurely stroll along the covered walk that skirts W. 38th Avenue inside Elitch Gardens. It was that time of year for a fine meal at the Orchard Cafe before attending the summer Theatre and perhaps a few dances afterwards at the Trocadero before going home to bed.

Whitfield Connor returned for the first three plays of the season. He had recently appeared on Broadway in *There Was a Little Girl*. He "stepped into the play almost at the last minute when Louis Jean Heydt, playing the father of Jane Fonda, collapsed and died in the wings during the Boston run. Next morning Connor was asked to take over the role. He studied his sides on the plane from New York to Boston." [10-1] Mala Powers was the leading lady for the first half of the season. Boyd Dumrose was the new stage designer. John Holden returned as director.

The final play of the season featured Joe E. Brown in the role of Elwood P. Dowd in Mary Chase's *Harvey*. The play was awarded the Pulitzer Prize for Drama in 1945. Dowd's dearest friend is Harvey, a six-foot-plus rabbit, invisible to all but a select few.

The *Rocky Mountain News* review of the play favorably commented on the performance of Joe E. Brown.

> Joe E. Brown IS the lovable lush, Elwood P. Dowd. The enormous white hare becomes almost visible to the audience as Brown smiles at him ever so sweetly or smoothes down his long ears.
>
> Dowd's wise and philosophical view of life, as seen through a whiskey glass, also makes very good sense at times when expressed by Brown.[11]

Brown was no stranger to the role of Elwood P. Dowd.

> The comic said that sometime during the run of *Harvey* at Elitch, he'll have invoked the character of the lovable Elwood for the 2,000th time.

This means that he'll have played the part more than any other living person, in addition to performing it in more countries than anyone.

"I've performed it in Australia, Canada, England and Hawaii," said Brown. "I took over the part in the New York company when Frank Fay, the originator, gave it up, and played it seven months before it went on the road."[10-2]

The "In-Between" Boredom of an Actor's Life

Karl Malden, an Academy Award winner and highly regarded in his profession, is frank to admit the boredom an actor often faces loafing around the house between jobs.

Waiting is the most difficult part of the acting profession. It's the nature of our work and is a problem for me. I would like to be associated with a college or university as a teacher working with young people.

Right now I'm looking for the courage to do it. You need courage because ... an actor sits by the phone. I might be someplace else when the phone rings and miss out on a job. * [10-3]

Denver Public Library Western History Collection - *Rocky Mountain News Archives*

Whitfield Connor returned to Elitch Theatre in 1960 as leading man in the last five plays, having previously appeared as the leading man in numerous plays from 1949 to 1953.

* Of course, with the current availability of cell phones, this lessens the problem.

Chapter Twenty-Eight

(1964 - 1965)

Helen Bonfils Leases the Theatre
The "Star Package System"
The Larry Tajiri Awards

The 1964 Season

An Important Conversation

(In 1964, Arnold B. Gurtler told Helen Bonfils) that Elitch had been losing money hand over fist. For one thing, it was a resident company and these had become costly dinosaurs. Several years earlier, Helen had paid for a remodeling of the theater and she held a mortgage on it. Now Arnold was asking her to take it over altogether.

"If I don't, what will become of it?" she asked.

Arnold walked over to the window and gazed out. "I'll tear it down," he said.

For Helen, that was unthinkable.[1]

Helen Bonfils Leases the Theatre

The Elitch Gardens entire complex, including the Theatre, was owned and controlled by the Gurtlers under a corporation they established as Elitch Amusements, Inc. When the Gurtlers decided to resign from managing the Theatre following the 1963 season, Helen Bonfils offered to guarantee the ongoing program of summer theater productions. She was familiar with Elitch Theatre, having played numerous character roles in its plays. Her husband, George Somnes, had directed plays at Elitch for many years.

Miss Bonfils entered into an agreement with Elitch Amusements, Inc. to lease and operate the Theatre for one year, with a right to renew the lease from year to year. She became the founder of The Elitch Theatre Company, which she operated as an individual enterprise, and became the producer for the first season of operation at Elitch in 1964. It was agreed that the name of the Theatre was not to be changed, but would continue to be known and called the Elitch Gardens Theatre.

Helen Bonfils functioned as the producer and named Whitfield Connor as her executive administrator and general manager of theater operations for the 1964 season. Whitfield Connor was well-suited for the responsibility, having had an extensive background in film and theater and having been a leading man from 1949 through many seasons at Elitch.[2-1]

On February 17, 1964, Helen sent a letter to Whitfield Connor, which was to become their agreement, outlining his responsibilities, among them being the following:

> In your capacity as Executive Administrator or General Manager, you will attend to the day-to-day functions and details associated with promoting and maintaining a successful theatrical season at The Elitch Gardens Theatre in Denver. Your duties will include making the necessary arrangements with actors and actresses of outstanding caliber and the hiring of theatrical troupes to present theatrical plays for one-week engagements only, with a different theatrical play to be shown the public each succeeding week during the theatrical season, as denoted above.
>
> We will endeavor to bring in only the best theatrical presentations, keeping in mind, however, the necessity of preventing expenses from getting unduly high, and with the objective of having a profitable operation ... You are free to negotiate with agents or agencies, or directly with theater companies, or individual actors and actresses for the purpose of securing high-quality dramatic productions during this summer season.* [3]

Whitfield Connor's salary for the 1964 season was $200 a week from February 3rd to April 30th and $300 a week from May lst to the closing of the season on about September 5, 1964, plus 50% of the net profits as determined before taxes at the end of the season.

Gurtler Announces Helen Bonfils Role as Producer

In the first Elitch Theatre Program of the 1964 season, Arnold B. Gurtler announced that Helen Bonfils was to assume the guidance of the Theatre. The letter addressed to the patrons of the Theatre stated:

> As you, our patrons, know, Elitch's Theatre has a long, proud heritage. However, with changing times and changing influences in the world of theater, we are content to let our past be prologue and to see the curtain go up on a new era in our historic Theatre.
>
> It is very gratifying to me, personally and professionally, that our beloved Theatre is going to be under the guidance of Miss Helen Bonfils, who has spent so many years with me at Elitch and who appreciates, as I do, the very special place the Elitch Theatre holds in the hearts of Denverites and the theatrical world. I'm sure our audiences are in accord with me on this.

* The letter provided further that Helen be consulted before entering into any written commitments or contracts; however, "where time and circumstances prevent my actively examining such contracts and signing the same, then it is understood that you will have the authority to do so and bind me. I will furnish to you, in such instances, telegraphic or letter authority for so committing me to a particular contract or contracts."

> I know of no one who could be more capable of assuming this obligation and of maintaining the traditions of the oldest summer theater in the country.
>
> The plays and stars they (Bonfils and Connor) are bringing us for our 1964 season will add great luster to our already brilliant past.

That summer, Helen Bonfils introduced the "Star Package System" of plays. The Theatre was profitable.

The "Star Package System"

> Denver's Elitch Gardens Theatre will feature the top shows touring the straw hat circuit this summer. Producer Helen Bonfils and Whitfield Connor, executive administrator, have switched the Elitch format from that of the resident company of professionals to the touring summer show.
>
> Heretofore, the summer packages, topped by stage, film and TV personalities, never ventured west of Chicago. Now Denver's entry into the field via Elitch may lead eventually to a national circuit. The trend in summer theater currently is to the touring show instead of the former pattern in which the same actors performed 10 shows in 10 weeks.[2-2]

With the popularity of television, a summer stock company became less appealing to theatergoers, who sought to see the television and film stars they had come to like.

Helen Bonfils and Whitfield Connor instituted what became known as the "star package system," wherein entire casts headed by a recognized star came to Denver for each new production of the season. At times, if a minor role or walk-on was needed for the performance, it could be filled by a local actor. The "star package system" proved to be a successful innovation among the fans at Elitch and they flocked to see their theatrical celebrities. Elitch was the first summer theater west of Chicago to book the summer package shows.[2-2] Larry Tajiri, drama editor for the *Denver Post*, wrote:

> Miss Bonfils' pioneering in this aspect of summer theater may inspire other of the West's leading summer theaters, such as those in Phoenix and La Jolla, Calif., to join in instituting a policy of importing the package shows which are touring such leading eastern summer theaters as those in Westport, Conn., Mineola, N. Y. and the Paper Mill in New Jersey.[2-3]

The "star package system" had a significant advantage, since the actors would have played together elsewhere in their tour earlier in the season or even during a prior season. It made for a successful ensemble performance. In ensemble acting there is an emphasis on an integration of all roles in the play, including that of the star performer, so that the actors gel with one another. Just knowing lines is not enough. For example, in the very favorable review of the play *Send Me No Flowers*, starring Van Johnson during the 1977 season, the drama editor commented.

> Most of this group have worked together on and off for the past two years in this show, and the professionalism and technique virtually guaranteed a show as successful as was opening night's.[4]

For many theaters, progression to a star package system was an unsuccessful learning experience. For some theaters "let's have stars" resulted in a "personal appearance star system" with a resident company. But while stars were attracted to the idea, they were not always interested in spending time rehearsing with resident companies.

> Instead, they wanted to arrive at the last possible moment, have a quick dress rehearsal with the company, and then perform. This scheme proved detrimental on several levels. First, there was no time to build an ensemble performance until, with any luck, the end of the engagement, at which point the star and the company had had a week of "rehearsals" before a paying audience. Second, many opening nights were a shambles because there had been little or no rehearsal and the stars were busy being stars rather than actors engaging in a role. Third, many Hollywood and, in the 1950s, television actors lacked stage training and could not really act.
>
> Their inadequacies were all the more prominent when supported by experienced performers.[5-1]

In such circumstances, audiences quickly tired of the result and stayed away from the theaters, causing some to fold.[5-2]

In Denver, the "star package system" was well-received by audiences. For many reasons, the Elitch management was able to engage top stars and plays for the season. The Elitch Theatre had acquired a national reputation and to have played here was a boost to a star's credentials. Denver's mile-high climate away from the humidity of larger cities was attractive to many stars. Also, Helen Bonfils was well known and respected in the business world as head of the *Denver Post* newspaper, and she was well-connected in theatrical circles as an actress and as a producer of shows on Broadway. Stars that played Elitch brought with them extensive experience in theater and often in film as well.*

The summer package tours usually did not travel with scenery or lighting, leaving the responsibility to the host theater to supply those elements based on detailed

* According to Mr. Gurtler, as a rule, "Elitch's has a code of long standing, that no actor or actress in the cast will be engaged without having a considerable background of Broadway experience." *Rocky Mountain News*, Jun 1, 1947, p. 24.

floor plans and designs provided by the packager, either by the star or by someone hired to organize the tour. The summer houses maintained a full technical staff so that the packages could tour without stagehands and other backstage personnel.

The staff at the theater arranged ahead of time all the necessary accommodations for the needs of the touring personnel. A list of hotel accommodations and even private residences was provided. Transportation was made available as well as medical doctors and nurses in the event of an emergency. Many actors who came to Denver for the first time were not prepared for the effect of being in a higher altitude. At times, the thin air affected their breathing, so oxygen was supplied until they got adjusted.[6]

Walter Pidgeon agreed to come to Elitch for this 1964 season to perform in *Take Her, She's Mine* only after Miss Bonfils and Connor convinced him that Denver's mile-high altitude was not a deterrent to acting.* [2-2] Media personnel were notified to arrange the interview of performers by the press to publicize the stars and the plays. Members of the press, special invitees and prominent local citizens would meet the actors at a party gathering in an area behind the stage following the opening night performance.[7]

The "star package system" format was expensive and for many summer stock venues, the expense was prohibitive. The hope was always that the expense for the package would be offset by the theater draw because of the stars. The economics of the system depended on many factors, which included the seating capacity, the location and the drawing power of the host theater. The economic factors favored Elitch Theatre for many reasons.[5-3] The response by the public to the new star policy was favorable and imminent.

Tickets for *Kind Sir,* the opening play of the season, were virtually all sold within three days after the box-office opened.[2-4] Arlene Francis, the star personality and actress of the play, was reported to have "conquered a Denver first night audience" and successfully launched the star policy.[2-5]

The Denver Post reported that Miss Bonfils' "highly successful 'big name-big play' policy has brought new luster to Elitch resulting in standing room only for many productions."[8-1]

* Walter Pidgeon expressed his concern about the high altitude in an interview. In 1923, when he was just getting his start in theater, "we got to Denver and I suddenly began to get awful headaches and nosebleeds. I was singing and dancing in the act and it probably was the strenuous nature of my performance in Denver's high altitude which precipitated my troubles." Pidgeon added, however, that the role in *Take Her She's Mine* "doesn't compare with that of *The Happiest Millionaire* in its physical demands. I knew I would have no problems with it in Denver and I haven't." *Denver Post*, Jul 2, 1964, p. 22.

Linda Purl, who appeared at Elitch in the feminine lead in *Snacks* during the 1984 season, noticed a difference between performing in Colorado and other places. "The altitude. We all felt it." She stated that in one heated scene during rehearsal, "I thought I was going to pass out." *Gazette Telegraph*, Aug 9, 1984, p. F2 (article is contained at History Colorado, Denver, Elitch Theatre Collection 1364, Box 9, File Folder 768).

Star Packaging Contracts

The "star package" engagements were accomplished by the signing of a number of contracts outlining the responsibility of the parties. Although each packaging agency had its own contract format and expression, they were similar in their differences. Essentially, the packaging agency would be responsible for providing the theater with a fully rehearsed production including costumes and sound effects. The theater would provide sets, stage manager and any and all related personnel required by unions, including a theater for a technical rehearsal.

Incident to this, the packaging agency would include the following:

(1) Contracts, bios, photos and published material for all actors in the production.

(2) Housing preference for all actors in the production.

(3) Routing sheet for entire tour.

(4) A property list, scenery floor plan, light plots, cue sheet and master script.

(5) Actors' Equity Association contracts of the actors in the play.

The theater would be required to provide the following:

(1) Submit to the packaging agency box office statements after each performance and final statement and payment at the conclusion of the last performance.

(2) Pay for the transportation of those persons in the production as provided in the Actors' Equity Association stock jobbing book.

(3) Provide living accommodations for all persons in the production, in accordance with standards and rules presented by the Actors' Equity Association.

The various contracts also contained specific provisions relating to the requests and desires of the actors, as for example:

> The ACTOR will have first choice of a dressing room in the Theatre and such dressing room shall be air conditioned.

When such a contract request was made by an actor, since Elitch Theatre did not have air conditioning, the contract condition was changed to read "shall be air cooled." *

> The THEATRE agrees that ACTOR shall have no liability in connection

* In a letter from Christopher Kirkland to Jack Bean dated Apr 16, 1987, regarding the engagement of Mitzi Gaynor, he wrote, "There is no air conditioning or heating in the Theatre, which is cooled, when necessary, by a swamp cooler. We supply fans whenever necessary." History Colorado, Denver, Elitch Theatre Collection 1364, Box 10, File Folder 808.

with salary paid to dresser, which shall be provided by the THEATRE.

In all billing credits ACTOR'S name shall appear in the center top line, immediately above the title in a type and size and boldness and prominence no less than 100% of type used in the title.

THEATRE agrees to obtain prior written approval from ACTOR for all biographical material concerning the ACTOR, before such material is released for programs.

THEATRE shall provide a car for ACTOR'S exclusive use for duration of ACTOR'S stay in Denver.

The contract of Keir Dullea for his appearance in *Same Time Next Year* in 1977 contained this provision for the exclusive use of a car. However, an earlier contract with the leading lady of the show, Rosemary Prinz, contained the provision "ACTRESS to share use of car with Keir Dullea," which was not binding on Dullea.[9-1]

Most important, the contract will state the total cost of the production (e.g., $11,000), plus a percentage (e.g., 33 1/3%) of gross receipts over (e.g., $51,000), with the understanding that the gross potential of the theater is (e.g., $60,000) in the event of full capacity.

Payment of Royalties *

In addition to the theater's expenses under the packaging contracts, it is responsible to pay royalties for the use of the play. This is arranged through Samuel French, Inc. publishers of the play scripts. As a general rule the royalties are as follows:

4% of the entire weekly gross up to $9,000.00

5% of the entire weekly gross if $9,000.00 but not more than $15,000.00

6% of the entire weekly gross if over $15,000.00

Stage Designers and the Advance Director

As previously noted, under the star package contract, it is the responsibility of the theater to prepare the set for each upcoming production. The stage designer is an important part of the process. Throughout the years, the Elitch management had the good fortune of having stage designers who fully understood and appreciated the critical role they played toward making a play a success. Among those who have appeared at Elitch was the soft-spoken native of Ireland, Harry Cummins. Cummins was one of the nation's top stage designers, having done sets on Broadway, such as the musical *Wonderful Town*, which starred Rosalind Russell,

* Information contained in this and the prior section is based on an examination of equity contracts and other documents in History Colorado, Denver, Elitch Theatre Collection 1364, Box 7, File Folders 647 to 656.

and for the NBCTV shows such as the Colgate Comedy Hour and the Jimmy Durante Show.

Boyd Dumrose was another set designer at Elitch for many years. Some of the Elitch stars, who performed the same plays on Broadway, said that the Dumrose sets "were more attractive and comfortable than the original ones." Dumrose was particularly sensitive to set design details because he had been an actor. He said, "I try to do a set in such a way that the actor can concentrate on the role - not technical difficulties."[10-1]

In preparing to design a set, the stage designer reads the script of the upcoming play and carefully scrutinizes the advance information provided by the touring company, such as the list of props, the lighting and the scenery floor plan - in essence, a complete blueprint for the set design. Antique shops, department stores, Goodwill Industries and other establishments, as well as other theaters, often cooperated to make furniture or items available on loan to Elitch, and, in doing so, benefited from free advertising as their cooperation was acknowledged in the Elitch Theatre program. Furniture items were also often rented for productions.

On Monday, the stage designer reviews the information provided with the carpenters and turns the construction over to the workmen. "Blocking" must be kept in mind by the stage designer. This involves the specific moves an actor or actress has to make on stage in predetermined areas. Where must an actor stare out a window? Where are the doors necessary?

> At times, special requirements of an actor also influence details. Olympia Dukakis, actress in *The Time of the Cuckoo*, broke her foot the first week the show was on the road. Miss Dukakis designed herself some long gowns, pulled a black stocking over her cast, and the audience saw a lovely graceful lady on stage. Part of the grace was due to the strategic placement of furniture. Miss Dukakis always had something to grasp unobtrusively, rising, sitting, or making an entrance or exit.[10-2]

Next, the stage designer and the prop man set out to obtain the necessary props, paint, and fabric material necessary to complete the set. Obviously, this has to be accomplished within a very short period of time.

> By Wednesday, the advance director for next week's play arrives. This director checks over the myriad of details of the setting plans and informs the backstage crew of any changes in the running schedule - lighting cues, sound cues, color of the star's clothing.[10-2]

Following the advance director's advice and approval, the appropriate changes and finishing touches are applied to finalize the set.

> Saturday night, when the curtain rings down for the last time on the current week's play, the theater explodes into activity almost before the

crowd has filed out. The old set is moved out into the wings, to be taken apart later, and the new set pushed into place.[10-2]

At that point, the electricians make the necessary connections for the doorbell to ring, head mikes to work, the lamp to light up and the spotlights to shine in the right places. The crew then runs through a technical rehearsal without actors, checking on lights, sound and the movement of props between scenes.

The previous company leaves by noon on Sunday, while the new cast of players usually arrives sometime between noon and 5:00 p.m. and is taken to the theater to check out the set and the dressing rooms, after which they are taken to their various accommodations. After dinner, the cast may hold a Sunday night rehearsal, followed by a technical dress rehearsal on Monday afternoon. They open with a full audience on Monday evening. Each show continues for a week, with a matinee on Wednesday and Saturday. Come Sunday, it starts all over again.

The advance director usually remains to see the opening of the play, and then travels to the city where the play will next open.

As one stage designer put it, "once the play opens, we consider it last week's production. I'll admit I feel a pang when a stage setting goes down. Our art is complete only when the actors are on stage, the lighting on, the music being played. Our work does not remain to be admired. A week, and it's gone. But, it lingers on in the minds of the audience and the actors. And there is always next week's play." * [10-2]

Stage Designers - Some General Comments

The role of the stage designer requires a highly developed skill. He must provide scenery that is "consistent with the play for which it is intended, that is, with the mood, style and meaning of the play" and the director's concept.[11-1] He must coordinate numerous elements, such as lighting, colors, costumes, furniture and styles, to create an environment within which the actor moves and releases the energy of the play. The stage designer's role is more than simply creating a pretty stage picture. The distinction between scenery as a large and pretty picture and scenery as part of a total stage production can never be overemphasized.

> Frequently in the theater - particularly in an elaborate production - the audience breaks into applause when the visual image of the set is revealed as the curtain rises. There is nothing wrong with admiring the beauty or excitement of a stage picture. Taken to extremes, however, the emphasis on illustration or a "pretty picture" runs counter to the purpose

* In a letter from Christopher Kirkland to Jack Bean, husband and agent of Mitzi Gaynor, dated Apr 16, 1987, he stated: "(T)he technical demands (of a set) rarely allow us to rehearse on stage until Monday afternoon. We found Debbie Reynolds a room with a piano at the Oxford Hotel, where she was staying. We are trying to provide Bernadette Peters with a rehearsal room for Sunday." History Colorado, Denver, Elitch Theatre Collection 1364, Box 10, File Folder 808.

> of scene design. If members of the audience spend their time admiring the beauty of the scenery, they may miss the words of the playwright and the actions of the performers, and as a result, they may not grasp the meaning of the play. This suggests how important it is to have a stage setting in tune with the total production.[11-2]

The scenic designer has imaginative flexibility in his ultimate design for his play. There is, indeed, "a difference between interior decorations in real life and set designs for the stage." Robert Edmond Jones (1887-1954), an outstanding American scenic designer, stated:

> A good scene should be not a picture, but an image. Scene-designing is not what most people imagine it is - a branch of interior decorating. There is no more reason for a room on a stage to be a reproduction of an actual room than for an actor who plays the part of Napoleon to be Napoleon or for an actor who plays Death in the old morality play to be dead. Everything that is actual must undergo a strange metamorphosis, a kind of sea-change, before it can become truth in the theater.[11-3]

While a stage signals an atmosphere to the viewer, "in the same way that rooms in real life do, the scene designer must go a step further ... the theater is not life; it resembles life. It has both the opportunity and the obligation to be more than mere reproduction ..."[11-3]

First Season of Plays Under the "Star Package System"

Needless to say, Denver audiences anxiously waited to welcome to the Elitch Theatre a season of familiar Hollywood, television and theater personalities and stars. The first season of stars and plays under the "star package system" were:

Arlene Francis in "Kind Sir"
Walter Pidgeon in "Take Her, She's Mine"
Roger Smith in "Sunday in New York"
Cesar Romero in "Strictly Dishonorable"
Peggy Cass in "Bachelor's Wife"
(titled "Lullaby" when first brought to Broadway)
Barbara Bel Geddes in "The Constant Wife"
Cyril Ritchard and Cornelia Otis Skinner
in
"The Irregular Verb to Love"
Hal March and Marjorie Lord in "The Wayward Stork"
Darren McGavin in "A Thousand Clowns"
Evelyn Wyckoff in "The Sound of Music"

Cesar Romero returned to the stage in Preston Sturges' comedy, *Strictly*

Dishonorable, the show in which he had appeared more than three decades earlier. The play was praised in the year it was first produced on Broadway as "the best comedy of the season." The show ran for 557 performances, during which young Romero was chosen to replace Tullio Carminati in the Broadway production. He was then called to Hollywood where he made a career in film. The Elitch performance was his first stage encounter since he had started film making. His performance was rewarded with plentiful applause by a near-capacity audience.[2-6]

> The fact that Romero has been able to step back into his stage role after such a long absence, during which he made films in Hollywood, testifies to his durability both as a performer and as a star personality.[2-6]

Barbara Bel Geddes, one of the American theater's foremost actresses, appeared at Elitch in Somerset Maugham's comedy, *The Constant Wife*. She appeared for at least two years in each of three Broadway plays: *The Moon is Blue, Cat on a Hot Tin Roof* and *Mary, Mary*. "I've wanted to come to Denver ever since Wink (Windsor Lewis) came home four summers ago with his pocket full of rocks and with silver buckles and western hats. This is my first tour and I love it," said Miss Bel Geddes. Lewis, her husband, had spent the summer of 1960 as director at the Elitch Theatre.[2-7]

Stage Design - Kind Sir

Sometimes, even with every possible precaution, things go astray and, in this regard, Elitch had its share of theater stories. For example, Boyd Dumrose had visited Arlene Francis in New York, in anticipation of her performance in *Kind Sir* to be played at Elitch, so his design colors would not clash. She showed him the royal blue dress she was going to wear. He chose a gold couch for the set. However, before the play arrived in Denver, Miss Francis decided to substitute a gold dress in place of the blue. In the play, she sat on the couch of identical color and disappeared except for her face and hands. Since the furniture could not be easily changed, she gracefully bought another dress to wear.[12]

Stage Design - Bachelor's Wife

There have been times when a traditional stage design touches upon an actor's personal stage superstition. While an actor's wishes are respected whenever possible, the stagehand crew cannot foresee every possible situation. In the stage setting of *Bachelor's Wife*, a decoration of fruit, fish, and fowl appeared. "Take it down," pleaded Peggy Cass. "Dead fowl or fish is bad luck on the stage."[10-2]

Neil Simon and the Denver Connection

Neil Simon returned to Denver after a 19-year absence to attend the opening of his play *Barefoot in the Park* in the Central City Opera House.

In an interview with Larry Tajiri, the *Denver Post* drama critic, Simon said, "Denver is where I learned to write." Simon went on to explain his connection with Denver.

I was 18 years old and had just gotten into the Air Force in August, 1945, when the war ended. Instead of going to gunnery school, I wound up at Lowry Field. A call went out for "anyone who wanted to write" and I volunteered. I was sent to see a captain and he said: "You're the sports editor of the Rev-Meter."

I hadn't done much writing before and I was pretty nervous, but I learned to write on the paper.

While I was at Lowry I used to come in to see the shows at Elitch Theatre. I guess I was interested in the theater even in those days.[2-8]

1965 Season - The Elitch Theatre Company Incorporates[9-2]

Helen Bonfils decided to incorporate The Elitch Theatre Company. This was done on May 26, 1965 as The Elitch Theatre Company, a corporation chartered to do business as a theater. Helen Bonfils was issued ownership of all the stock of the corporation and in exchange she assigned to the corporation all her right, title and interest in The Elitch Theatre Company, which included the lease of the Theatre and the right of renewal, and "all advance bookings of attractions and all advance ticket sales for the 1965 season and all physical assets owned by her and used in connection with the business of The Elitch Theatre Company." The lease agreement for the Theatre provided that the name of the Theatre not be changed and that it continue to be known as and called Elitch Gardens Theatre. In addition to the stock issued to Miss Bonfils, further consideration to her included the corporation's assumption "of all outstanding commitments and liabilities of the business and the agreement of the corporation to hold her (Miss Bonfils) harmless on account thereof."

Whitfield Connor continued to be executive administrator and general manager of the Theatre. Miss Bonfils was designated as president of the corporation and producer of the attractions to be presented by the corporation.

Whitfield Connor's duties and responsibilities for the 1965 season were the same as for the 1964 season, while his salary was slightly increased to $300 per week retroactive to February 1, 1965, and continuing until the close of the theatrical season on or about mid-September, plus 50% of the net profits, as determined before taxes at the end of the season.

The Season and the Stars

Among the stars in the 1965 season were Eve Arden, Jean Pierre Aumont, Hermione Gingold, Kitty Carlisle, Hal March, Arlene Francis and Ralph Meeker

Overall, Elitch had a successful season for its audiences, who were able to enjoy an evening with some of their favorite movie and television stars, while getting caught up on recent Broadway hits, such as *Two for the Seesaw*, the two-character play which appeared on Broadway with Henry Fonda and Anne Bancroft, and *Ready When You Are, C.B.* The audiences were also treated to *Mrs. Dally Has a Lover,* a new play by William Hanley that was slated for Broadway.

> In contrast to presentations by resident stock companies which must rehearse the next week's play while performing nightly in another production, touring companies, like those appearing this year at Elitch Theatre, have the advantage of being perfectly rehearsed. Cast members are completely familiar with their play because they have been presenting it for many weeks, sometimes years, and are able to give the audience the ultimate interpretation of each role, each situation, each line.[8-2]

Hermione Gingold - Comments in an Interview

Hermione Gingold, Britain's gift to comic genius, appeared at Elitch in the comedy *Oh Dad, Poor Dad, Mama's Hung You in the Closet and I'm Feelin' So Sad.*

In an interview, she stressed the importance of audiences to actors - particularly how much it means if an audience is receptive and warm in its attitude.

> "If only audiences knew how much they mean to a play, how much its success depends on them," she said. "They must give warmth and even love. And hold off the coughing! If I owned a theater, I'd have a doctor in the vestibule to examine everyone before they were allowed to go in. Maybe that's why college students are fabulous to play for: they don't cough."[8-3]

She then commented on the mindset of an actor, how it is centered in the theater, and how different it is from the "world outside."

> "I remember doing a show in England during the war," she said. "Someone came in with news of a disaster and said, 'Something terrible has happened.' My first reaction was, 'Don't tell me the scenery hasn't arrived!'"[8-3]

Stage Design - Beekman Place

Occasionally the stage crew had a bit of fun with the actors. In *Beekman Place,* the view from the stage through the apartment windows revealed a number of factory signs. Although the signs were too small to be read by the audience, they were quite legible to the actors, and each sign carried the name of one of the performers. Eve Arden, for instance, could see a sign reading "Eve's Lumber Company."[10-2]

The Larry Tajiri Awards

Larry Tajiri, the drama editor of the *Denver Post* for nine years, passed away on February 12, 1965. On August 30, 1965, about 400 persons attended the first Larry Tajiri Memorial Awards banquet at the Albany Hotel in Denver. Five awards were presented to five persons or troupes who had made outstanding contributions to the living theater in the Rocky Mountain area. It was the first such major award established in that part of the country. The entertainment for the evening was a musical revue titled *The Highlights of Broadway*. A host of telegrams paying tribute to the event were received from such celebrities as Henry Fonda, Paul Newman, Natalie Wood and Victor Borge. Producer Harold Prince wired: "The shows I sent to Broadway were always judged constructively by Larry Tajiri."[8-4]

History Colorado - # 10039861

Barbara Bel Geddes (1964)

Chapter Twenty-Nine

(1966 - 1969)

June Allyson and "Goodbye Ghost"
Another Evening With Someone
Gloria Swanson and "Reprise"
More Packages of Stars and Plays
The Increasing Cost of Broadway Financing
Ticket Outlets
Boyd Dumrose - Set Designer
The Larry Tajiri Awards - Special Guest

The 1966 Season

Whitfield Connor continued as executive administrator and general manager of the Elitch Theatre, importing packages of stars and plays, and even entertainment other than plays such as an evening with Joni James.

Theatergoers were introduced this season to Robert Alda, who they may have known as an actor with a disappointing film career.* They were aware of his success as Sky Masterson in the Broadway production of *Guys and Doll*s more than a decade earlier. Now, he was featured at Elitch with Lisa Kirk in the musical comedy *Riverwind,* which played to much acclaim for more than two years off-Broadway.

Other stars that appeared during the season included Maureen O'Sullivan, Chester Morris, Lisa Kirk, Louis Nye, Cliff Arquette, Tom Ewell and Vivian Vance.

June Allyson and "Goodbye Ghost" [1-1]

The 75th summer season at Elitch was launched with a pre-Broadway bound comedy called *Goodbye Ghost* by playwright Harold Kennedy, who also appeared in the production. June Allyson played the lead. Her two children, Dick Powell Jr. and Allyson Powell, also appeared in the play as the children of Miss Allyson and Bill Morey, the middle-aged couple in the play who have forgotten the fundamentals of love. June Allyson endeared herself to the audience when she flubbed a line at the close of Act II.

> Though Miss Allyson appeared somewhat nervous opening night, a flub of lines proved that she is a solid professional. At the close of Act II, in a spirited dialogue with (Harold) Kennedy, she said, "Casanova" instead of "Dracula."
>
> The flub broke her up and she began laughing about her mistake, so

* Robert Alda is the father of Alan Alda, who was born Jan 28, 1936 in New York City. Alan Alda was educated at Fordham University and was the star of the television series M*A*S*H, among other theatrical achievements. See Katz, *The Film Encyclopedia* (Thomas Y. Crowell, Publishers 1979), p. 17.

much so that the audience joined in. Then, turning to Kennedy, she said: "You say it." He picked up her lines and proceeded as Miss Allyson tried, but not very successfully, to stifle her laughter. She got a good round of applause for her honesty.

Pre-Broadway summer stock presentations of a play are significant to the progress and success of a play moving in the direction of Broadway. For example, the review of the performance at Elitch contained some worthwhile suggestions and encouragement.

> The opening was slow and a couple of scenes in which Morey and Miss Allyson are discussing their lives seemed to drag.
>
> More bright and sparkling dialogue is needed in those particular instances to keep the humor alive, to prevent the audience from yawning and looking at their watches.
>
> *Goodbye Ghost* is only a step away from being a solid comedy, one that would stay alive for years in stock companies and community theaters.

Another Evening With Someone

The 1965 season had presented *An Evening of Music and Laughter* with Phil Ford and Mimi Hines. The 1966 season presented *An Evening of Music and Laughter with Joni James*. Future seasons were to have other evenings with other nightclub style acts.

Joni James' act was described by her manager, Tony Acquaviva (also her musical director and husband), as a "spontaneous show. She sings some of her biggest hits, sings in several foreign languages, talks with the audience, just whatever happens to appeal to her at the time." According to the review, "that pretty much sums up the two-hour show."[1-2]

You Can't Take It With You

You Can't Take It With You, the 1937 Pulitzer Prize comedy by Moss Hart and George S. Kaufman is a must for all theatergoers. The audience was introduced to the wacky Sycamore family's New York City household.

> Grandpa is a man who gave up his job one morning 35 years ago and has done nothing since except collect snakes, attend commencement exercises, take midnight walks with the neighborhood policeman, and refuse to pay his income tax.
>
> (His daughter), Penelope Sycamore writes plays (plays that she never finishes) because a typewriter was left at the house by mistake eight years previously.
>
> There is her husband, Paul and Mr. De Pinna who manufacture fireworks in the basement.

There is her daughter, Essie, an aspiring ballet dancer (who practices in the living room while her husband plays his xylophone and runs his printing press).[1-3]

Cliff Arquette played the principal role of the grandfather in the Elitch play, and his fans were treated to an extra bonus. Following the third act curtain, Cliff Arquette spent about ten minutes reading one of his Charley Weaver famous "letters from momma."[1-3]

The 1967 Season

Theater has been an integral part of Colorado's cultural life since the days of the Gold Rush, when the miners with their new-found riches wanted better entertainment than was supplied by the saloons.[2-1]

Notwithstanding the growth of theaters in Colorado, Elitch Theatre continued to maintain a foothold among the ranks of summer entertainment. It was evident from the plays and actors presented for this 76th season.

Gloria Swanson in "Reprise"
Paul Ford in "What Did We Do Wrong?"
Joan Fontaine in "Spider's Web"
George Jessel in "An Evening With George Jessel"
Ronnie Graham and Giselle MacKenzie in "Luv"
The National Touring Company of "The Fantasticks"
Myrna Loy in "Barefoot in the Park"
Stephan Boyd in "The Bashful Genius"
Henry Morgan in "The Odd Couple"
Hal Holden in the musical based on H. G. Wells' novel *Kipps,* "Half a Sixpence"

Gloria Swanson and "Reprise"

Harold J. Kennedy authored and directed the play *Reprise* and also co-starred with Gloria Swanson. This was the second consecutive season that Kennedy wrote the opening night play and co-starred as well. The prior season, the play was *Goodbye Ghost* with June Allyson.

A letter dated July 9, 1967 to Whitfield Connor, written by someone on behalf of Gloria Swanson, concerned the accommodations for her stay in Denver while performing *Reprise* at Elitch Theatre.

Among other things, the letter included the following comments:

I am sure Miss Swanson has talked to you regarding what kind of accommodations she will want - the most important item of course is a kitchen. Will you please arrange to have bottled water delivered for her use during the one week - what we have here in Chicago comes in two-quart decanters which are very convenient. Probably two cases, or 12

> decanters, will be enough for the week.
>
> Also we will have food shipped to Miss Swanson care of the Theatre, so we would appreciate your taking care of this until Miss Swanson's arrival.[3-1]

In the files of the Theatre, a "to do" list noted to "get yellow page of Health Foods" and "shop for organic foods produce -carrots."[3-2]

Harold Kennedy described Gloria Swanson as a "perfectionist," and stated:

> When she sends the scenic designer explicit instructions that the mantel on the fireplace is to be four feet six and a quarter inches high, that is what she means. And it better not be six and one eighth. She will know in a second and if there is any discussion she'll bring her tape measure out on the stage with her ... She is a meticulous actress and she knows how to posture herself well and effectively ... If she plans to lean an elbow on the mantel she wants it to be the exact angle that is flattering [4-1]

Who else but Harold Kennedy should know Gloria Swanson better. He participated in at least seventeen separate productions with her, with two of the plays written by him especially for her: one being *A Goose for the Gander* (which got to Broadway) and the other being *Reprise*.[4-2]

In her autobiography, Gloria Swanson credits Harold Kennedy for her career in theater. She stated,

> I had an absolute terror of the stage ... and through the years I continued to turn down all comers who tried to lure me to Broadway. Even when I had no movie career left to jeopardize, I refused to go on the stage.[5-1]

Then Harold Kennedy offered her a challenge, even though he knew she was petrified at the thought of acting on stage. He selected the George Kelly play *Reflected Glory* as being right for her and arranged to have it performed in Poughkeepsie, New York.

> Harold Kennedy selected a cast and put me to work early learning lines because he sensed without my telling him what I feared most about those thousands of words ... (On opening night) as I walked onstage, my heart was pumping so outrageously that I was sure it was visibly lifting me up and down off the ground. There was a thunderclap of applause that lasted a minute, and I blessed all the people of Poughkeepsie. Then I opened my mouth, and the words came out, all of them, in the right order, by the thousands.[5-2]

In Denver, following the Wednesday and Saturday matinees, Miss Swanson remained on stage for a quiz session by the audience.

> Understanding the wide interest in her youthful appearance and

> apparently unlimited energy, Miss Swanson has question-and-answer periods following her matinees when the audience may ask about her health, age, looks and physical regimen.[2-2]

When asked about her age Miss Swanson rightfully admitted to being a youthful 68 years, but she pleasantly reminded people that Oliver Wendell Holmes wrote *Over the Teacups* at age 70, and Verdi wrote some of his greatest operas in his 80s. Years later, in 1975, during a visit with friends, a *Denver Post* article referred to her as the "Spirit of 76" noting:

> Gloria Swanson is unhappy about a number of things - but having lived to 76 and "being still vertical while so many are horizontal' is not one of them. "People expect a sugar limp old lady," she says with a laugh that sets the red carnation she clutches into spinning circles in the air. [2-3]

An Evening With George Jessel

An Evening With George Jessel was an experimental venture, sort of a Johnny Carson impromptu show without commercials. A number of artists came along and the evening was interspersed with songs and music. Nostalgia was the heart of the evening. In the first part of the show, Jessel recounted some of his early days in show business, told some of his best jokes and sang some songs. He closed before intermission by doing an imitation of the late Al Jolson singing "California Here I Come" and an imitation of the late Eddie Cantor doing "If You Knew Susie."

The second part of the show was similar to the first. Jessel deviated from the show format for a moment "to explain his beliefs on the Vietnam war, the only serious point of the entire evening."[2-4]

George Burns, in his book entitled *All My Best Friends*, stated that George Jessel "got so involved in politics that he forgot he was supposed to be a comedian ... He had always been someone who believed so much in peace that he was willing to fight anyone to get it."[6] In the past year, Jessel had traveled to Vietnam on three occasions to entertain American servicemen there.[2-5]

The 1968 Season

Patrons of Elitch Theatre had grown used to the star package summers and anxiously awaited a glimpse of a favorite movie or film star in an almost Broadway stage setting. Following each performance a small gathering of fans waited near the stage door for a closer off-stage look at their star, and perhaps an autograph, as they watched the star disappear into the crowds of the Gardens or into an automobile headed toward the Brown Palace Hotel where actors customarily stayed. While the stage door and the scene wasn't Shubert Alley, to many, it was a taste of it.

The stars that came to Elitch included Shirley Booth, Ann Sothern, Morey Amsterdam, Joan Fontaine, Rosemary Prinz, Robert Cummings, Barry Nelson, Julie

Newmar, Forest Tucker and Marian Seldes. Ford and Hines returned for *An Evening of Laughter and Music*, having previously appeared during the 1965 season.

The Desk Set

Elitch Theatre chose *The Desk Set* to open its season, a brilliant comedy about automation, which was first presented on Broadway in 1955. The play is about "a group of researchers in the library of a large television network who are about to be replaced by an electronic brain."[7-1]

Shirley Booth was chosen to star at Elitch in the part she originated in the Broadway production. Among her Broadway hits were *Come Back Little Sheba, A Tree Grows in Brooklyn, By the Beautiful Sea* and *The Time of the Cuckoo*, for all of which she received Tony awards.[7-1]

An amusing moment occurred during a performance when a door of the set jammed. The stage for *The Desk Set* consisted of two rooms separated by a door. On one side of the door was Shirley Booth and on the other side an actor. After a time exchanging their lines, the actor attempted to open the door. After a minute of trying without success, the actor walked around the door and the set into the other side of the stage. Shirley Booth looked up at him and said, "Do you walk on water, too?"

Two Plays From the 1930s

The Elitch management selected two plays that had first been presented on Broadway in the 1930s, *Private Lives* (1931) and *Room Service* (1937). They had been favorites with theatergoers ever since.

> Thirty-eight years have passed since Noel Coward wrote *Private Lives* and it still remains one of the most sophisticated comedies in the theatre. The passing years have not dimmed its luster in the slightest.
>
> Coward's ironic sense of humor compelled him to write a play about two ex-mates who meet on their honeymoon, discover how wrong they were to divorce each other, and go back together and try for a reconciliation - leaving their new spouses to ponder.[7-2]

Coward appeared with Gertrude Lawrence in the original Broadway production. The play had several Broadway revivals.

Room Service was a family affair for comedian Morey Amsterdam. He was featured in the play and appeared with his wife Kay, his 17-year old daughter Cathy and his brother-in-law Craig Thomas, as part of the cast. At the conclusion of the performance, Amsterdam made an after-curtain appearance and delivered ten minutes of personal comedy and, in addition, informed the audience why he had chosen to do a 30-year-old play because "comedy - really good comedy - never grows old."

The whole precept of the play is simple in the extreme. A ne'er do-well theatrical producer plots ways and means of sustaining a cast of 20 persons in a hotel without funds.[8]

Who Is Rosemary Prinz?

Rosemary Prinz was cast for the lead role at Elitch in *A Girl Could Get Lucky*. Del Carnes, the *Denver Post* drama editor, was frank to admit that he missed a TV soap opera called *As The World Turns* during the past years, in which Rosemary Prinz appeared. After viewing the Elitch opening of *A Girl Could Get Lucky*, Carnes vowed to be looking at the soap opera from now on, and all because of "a young lady named Rosemary Prinz."

> I got my first glimpse of Miss Prinz Monday night at the Elitch Theatre opening of *A Girl Could Get Lucky*, and she's about the cutest, most devilishly charming little actress who has graced the Elitch stage in quite awhile.
>
> Millions of housewives know Miss Prinz as the serious heroine of the above-mentioned soaper. But I wonder how many are aware of her talents as a stage comedienne?[7-3]

Briefly, the two-person comedy at Elitch is about a scatterbrained secretary played by Miss Prinz, and a practical, thrifty cab driver who fall in love, get married and almost divorce because of clashing idiosyncrasies.

> (For example,) where he will save money using paper linen, and stocking up his grocery shelves with supermarket sales, Miss Prinz will use real linen at every meal (sending it out to be cleaned each time) and order steaks from the butcher without asking the price or selecting the meat.[7-3]

However, as in all good comedies, before the final curtain, the end is pleasant. And as the drama critic promises, "the adroit, polished performances (of the actors) are the kind you savor for more than just a few hours after the curtain has gone down."[7-4] Rosemary Prinz returned to Elitch Theatre and appeared with Keir Dullea during the 1977 season, during which she played the female lead in the comedy *Same Time Next Year*.

Generation [9]

William Goodhart's play *Generation* about "the differences between parents and their grown children was one of the first of the recent generation gap comedies, and it is still the best." The Elitch production was directed by and starred Robert Cummings. Because of the mile-high altitude, which Robert Cummings discussed with the audience following the show, "the opening night production was a little rough in that actors tossed away lines because they were not savoring the audience laughter to the fullest."

A Bit of Miscasting

Fortunately, a well-written comedy could even withstand a bit of miscasting. Such was the case in the Elitch production of Neil Simon's *The Star Spangled Girl*, the headline of the review stating, "Neil Simon Comedy Proves Rib-Tickler." Notwithstanding, the drama critic could not resist offering his view of the lead roles as performed by Edd Byrnes and Diane McBain, graduates of the Warner Brothers TV stock company.

> It appears, unfortunately, that in Edd Byrnes as Andy, and Diane McBain as the "Star Spangled Girl," a bit of miscasting has occurred.
>
> Byrnes simply has not grasped his role with forcefulness or conviction. He delivers a comedy line with the dourness of a tragedian.
>
> Miss McBain is so fair of skin and pretty of face that only a cad would give her a bad notice. Yet, it must be said that she is uneasy in the role and something less than convincing as a young Southern lady who was an Olympic swimmer.
>
> (It goes to show that) "a television series ... does not always a stage actor make."[7-4]

In Frank Gilroy's *The Only Game in Town*, Julie Newmar is cast opposite Barry Nelson. She had previously won the Tony Award in her Broadway debut for her role in *The Marriage-Go-Round*. The headline of the drama critic's review of the Elitch play reads "Nelson's Performance Outstanding." The following comment addresses the performance of Julie Newmar.

> Miss Newmar looks marvelous but gets involved in too many visual and vocal mannerisms. She's most effective at her most simple and direct, when she isn't overplaying the coyness in the role.[7-5]

Moscow Theaters/Tighter Controls/Echoes of the Past [7-2]

In Moscow, Russia, theater presentations were subjected to tighter controls after a controversial season. The center of the controversy was a modernized version of Chekhov's *Three Sisters*, staged at the Moscow Drama Theatre by Anatoli Efros.

> Chekhov's critical lines about Czarist society at the turn of the century were presented in a setting applicable to the present day.
>
> The play was abruptly withdrawn from the theatre's repertory several weeks ago. Efros was reported to have been transferred to a minor administrative post in the Ministry of Culture.

As a further result, a decree by the Moscow City Council complained that too many ideologically and artistically weak plays were staged during the last season.

> The decree ... demanded more plays about "the heroes of our time" - workers, collective farmers, soldiers, Communist party officials, scientists and industrial managers.
>
> Theatres were also ordered to present more plays about the class struggle of workers in capitalist countries ...
>
> The decree follows a demand by the Communist party Central Committee for an intensive ideological campaign to combat "subversive influences" from the West.

The action taken by the Moscow City Council raised echoes of the past in America and The House Committee on Un-American Activities, a government committee formed in 1938 to investigate alleged communist influence in Hollywood. In 1947, the Committee turned its attention to Hollywood screenwriters, claiming they had slipped subversive messages into the films they made for major studios. Screenwriters, playwrights, actors and others were subpoenaed before the committee, many of whom were condemned by the Committee, such as *The Hollywood Ten,* screenwriters who challenged the committee by the assertion of their First Amendment rights. Many individuals were blacklisted, such as actor Zero Mostel who was without work for some time.

The Increasing Cost of Broadway Financing

Like the rising costs for food and other necessities at grocery and department stores, the industry of theater was not immune from inflation. Theatergoers who pay hard-earned dollars at the box office for a ticket occasionally ask: Where does all the money go to make a Broadway show?

> Back in 1949, when the big musical *South Pacific* cost $225,000, an orchestra seat went for $6. Now there's nothing unusual about a production costing more than $700,000.
>
> In addition to the upsurge in basic show financing, the weekly operating expenses have risen. In 1957, *The Music Man* broke even at $36,000 weekly. Just 10 years later, *Hallelujah, Baby!* had to take in $53,000 each week before starting to show a profit for the backers who financed the project.[7-6]

The many costs of a theatrical production include sets, costumes, lighting, props and furniture, union bonds and theater rent guarantees, script rights, travel, auditions, legal fees, actor compensation, rehearsal payrolls, out-of-town openings, advertising and posters.

The 1969 Season

Ticket Outlets

An added service for Elitch theatergoers was the establishment of eleven area Elitch Theatre box office outlets throughout the Denver area. Box office outlets were also set up in Boulder and Greeley. In this manner Elitch patrons did not have to go downtown in Denver or drive to the Theatre to purchase tickets for shows.[10-1]

The Season

Again, the season brought many known actors aboard, such as Tom Poston, Sam Levene, Hurd Hatfield, Jeanne Cagney, Tom Ewell, James Whitmore and Arlene Francis. Barry Nelson returned to appear in *Cactus Flower*, a comedy.

Boyd Dumrose - Set Designer [11]

Throughout its history, Elitch Theatre productions had been enhanced by well-chosen set designers, such as Harry Cummins and Victor Paganuzzi. For the past seven years, the sets had been designed by Boyd Dumrose. Dumrose would begin to work on his sets about a week in advance of the show.

> He first reads the script of a play and, using a basic ground plan sent him by the touring company, starts to design the set.
>
> First, the period has to be right for the play. Dumrose researches different eras during the year because there's no time to do it in the week allowed in summer stock.
>
> "Blocking" has to be kept in mind. This comprises the specific moves an actor or actress has to make on stage in predetermined areas.
>
> Also, in order to be believable, stage doors, railings and steps should be sturdy. Dumrose, a lean but strong man, builds the type of sets that could survive a stampede of cattle.
>
> The hunt for props would give a treasure hunter a challenge.
>
> "I rent furniture from Denver stores and comb antique shops and even Goodwill stores for what we may need," Dumrose says. "Also, I've made quite a few friends in Denver and they are always happy to lend me furniture or art pieces - especially if a favorite star of theirs will use the prop."
>
> Dumrose also keeps in mind the general build of a star when choosing furniture.
>
> "If an actress, for instance, isn't as graceful as another, I get chairs and couches that don't sink too low," he said.

Tom Ewell

The comedy, *Don't Drink the Water*, Woody Allen's first Broadway play, was a favorite among summer stock theaters. At Elitch, Tow Ewell was chosen to play the part of the New Jersey caterer. The plot, which details the caterer's trip abroad, is a Woody Allen classic.

> It's an implausible plot ... about a caterer from New Jersey mistaken by Communists for a spy. Chased into the American Embassy (in an unnamed Iron Curtain country), the caterer ... and his family find themselves amidst the darndest assortment of people.
>
> First, there's the ambassador's bungling son, Axel, who's in charge while father is away. Axel is, by his own admission, the biggest failure since the New York World's Fair.
>
> An excitable chef who doesn't know how to cope with an American caterer is part of the crowd, as well as a Sultan of an oil-rich country with whom America is trying to establish good relations while Ewell is busy tearing them down.
>
> And you wouldn't believe the situations. The Communists, convinced Ewell is a spy, believe equally that a list he has for a wedding reception back home is a code for troop movements. The Communists and this country decide to effect a trade - their master spy the Americans have captured for a master caterer.[10-2]

Try to imagine Tom Ewell's dead-pan glances and stony-cold retorts, in the role of the caterer trying to fend off the Communists. Try to remember how marvelously funny he was in both the stage and film versions of *The Seven Year Itch*.

Tom Ewell was born in 1909 in Owensboro, Kentucky. His initial desire was to become a lawyer, and he prepared for law school by majoring in political science in college. But, instead, he went into acting and it had been his career for over 40 years. He was best known as Richard Sherman, the summer bachelor who falls in love with his upstairs neighbor in *The Seven Year Itch* (1952). In an interview with a *Denver Post* reporter Tom Ewell centered largely on his wife's enrollment in cooking school. Notwithstanding his great love for the theater, Ewell refused "to discuss acting because, he says, like Somerset Maugham, he finds nothing more boring than an actor discussing acting."[10-3]

Milo Boulton

Milo Boulton appeared at Elitch with James Whitmore in the pre-Broadway tryout of *Chic Life*. The last time Milo Boulton played at Elitch had been in 1936 in *The First Legion*. Denver was Boulton's home for a long time. He graduated from

North High School and attended the University of Colorado where he became the first freshman to be accepted in the Drama Club. He achieved fame during World War II, when he became emcee of the popular CBS radio show, *We, the People*. His stage credits read like a "Who's Who in Show Business."

> He was with Humphrey Bogart in the play that started Bogart's film career - *The Petrified Forest* - and in later years, played Horace Vandergelder in *The Matchmaker* opposite Gertrude Berg.
>
> He later essayed the same role in the national tour of *Hello Dolly* (a musical version of *The Matchmaker*) with Carol Channing.[10-4]

Pal Joey

The musical *Pal Joey* was chosen for the final play of the season. It starred Arlene Francis, who had appeared in many Broadway shows and had been a panelist on the television show *What's My Line?* since 1950; however, *Pal Joey* was her debut in a musical.[10-5] The reviewer of the play commented on her singing.

> It seems a little ungallant for us to point it out, but Miss Francis is a far better actress than she is a singer. Granted that one doesn't have to be a Metropolitan Opera star to do musicals, it does seem in order to require some singing talent. Miss Francis' voice is flat, and she would do far better to talk-sing, a technique Rex Harrison perfected in *My Fair Lady*.[10-6]

On the other hand, it was actor Joe Masiell, as Pal Joey, who was the hit of the evening with his portrayal of the brash night-club performer.* The play is gifted with wonderful songs from the fabulous team of Lorenz Hart and Richard Rodgers, such as *I Could Write a Book* and *Bewitched, Bothered, and Bewildered*.

The Larry Tajiri Awards - Special Guest

Actress Jean Simmons, whose rise to stardom came when Sir Laurence Olivier chose her to play Ophelia in his screen production of *Hamlet* in 1950, was a special guest at the fifth annual Larry Tajiri Memorial Foundation Awards held on September 15, 1969 at the Cosmopolitan Hotel in Denver.[10-7]

* *Denver Post*, Aug 19, 1969, p. 12.

Masiell's father was also named Joe, but had Masiello as his last name. The father was a singer and acted in Italian theater in New York for many years. This author, as a youngster, had the good fortune of having seen him on many occasions in Italian theater presentations. See interview with Joe Masiell in *Denver Post*, Aug 27, 1969, p. 87.

Chapter Thirty

(1970 - 1972)

The Death of Arnold B. Gurtler Sr.
A Big Change - Only Five Plays a Season
Mourning the Death of Maude Fealy
The Death of Helen Bonfils
The Whitfield Connor Option
The Death of Brandon de Wilde

The 1970 Season

The Death of Arnold B. Gurtler Sr.

Arnold B. Gurtler Sr. died at his home at 710 So. Garfield Street on February 19, 1970 after a long illness. He was 74 years of age. He was born in Leadville, Colorado on January 17, 1896. Before his work at Elitch Gardens, he was a decorator for a downtown Denver department store. He married Marie Mulvihill, daughter of John M. Mulvihill, on October 5, 1916. Upon the death of John M. Mulvihill in 1930, he was named President of The Elitch Gardens Amusement Park.

Under Gurtler's management the park and Theatre grew and prospered. The Trocadero Ballroom was redecorated, and new rides were added to the park's amusement area. He was two-term president of the International Association of Amusement Parks and a leader in amusement park innovations. He also participated in many community activities and organizations.

Gurtler's first wife preceded him in death on January 27, 1960. She was 64 years of age. In 1961, Gurtler married Agnes M. Miller, a former nursing supervisor at St. Joseph Hospital in Denver. She survived him, along with his two sons, John and Arnold Jr., a sister and six grandchildren, all of Denver.[1]

A Big Change - Only Five Plays a Season

The new season brought about a significant change in the number of plays to be presented each summer. Rather than the usual ten plays, the number of plays was reduced to five, with the final play customarily being a musical. Each play would run for two weeks. More than in the past, play selections would occasionally include the one-star type performer show, such as *Jim Nabors in Concert*, Debbie Reynolds in *The Debbie Reynolds Show* and Mitzi Gaynor in *The Mitzi Gaynor Concert*. Such presentations smacked of nightclubs in effect but were entertaining and well-received nevertheless. The 1970 season offered two such shows.

The season's presentation of *Another Evening of Laughter and Music* with Phil Ford and his wife, Mimi Hines, was met by favorable comments, a reviewer stating that "it is difficult to see how a Denver summer evening could be passed more pleasantly in the theater than at Elitch's during this engagement."[2-1]

Ford and Hines had been comic partners for 14 years and married for 12 years. They first met in Anchorage, Alaska, when Miss Hines was appearing as a singer and Ford as a comedian.

> Their successful partnership began when Ford asked Miss Hines to join him in several gags during an act. That night the antics went over so well that the club owner told Ford to cut out the first part of his act and start right out with Miss Hines on the comedy bit.[2-2]

Also presented during the Elitch season was Victor Borge in *An Evening of Music and Mirth*.

> Borge's own platform manner is inimitable, as always. He is deft in his earnest moments at the piano - outrageously funny when he finds himself trapped in convoluted classical passages able to escape, eventually, only by strumming a few bars of "Happy Birthday."
>
> Borge's by-play with the audience, much of it spirited ad lib, is utterly engaging. His chuckles, winks, leers and grimaces are worthy of a Bert Lahr or a Bobby Clark.
>
> No matter how often one sees Borge, he is always an enchanting artist - ever fresh in appeal and the more enjoyable for the air of amiability which he so successfully communicates.[2-3]

The Season of Plays - Some Comments

The opening play of the season was Noel Coward's 1954 success, *Blithe Spirit*, whose story line involved a ghost in a worldly romance. Noel Harrison, son of the famed actor Rex Harrison, starred in the central role of the writer bedeviled by the ghostly appearance of his first wife, an engaging spook in gray draperies and makeup, while wife number two faces the return of her deceased predecessor. The drama critic's reaction was clear: "America's most venerable summer theatre has made an auspicious start on its new season."[2-4]

Light Up the Sky was written by the talented Moss Hart. The play opened on Broadway on November 18, 1948, with the lead role of Irene Livingston played by Virginia Fields. The play had originally been written for Kitty Carlisle, Hart's wife. In the Elitch presentation, Miss Carlisle played the lead role and performed it well.

> Miss Carlisle sails through the comedy's central role as Irene Livingston, a reigning lady of the American stage. In the beauty of her maturity, with enchanting voice and presence, with exquisite timing and delightful shadings of characterization, Miss Carlisle heads her company with bewitching allure.[2-5]

Light Up the Sky is a story of backstage life, about a play that has had a bad out-of-town tryout and is now a play in trouble. Its characters are the Broadway insiders assembled in a suite of the Ritz-Carlton Hotel in Boston before and after the play's first performance. Everyone blames everyone else for the audience's having stampeded the exits before the final curtain. The characters in the play were patterned by Moss Hart after well-known, easily identifiable theatrical personalities, which comparisons did not sit well with those individuals.

> This too-easy mockery suggested that Moss's real purpose in *Light Up the Sky* was to settle scores with postwar Broadway, especially its theater parties and the hit or flop economics he had been burned by, as had everybody else.
>
> It was a comedy of bad manners punctuated by backstage jokes and soured by cynicism.[3-1]

The play's poor reception in its out-of-town opening necessitated a rewriting of the play prior to its opening on Broadway, where it ultimately appeared as a moderate hit.

> Moss put the most confident face possible on his New Haven and Boston debacle as he labored around the clock to save a play that audiences found confused and unfunny. Life was imitating art with a vengeance.
>
> Turning his comedy into even a nervous hit had so exhausted Moss that he swore never again to direct a show he had also written.[3-2]

Notwithstanding the history of this play, the *Denver Post* drama editor concluded that "It is altogether fitting that Hart's widow, the stunning Kitty Carlisle, is engaged in bringing her late husband's show-business Valentine back to the boards."[2-5]

The season closed with the musical *Carousel*, a story centered on the character Billy Bigelow, a carnival barker in an amusement park, a role made famous in its 1945 Broadway opening by John Raitt. The drama editor of the *Denver Post* amusingly noted that when the play ended and the audience exited the Theatre, it found itself in another amusement park.

The Reliability of Whitfield Connor

Harold J. Kennedy was a familiar face on the summer circuit as an actor, director, producer, and playwright for over 40 years. He was a graduate of Dartmouth College and the Yale Drama School. He frequently arranged "star package" plays for the Elitch Theatre and at times directed and acted in some of the plays. This season he packaged and directed the *Light Up the Sky* presentation. In a letter to an Elitch Theatre representative dated July 8, 1979, he wrote:

> What a joy it always is to deal with Whit Connor and the people who work for and with him. When he says that old bromide, "The check is

in the mail," it is as good as money in the bank and you can proceed accordingly. Not that some of the others are dishonest but they are not very well organized and I often marvel that they get one play a season on, let alone ten.[4-1]

The 1971 Season

Attendance at Elitch Theatre

The attendance at Elitch Theatre was significantly higher than in the two previous years. The attendance figure at the Theatre for the 1971 season, excluding passes and theater personnel, was 91,250, as compared to 73,000 for 1969 and 67,500 for 1970.[4-2]

Neil Simon Comedies

The season brought two Neil Simon laugh-filled comedies to Denver audiences, *Last of the Red Hot Lovers* and *Plaza Suite*, the former being the season opener starring Sid Caesar. Those familiar with Sid Caesar's talent would agree with the *Denver Post* drama critic that he was an excellent choice for the role of Barney Cashman, an aging married man yearning for the last "fling" to "prove" he is still young and a Lothario.

In his popular television program, *Your Show of Shows*, with Imogene Coca and Carl Reiner, Caesar was known for his double-talk of foreign languages. While in his teens he worked in his father's luncheonette in Yonkers, New York. The clientele consisted largely of foreign laborers, whose dialects and accents carved indelible images in Caesar's creative mind, resulting in hilarious television sketches.[5] In his autobiography, he wrote:

> I would go from table to table, listening to the sounds. I would hear the groups speak Italian, Russian, Polish, Hungarian, French, Spanish, Lithuanian, and even Bulgarian. I would pick up words and the nuances of the dialects and the tones, and would speak to them in double-talk, which was as close as I came to actually learning the language. The first time I tried it out was in front of a table of Italians. I was so young, my head barely reached above the table. When I rattled away in fake Italian, they listened to me and smiled, certain I was one of their own. Then they tried to figure out what I was saying, and quickly realized I was speaking gibberish. They loved it.[6]

Douglas Fairbanks, Jr.

The Pleasure of His Company by Samuel Taylor and Cornelia Otis Skinner pleased its first night audience. "They were also charmed by Fairbanks' curtain speech in which he expressed happiness at having the opportunity to play upon the stage where his father's career began."[7]

Douglas Fairbanks, Jr. was born to Douglas Fairbanks, Sr. and Anna Beth Sully on December 9, 1909. He was raised by his mother from the age of nine after his parents divorced. His father married Mary Pickford. They were for some time the dream couple of Hollywood but later divorced, and Mary Pickford married Buddy Rogers. Although Douglas Fairbanks, Sr. had only a distant relationship with his son for some time, they later became good and lasting friends.[8]

A photograph of Mary Pickford had mysteriously disappeared from the photo gallery in the foyer of the Theatre. Whitfield Conner sent a letter to her on July 20, 1971 after receiving an 11x14 photograph from her to replace the missing photograph. He wrote as follows:

> Thank you very much for the lovely picture you sent to us to replace the one which was stolen from our collection. Please know that it will have an honored place in our gallery alongside Douglas Fairbanks, Jr. and his father.
>
> Mr. Fairbanks was a delight both on stage and off, and he brought with him a first rate production of *The Pleasure of His Company*. He spoke of you and Mr. Rogers and all at Pickfair with heartfelt warmth and admiration.[4-3]

Mourning the Death of Maude Fealy (1881-1971) [9]

On November 9, 1971, the theatrical world mourned the death of Maude Fealy. She passed on in her sleep at the Motion Picture Home and Hospital in Woodland Hills outside of Hollywood, California. The veteran actress was 90 years of age.

She appeared on the stage of Elitch Theatre in 1899 and for several seasons thereafter in the early 1900s. For many years she appeared in London and on the American stage. She lived in California for a while and was associated with Cecil B. De Mille in the film industry. Notwithstanding, some of the happiest days of her career were those spent in summer stock at Elitch.

Her mother was Margaret Fealy, an actress who conducted the Fealy School of Acting in the Brown Palace Hotel in Denver for many years. Margaret was married to Rafaello Cavallo, a pioneer musical conductor at the Tabor Grand and Broadway theaters, a conductor of the Denver Symphony Orchestra, and founder of the Pueblo Symphony Orchestra. He also performed concerts at the Elitch Theatre.

After being in California for several years, Maude Fealy moved back to Denver in 1937 and alternated between the city and Pueblo in order to be near the ill Cavallo. Her mother and stepfather had separated but were never divorced. After the death of her stepfather in 1942, Maude and her mother moved to California and opened a studio in Hollywood. Following her mother's death in 1955, Maude Fealy returned to Denver in 1957 to "retire." She lived at 1000 Grant Street. However, she continued to remain active, appearing before various clubs and organizations, recalling the magic of the glorious years of the theater that she had experienced. At one time she gave a series of lectures at Loretto Heights College. In her last interview in Denver in 1961, she was quoted as saying - "Actors never give up acting - it gives them up."

She later returned to California to live out her later years. She is interred in the Abbey of the Psalms Mausoleum in the Hollywood Forever Cemetery in Los Angeles County, where many notable Hollywood theater and film personages have been laid to rest. The endless list of such personages at Hollywood Forever Cemetery includes Douglas Fairbanks, Sr., Tyrone Power, Rudolph Valentino, Mel Blanc, Hattie McDaniel and Jayne Mansfield.

The 1972 Season

The Death of Helen Bonfils

Helen Bonfils died on June 6, 1972, at the age of 83, at St. Joseph's Hospital in Denver after a long illness marked by heart trouble. The Mass of the Resurrection was celebrated for her by Archbishop James V. Casey at the Church of the Holy Ghost in Denver, the construction of which she financed as a memorial to her father. Her casket was placed in the family mausoleum at Fairmount Cemetery, where her father and mother and her first husband, George Somnes, were also buried.

The Whitfield Connor Option - A New Corporation [10]

At the time of her death, Helen Bonfils still owned all the stock of The Elitch Theatre Company. At the time of the incorporation of The Elitch Theatre Company in 1965, Helen Bonfils and Whitfield Connor entered into an option agreement which contained the following clause:

> In the event the Company should at any time terminate its operation of said Theatre without intent to resume operations at a subsequent date or season ... it is the desire of Bonfils and the Company that Connor have the right to purchase the physical assets of the Company useful to him in such enterprise, or to purchase the capital stock of the Company.

On August 9, 1972, a letter was sent to Whitfield Connor from Donald R. Seawell and Earl R. Moore, executors of the estate of Helen Bonfils, that informed Connor of his option to acquire the interest owned by Helen Bonfils in The Elitch Theatre Company in accordance with the option agreement, which included the right to assume the lease on the Theatre, to use the Elitch name, and to continue the operation of the Theatre under Connor's direction or under a new corporation setup.

Whitfield Connor accepted the option and notified the Gurtlers that after the final audit of the 1972 season, The Elitch Theatre Company was to be dissolved, and a new corporation was to be formed using the same name. Under the option agreement, "the price payable by Connor upon exercise of this option shall be the current book value of the assets to be transferred."

The old corporation was liquidated on December 26, 1972, and a new corporation was established and filed with the Office of the Secretary of State on the next day, with 51 shares of stock issued to Whitfield Connor and 49 shares to Haila Stoddard. The corporation elected to operate as a Subchapter S corporation.

Whitfield Conner informed John M. Gurtler and Arnold Gurtler Jr. by letter dated September 7, 1972, that:

> It is my intention that the Elitch Theatre will continue to operate on the same high level it has enjoyed during the years since Helen Bonfils and I began running it in 1964.
>
> I want you both to have ease of mind about your great Theatre. In the years to come I want it to be ever more successful - ever more the flagship theatre of the nation. I will always do my best to fulfill its great tradition.

The Directors of the new corporation were Whitfield Connor (President), Haila Stoddard Connor (Secretary-Treasurer), and Christopher Kirkland (Vice-President). Christopher Kirkland was the stepson of Whitfield Connor, born to Haila Stoddard from her former marriage to Jack Kirkland, author of the play *Tobacco Road*. Christopher Kirkland was designated Producer-Director of the Theatre and remained in that capacity until the Theatre's final season in 1987.

The new corporation entered into a new lease for the Theatre, which contained the same provisions as the old lease with some minor changes. For example, under the old lease, the lessee had the right to offer such type of entertainment which its Board of Directors, in its sole discretion, deemed advisable. The new lease still allowed the entertainment at the Theatre to be at the lessee's discretion; however, the new lease added the following:

> ... but the lessee agrees that the shows presented shall be such as to maintain the standards of excellence and morality which have been characteristic of its past performance.

The Season

Five plays were presented during the 1972 summer season, with the final three being musicals, a rarity for an Elitch season.

The musical *Do I Hear a Waltz?* was adapted by Arthur Laurents from his play, *The Time of the Cuckoo*, the Broadway production of which starred Shirley Booth in the role of a lonely American spinster, Leona Samish, who goes to Venice to look at the sights and for romance. Richard Rodgers (music) and Stephen Sondheim (lyrics), in their only collaboration together, provided the score. *Summertime* (1965), starring Katherine Hepburn, was the film version of the play.

In the Elitch presentation, Patrice Munsel played the role of Leona Samish. Miss

Munsel began her professional career at the age of 17 by winning a contest of the Metropolitan Opera "and became the youngest diva ever to appear at the Met."[11-1]

The musical *Fiddler on the Roof* (1964) is based on Sholom Aleichem's novel *Tevye's Daughters*. The musical was a surprise hit on Broadway, and established a long-run record (3,242) of performances that held for a decade. It has since been seen throughout the world in venues from Broadway to churches.[12] The drama editor of the *Denver Post* noted that the songs from the musical "are now so familiar that it's difficult for an audience not to hum along with the players."[11-2]

The award-winning musical *1776* was chosen for the final play of the season. The theme of the musical centers around the Continental Congress of 1776, "with the suspense built upon the pro and con arguments of revolution, leading to the signing of the Declaration of Independence."[11-3]

The Death of Brandon de Wilde

On June 21, 1972, the *Denver Post* reported:

> Brandon and Janice de Wilde declared Tuesday that they will always remember Denver because it is here that they will celebrate their third anniversary. On June 25, they will have been married exactly three months![11-4]

The 1972 season brought sadness to theatergoers worldwide. The play *Butterflies Are Free* starred Brandon de Wilde as the blind lad and co-starred Maureen O'Sullivan as the mother. In the 1953 classic western film *Shane*, the young de Wilde stood on a barren plain and called out to a stranger (Alan Ladd) who had helped him and his mother (Jean Arthur), "Shane ... Shane, come back." It was a line that filmgoers could not forget. De Wilde was 11 at the time. He continued to find success in films, including *Mrs. McThing, In Harm's Way* and *Hud*, just to name a few. But even earlier, at age 7, de Wilde was presented the Donaldson Award for "Best Debut Performance" on Broadway when he starred with Ethel Walters in *Member of the Wedding*. This author attended de Wilde's final Elitch performance of *Butterflies Are Free* on July 1, 1972. It was to be the final performance of his life.

A week later, while en route to Colorado General Hospital in Denver to visit his ailing wife, Janice, the camper he was driving went out of control on West 6th Avenue and Kipling Street, struck a guardrail and caromed into a flatbed truck, resulting in multiple injuries to de Wilde. It was raining slightly at the time. He was taken to St. Anthony's Hospital, where he died several hours later at the age of 30.[11-5] Brandon's body was flown to San Fernando, California, on July 8, 1972.[11-6] Funeral services were held in Los Angeles.[11-7]

On July 14, 1972, a matinee benefit performance of *See How They Run*, starring Mickey Rooney, was held at Elitch to honor de Wilde. The proceeds from the performance offered by the cast, the crew, and the Theatre staff were divided equally between Janice de Wilde (for her immediate needs) and for use in starting an educational trust fund for Jesse, Brandon's young son from an earlier marriage.[11-7]

In the *Denver Post* review of the opening night performance of *Butterflies Are Free,* it was stated:

> Brandon de Wilde ... is giving one of his best performances ... In his virtually flawless playing of the part (of the young blind man), de Wilde proves that the training he has received and the background from which he has emerged works for him with sound effectiveness. His is one of the best interpretations by a young leading man to be seen in Denver for some time.[11-8]

Douglas Fairbanks, Jr., viewing photograph of his father in Theatre lobby (1971)

Brandon de Wilde and his wife, Janice (1972)

Chapter Thirty-One

(1973 - 1975)

"Under the Yum Yum Tree" - Contract Issues
Play and Star Selection - Comments by Whitfield Connor
Mickey Rooney and Steve Allen
Not a Favorable Season

The 1973 Season

Rooms to Rent

Robert Downing, drama editor of the *Denver Post*, included the following in one of his columns:

> ELITCH THEATRE management hopes that residents in the vicinity of the Theatre may be able to rent rooms to supporting members of visiting casts who don't make astronomical salaries.[1-1]

Under the Yum Yum Tree - Contract Issues

The first "star package" to open the new season at Elitch was Lawrence Roman's *Under the Yum Yum Tree*. The "star" of the package was actor Gig Young.

> Briefly, the story concerns a school teacher who is renting her San Francisco apartment to a young friend while she goes to Sacramento on assignment.
>
> The apartment, apparently, has been a playground of sorts for the landlord of the building who lives across the hall. This chap has found considerable delight in the succession of single girls who have been his neighbors.
>
> The aging roué has less success with the new tenant, principally because the girl's boyfriend moves in with her - as part of a "platonic" experiment the lass wishes to conduct before their marriage.[1-2]

Prior to coming to Denver, the "star package" play was presented at the Falmouth Playhouse in Falmouth, Massachusetts. The producer of that summer theater had a problem with the "understudy clause" in the contract proposed by Gig Young's agent. The producer sent a letter to the agent, which read as follows:

> Under no circumstances can I sign any contract that has an understudy clause in it for the star. In my theatre, if the star does not appear, we either replace him with a star of equal magnitude or cancel the performance.
>
> My public, as you know, comes first to see the star, which is why we are paying Mr. Young such a very large salary. I am sure you understand

an audience reaction to a star replacement. Let's just pray it never happens again.[2-1]

The producer also had problems with charges submitted by Gig Young's agent for payment and wrote the following:

> I have just received your package agreement and breakdown. At no time have we ever paid more than $300 for a booking fee.
>
> Since there are no costumes in the show, why are we paying not only $573 for costumes as well as a costumer's fee of $300.07. The total bill for the hundreds of costumes in "Cyrano" is $706.00.
>
> I don't care if you talk to Gig Young every day for two hours, a telephone bill of $1,320.00 is not possible.
>
> As for the acting and rehearsal hall figure, that's too ridiculous to even try to break down.[2-1]

A copy of the letter regarding the charges was sent to Whitfield Connor in Denver, where the "Yum Yum Tree" was to next appear, informing him that the "pre-production costs are so ridiculously padded, we would be idiots to pay it" and that "at no time was a $500 booking fee mentioned."

The issue of costs became even more significant following a harsh review of the play in the *Denver Post*, noting as follows:

> Gig Young plays the older man across the hall with more of a sense of wistfulness than an appreciation for the need to get on with the farce.
>
> Laugh after laugh was missed by the cast opening night - largely because of ineffective timing.

The drama editor further stated that the comedy was "precariously suspended" on "slender threads."

> Lawrence Roman's comedy *Under the Yum Yum Tree* is thin theatrical fare at best and very contrived. If the performance spins along at the brightest pace director and actors can achieve, the piece can suffice as a bit of frothy entertainment.[1-2]

Under these circumstances, when cost issues are challenged, they may be submitted to COST (Council of Stock Theatres, Inc.) for review and resolution.

Shelley Winters and the Effect of Gamma Rays and the "Ghost"

Paul Zindel's *The Effect of Gamma Rays on Man-In-The-Moon Marigolds* was awarded the Pulitzer Prize for Drama in 1971. It was only the second Off-Broadway production to receive the Prize. Zindel (1936-2003), a native of New York City, had been a high school teacher and novelist.[3-1]

In the play, Shelley Winters "portrays a middle-aged widow who is tormented by the frustrations and failures of her life and who, in turn, torments her teen-age daughters." The play is "of character, of heartbreak, and of small human victories on many levels."[1-3] Miss Winters, a recipient of two Oscars for best supporting actress, smiled in an interview and said, "I may go on playing 'Marigolds' forever, (as) I love the part."[1-4]

And what about the "ghost"? It was customary for members of the resident company at Elitch to hang pictures of the season's leading man and woman outside the Theatre. At the end of each season, the pictures were ceremoniously removed and primarily hung from the high beams backstage.

Christopher Kirkland, in an interview, stated that it "created a ghostly atmosphere. You look high up in the shadows and could swear Douglas Fairbanks is there watching you. Shelley Winters was absolutely convinced she saw a ghost while she was rehearsing by herself in 1973."[4]

Jose Ferrer in Cyrano [1-5]

Jose Ferrer starred in the title role of *Cyrano* at Elitch and also directed the production.

> *Cyrano* has been something of a saga for Ferrer. He first did it on Broadway, to considerable acclaim in 1946. In 1949, he repeated the role for the Philco TV program. In 1950, Jose starred in the film version of the play, and won an Academy Award for his portrayal. It was also in 1950, that he recorded the play for Capital Records. The disc is now a collectors' item.
>
> The year 1953 found Ferrer doffing the white plume in a Producers' Showcase production of *Cyrano*, and in 1953-54, he revived it at New York's City Center.

The reviewer of the play recognized Ferrer as "one of the last of the great American actors ... (one) who can act the range of comedy, drama, farce; who can play with distinction in every entertainment medium. Here is an actor who also sings, dances, directs and who, in the estimation of his professional peers, stands at the very top."

In addition to his acting chores in Denver and his press and broadcasting obligations, Ferrer happily escorted five of his children and the guest of one of his sons around the environs of the city.

The 1974 Season

Play and Star Selection - Comments by Whitfield Connor

Whitfield Connor was responsible for finding five plays for the season. The search began in February, when Connor began "digging around, loosening the ground so to speak," finding out what was possible or not possible. The serious consideration began the first of March. Connor described the not-so-easy task:

> I want them to be good ... It takes a lot of patience. For every one I sign I turn down perhaps 25. Every year I think I have something special and all too often it slips away. A star says "no" or perhaps gets a big movie deal. I thought I had Julie Harris this year in one of two plays. Then she decided she was too tired and she wanted to stay close to an ailing mother.[5]

The Season

Sandy Dennis and Gary Merrill in "Born Yesterday"
Patty Duke Astin and John Astin in "The Marriage Gambol"
Steve Allen and Jayne Meadows in "Tonight at 8:30"
(Three One-Act plays by Noel Coward)
Mickey Rooney in "Three Goats and a Blanket"
Sid Caesar in "The Prisoner of Second Avenue"

The Marriage Gambol - A Two-Character Play [6]

As thing's turned out at Elitch, *The Marriage Gambol* was a gamble. As the drama editor for the *Denver Post* noted, "It is difficult to write a play for two characters. It is difficult for two players to sustain an entire evening in the theater." Throughout the evening, the play had many set changes, and it was obvious to the audience that the backstage crew outnumbered the cast. As a generous gesture, the Astins brought the crew onstage to share one of their curtain calls.

Mickey Rooney

The title of the play *Three Goats and a Blanket* is taken from an ancient Greek custom of a husband dissolving a marriage and buying his freedom by giving his wife three goats and a blanket. These humble beginnings have been abandoned in favor of alimony, the subject of the play. After the show, Rooney made "a curtain speech likening the plot to his personal history (of many marriages), (and stated) 'You'll see an exhibit of my wedding cakes in the lobby on the way out.'"[7]

However, it was on the way into the Theatre that patrons were caught off guard. Rooney greeted them as they entered the Theatre lobby and was personally peddling souvenir copies of a booklet of his long theatrical life entitled *Photo Memories*. In his curtain call speech, he closed by inviting the patrons who had purchased copies of his booklet to meet him for his autograph and to reminisce with him near the picture gallery in the lobby.[8]

The play was written for Mickey Rooney by television writers Bo Hillard and Woody Kling, whose credits include many of the Jackie Gleason shows and other television comedies.[9-1] Unfortunately, the review of the play may be something that Rooney may wish to exclude from future reminiscing.

> (In his performance of the play's character), Rooney is a walking hangover. He is the leftover taste of the onion in yesterday's hamburger.
>
> He is - in short - rather gross. Rooney's face changes shape as easily as a sopping wet, scrunched up washrag. He is all physical and facial mannerisms and grotesqueries; and he has no hesitancy about turning directly to the audience for an aside or two.[9-2]

Christopher Kirkland described Mickey Rooney as one of the most interesting people ever to play Elitch. Rooney loved the races.

> During matinees, he would say every word of the show as fast as he could, so he could get out in time to bet the end of the card at Centennial Race Track. He'd run out 15 to 20 minutes ahead of the scheduled curtain, shouting, "I said every word. I said every word!"[10]

Steve Allen

Steve Allen was the first host of the long running *Tonight Show* on television, a distinction that won him a place in television history as the founder of late-night talk shows. He appeared at Elitch with his wife, the talented Jayne Meadows, in three short plays from Noel Coward's *Tonight at 8:30*. It was the first time for each on the Elitch stage. Allen charmingly engaged the opening night audience with a curtain speech before the performance began.[9-3] During their stay at Elitch, the couple celebrated their 20th wedding anniversary at a backstage party held in their honor.[9-4]

The general public is aware that Steve Allen is a multi-talented individual who, among other things, has an enduring love of music, which provides a built-in-release of energy for him. It relaxes him. Harold J. Kennedy, noted actor and director, in his book *No Pickle, No Performance*, recalled the following incident in Denver.

> When we were playing Elitch Gardens, after the show every night he would sit at the piano with the combo at the Denver Continental and play for hours. He was rarely recognized, but one night I was sitting at the bar and a tourist sitting next to me said in some surprise, "Isn't that Steve Allen?" I said that it was.
>
> "My God," he said, "what a shame to have him wind up in a dump like this."[11]

Loretto Heights College

In the 1974 season, Loretto Heights College began a summer theater program in their May Bonfils Stanton Center of Performing Arts and brought in "packaged shows" just as was being done at Elitch Theatre and in Central City. However, Loretto Heights College was not using union members for its crew.

On April 26, 1974, Whitfield Connor, concerned about the situation, addressed a letter to the Business Agent of Denver's Theatrical Stage Employees Union, stating:

> It is highly unfair to the other professional operations to have this new theatre open with no union personnel backstage. Further, it gives them a competitive edge over the other two long established theatres. This is a situation which you must deal with promptly and vigorously.[2-2]

The opening play was the musical *No, No, Nanette*, starring Helen Gallagher in the feature role.

> (However), the opening was somewhat dampened by picket lines at the entrances to the Loretto campus, lines thrown up by members of the stagehands' union who haven't been able to reach a working agreement with the Loretto management.[9-5]

The seating capacity at the Loretto Heights theater was 900 seats, while Elitch was designed to seat 1,440.

The 1975 Season

Not a Favorable Season

Notwithstanding the reputation and experience of the featured stars of this season, the comments by the critics were not always favorable, a rare happening for the historic playhouse.

In Praise of Love [12-1]

The *Denver Post* drama critic began her review of the opening play of the season by describing Terence Rattigan's *In Praise of Love* as "a silly play about a serious subject which could have been entitled 'In Praise of Phoniness.'" As to the performances by Kim Hunter and supporting actor Edward Mulhare, who plays her husband, she writes that "their acting does little to add any depth to the characters they portray."

> Somehow, in the play, despite Lydia's impending death and her efforts to keep the news from her husband; despite the fact that her husband already knows, but he thinks he is protecting her from that information; despite references to Lydia's survival of Nazi tortures, all feeling settles into sheer schlock.
>
> The saddest thing about the couple ... isn't that the Cruttwells are facing death, but that the husband and wife can't be honest with each other.
>
> Apparently being phony with each other and the rest of the world has been a way of life during their 28-year marriage. And Lydia offers justification for such behavior ... on grounds that it is kinder than the truth.

Rattigan's play was said to be based loosely on the lives of the then late Kay Kendall and her husband Rex Harrison. Kendall died of leukemia. Harrison maintained that she never knew she was fatally ill, insisting to her that she was ailing from anemia.

Forty Carats

Late night television viewers were able to see Ginger Rogers in the flesh, the lively, versatile, and durable star of Hollywood films of the 30s, 40s, and 50s, her last film role playing Jean Harlow's mother in the film *Harlow* in 1965. In the 1960s, she starred on Broadway in *Hello Dolly*. She later took *Mame* to London's Royal Drury Lane Theater for a 14-month engagement that included a command performance for the Queen.[13]

Forty Carats is the story of a love affair between a young man and a considerably older woman, played by Ginger Rogers. The *Denver Post* review of opening night had the following comments:

> Opening night Monday, (Ginger Rogers) was stagey, melodramatic and her voice at times sounded like the Honda owned by her young suitor in the comedy.
>
> Miss Rogers is no great shakes as a comedienne, but the character she plays is stuck in amusing situations. She is aided by a fine supporting cast, and the comedy, itself, is good.
>
> Director Lucia Victor has done well with her cast, and her cast will do better for her after it learns all the lines.[12-2]

Life on a Limb

The play *Life on a Limb* was an adaptation by Haila Stoddard from the writings of James Thurber. For the Elitch Theatre presentation she received one and one-third percent of the gross receipts.[14]

For the first time in many years, a show was cast with Denver area actors. Auditions were scheduled for July 1st and 2nd at the Theatre, and prospective cast members had to be available for all-day rehearsals from July 11th through the 21st, with opening night scheduled for July 21st.[12-3]

Haila Stoddard had co-produced *The Thurber Carnival* with the late Helen Bonfils, in consultation with Helen Thurber, Thurber's widow. Helen Thurber was in residence at Elitch during the two-week engagement of *Life on a Limb*.[12-3] Fortunately, the drama critic welcomed the play, noting that "Elitch Theatre ended its summer drought Monday night with the opening of a play that is as welcome as soft rain breaking a hot afternoon."[12-4]

Yet, the drama critic could not refrain from suggestions to improve the evening.

> The only major problem with the production (assuming that opening-night delays and lighting mix-ups are a thing of the past) is that it runs a little too long.
>
> Trimming wouldn't hurt. "Brother Endicott," for instance, might make more of a contribution to the show by its absence than its presence.
>
> Also, the program not only isn't an accurate running account of the show, but it contains sloppy errors which are below Elitch Theatre's dignity.
>
> Instrumental music, by the way, is on tape.[12-4]

Life With Father

Thirty-Six years had passed since Howard Lindsay's and Russel Crouse's play *Life With Father* (1939) opened on Broadway. The play went on to set a record for the longest running nonmusical play in Broadway history - 3,224 performances. The comedy is based on Clarence Day Jr.'s recollections in the *New Yorker* about his family's life in New York in the late 1880s. The play's popularity is in part attributed to the unsettling times.

> Arriving as war broke out in Europe and while America was still feeling the effects of the Great Depression, its affectionate portrait of 19th-century home life evoked a past of simple values.[3-2]

The *Denver Post* staff writer who reviewed the play was not the same individual who reviewed the other four plays of the season.* He found favor throughout with the play and its performances.

> To see the play performed so delightfully once more makes it easy to understand its original longevity, to say nothing of numerous revivals since then.
>
> It would be hard to believe that any serious theatergoer has never seen a production of *Life With Father*, but if any such exists, young or old, they should see this one. Those who have, should see it again to recall how much the play undoubtedly delighted them the last time.[12-5]

The Two of Us

Lynn Redgrave's appearance at Elitch in *The Two of Us* received a more glowing review than Ginger Rogers. She was born and raised in a theatrical home environment, being the daughter of Sir Michael Redgrave and younger sister of Vanessa Redgrave.

* It appears that the position of reviewer of plays by the *Denver Post* was in transition. Robert Downing, the designated drama editor in 1974 did not review plays in 1975; instead it was handled by two staff members, with James Mills reviewing *Life With Father*, and Arlynn Nellhaus the other four plays. Barbara MacCay would review plays in 1976 as the designated drama editor.

The *Rocky Mountain News* reporter, commenting on her performance, wrote:

> Let me state, straight out and with no reservation at all, that my favorite Redgrave is named Lynn.
>
> Lynn Redgrave is that rarest of birds, British or otherwise, a comedienne who is felicitously feminine, incisive, funny and uniquely herself. Hers is no jokey, unprobing manner of playing.
>
> She is a special lady, a true star, and one of the finest living actresses and comediennes.[15]

However, notwithstanding Lynn Redgrave's talent as an actress, the play was described as "One Big Zero" by the drama critic of the *Denver Post*. More specifically, she wrote:

> It's a sad evening when the nicest thing to be said for an opening-night play is that the sets were lovely.
>
> Even Lynn Redgrave's starring presence in all four parts of the play couldn't save it from being a dreadful bore.[12-6]

Demolishment of the Trocadero Ballroom [12-7]

The famous Trocadero Ballroom, introduced at Elitch's in 1917, was demolished after Labor Day. The Trocadero attracted many famous bands to Denver, such as Harry James, Dick Jurgens, Tommy and Jimmy Dorsey, Louis Prima, Guy Lombardo, Gene Krupa, Lawrence Welk, Eddy Howard, Stan Kenton, Tex Benecke, Les Brown and Buddy Rich, as well as singers such as Dick Haymes and Perry Como.

The decision to demolish the Trocadero was a difficult one for Jack and Budd Gurtler. With "nostalgic regret," Jack Gurtler said:

> We've delayed the decision for years, hoping that ballroom dancing would make a comeback. We've maintained a beautiful setting ... offered the finest dance music available, and we've insisted upon a high level of decorum in the ballroom.
>
> However, instead of a resurgence, ballroom dancing keeps going in the opposite direction.

In the mid-1930s, there were up to 1,500 couples that packed the Trocadero Ballroom on Saturday nights and nearly filled the dance floor on the six other evenings of the week and during a matinee. However, in recent years the Trocadero had been operating only four to eight hours a week and couples rarely exceeded a few hundred persons. Equally saddening to the Gurtlers was the dwindling number of dance bands and their reluctance to travel.

While fans of the famed ballroom began circulating petitions to stop the landmark from being razed, Gurtler appropriately noted that the efforts of those interested in signing the petition would have been better served had they showed up *en masse* in the past years to dance.

However, the demolishment of the Trocadero cannot demolish the many memories and stories by patrons of the Gardens of times gone by, such as the filming of scenes at the Trocadero for Hollywood's movie of *The Benny Goodman Story*. The Gurtlers recalled another story.

> They remember with a smile that a Denver teen-ager named Mamie Dowd (*sic*) once was told by the ballroom manager to quit dancing cheek-to-cheek with her partner - or get off the floor. She later married a guy name Dwight Eisenhower.

Mamie Doud Eisenhower

Mamie Doud Eisenhower was born in Boone, Iowa, on November 14, 1890. Her family moved to Denver, Colorado when she was seven years old and lived in a large house at 750 Lafayette Street. On July 1, 1916, she and Dwight D. Eisenhower were married in Denver at 12 noon in the first floor music room of the Doud family home. The family maintained an interest in the home until after the death of her mother in 1960.

Denver Public Library Western History Collection - *Rocky Mountain News Archives*

Jose Ferrer in *Cyrano* (1973)

Chapter Thirty-Two

(1976 - 1979)

Play Selection - Some Thoughts
Lana Turner
Compensation of the Stars
Farley Granger and Julie Harris
Van Johnson, Vincent Price and John Raitt

The 1976 Season

The Elitch Theatre celebrated its season with a variety of plays ranging from mystery to politics, romance and a musical with a Bicentennial flavor - *Shenandoah.* A host of theatrical stars spanned the season. Among them were Richard Kiley, Teresa Wright, Jan Farrand, John Raitt, Sandra Dee, Maureen O'Sullivan, Sylvia Sidney, Victor Jory and Peggy Cass.

Agatha Christie's most popular murder mystery, *The Mousetrap,* was selected to open the season. At the time, *The Mousetrap* had been running in London for 24 years and was still a strong box-office attraction.

Jan Farrand appeared in *Noel Coward in Two Keys.* Her story was that of a local girl who made good. She was raised in Denver and got her first look inside Elitch Theatre when she was six years old and her parents took her to see *Watch on the Rhine.* Her father had been a member of the Metropolitan Opera chorus but came to Denver for his health. Jan had planned a career in music, but her ambitions changed when she studied drama at North High School with Kathleen Ommaney whom she recalls as being "a marvelous, exciting teacher." After graduating as valedictorian from North High School, she attended the University of Colorado where she continued her study of theater.

She later moved to Cambridge, Massachusetts and helped start the Brattle Theater in Harvard Square. She made her Broadway debut with Cyril Ritchard in *The Relapse* and later appeared with Louis Jordan in *Tonight in Samarkand.*[1]

Richard Kiley made his first appearance at Elitch this season. He commented in an interview, "I love the atmosphere of the old Theatre. It has lovely old ghosts."[2]

Following the opening night performance of the musical *Shenandoah,* John Raitt left his dressing room in time to catch the theater patrons in the lobby as they filed out. He shook hands with them, joked with them, answered questions and signed autographs.[3-1]

The 1977 Season

Play Selection - Some Thoughts

Theatergoers often wonder how a theater manager or artistic director goes about selecting plays for a season. On the surface, it would seem to be an easy task. However, in an interview with Elitch Theatre's producer Whitfield Connor regarding play selection for Elitch's season, the reporter stated that Connor sometimes found himself in an awkward position.

> Many of Denver's theatergoers don't particularly take kindly to the growing stage-use of four-to 12-letter words describing everything from anatomical functions and aberrations to one's ancestry.
>
> But what is unacceptable to some is perfectly acceptable to others. With the presentation of *California Suite*, Elitch's season opener, Connor received more than 15 letters, at least as many telephone calls, from patrons who objected strenuously to the language therein.
>
> Figuring, as Connor does, that only about 10 per cent of those who were offended bothered to write or call, that places the number of offendees (sic) somewhere around 300 for the opener.
>
> (As to the problem of explicit language, Connor is far more philosophical). "A word in and of itself, poor thing, is neither dirty nor clean," Connor commented. "We have to salute our young people who, a long time ago, began teaching us. One thing they have taught us is that obscenities are in actions, not words."
>
> "Those words we seem to object to so much are the oldest words in the language. They have been there ever since the Anglos (sic) and the Saxons put them down. One of Shakespeare's characters refused to take an offered seat 'because a dog pisseth there.'"
>
> Connor wanted to bring *Equus* to the Elitch stage as one of this summer's attractions, but the plan was nixed by Elitch owners because of the play's necessary, even vital, nude seduction scene.[3-2]

"Surprisingly, there have been no complaints whatsoever on *Same Time Next Year*," Connor said, a play that deals with marital infidelity and which contains some of the words uttered in *California Suite*.

> "The difference," Connor commented, "is that *California Suite* contained four playlets. The time for each doesn't allow you to get so totally involved in any one of them. So, the words stand out more."[3-2]

Same Time, Next Year

Same Time, Next Year is a comedy by Bernard Slade which opened on Broadway in 1975 and ran for 1,453 performances. Although the play is about adultery, there was very little objection to the basic premise of the play. As to the play's use of four-letter words, director Crane was straightforward in his comments.

> Sooner or later, we have to face up to the fact that they are just words.
>
> Every modern play has some four-letter words in it. My feeling is that you can't change everything in the show, so why change anything? I apologize to the people who are offended.
>
> Even in Boston, the audiences didn't mind that the play was about adultery, because it's a sweet play. The affair doesn't affect either person's marriage negatively. It strengthens them.[4-1]

Van Johnson

Send Me No Flowers is a comedy by Norman Barasch and Carroll Moore about George Kimbell, a hypochondriac who is certain he is going to have a heart attack, occasioned by his overhearing a telephone conversation by his doctor about another patient with a real, and not imagined, heart problem. Kimbell mistakenly believes it is his diagnosis.

> He is so convinced about his immediate demise he arranges all the details of his death. He even picks a second husband to take care of his bereaved wife after he is gone.[4-2]

Of course, everyone in the audience knows Kimbell is perfectly healthy. The role of Kimbell is not an easy comedic role, for he must appear to be something of a fool, without being a buffoon, while at the same time calling for sympathy. The critics approved the performance.

> Johnson, that warm appeal not appreciably damaged by time, takes his share of comedic control of the play as he sets about reorganizing his wife's life so that it will function smoothly after he "departs." The actor always has had an amazing aptitude for comedy, and it comes through intact on the Elitch stage.[3-3]

On August 25, 1977, following his performance in *Send Me No Flowers*, Van Johnson was confronted with a surprise celebration for his 61st birthday. Denver Mayor Bill McNichols appeared at the Theatre with a band, balloons and champagne.[5] This author was among the members of the audience that evening and recalls Van Johnson jokingly commenting, "It is a pleasure to play at Elitch. It reminds me of something my mother said to me. 'Son, I know you'll some day wind up in an amusement park.'"

Van Johnson still appeared on stage wearing red socks as his trademark, sort of as a good-luck charm for him. He also signed his equity contracts in red in large script.[6-1]

Lana Turner

In an interview with Josephine Gonzales, the matron and first aid nurse of Elitch Theatre, in sharing her fond memories of the performers who played Elitch, the news reporter wrote:

> Lana Turner was the only "difficult one," she said. "She didn't want anyone backstage for hours before a performance ... because of her make-up ... she was kind of standoffish ... she wouldn't give any autographs ... But I can understand that ... some people are so rude ... But she was very attractive in her make-up."[7]

In a review of *Bell, Book and Candle,* the reporter made the following observations about Ms. Turner.

> Ms. Turner looks lovely, despite the unflattering lighting, at least from her upper eyelashes down and from her eyebrows up. In between, there is a rather garish turquoise cast to her eyelids, which lasts and lasts and lasts, from the first act to the second (two weeks later) and on into the third (two months later).
>
> The main problem with the bizarre eye shadow is that it is totally out of synch with the rest of Ms. Turner's elegant dress, perfect coiffure and general physical grace. The rare appearance of a stage-film legend deserves somewhat more attention to detail.[4.3]

Compensation of the Stars [8]

The salaries of the star performers for the 1977 season were as follows:

Lynn Redgrave - $4,000 a week
Keir Dullea - $3,500 a week
Rosemary Prinz - $2,000 a week
Lana Turner - $8,000 a week
John Raitt - $5,000 a week
Gaylea Byrne - $1,200 a week
Van Johnson - $5,000 a week

The contract read, however, that the weekly salary did not include rehearsal pay or any other sums that were due or became due the actor. Rehearsals of the plays were usually accomplished in the cities where the play was packaged. Accordingly, rehearsal fees at Elitch were not extensive, if any. In *Same Time, Next Year,* Rosemary Prinz received a rehearsal payment of $300.

The contract usually provided for additional compensation depending on the attendance. For example, Keir Dullea's contract provided that he would receive, in addition to his weekly compensation of $3,500, 25% of the gross weekly box office receipts over and above $52,000 (exclusive of admission taxes), with the understanding that the Theatre had a gross proceeds potential of $66,000 for the week.

In addition to monetary compensation, the manager provided the performers with other benefits, such as air transportation, a star dressing room for the actor's exclusive use, as well as suitable living accommodations. For example, in the case of Lana Turner, Whitfield Connor noted that reservations were made at the "Radisson Denver Hotel (two bedroom, two bath, with kitchen and separate living area) which we consider to be the top of the town."

Compensation for Cast Members

Generally, compensation for supporting cast members was substantially less than that received by the star performers, as it was the "stars" who drew audiences. Cast members usually averaged between $300 and $600 a week. For example, Bob Moak, an excellent comedic actor in the supporting cast of *Send Me No Flowers*, received $525.00 a week.

The 1978 Season

Robert Carello in "The Magic Show"
(a musical of magic)
Peggy Cass in "An Almost Perfect Person"
Patrice Munsel and Edward Mulhare in "The Play's The Thing"
Farley Granger in "Count Dracula"
Julie Harris in "The Belle of Amherst"

The following is a brief walk-through of two of the theatrical offerings at the Elitch Theatre during its 1978 season. Other than the names of stars and plays, the season did not have any extraordinary history assigned to it - no changes in policy or shift in emphasis.

Another Dracula

> There are a variety of Draculas on stages throughout America these days. In New York, the Broadway production of *Dracula* and the off-Broadway production of *The Passion of Dracula* have created a cult of vampire buffs.
>
> But seeing one Dracula doesn't mean you've seen them all. The *Count Dracula* which opened at the Elitch Theatre Monday night may be the world's first soap opera "Dracula." In fact, it might be filmed and run on daytime television, retitled "One Neck to Suck."[9]

Farley Granger played the role of Dracula. Early in his career he appeared in two Hitchcock films: in 1948 as a brooding young psychopath in the film *Rope*, and later in the Hitchcock thriller *Strangers on a Train*. For some reason, in the early 1950s his movie career was cut short and he returned to the stage, appearing in repertory with Eva LeGallienne, playing such roles as Luvborg in *Hedda Gabler* and Proctor in *The Crucible*. He returned to films in the 1960s appearing mostly in obscure Italian productions. [10]

> (In *Count Dracula*), Farley Granger's Dracula is anything but a monster. He's a sophisticated velvet-suited aristocrat, a man who looks more like an opera singer bored with his admirers than a vampire on the trail of a beautiful young jugular.
>
> At the very worst, this Dracula is a snob you might not want to invite to your next lawn party, with all his affected cape swishing and funny hand gestures.[9]

Whether the audiences enjoyed the play is not clear from the newspaper accounts. However, one may judge from the following observations:

> In the current version traveling the summer-stock circuit, the sets are impressive, and the company onstage is first-rate. But the story of the blood-sucking villain, who preens like a graveyard Romeo, smells of high camp.
>
> No one would have thought of making (Dracula) ... into the matinee idol (for women of all ages) he has become in the 1970s.
>
> But it does make perfect sense that Granger's brooding young psychopath of *Rope* and elegant villain of *The Heiress* should find maturity, finally, in the irresistibly ghoulish and charmingly dreadful Count from Transylvania.[11-1]

Julie Harris

Julie Harris was born in 1925 in Grosse Pointe, Michigan. She was educated at the Yale School of Drama and made her Broadway debut in *It's A Gift* (1945). She appeared in many other Broadway plays, among them being the gamin Joan of Arc in *The Lark* (1955), Mary Todd Lincoln in *The Last of Mrs. Lincoln* (1972) and poet Emily Dickinson in *The Belle of Amherst* (1976).

The Belle of Amherst had its only production of the summer on the Elitch stage. The only other productions of this one-woman play during the year were in Florida at Easter and at Harris's old school in Grosse Pointe, Michigan in May.[11-2] Whitfield Conner, a long-time friend of Harris stated that at Grosse Pointe, Harris "thought it would be an opportunity for her mother, who lives there to see it before she died, but sadly, she was too ill to attend."[11-3]

The drama critic of the *Rocky Mountain News* called the play and the performance of Miss Harris at Elitch a triumph.

> Julie Harris lives among the mementoes of the poetess' life onstage. She calls herself, as Emily called herself, "plain, but with bold hair."

She uses her hands and her crescent blue eyes and her narrow feet to bring back the luminous figure that was Emily Dickinson for all to know in her eccentricities onstage.

Miss Harris brought the opening night audience, accustomed to remaining comfortably in its seats, to its feet and then rewarded each member thereof with an exultant closing cry, arms outstretched, of Emily Dickinson's verse.[11-4]

It was a coincidence that 1890 was the year in which the first collection of Emily Dickinson's poems was published, four years after her death, and one in which John and Mary Elitch opened their lovely Elitch Gardens and Theatre.[12]

The 1979 Season

Van Johnson in "Boeing-Boeing"
Paxton Whitehead in "The Crucifer of Blood"
Vincent Price in "Diversions & Delights"
Dirk Benedict in "The Rainmaker"
John Raitt in "Man of La Mancha"

The season included plays that dealt with personages known in history and in literature, such as Sherlock Holmes and Dr. Watson, Oscar Wilde and Miguel Cervantes and his servant Sancho.

Boeing-Boeing [13]

Boeing-Boeing is a four-bedroom farce featuring Van Johnson in the leading role and three well-stuffed ladies wearing towel wraps and stretch undies.

Johnson ... keeps a revolving roster of international stewardesses happy between their global hops.

There is one double door in the set, three bedroom doors, and one which swings wildly as the stews-in-residence show up at awkward times and flit in and out in negligees.

Notwithstanding the plot, the review stated that the play "barely squeaks by as an evening of theater," but "is saved from insignificance by a very funny second banana named Bob Moak." As to the performance of Van Johnson, the critic wrote that he "acts as if he had just dropped by to watch" and "seems breathless and almost a spectator on stage."

In contrast, in commenting on Moak, the following is stated:

Moak carries the burden of the plot and of the entire evening. He is the one who frantically switches the photographs of the visiting ladies as they pop up unexpectedly.

And he has perfected a system of mannerisms which are sublime and ridiculous. He drags his pants up over his shoe tops, spins in erratic circles, stammers and tapers off vaguely at the end of his *faux pas*. Each of the gorgeous women confides in him or kisses him and he ends up bafflingly engaged to one of them at the end.

To add to matters, on opening night, a "leg snapped off an essential piece of furniture" and "a bank of overhead lights flickering on and off, fazed no one on stage. The plot ran on, gathering steam like a sturdy old locomotive."

> Everyone on stage seemed secure enough near the end to stop for a sly aside or two. "You take this one," Moak told Johnson as he groped for a line. "You make the big money."

Vincent Price

The *Denver Post* reporter noted that actor Vincent Price is quite comfortable portraying Oscar Wilde in his one-man show, *Diversions and Delights*. The play takes place on November 28, 1899, while Oscar Wilde was in exile in Paris, a year before his death, and he stands alone on the stage, offering reminiscences and observations of himself, one of the most fascinating lives in all of English literature.

Price's contract salary for his performance at Elitch was $15,000.00 a week (not including rehearsal pay or any other sums that may be due or become due the actor). This was considerably higher than other salaries paid to actors in the "star package system."[6-2] With regard to the compensation paid to him, in addition to Vincent Price's experience and popularity as an actor in the role, another factor may have been that no other actors had to be compensated. Clearly, however, his compensation was evidence of his talent, as reflected in an article that identifies him as a "major theatrical talent" performing a most difficult role. Price's success in playing the role was evident in his comment about the mail he received: "Half the mail I get is addressed to Oscar Wilde. That shows me the audience has lost me, which is exactly what I want to happen."[14]

Vincent Price was a noted artist and art collector. Price had donated paintings from his collection to Yale University and to a museum in Albuquerque. During his appearance at Elitch Theatre, Price was honored at the Denver Art Museum. Price could see the museum from his hotel room and admired its roof line. "It's wonderful," he said. "There should be knights standing on its roof."[15-1]

The Local Artist and Vincent Price

In an interview with Christopher Kirkland, producing director at Elitch Theatre, he recalled an incident when Vincent Price's car was broken into right outside the Theatre. Kirkland reluctantly informed him that "with all those canvasses and sculptures in the car, I have no way of knowing what's been taken." Vincent Price looked at him oddly and said, "What? The car was empty." It turned out that a local artist who wanted to get Price's attention had broken into the car and left his work there.[16]

Dirk Benedict

In a letter to Harold J. Kennedy, who was planning a summer circuit tour in which Dirk Benedict would perform in one of three plays being considered - *The Rainmaker, Bus Stop* or *Deathtrap* -Benedict wrote:

> It was very much appreciated ... your letter explaining in some detail the theaters I would be playing this summer. It is very attractive to me for several reasons ... foremost because I am hungry to get on a STAGE in front of a LIVE audience and do what it is I chose this profession for in the first place ... ACT. How far removed film and television are from the original dream.[17]

The play selected for Dirk Benedict at Elitch was *The Rainmaker*, performing the role of Bill Starbuck. Benedict was well-known for his television role as Lt. Starbuck in *Battlestar Galactica*. In a minor scene, set in the corner of a barn, the script of *The Rainmaker* called for Benedict to take off his shirt. Prolonged whistles and stamps and feminine squeals erupted from the audience, and Benedict hung his head while he waited.[15-2]

John Raitt

Denver audiences were pleased to welcome the services of musical comedy legend John Raitt for their *Man of La Mancha*.

> On the opening night of "La Mancha" at Elitch, Raitt had come out for a curtain call and chatted from the footlights. He was considering touring in a revival of *Carousel*, he said, adding that he might have to do it with the help of a couple of bottles of a certain colorless, slow-working hair dye. The audience whistled and applauded wildly.[15-3]
>
> Raitt halted his final curtain call with a benevolent spread of his arms, said a few introductory words and launched into a full rendition of "My Way."[15-4]

A Denverite on Broadway [15-5]

In October of 1979, Patricia Elliott, a Denver native and a graduate of South High School, took over the role of Mrs. Kendal in the Broadway presentation of *The Elephant Man*. Miss Elliott studied at the London Academy of Music and Drama. She returned to America and attended Harvard and began to act at the Loeb Theater in Cambridge. In 1973, she created the role Countess Charlotte in the Broadway musical *A Little Night* Music, which won her a Tony award. In 1978 she received a Tony nomination for her performance in *The Shadow Box*.

When she was interviewed by a *Rocky Mountain News* Reporter as she was about to start rehearsal for *The Elephant Man*, Miss Elliott stated that she didn't think she had ever been interviewed by anyone in her hometown of Denver. She exclaimed, "My mother will be thrilled."

Photo by Kenn Bisio, *Denver Post,* 1977

Actor Van Johnson toasts the Elitch Theatre audience during his surprise 61st birthday celebration on the Elitch stage following his performance in *Send Me No Flowers* (1977).

Denver Public Library Western History Collection - *Rocky Mountain News* Archives

Following his opening night performance of the musical *Shenandoah,* John Raitt appeared in the outer lobby of the Theatre to meet theater patrons as they filed out, shook hands with them, answered questions and signed autographs (1976).

Denver Public Library Western History Collection - *Rocky Mountain News* Archives

Richard Kiley in *Noel Coward in Two Keys* (1976)

Denver Public Library Western History Collection - *Rocky Mountain News* Archives

Julie Harris as Emily Dickenson in a scene from the *Belle of Amherst* (1978)

Denver Public Library Western History Collection - *Rocky Mountain News* Archives

Dirk Benedict starred in *The Rainmaker* (1979)

Chapter Thirty-Three

(1980 - 1982)

Pat O'Brien - A Dream Realized
"Favored Nations" Clause in an Actor's Contract
"The Streets of New York" - Mary Elitch's First Play
The Shift in Emphasis
Joslin's Department Store
The Death of Mary Coyle Chase
The Show Will Go On For Theater Buff

The 1980 Season

Sada Thompson in "Children"
William Shatner in "Deathtrap"
Pat and Eloise O'Brien in "The Second Time Around"
Farley Granger and Orson Bean in "The Streets of New York"
Charles Repole and Cast of the Broadway Musical in "I Love My Wife"

Children

A review of *Children* in the *Denver Post*, the opening play of the season, was unfavorable, the headline reading "*Children* Never Rises Above the Shallowness of Its Characters."[1-1] It is rare that a script of the talented playwright A. R. Gurney, Jr. is criticized. Gurney had previously received the 1971 Drama Desk Award and a 1977 Rockefeller Playwriting Award. Among his many later plays were *The Dining Room* (1982), *The Perfect Party* (1986) and *Sweet Sue* (1987).

However, the *Rocky Mountain News* review was more favorable, stating that "under Sada Thompson's glowing spell, it is an evening finely-honed of theater."[2-1] The setting of *Children* was the front of the family's shingled summer house on the island of Nantucket. The widowed mother, a matron of proper New England tradition steeped in custom, had summoned the children to inform them that "in September, in the fall, when I marry, the house will belong to you." It was a weekend of mixed feelings. The children were born during the baby boom "that produced runaways, seekers and oracles." It was a meeting on the terrace "remembering the bunk beds and back stairs of growing up. A visit, one more time, to see if mother still loves you best." The play dealt with the tensions arising out of the situation.

> But Sada Thompson presides - predictably obtuse and entirely composed - as mother. Gurney has given her a wonderful scene of aberrant rage. "I don't want to know your phone numbers," she tells the children, suitcase in hand, "and I won't give you mine. Go ahead and hurt yourselves," she shouts at the grandchildren as she watches them setting off Fourth of July fireworks in the distance.[2-1]

However the audiences may have felt about the play, a consoling contribution was contained in the theater program which featured a recipe for Sada Thompson's New England Style Clam Chowder.

Pat O'Brien - A Dream Realized

Pat O'Brien acknowledged that it took him a long time to fulfill a dream. In fact, it nearly took him 61 years in show business. He realized that dream when he appeared in a play on the historic stage of the Elitch Theatre.

Following his opening night performance in *The Second Time Around*, Pat O'Brien, now a deceptive 81 years young, "remained on stage and told the opening night audience of his dream to perform at Elitch after a career in the theater that has spanned more than half a century."[1-2]

> Before the curtain rang down on *The Second Time Around*, Mrs. Pat O'Brien made a graceful exit and Pat himself lingered on stage to explain that he has a bit of arthritis in his hip, that he turned 80 last November and that he will "sail to London with Mommy (Eloise) and the Jimmy Cagneys in September" to begin filming of E. L. Doctorow's *Ragtime*.
>
> And then Pat ... reeled off a trio of "shaggy-dog" stories, two in Irish brogue and one in Yiddish. At the end of this scrap of stand-up comedy ... he recited the Gaelic blessing which invokes soft winds at the back and hopes you'll beat the devil when you die.[2-2]

The Second Time Around had been a tour de force for Pat and his wife, Eloise. The O'Briens had been married 49 years and *The Second Time Around* is one of the many shows they had performed together since Mrs. O'Brien had come out of retirement 20 years earlier. She was an actress when Pat met her in a Chicago performance of *Broadway* in 1927. In an interview, they briefly described their meeting and courtship.

> "I thought she was absolutely beautiful as she walked through the door. As she passed by I reached out and patted her on the backside. I don't remember if it was a left or right hook, but she responded in kind."
>
> Mrs. O'Brien said it was a couple of years before he got around to proposing. "He said, 'Let's get married or something.' I said, 'Let's get married or nothing.'"
>
> Feeling that two careers weren't manageable, Mrs. O'Brien left the stage to raise two sons and two daughters.[2-3]

The "Favored Nations" Clause in an Actor's Contract

In the play *The Second Time Around* with the O'Briens, William Lithgow played the part of Dr. Arthur Morse, a psychiatrist married to the daughter in the play. His contract with Elitch Theatre contained a "favored nations" clause which stated that except for Pat and Eloise O'Brien, "no other actor in the company shall receive more money than Mr. Lithgow (this is to include salary and per diem compensation), before or after the signing of the contract for employment in *The Second Time Around* at Elitch Gardens in Denver, Colorado, from July 21 through August 3, 1980."[3]

William Shatner

William Shatner was well-known for his role as Captain Kirk in the television series, *Star Trek,* when he reported to Elitch for the 1980 season. He appeared in Ira Levin's comedy/thriller *Deathtrap*, performing the role of Sidney Bruhl, the mystery writer suffering from a dry spell. At the time of the Elitch performance, William Shatner had three daughters, one of whom was in her senior year at the University of Colorado.[1-3]

On July 16, 1980, the Elitch management held a Star Trek costume contest, and William Shatner appeared as Captain Kirk to judge the finalists of the contest.[1-4]

The Streets of New York - Mary Elitch's First Play

The Streets of New York was the very first play that Mary Elitch had seen, and the experience made Mary determined to become associated, in some manner, with the life of theater. It was in San Francisco in 1872, following their marriage, that John took her to see the play which, at the time, starred Frank Mayo.

The play as written in 1857 by Dion Boucicault, a French-born playwright of Irish descent, was adapted from Edouard Brisbarre and Eugene Nus' *Les Pauvres de Paris*. The play was presented on Broadway as *The Poor of New York* and was later revived frequently, usually with the title *The Streets of New York,* and in England as *The Streets of Liverpool* or *The Streets of London*.

Boucicault left his native Dublin to study in London. He began to act and write in 1836, made his American acting debut in Boston in 1854, and two months later on Broadway in one of his own plays. He is said to have written over 200 plays.[4-1]

The original New York production of *The Streets of New York* opened at the Forty-Eighth Street Theater and played over 2800 performances. The play's historical significance lay in its use of contemporary events, the financial panic of 1857, and its thinly veiled caricatures of well-known citizens of the day. It was the first indigenous American play to utilize actual social/political events as a framework for a fictional story. *The Streets of New York* stands today as a landmark in the evolution of American theater and its appearance marked a significant new beginning in American theatrical history.

I Love My Wife

Outside of the Elitch Theatre, there were roller coaster type rides in the amusement park. Within the theater, there were some roller coaster bumps and rides provided by the play selection, perhaps a few too many. For the final performance of the season, the theatergoers welcomed a musical. Michael Stewart and Cy Coleman's *I Love My Wife* was selected to close the 1980 season. While this musical had not been categorized with those of Rodgers and Hammerstein, it nevertheless provided an evening of relaxation, without mystery, murders, family tensions, or the streets of New York.

Charles Repole, a member of the cast of *I Love My Wife,* was described as "a consummate, versatile singer/dancer/actor." Indeed he was! Repole had worked as stage manager for Ben Vereen and Joel Grey and had starred in *Whoopee* on Broadway. Opening night at Elitch was successful except that "a recalcitrant lamp wouldn't light, then came on unexpectedly." Repole noted that audiences are amused and forgiving of that kind of problem. He recalled a show in which he was previously cast "when a piece of scenery didn't work, I just did a little dance until it appeared," and the show continued as planned.[1-5]

The 1981 Season

The Shift in Emphasis

The "star package" season began at Elitch in 1964 with ten plays a season. This continued until 1970 when the number of plays per season was reduced to five, with the last play usually being a musical. In more recent years, a musical had not always been a part of the season, most likely due to increased cost because of the large number of players that usually make up the cast of most musicals. A musical with few performers was more likely to be selected, such as the one in the 1982 season, *They're Playing Our Song* with two players. A musical concert by a single performer was from time to time a part of the season offering. Notwithstanding these changes, to most theatergoers, Elitch Theatre remained the centerpiece of their summer experiences.

The Season

While this season did not offer a musical or a musical concert as part of its regular season, a preseason ballet was presented of *Giselle* starring Giselle Kirkland, the half-sister of Christopher Kirkland, the producer-director of Elitch Theatre. A reviewer of her performance stated that she is "arguably, the greatest ballet talent currently performing."[5-1]

The following were the five plays selected for the regular season. Lanford Wilson's *Talley's Folly* (1980) and Donald L. Coburns' *The Gin Game* (1978) had each been previously awarded the Pulitzer Prize for Drama.

Judd Hirsch in "Talley's Folly"
Pat and Eloise O'Brien in "On Golden Pond"
Jane Powell in "The Marriage-Go-Round"
Gene Rayburn in "I Ought To Be in Pictures"
Nancy Walker and Pat Hingle in "The Gin Game"

Talley's Folly

Talley's Folly, the opening play of the season, is a two-character play that starred Judd Hirsch and Veronica Cartwright. The play is part of a trilogy of plays about the Talleys, a wealthy Lebanon, Missouri family, owners of the local garment mill. Lanford Wilson, the playwright, wrote *Talley's Folly* with Judd Hirsch in mind. *The Fifth of July* (1978) was the first play of the trilogy. It ran for 158 performances at the Circle Theatre off-Broadway. *A Tale Told* (1981) was the last play of the trilogy, and not as popular. Hirsch was in the off-Broadway production of *Talley's Folly* in 1979, and he played the principal role when it moved to Broadway in 1980.[4-2] At Elitch, Hirsch directed and starred in the play.

Colorado figured largely in Hirsch's career. It was at the "Back Room Theater" at Estes Park, Colorado, in 1962, that the future Broadway and television star and Academy Award nominee made his acting debut.

> Besides playing the villain in "terrible" melodramas, (Hirsch) directed the 1928 communist farce, *Squaring the Circle,* for the summer tourist crowd. Now he cheerfully admits it may have been the most misguided production ever to hit that town and he wasn't paid the $80 he should have earned for the summer.
>
> "Not a grandiose beginning for an actor," he said.[5-2]

In *Talley's Folly*, Hirsch played the role of Matt Friedman, a forty-two year old man, dark-complexioned, rather warm and unhurried, and of whom the playwright wrote, "In his voice there is still a trace of a German-Jewish accent, of which he is probably unaware."[6] The play has an engaging beginning as Friedman speaks to the audience in a monologue, which the drama critic states is "seemingly designed more to entertain the rest of the audience while the late arrivals make their own entrances."[5-3] With the curtain up, the following comments are interspersed with descriptions of the set and the neighboring area.

> They tell me that we have ninety-seven minutes here tonight - without intermission. So if that means anything to anybody; if you think you'll need a drink of water or anything ...
>
> You know, a year ago I drove Sally home from a dance; and while we were standing on the porch up at the house, we looked down to the river and saw this silver flying thing rise straight up and zip off. We came running down to the river, we thought the Japanese had landed some amazing new flying machine, but all we found was the boathouse here, and - uh, that was enough.
>
> I'll just point out some of the facilities till everybody gets settled in. If everything goes well for me tonight, this should be a waltz, one-two-three, one-two-three; a no-holds-barred romantic story, and since I'm not

> a romantic type, I'm going to need the whole valentine here to help me: the woods, the willows, the vines, the moonlight, the band - there's a band that plays tonight, over in the park.

The monologue is interrupted by Sally Talley's voice off stage saying "Matt? Matt? Are you in that boathouse? I'm not going to come down there if you're not there 'cause that place gives me the creeps after dark. Are you there?"[6]

And the play begins. It is about Matt Friedman and Sally Talley. After a long absence, he has returned to the Talley farm in one last effort to woo and marry her.

> Friedman's problem is that he's Jewish, over 40, has a beard, and takes a dim view of World War II. How, one might wonder, would a character like Friedman ever conceivably get past the point of social amenities with a woman coming from a Missouri WASP background.
>
> The answer is that Sally is a bit of a maverick herself. At 32 and unmarried, she holds the distinction of being fired as a Sunday school teacher for trying to explain to her students the workers' point of view toward a strike at her family's mill.[5-3]

In the end, love conquers all!

Veronica Cartwright was cast as Sally Talley. Cartwright had appeared in a number of films, including *The Birds* and *Invasion of the Body Snatchers*.

On Golden Pond

Pat O'Brien had appeared at Elitch for the first time in 1980 in *The Second Time Around*. In an interview with him at that time, he expressed his love for Elitch Theatre, stating that he and Eloise, his wife, "always wanted to play here at Elitch because it's one of the most traditional theaters in America ... This is a real nostalgia trip for us."[7]

In his return to Elitch in *On Golden Pond*, it was truly a family affair, with Pat and Eloise playing the roles of husband and wife, and their daughter Brigit O'Brien, playing the role of their daughter in the play.

In the star package contractual arrangements, it was the theater's responsibility to prepare the sets for the production in accordance with plans provided by the star package company. Jeffrey Beecroft, who had designed sets for Broadway and off-Broadway plays, was selected to be the Elitch set designer for the 1981 season. Beecroft was familiar with the play's set design, as he was the assistant designer for the play on Broadway; however, at Elitch the set had to be changed. From time to time, a successful stage design on Broadway must be changed to accommodate the needs or deficits of an actor. He said of the Elitch presentation, "I was given a 10-foot stage depth to work with because of Pat O'Brien," inasmuch as the 81-year old

O'Brien was partially disabled with an arthritic hip, and was not able to traverse more than a 10-foot radius on stage.* It had its effect on the performance.

> On a cramped, pallid set designed by Jeffrey Beecroft, director Jack V. Booch has his actors meander lethargically through a maze of furniture, the armchairs and sofa and tables that clutter the living room of a musty old house on Golden Pond in Maine.
>
> Eloise O'Brien looks particularly uncomfortable with Booch's blocking. She seems to be forever hiding behind sofas and chairs.[5-4]

Joslin's Department Store

From time to time, Elitch performers would appear at social gatherings, such as at a meeting of the Rotarians, and speak about their experiences as actors.

This season, Joslin's Department Store arranged through the Elitch management for Nancy Walker and Pat Hingle to appear at 1:30 p.m. for customers to meet and chat with the stage and screen notables.[5-5]

The Death of Mary Coyle Chase [5-6]

On October 20, 1981, Denver playwright Mary Coyle Chase died of a heart attack at Denver's University Hospital. She was best known for her Pulitzer Prize-winning play *Harvey,* which became the fourth-longest running play in Broadway history. She was born in Denver on February 25, 1907, attended West High School, the University of Colorado and the University of Denver. She worked as a reporter for the *Rocky Mountain News* before writing her first play, *Me Third,* for the Federal Theater Project in 1936. *Me Third* was presented on Broadway the following year. While at the *News,* she met Robert L. Chase, a reporter (who later retired as associate editor of the newspaper), and they were married in Denver on June 7, 1928.

After her marriage, Mrs. Chase worked for the International News Service and United Press. She was a member of the board of trustees of the Bonfils Theater, the Denver Center for the Performing Arts and an honorary life member of the Women's Press Club in Denver.

In addition to *Harvey,* Mrs. Chase wrote a number of other plays, among them being *Mrs. McThing, Bernadine, The Next Half Hour* and *Midgie Purvis.*

Donald R. Seawall, then chairman of the board of the Denver Center of Performing Arts, characterized Mrs. Chase as "Colorado's first lady of theater."

* *Rocky Mountain News* (Now Section), Aug 2, 1981, p. 28.

Beecroft was careful to note, however, that he considers Elitch Theatre "a wonderful theater in terms of space. And the prop crew is as good as any in New York."

The 1982 Season

James McArthur and Cybil Shepherd in "Lunch Hour"
Sandy Dennis and Barbara Rush in "The Supporting Cast"
Timothy Bottoms and Marsha Skaggs in "They're Playing Our Song"
James Lawless in "Dear Ruth"
Barbara Feldon and Eileen Heckart in "What I Did Last Summer"

Some Observations on the Season

The light-hearted comedy *Lunch Hour* was written by Jean Kerr.

> The play is about a woman (Shepherd) and a psychiatrist (MacArthur) who get to know each other because their spouses are having an affair ... When the woman and psychiatrist decide to make it seem as if they too are having an affair to get their spouses back, "all hell breaks loose."[8-1]

James McArthur was first involved with Colorado theater thirty years prior as an usher in Central City, ringing a bell to announce to patrons outside the theater that it was curtain time for his mother's performance in *Mrs. McThing*. His mother was actress Helen Hayes, and his father the late playwright and journalist Charles MacArthur, co-author of *The Front Page*.

> Colorado has been a regular part of MacArthur's itinerary for several reasons. One is that he has a son at the University of Denver ... majoring in psychology.
>
> MacArthur also has a place at Crested Butte, where he not only goes to ski, but to check up on the lodge there in which he is a part owner.[8-2]

Actor James Lawless returned to Denver to play a leading role in *Dear Ruth*, a well-known comedy by Norman Krasna from the 1940s. Lawless had appeared with the Denver Center Theater Company founded in 1972 by Donald E. Sewell, performing in various plays during the Center's first two seasons. In *Dear Ruth*, he played the father of Miriam, his precocious 16-year old daughter who is the cause of the romantic complications in the play. More than by coincidence, Miriam's role was played by his real-life daughter, Wendy Lawless.[8-3]

The Show Will Go On For Theater Buff[8-4]

Frances Byers Hamil, 84, was an ardent fan of Elitch's summer theater. She had not missed a Saturday matinee performance in 74 years, having started attending matinee performances at the age of 10 with her mother. When she was not in her usual seat at the opening play of the season, her theater friends were concerned.

Elitch staffers disclosed that Mrs. Hamil had not renewed her season tickets. Upon being contacted, Mrs. Hamil disclosed that surgery about a year ago had slowed her down a bit, and when she was unable to find transportation to the

Theatre, she gave up her season tickets. Mrs. Marlene Ospina, a friend, promptly offered to arrange getting her to the Theatre and to keep Mrs. Hamil's passion for the Theatre alive and well.

When Elitch producer Whitfield Connor learned of the situation he provided complimentary season matinee tickets for Mrs. Hamil and for Mrs. Ospina and her daughter, Monique. Although Mrs. Hamil had missed the season's opening play, she was happily on hand in her same parquet row at Elitch for the Saturday matinee performance of *The Supporting Cast,* and looked forward to the remainder of the season.

Denver Public Library Western History Collection - *Rocky Mountain News* Archives

Judd Hirsch and Veronica Cartwright in *Tally's Folly* (1981)

Denver Public Library Western History Collection - *Rocky Mountain News Archives*

Pat O'Brien and his wife, Eloise, relax beginning a two week Elitch Theatre production of *Second Time Around* (1980).

Denver Public Library Western History Collection - *Rocky Mountain News Archives*

Pat O'Brien and his daughter, Brigit O'Brien, in a scene from *On Golden Pond* (1981)

Chapter Thirty-Four

(1983 - 1985)

84 Charing Cross Road - The Shelley Winters Debacle
The Theater Critic
Cloris Leachman and Richard Kiley
Musicals and Other Plays
The Warning Sign
The Fatal Announcement

The 1983 Season

This season was a roller coaster ride of entertainment. It began with the Shelley Winters debacle, was uplifted somewhat by the play *Outward Bound* and its stars, then dropped to a level of disappointment by the performance of Gabe Kaplan in *Groucho*, and salvaged somewhat by stars like Cloris Leachman and Richard Kiley. All in all, however, there were still the cool mile-high summer nights, good dinners at the Orchard Cafe, the beautiful floral displays of the Gardens and sufficient moments of theatrical accomplishment to rate the season with far more than just a passing grade.

84 Charing Cross Road - The Shelley Winters Debacle

It would be difficult for any Elitch theatergoer to remember any performance in the Theatre's history that resulted in such scathing remarks about the performance of an actress as did Shelley Winters' attempt at acting in *84 Charing Cross Road*. The reviews, letters to the Theatre, and performances later by Miss Winters on the tour did not escape stinging criticism.

The Boulder *Daily Camera* wrote as follows:

> Shelly Winters' best line in *84 Charing Cross Road* ... was an impromptu statement the illustrious actress blithely added to the script.
>
> "I can't hear you," Winters said plainly, turning not to another character, but to the prompter just offstage.
>
> Unfortunately, the audience sitting close to the stage could hear the prompter all too well and all too often. The constant prompting was to no avail, however.
>
> Sputtering and stuttering, Winters stumbled through her performance, distractedly groping for words. The already long play became interminable, lengthened by countless "ums" and "uhs."
>
> If Winters did not have enough time to learn her lines (the play is rumored to have been in rehearsal for two weeks), she certainly did not have time to develop a character. Nor did she apparently have time to

think about pacing, timing, delivery, physical comedy or motivation - leaving the audience cringing in embarrassment that a star of Winters' stature would go on stage totally unprepared.[1]

The *Rocky Mountain News* reviewer stated that the play "suffered untold atrocities ... From the outset, the evening became a farce of watching Winters snap her fingers for cues ... it really wasn't fun at all ... There were moments ... when the audience held its breath and waited for her to call it all off."[2-1]

The *Denver Post* reviewer wrote that "the star of the show was there in ample body only. Her mind obviously wasn't, as she stumbled over words and looked pleadingly toward a prompter in the wings."[3-1]

Another Denver-based writer who reported on entertainment and the arts wrote the following:

> In the beginning, it seemed possible that her hesitation, indecision, quickly changed words and lines, and puzzled looks might represent the peculiarities of her role. However, it soon became painfully apparent that the missed lines, skipped cues, rudimentary attempts at acting and atmosphere of bewilderment sprang from Winters' own inadequacies. If any doubts remained, they were shockingly resolved by the audible dialogue between Winters and her offstage prompter.
>
> (Shelley Winters) ... turned out to be the Winters of our discontent.[4]

Numerous letters were written by theatergoers and sent to the Theatre expressing their disappointments. The following are a few of their comments:[5]

> - Why was she allowed to go on stage? It would have been far better for Elitch's fine reputation, to say nothing of the sanity and dignity of the other fine actors, for you to have simply cancelled the run. It would have been infinitely better for the audience which was put in the unbearable situation of being embarrassed for those on stage, hoping it would get better, wanting to do something to make it better, holding their breaths every time there was a pause, trying to decide whether to leave or stick it out, and feeling generally miserable, anxious, and finally angry. I think it is unconscionable to accept money from innocent ticket buyers for such a fiasco.
>
> - I only hope Ms. Hanff (author of the play) remains happily ignorant and never sees the unrequited demolition of her delicate little story as I did last Friday in which Ms. Winters, with the careless authority of a movie star, chopped and hacked her way through the lines in a manner that would make a junior high school drama coach blanch.

One theatergoer acknowledged having seen Ms. Winters a number of years before at Elitch in *The Effect of Gamma Rays on Man-in-the-Moon Marigolds* and noted that she did a memorable job in that play, ending the letter with the comment, "I will chose to remember her acting abilities based upon that role and not the one I suffered through this past week."

The play was the first stop of a scheduled summer tour at other venues. The weakness in Shelley Winters' overall performance should have improved with the show's continuous performances. However, it did not! The following is a review of Shelley Winters' performance at the Westport Playhouse in Connecticut, many weeks later that summer while on the tour:

> (Winters') mutilation of the Hanff role is beyond words. But then, what possible success could she have with lines she didn't know? The stumbling about for the next line, the groping for the next word - gaps that came sometimes just under a full minute's duration - were filled in with such jerky, uh, uh, uhs and mmm, mmmm mmmms that at times she gave the impression of a mute endeavoring to speak. Her verbal flopping about on that stage, the light years between her and anything resembling a performance, provide previously unthought-of definitions for "deplorable," "embarrassing" and "inexcusable."
>
> When one ponders on the availability of creditable actresses and actors, both unknown and known, worthy of the price of the ticket, one further ponders on the wrong-headed persistence of producers and directors - especially of summer theater - in dragging in "names" regardless of their want of talent, or ability to learn lines for that matter.
>
> Such wanton, cavalier casting is a rip-off of the audience and cruel and unusual punishment for the professionals who must rush to their typewriters to report on all as honestly and fairly as possible - and meet a deadline. In the case of Shelley Winters' fiasco at the playhouse, the free press ticket was outrageously priced.[6]

Christopher Kirkland, in an interview in the *Denver Post*, reflected upon this season with Shelley Winters aboard and revealed his dilemma. He stated that:

> A big and delicate ego is stock in trade here. With the likes of a Shelley Winters, it's hellacious ... She was about the most difficult person we've ever had to deal with. I don't think she ever learned her lines; she didn't seem to have the vaguest grip on her part. The only time we've really rehearsed and hired an understudy was when Winters was playing in *84 Charing Cross Road*. I secretly flew in Elizabeth Perry, who had understudied the part for Ellen Burstyn. We secluded Perry in a Denver motel, where we had arranged the furniture to resemble the set, and rehearsed her there for three days - without, of course, letting Miss Winters know.

When she was ready to replace Winters, I went around during an intermission talking to the audience about the possibility of replacing Shelley Winters. They were horrified! People would say "Oh everybody thinks she doesn't know her lines, but they've never watched her on 'The Johnny Carson Show.' That's just the way she is." So we kept her in the show.[7]

The Theater Critic

In view of the debacle of Shelley Winters, a comment by Eric Bentley on the role of the drama critic may be appropriate. Bentley is a renowned drama critic and author of *In Search of Theatre, The Dramatic Event* and *The Playwright as Thinker*.

> To write theatre reviews is worse than walking on eggs; it is to walk on live bodies and make them bleed. The critic's comments may be far less harsh than those that are heard in every cocktail party in New York. But, while the party-goers only commit the venial sin of stabbing their fellow men in the back, and their victims will never find out who did it, the critic commits the unpardonable crime of striking right between the eyes and taking the responsibility in public. His victims know whom to hate, and receive abundant sympathy to their face from those who, behind their back, agree with the critic. I sometimes feel that theatre reviewing is the art of making enemies and failing to influence people.[8]

Outward Bound

Outward Bound was written by Sutton Vane in the 1920s. It has been produced by many community theaters because of its equal number of strong characters. The setting of the play is an ocean liner with very few passengers. They are a wide mix of people who seem vague about their destination. The mystery of where the ship is headed deepens until each passenger learns that their journey is guided by their own mortality. Director Harold J. Kennedy appeared as an actor toward the end of the play as the one who orders each passenger to heaven or hell - with no second chance.[3-2]

To the delight of the audience, the play was packed with favorite stars, which included John Ireland, Keir Dullea, Tyrone Power IV, Tammy Grimes, Maureen O'Sullivan and David McCallum.

The play offers a good example of ensemble acting, with each player using timing, moods and tempos of the other actors to help shape each of his own lines in some interesting manner. Ensemble playing can help an actor get rid of bad habits that tend to upstage other actors. In ensemble work, "while one actor is speaking the rest of the actors on stage have to efface themselves. Any ill-timed movement can be very destructive."[2-2]

Laurence Olivier is said to have known how to avoid distractions from his performance. Tammy Grimes said, "When Laurence Olivier played Othello, he wore a white caftan with a red rose pinned on it. You couldn't take your eye off the rose."[2-2]

Tammy Grimes' appearance in Denver echoed many memories of her past. She appeared at the start of her career in the national company production of *The Lark* with Julie Harris and Christopher Plummer, which played at the Central City Opera House in 1956. She and Plummer were married by a justice of the peace in neighboring Blackhawk in August of 1956. They were divorced in 1960.[3-3] Miss Grimes next appeared in Denver in 1963 at Denver's Auditorium Theater in the title role of the musical hit *The Unsinkable Molly Brown,* a role that brought her stardom.

During the season at Elitch, on July 18th, Miss Grimes appeared at the Molly Brown House in Denver for a garden party that rekindled the memories of her role as Molly Brown.[3-3]

The cast member of *Outward Bound* known as Tyrone Power IV was the fourth generation of actors in the Power family, his father being Tyrone Power, Jr. of films such as *Jesse James, The Sun Also Rises,* and *Witness for the Prosecution.* His grandfather is Tyrone Power Sr., who appeared at the Elitch Gardens Theatre as an actor during the 1905 summer season. His great-grandfather was the famed Irish actor Tyrone Power, who was born in 1797 and died in 1841. Tyrone Power IV's initial appearance on stage "brought an embarrassing round of applause merely because of his name and resemblance to his handsome late father."[3-2]

Groucho

Groucho was a play written by Arthur Marx (Groucho's son) and Robert Fisher (who used to write material for Groucho). The anticipated success for the play felt flat, even phony. Groucho was played by Gabe Kaplan, best known for his role as Mr. Kotter, the teacher, in the television series "Welcome Back, Kotter"

> With those eyebrows and mustache that seem to have been applied with Magic Marker, who could mistake Gabe Kaplan for Groucho Marx? ... Kaplan looks phony.
>
> The performance seems phony, too. Though he tries to approximate Groucho's grainy, quasi-Yiddish voice, the timing and delivery are Kaplan, not Groucho. The smile that ought to be wide and zany is frozen - part smug, part seasick. The trademark stooped walk is tired and perfunctory. Even when Kaplan raises his eyebrows, it seems an enormous effort.
>
> Kaplan, in keeping with his background, plays the role the way a stand-up comic would. His performance is guided by laughter rather than character.

> Unfortunately, Kaplan's interest in laughs and only laughs prevents him from developing a character that can hold the stage for over two hours.[3-4]

Cloris Leachman

Cloris Leachman is a versatile actress who absorbs the challenges of any new play. She claims to have loved every role she has played. And the Denver audiences loved her. In describing her role in *The Housekeeper*, Leachman stated:

> She portrays "an incipient bag lady who pulls herself together and gets herself a job as a housekeeper to an eccentric millionaire, whose mother has just died. He thinks he's a writer, but she destroys that illusion and then she builds him up again. We go from the shady side of the street to the sunny side."[3-5]

She costarred with Noel Harrison, son of the famed actor, Rex Harrison. Leachman enjoyed working with Harrison, whose life path was quite different from hers. While Harrison was absorbing theater in England from his father, she was growing up in Middle America and gained notoriety as a Miss America beauty pageant finalist.

Richard Kiley [3-6]

Richard Kiley was a versatile actor who was steadily employed throughout his career. The final play of the season featured him in the non-musical, *Mass Appeal*. Those members of the audience only familiar with Richard Kiley in the *Man of La Mancha* soon learned of the completeness of his acting skills. The drama critic wrote:

> If you've wondered whether Richard Kiley can do anything more than sing "The Impossible Dream" in a quivery baritone, his performance as Father Farley should allay all doubts. It's easy to overplay this role, which lends itself to the full array of "cute drunken Irish Catholic priest" mannerisms ... But Kiley foregoes the cuddly distractions, laying bare the priest's cowardice and genial corruptibility from the beginning. And oddly enough, we respect the character more for it.
>
> (Kiley) handles the play's final and weakest scene - in which Farley disrobes before his congregation, giving a pat and smarmy "I lost Christ" speech - with such conviction that it sends a small shiver up your spine.

The drama critic's overall assessment of the play was reflected in the headline of the review: "Elitch's *Mass Appeal* Beautifully Performed."

(1984 - 1985)

Hovering in the background of the 1984-1985 seasons of musicals and other plays, some of which did not receive flattering reviews, was the road moving toward the final days of the historic playhouse.

The 1984 Season

Gary Dandy, Marcia Rodd and Avery Schreiber
in "A Luv Musical"
Phyllis Thaxter and Jeff Conaway in "Foxfire"
Nancy Dussault and Howard Platt
in
"I'm Getting My Act Together and Taking it
on the Road"
Linda Purl and Thomas Calabro in "Snacks"
Margaret Whiting and Sheila Smith in "Taking My Turn"

The season at Elitch was somewhat different in that three of the five plays were musicals. *Snacks* and *Foxfire* were not.

A Luv Musical

A Luv Musical is the musical version of Murray Schisgal's play *Luv* and reiterates the neurotic relationship of the three characters in that 1964 hit.

Having an opening play of a season fail was not what was hoped for by the producers at Elitch. *A Luv Musical* opened in New York in the spring and failed. In commenting about the play, a reviewer wrote, "The musical opened in New York in the spring and failed. Perhaps after tinkering and tuning, everyone thought it deserved another chance at the starting gate. On opening night at Elitch, it proved them all wrong as it sputtered and rolled into a ditch."[9]

The play details a rather peculiar love triangle among the three characters in the play. The principal interaction among the three cast members occurs on the Brooklyn Bridge.

> As the show opens, we see Harry preparing to throw himself off the Brooklyn Bridge; life just isn't what it was cracked up to be. Along comes Milt, an old school chum of Harry's, who offers him a reason to go on living: Harry can take Milt's wife, Ellen, off his hands. After all, Milt has been looking for an excuse to leave Ellen and run off with Linda.
>
> The arrangement sounds ideal, but at the beginning of Act II, several months later, we find Ellen on the Brooklyn Bridge, bemoaning the fact that life with Harry isn't all it was cracked up to be. Along comes Milt, who, after putting up a brave facade, confesses that life with Linda isn't all it was cracked up to be. Needless to say, complications ensue - with that railing on the Brooklyn Bridge providing an ever-convenient escape route.[10-1]

In another review, the comments were harsher.

> *A Luv Musical*, the first production at Elitch's this summer, is not a bad

> experience. It is a non-experience - no experience at all. It does not even rise to the level of boredom, for boredom in the theatre usually results when the artists are actually trying to do something significant. There is nothing significant about *A Luv Musical*, nothing arresting or compelling, amusing or hilarious.[11]

Snacks

The parents of Linda Purl, the female lead in the play *Snacks*, lived in Colorado Springs and were able to see her perform at Elitch. The playwright had previously written *Butterflies Are Free*, and the lyrics of the song *Born in a Trunk* for Judy Garland in the film *A Star is Born*.

> *Snacks* ... is a sentimental comedy that asks the age-old question: Can a Philadelphia Main Line beauty find true happiness with a dumb but sweet Italian from the Lower East Side?[10-2]

Much was expected of *Snacks*. However, it didn't turn out that way. Another local reviewer of the play stated:

> *Snacks* turns out to be what its title connotes - a little something to tide one over, without much substance.[12]

As for Linda Purl, in addition to her wholesome good looks, her stage technique was viewed favorably. The reviewer wrote:

> What is substantial, however, is the talent of Linda Purl. She brings a moving intensity, sincerity and strength to the role of Betty that is substantially superior to what she has to work with.[12]

Taking My Turn was the final production of the season. The musical ran seven months off-Broadway the prior season. The play deals with aging. The musical doesn't have a plot, so to speak, or no more than a thin one, but rather a string of subjects on aging to be examined by one of the older men and women in the cast. Margaret Whiting tells of having to bury her child, while Sheila Smith tells of the *Two of Me* - "the young girl that's always inside and the woman she sees in the mirror."[10-3]

The Broadway Season

The news from Broadway and new plays for the 1983-1984 season were a bust.

> Those still maintaining the illusion that New York was the main source of new plays in the American theatre were sorely shaken this season. Not only did fewer works open on Broadway than in any season in the past century and a half, but those that did were mostly from Europe and regional theatres. Only eight new American plays appeared on Broadway (a drop by almost half from the previous season) ...

As was often the case, British actors and playwrights dominated the season. Even the best American play of the season, David Mamet's *Glengarry Glen Ross*, had been seen in London first.* [13]

The 1985 Season

A Warning Sign

As the season approached there were whispers in the wind, a concern about future profitability. The prior season had sustained an $80,000 loss.

> The previous season, which emphasized new shows and semi-famous actors, was a financial disappointment, and over the winter (producer director Christopher Kirkland) has had to rethink Elitch's entire strategy.
>
> "We have more star power and bigger shows this year," Kirkland said, "and I've had more time to recruit and negotiate with actors."
>
> But the current season is still the big question mark. Although subscriptions are running about 25 percent ahead of last year, Kirkland is counting heavily on revenues from single-ticket sales. Last year, he said, "We budgeted to break even at 65 percent attendance, and we lost $80,000. This year, we'll break even at 75 percent. It's a gamble. But we've found that we can't cut corners anymore. There really didn't seem to be any other choice than to go for it."[14]

The Season of Plays - Some Comments

Mary Jo Catlett in "Harvey"
Leslie Caron in "One for the Tango"
Jim Nabors in "Jim Nabors in Concert"
Larry Kert in "The Music Man"
Keith Baxter and Milo O'Shea in "Corpse!"

Richard McKenzie, who played Dr. Chumley in *Harvey*, said that before he became an actor, he was a linotype operator and once worked at the *Rocky Mountain News*. Mary Jo Catlett, a Denver native, lived at home with her parents while appearing at Elitch. She looked favorably upon her early acting experience with the Windsor Players resident melodrama company originally housed in the historic Windsor Hotel on Denver's Larimer Street. She joined them in the early 1960s after the Players moved to Henritze's on South Colorado Boulevard and later to the Red Ram in Georgetown. Later in her career while performing in *Hello Dolly* on Broadway, she was professionally reunited with Ann Richardson, a founder of the Windsor Players melodrama group, and who was then the associate producer of *Candid Camera*.[15]

* Broadway presented seven revivals of former plays.

Denver audiences responded well to *Harvey*; in fact, for Denverites, the Pulitzer Prize-winning play was said to be "ours," written by the late Denver playwright Mary Chase. Denver audiences were all too familiar with Elwood P. Dowd and his tall and invisible rabbit named Harvey.

> A psychiatrist asks Dowd if he didn't think it was strange that when he encountered Harvey for the first time, Harvey addressed him by his first name. "No," Dowd answers, "you know how it is in a small town, everybody knows everybody else."[16-1]

The review in the *Rocky Mountain News* of the play *One for the Tango* had much to say about the translation from French into English.

> The team that translated *One for the Tango* from French to English should have wine poured in their typewriters, and a croissant stuffed in their mouths.
>
> The play, which is said to have delighted French audiences in its native tongue, lands on the Elitch stage with a thud. The reasons for seeing *One for the Tango* might include inspecting Caron from a 10th row seat and supporting the Elitch Theatre season, which opened with a solid hit in the form of *Harvey* and now has three more chances to redeem itself.[17-1]

Jim Nabors connected with the audience. "He climbed down into the audience, shook hands with the folks on the aisle and sang in front of a classy 17-piece stage band. He also just generally made his audience feel good."[17-2]

> He also recruited a chorus line of women from the audience and sent them off stage to get feather boas. When they returned, they did an astonishing variety of dance steps to a mild "stripper" song.
>
> It is a measure of Nabors' unique rapport with his fans that all six of the women got up and displayed a taste for show biz.[17-2]

The Music Man

There is one major obstacle to any presentation of *The Music Man* on tour. There is only one authentic Harold Hill, and that is Robert Preston, who created the character on Broadway and later in film. In the Elitch production, Larry Kert, best known as the original Tony in *West Side Story*, played Harold Hill, "the sugary con man who captivates a straight-laced Iowa town in the summer of 1912."

> Even Kert would probably agree that he isn't ideal casting as Hill; his voice is higher and lighter than the role calls for, and he doesn't have the authoritative, charismatic presence of, say, Robert Preston. But the actor compensates with a sprightly, pixie charm.[18]

The Music Man was a rare attempt at a large musical. Christopher Kirkland said,

"We're going to do it on a grand scale. We'll be taking out $5,000 worth of seats and putting in $10,000 worth of musicians."[16-2]

The Fatal Announcement

In 1985, the park management was handed down to Sandy Gurtler, Budd Gurtler's son. He was the fourth generation of the Mulvihill-Gurtler family to manage Elitch Gardens. Sandy Gurtler had grown up surrounded by the happenings in the Elitch amusement park and was well-acquainted with the demands and responsibilities of being its president. His uncle, Jack Gurtler, had retired in 1979.

> Sandy's first challenge was to carry out the family's long-range plans to move Elitch Gardens to a more central location. There were several reasons necessitating this. The Park had reached its limits - it simply had no more room to expand. For example, the new Spider ride was constructed atop the bumper-car building.[19]

In 1960, the former home of Mary Elitch Long located in the park had been demolished.* It was replaced by an amusement ride acquired from West Germany that had been an attraction at the Brussels World Fair the previous year. Although the 16-acre Chilcott Farm purchased by John and Mary Elitch had gradually "grown" to 32 acres, the Gurtlers concern for a continuing need for space did not subside. An announcement was made that the amusement park was seeking a new location.

* After the death of Mary Elitch Long in 1936, the house was used as a spook house, with ghosts, witches and goblins, until 1944. It had not been used since 1944. *Denver Post*, Feb 10, 1960, p. 51.

Whitfield Connor and Haila Stoddard, along with her son, Christopher Kirkland, ran the Elitch Theatre from 1972-1987.

Denver Public Library Western History Collection - *Rocky Mountain News* Archives

Noel Harrison and Cloris Leachman in *The Housekeeper* (1983)

Denver Public Library Western History Collection - *Rocky Mountain News* Archives

Christopher Kirkland, Producer-Director

Chapter Thirty-Five

(1986 - 1987)

The Expression of Concern
The Cloud of Relocation
Elitch Theatergoers' Last Season
Goodbye

The 1986 Season

The Expression of Concern

The minutes of the annual meeting of The Elitch Theatre Company held on January 26, 1986 expressed concern over the announcement by the management of Elitch Gardens that the amusement park was seeking to relocate. The minutes expressed the effect on the Company.

> The Directors will decide to commit to the production season for the summer of 1987, but thereafter only pending a Corporate reaffirmation by the Directors following a mid-year evaluation of the Corporation during the summer of 1987. It is our current anticipation, especially given the past year's history of uncertain and difficult relations with the Elitch Gardens Corporation since the announcement last April of their intentions (to) relocate and given our current and sustained uncertainty about their future plans for the Theatre, that The Elitch Theatre Company will not be extending contractual agreements with the Elitch Gardens Company following the one year contract currently under negotiation.[1]

Inappropriate Noise or Disturbance

The Elitch management was always conscious of making the Theatre patrons most comfortable in their attention to the performance of the play. Caveats have been noted in the Theatre programs against latecomers being seated, women wearing hats, and crying children. The Theatre program this season contained the following caveat.

> Any persons causing inappropriate noise
> or disturbance during the performance will be
> asked to leave without refund or exchange.[2]

The Season of Plays

The season continued as usual, notwithstanding the dark cloud that hovered above the Gardens and the Theatre. The following plays were presented.

Debbie Reynolds and Harve Presnell in "The Debbie Reynolds Show"

Michael McGuire in "Bus Stop"
Cloris Leachman in "Grandma Moses, An American Painter"
(World Premiere)
Conrad Bain in "Country Cops"
Marion Ross and Gavin MacLeod in "Never Too Late"

The Debbie Reynolds Show

Debbie Reynolds was joined in *The Debbie Reynolds Show* by Harve Presnell, who co-starred with her in the film *The Unsinkable Molly Brown*. It was convenient for Presnell to join her in the show, as he was residing at the time at 8356 Sunburst Trail, Parker, Colorado.[3]

On the opening night performance, while patrons of the park cleared out from under a heavy rain, the Elitch Theatre faithful, sheltered under umbrellas, remained to see Debbie Reynolds, their favorite entertaining star.

> They were rewarded with a warm dose of nostalgia and comedy from Reynolds, whose strong suit is a genuine sense of comic timing and an apparent ease in front of a damp and disheartened audience. Reynolds immediately chased the clouds away.[4]

An editor of the *Rocky Mountain News* and his wife saw Debbie Reynolds at Elitch and he described her performance as follows:

> We joined a packed house at the Theatre for Debbie Reynolds' show. Debbie was just as we remembered her in *Tammy, Singin' in the Rain,* and *The Unsinkable Molly Brown* - cute, feisty, vivacious and energetic as a small volcano. Pure dynamite.
>
> She sang. She danced. She joked with the audience. Even came down from the stage to mingle and visit. She reminisced about filming *Molly Brown* and *How the West Was Won* here and wound up introducing her mother, who has a home in Ouray.[5-1]

While performing at Elitch, Miss Reynolds stayed at the Oxford Hotel and was present in the hotel when the fire alarm went off at 2:30 of a Sunday morning. She shared the event with Alan Stern, the *Denver Post* drama critic.

> "All the guests were in the lobby in our pajamas and nightgowns ... What were we going to do, stare at each other? So we all went into the bar and I started singing. Pretty soon everybody was joining in with 'Roll Out the Barrel.'"[6]

Stern commented that it sounded "like a scene from *The Unsinkable Molly Brown*, in which Reynolds - playing Colorado's leading legend - kept up morale in the lifeboat after the Titanic sank."[6]

After the final performance of *Never Too Late*, Debbie Reynolds and Harve Presnell were brought back by popular demand for 6 days of their Las Vegas style of singing entertainment.

Cloris Leachman and Grandma Moses

Cloris Leachman had appeared at Elitch during the 1983 season as the bag lady in a play called *The Housekeeper*. Denverites welcomed her return for the portrayal of the American-primitive artist, Grandma Moses, from her age 45 to age 100. Playwright Stephen Pouloit reportedly said to Leachman, "You're the only one who could play this role." To which Leachman amusingly acknowledged, "And he's right. I'm the only one who could be 100."[5-2] After the final curtain, Leachman appeared before the house for a 100-candle birthday cake and a tribute from the audience. Jackie Campbell wrote that "all honors go to Leachman ... (who) has worked the actor's most mysterious art, that of becoming a character far in age and spirit from her own but nonetheless real."[5-3]

Leachman's connection with Colorado went beyond the Theatre. Her son, Morgan Englund, attended the University of Colorado. While in Boulder, he auditioned for the Circle in the Square Theater training program in New York, was accepted and after a year joined the road show of *Picnic*. Another son, a musician, attended the University for a year. A third son who became a lawyer, recently turned actor, had also attended the University.[7]

While in Denver during this season, Leachman sang the national anthem at Mile High Stadium before an important baseball game between the Denver Zephyrs and the Oklahoma City 89ers.[5-2]

The Cloud of Relocation

In 1986, the management of Elitch Gardens had been negotiating a move from its present location to Highlands Ranch in Douglas County.[8] However, in the fall of 1987, the *Denver Post* reported that the negotiations had fallen through, and that a move elsewhere by Elitch Gardens was at least three years away.[9-1] In fact, however, Elitch Gardens remained open until October 1, 1994, its final day of operation before relocating elsewhere. As for the Elitch Theatre, its demise was more imminent than anyone might have realized.

The 1987 Season

The Final Season

Mary Jo Catlett in "Nunsense"
Barbara Rush in "A Woman of Independent Means"
Barbara Cook in "A Concert for the Theatre"
Michael Learned in "No Time for Comedy"
Mitzi Gaynor in "The Mitzi Gaynor Concert"

The rather unusual season at Elitch included concerts by Barbara Cook and Mitzi Gaynor and a one-woman monologue by Barbara Rush about the life of Bess Steed Garner, the subject of Elizabeth Forsythe Hailey's novel, which was reportedly based on the life of her grandmother, a wealthy Dallas matron. The opening play of the season, *Nunsense,* was a musical comedy. When the play *No Time for Comedy* was presented, Alan Stern, the *Denver Post* drama critic wrote:

> With *No Time for Comedy,* its fourth production of the season, the Elitch Theatre offers the novelty of a real play, in which nobody sings, or dances, or stands alone on stage to tell the audience his life story. It's a refreshing change for America's oldest summer theater, which once specialized in this sort of fare.[9-2]

This was to become the final summer season of plays for the Elitch Theatre. A number of factors contributed to the ultimate demise of the Theatre. The building was badly in need of repairs. It lacked air conditioning. The economy had lagged. Modern theaters, sporting arenas and skyscrapers changed the face of Denver. The Theatre had suffered financial losses in recent years. In 1983, the loss reported was $71,506 and in 1985, the loss was reported at $10,080. In 1986, the liabilities of the corporation exceeded its assets.

Most important, however, the announcement the prior year by the Gurtlers that the amusement park was seeking a new location created doubt as to the future of the 97-year-old Theatre building.

In recent years, another problem for summer theaters was that most stars would only agree to a contract that contained a cancellation clause, an escape clause for them in the event a better offer came along, making the summer theater producer have to scramble for a last minute replacement. For example, the contract engagement of Debbie Reynolds for the 1986 season contained the following provision:

> Artist reserves the right to cancel engagement hereunder in the event her services are required for a motion picture, television special, television series, or legitimate stage play, which might conflict with the date of engagement hereunder, upon thirty (30) days written notice.

The economic effect of a cancellation clause was significant during the 1987 season with regard to the engagement of Bernadette Peters. She was to appear *In Concert* for sixteen performances. The contract of engagement submitted to Christopher Kirkland, producing director of Elitch, had a 45-day cancellation clause. The contract was returned and signed with the understanding that the cancellation notice would be 60 days instead of 45 days.

Kirkland received a notice of cancellation from Miss Peters' agent that was within the 45-day period but less than 60 days. He immediately addressed a letter to Roger Vorce, president of the agency handling Miss Peters' bookings, stating that "This cancellation is not acceptable," for the following reasons:

> We would point out that your agent Ed Kasses, with whom we negotiated in good faith the contract for Miss Peters, agreed to and directed that we change and endorse the cancellation clause to sixty days. Per his instructions we so changed and so endorsed and returned both the original contract sent to us, and a second set. We have proceeded on the basis of that agreement. The imminent return of the signed contract, as negotiated and endorsed, prior to May 15, was verbally assured again and again during the winter and spring by Mr. Kasses of your office.
>
> We have sold, and distributed within the last two weeks, $97,989 worth of tickets marked "Bernadette Peters." We have, since December, committed over $35,000 promoting and advertising Miss Peters. We have contracted and engaged through Denver Musicians Association Local 20-623 $20,000 worth of musicians for this engagement. These are but the more immediate of the damages which the cancellation will cause The Elitch Theatre Company.
>
> The future of this Theatre is, at best, precarious. Given the current extremely depressed economy in Denver, Miss Peters' cancellation assures the termination of The Elitch Theatre Company and the ninety-seven year history as "America's Oldest Summer Theatre."[10]

The response to Kirkland's letter by Roger Vorce was immediate:

> I have carefully investigated the matter of the cancellation clause and have discussed it at great length with Bernadette Peters' management. I assure you, nowhere do I find any evidence that there was any agreement to your asking for a sixty day cancellation clause.
>
> Most important - I also guarantee you that if there is any possibility of changing the pre-production conflict within the next few days, we will do so, but failing that, the right of Bernadette to exercise the cancellation clause must stand.[10]

Fortunately, The Elitch Theatre Company was able to engage Barbara Cook in *A Concert for the Theatre*, the show that she presented in London and more recently on Broadway and for which she received the 1987 Drama Desk Award and a nomination for the Tony Award.

On June 5, 1987, Christopher Kirkland addressed a letter to "Subscribers and Friends" informing them of the change. To encourage their support, he wrote:

> Frankly, we were devastated.
>
> We made every possible effort to hold Bernadette Peters to her Elitch commitment, every effort short of jeopardizing our chances of presenting

her in a future season.

Our devastation lasted no longer than it took us to engage the incredible talent of Barbara Cook to replace Miss Peters.

We'll be presenting the show that catapulted Barbara Cook back to the top of the heap in London last fall and on Broadway this spring -- the show that just won Miss Cook the 1987 Drama Desk Award and the Tony Award nomination.

Never in her long history has the grand old Elitch Theatre been able to present such a radiant international theatre sensation so freshly, so immediately. In *A Concert for the Theatre* Miss Cook, recently proclaimed by the London Times "the greatest theatrical singer in concert at the moment," sings all-time favorites by Gershwin, Berlin, Coward, Rogers and Hammerstein, Sondheim, Bernstein and many others. The New York Times says of this performance: "There is currently no other voice of such magnificence in popular music."

Frankly, we're delighted. You won't be disappointed.[10]

Broadway Insurance

There are many things that can go wrong with a theatrical production for which insurance is available. As a leading broker for entertainment insurance said, "You can take out insurance against anything except bad reviews." Insurance for the non-appearance of stars and abandonment of a show is usually obtained for one-person shows such as Lily Tomlin and for stars who are not easily replaced such as Jim Dole in his acrobatic role in *Barnum*. Such insurance is important for stars who are synonymous with their shows, such as Anthony Quinn in *Zorba* and Richard Kiley in *Man of La Mancha*.[5-4] It is unlikely, however, that such insurance would cover a situation where the non-appearance of a star is consistent with her rights under the contract. Moreover, insurance does not solve the disappointment to theatergoers who support and routinely look forward to seeing the scheduled offerings.

The Press Release by Christopher Kirkland

After evaluating many factors, on August 24, 1987, Christopher Kirkland issued a press release with the news that The Elitch Theatre Company does not intend to renew its lease of the Elitch Theatre for another summer season of plays.

The press release by Christopher Kirkland read:

It has become increasingly difficult to produce popular shows at populist prices, particularly in a facility as decrepit and continually neglected as this one has become in recent years. It is also apparently impossible to hold major stars to major commitments creating an understandable gap in the company's reliability and credibility. Additionally, the forced

> switch from Datatix to the Ticketmaster ticketing service at mid-season resulted in insupportable losses exceeding $40,000.[11]

A spokesperson for Christopher Kirkland stated that the losses relating to the change in ticketing service resulted from confusion over the new ticket outlets as well as the cost of retraining box office personnel. Moreover, the total losses for the season were expected to reach $80,000.[12]

> Our hopes for a brighter season next summer were dispelled by a 27% drop in early subscription renewals. Given Denver's current economy and the resulting lagging ticket sales, we really can't undertake another deficit cycle in a building without a discernible future.
>
> The final performance of the Elitch Theatre Company's 1987 season will be the Sunday, August 30, 6:30 performance of *Nunsense*, starring Mary Jo Catlett.[11]

With regard to any losses sustained by the Theatre, and of the Theatre's dismal future, Kirkland stated:

> Luckily, we have a very fortuitous stock portfolio that we are selling off to handle that (deficit of the season). Nineteen eighty-three was a profitable season, and we went into deficits in 1984 and 1985. It seems to go in three-year cycles, and we don't have unlimited resources so that we can continue. If next year and the year after were good seasons, just about the time we would pull out of debt, the bulldozers would arrive.[12]

The Response by Sandy Gurtler

Sandy Gurtler said that he and his father Budd, were "more involved with the Theatre" when it was under the direction of Helen Bonfils. "We stayed active then but we really fell behind the times when she deceased (in 1972)."

He further stated that:

> The Theatre hasn't made money in years. The lease has been so minimal that it has not provided any funds to repair leaks and faults in the substructure.
>
> We are in the amusement-park business, and the Theatre doesn't generate any revenue for Chris (Kirkland) or for us. We believe in the Theatre. It's part of our heritage, but it has been a labor of love as far as Chris is concerned.[12]

Elitch Theatergoers' Last Season

While the struggles for the Theatre's future were being sorted out and evaluated by everyone affected, the tradition of the theater, that the show must go on, received careful attention.

Theatre patrons were entertained by Barbara Rush's one-woman show, *A Woman of Independent Means*, which became a signature role for her, a role she had been performing around the country for the past three years.[9-3]

Barbara Cook was remembered for the many Broadway musicals in which she delighted audiences, such as *Plain and Fancy* and as Marian the Librarian in *The Music Man*. Cook, now sixty years of age, successfully made the transition from Broadway musical star to cabaret and concert performer "after a difficult period in the late 1960s (when) Broadway was in a slump, (and) roles for older women were hard to come by ..."[9-4]

Audiences were particularly attracted to Mitzi Gaynor, more known to them from her movie musicals, in which she had starred opposite Bing Crosby, Gene Kelly, and Frank Sinatra. The 56-year old singer/dancer/actress decided on a Las Vegas act in 1961 and had been performing it since then, periodically revising and keeping the material fresh.

> (Gaynor) admits that when she made the transition from Hollywood to Vegas, she was at an awkward point in her career ... In the 1950s, Hollywood was making fewer musicals, and 20th Century-Fox, the studio she was under contract to, was more interested in another blonde they had signed named Marilyn Monroe.[9-5]

The success of her two-hour show is reflected in a drama critic's review of her performance.

> Although her voice wavers and she isn't the dancer she once was, the 56-year-old star takes unerring command of the stage. With her tight features, too-wide eyes and pneumatic breasts, Gaynor may look like a caricature, but it's impossible to take your eyes off her.[9-5]

In addition to Kirkland's preparing staff personnel at Elitch to get a show presented in a proper and timely manner, there were other details that arose that needed to be addressed. For example, in a letter written by Christopher Kirkland to Jack Bean, Mitzi Gaynor's theatrical agent, in response to an inquiry about dressing rooms and telephones, he stated:

> Although we have two dressing rooms, one down and one up, with both commode and basin, there is no shower in the dressing room area. Four dressing rooms, each with a basin, and a small foyer can be curtained off into one dressing room suite ... but none of them have a commode. There is a recently tiled shower off the prop room a few steps from the dressing room area which Cloris Leachman and Debbie Reynolds (when she stayed at the Theatre between shows) used last year.
>
> Due to phone line limitations by the local phone company, we cannot provide dressing room phones. We are happy to have Miss Gaynor

and her company use our telephones in the Production Office just off stage right, and we gladly take messages, make calls, and help make communications facile.[13]

Jack Bean had been Mitzi Gaynor's manager, producer and husband for the past 33 years. They spent part of their honeymoon at Ethel Merman's house in Denver. It was Jack Bean who convinced Gaynor to put a stage act together. At the conclusion of their run at Elitch, Bean wrote the following letter to Christopher Kirkland.

> Mitzi and I and our whole group had such a good time in Denver, and we want to thank you most particularly for all of it. I know that there are plenty of people around you who added their help to the general picture, and thank them as well. I am delighted that we had a chance to get together and work together ... Much good luck the rest of the season, Chris.[13]

The opening play of the season was the musical comedy *Nunsense*. By popular request, *Nunsense* was scheduled for a return special engagement for the final two weeks of the season. While the play was rich with laughter, the audience was acutely aware that with every line uttered by an actor, it brought them that much closer to the end of a romance that began in 1890 between this celebrated and time-honored Theatre and its faithful patrons.

An Empty Gesture

Following the last performance of the 1987 season in the famous Elitch Theatre, a spokesperson for the amusement park stated that Elitch Gardens had every intention of keeping its Theatre open the next season.

> "We have absolutely no intention of closing or tearing down the Theatre," said Connie Schafer, a spokeswoman for the Gurtler family, which owns the Theatre and the adjacent amusement park.
>
> Although the Gurtlers haven't decided what sort of entertainment they will put there, "the only thing we know for dead certain is that we are going to run that Theatre next season."
>
> As for programming, "We have a whole winter to decide how to make next season the best Elitch has ever had." Some of the possibilities include musical revues, a pop series, comedy shows and legitimate theater.
>
> If and when they do move, she added, the Gurtlers will make every effort to move or build a replica of the historic Theatre.
>
> "The Theatre is as important to the Gurtlers as it is to any other person in town," she said. "It's their heritage."[9-1]

The promise became an empty gesture, and the Theatre became an empty building. An earlier statement made by the Gurtler management stated that the

Theatre would probably not continue as a "legitimate theater."[13] It did not. *Nunsense* was indeed the final performance.

The Elitch Gardens were ultimately sold and moved to a new area. The Theatre was not moved, nor was a replica built.

A Realistic Assessment

Alan Stern, the drama critic for *The Denver Post* prepared the eulogy for summer stock theaters in an article on August 24, 1986. He wrote:

> The summer stock format that gave Elitch its national reputation is virtually dead.
>
> Summer stock has been "all but dead" for at least a decade now ... Without a contingent of summer touring packages, its takes heroic stamina to line up a 10-week season of five plays.
>
> Christopher Kirkland, the producing director, has kept the Theatre afloat with a bagful of stopgap tactics: variety shows featuring such golden-oldie stars as Debbie Reynolds and Jim Nabors and an assortment of unexciting plays - *Country Cops* was one of them - buoyed by an actor familiar from television.
>
> But the TV-star strategy is probably more aggravation than it's worth. Most stars sign contracts giving them an escape if a better offer comes along, and when it does, Kirkland is forced to scramble for last-minute replacements.
>
> Aside from the headaches of lining up a new "name," it must be demoralizing for the rest of the cast when the lead bails out.
>
> The problems that Elitch faces are, of course, typical of theaters all over America. With hefty salaries being paid by Hollywood, even Broadway has trouble attracting stars - and it's virtually given up on cultivating them. Producers today are reluctant to commit to a project that doesn't star Robert DeNiro or Marlo Thomas. But if theater - particularly summer theater - is to survive, it's got to find a better way.[14]

Goodbye

As the theatergoers left the Theatre for the last time, their pace was slow, their faces sad as they glanced once more at the photographs that lined the entrance to the Theatre, photos reminding them of all the yesterdays as they walked away somewhat puzzled, as if in a state of disbelief, wondering if it was all really happening, that it was really goodbye.

The Last Performance

History Colorado - # 10039865

An empty stage - a lifetime of memories

Chapter Thirty-Six

(1988 and the Years After)

The Sale and Relocation of Elitch Gardens
The Elitch Gardens Theatre
A Precious Memory

The Sale and Relocation of Elitch Gardens

What's in a name? That which we call
a rose
By any other name would smell as sweet.

... William Shakespeare

Romeo's promise to Juliet does not apply to the new Elitch Gardens Amusement Park, now located miles away from the Chilcott Farm, where it all began more than a hundred years ago.

Those baseball fans who frequented Ebbets Field in Brooklyn to see their "bums" play baseball and to listen to the Brooklyn Sym-phony band (whose love of the Dodgers way outpaced their musical skills) marching through the stands and to Hilda ringing her cowbell every time the Dodgers needed encouragement did not feel that the new Dodger stadium in Los Angeles was an adequate replacement. Like most change these days, the relocation of the Gardens is best described as a monetary transaction. Elitch Gardens has become just another streamlined amusement park.

The Gurtler family considered several sites in their search to relocate Elitch Gardens.

> Then, in 1989, Denver voters approved $14 million worth of bond subsidies for floodplain and road improvements in an area of lower downtown in the Central Platte River Valley. The city had ambitious plans for a complete revitalization of this area, adjacent to the popular Mile High Football Stadium. The plans included a world-class baseball park, a new basketball/hockey/concert arena, and a state-of-the-art aquarium - a perfect place for Elitch Gardens Amusement Park. Further, city officials enticed the Gurtler family with a promise of $21 million in public funds to help offset their cleanup and construction costs.
>
> (The area had been used) as a railroad yard for over a hundred years. It was covered with contaminated soil that had been long and thoroughly saturated with spilled kerosene, oil, and coal.[1-1]

In June 1994, the Gurtlers' search for a relocation site reached fruition. The Elitch

Gardens management purchased the 6.7-acre plot of land from the city for $6.1 million and announced that they were going to move their Elitch Gardens from its original location to the new location in downtown Denver.

To successfully effect the move, a $95 million financing package was finalized. Sandy Gurtler lacked the necessary investment capital, and formed several limited partnerships to make the move happen.

October 1, 1994 was the last day ever for the old park and for some classic rides as well. Soon after, many of the rides were moved from the original site in the Gardens to be restored and installed in the new park. Elitch Gardens closed its gates forever in northwest Denver.

May 27, 1995 was the opening day for Elitch's new location in downtown Denver. The entrance to the new Elitch is a large bell-shaped pavilion housing the 1925 carousel and its 67 hand carved horses. Fifteen of its 18 major rides were brought to the new location. The old "Swing Ride" was repainted and kept. Also relocated from its old location were the "Sea Dragon," "Troila" and the "Rainbow." New rides were added.

Sandy Gurtler had high hopes for the park during its first season at its new location. Instead, attendance was weaker than the projected 1.2 million guests the park expected. Most likely, the Denver community could not so easily adjust to the closure of the park that nurtured its summer nights with its huge shade trees and floral decorations and, of course, its Theatre of stars. To most citizens, Elitch Gardens was more than just a roller coaster ride. It was a cultural staple of Denver. It was home, and hard to leave behind.

> So, the verdict was in. The good people of Denver stayed away in droves. Then, when Gurtler's new partners began to pressure him for their money, he unsuccessfully pleaded for time - time to let the Park's trees mature and for Denverites to get used to its new features. But they refused.
>
> The unthinkable was happening. Sandy Gurtler's options first narrowed and then were exhausted. He would be forced to sell Elitch Gardens, his family's business for four generations, in order to satisfy creditors who neither understood nor cared about the peculiarities of the amusement park business.[1-2]

During the mid-nineties, growing park chain Premier Parks, Inc., an Oklahoma City-based company, began purchasing regional amusement parks across the country. In October 1996, the Gurtler family sold the Elitch Gardens Amusement Park to Premier Parks, Inc. for $65.2 million.

In January 1997, Premier Parks, Inc. announced a huge multi-million dollar Elitch Gardens improvement program. In May 1997, three popular rides were added: The Mind Eraser (a suspended, inverted, looping roller coaster), Tower of Doom (a giant vertical free fall ride) and Shipwreck Falls (a family water ride). Improvements in the park continued, including a Trocadero Theater seating 700 for concert performances. This venue was also capable of being converted into a ballroom.

In 1998, Premier Parks, Inc. purchased all of the Six Flags Amusement Parks, and Elitch Gardens in Denver become known as Six Flags Elitch Gardens. In 1999, Six Flags Elitch Gardens opened its theme park with even more sensational new rides and attractions, including the Boomerang roller coaster.

In December of 2006, the Six Flags corporation sought to reduce $2.2 billion of its debt by selling its nine theme parks, which included Elitch Gardens in Denver, as a package or individually. In January 2007, Six Flags Elitch Gardens was sold to a Jacksonville, Florida-based park operator known as PARC 7-F-Operations Corp.* On April 10, 2007, it was reported that the closing on the sale had been finalized. PARC immediately sold the property to CNL Income Properties Inc., an Orlando, Florida-based real estate investment trust, which leased the attraction back to PARC to operate under 20-year renewable leases.

"Six Flags" was dropped from the name of the amusement park by the new owner, and it is now known again simply as "Elitch Gardens." Sadly, the names of John and Mary Elitch, their love and their struggles in bringing their dream to fruition, have been relegated to rides at an amusement park simply known as "Elitch Gardens," miles from their Chilcott farm, their flower gardens, their Theatre and their dream.

The Elitch Gardens Theatre

From 1891 to 1987, the Elitch Gardens Theatre was Denver's prime destination for an evening under the stars - Broadway-bound stars. The Theatre's last season of plays was 1987. When the amusement park relocated in 1994, the Theatre remained amid the vacant Chilcott land awaiting its future, its destiny. In 1991, the doors were reopened and a play presented to acknowledge the Theatre's 100th anniversary, and thereafter the doors were forever closed.

The Robber Bridegroom was the play presented. It was produced and directed by Coloradans. The cast consisted almost entirely of locally trained actors. It was a musical that kept the whole cast onstage from beginning to end. It was the Theatre's 100th birthday, "and the occasion for lots of Colorado talent to come together and celebrate."[2]

There was a community concern about the future of the Theatre, whether it would

* The sales price of $312 million dollars encompassed six other Six Flags amusement parks as well. Six Flags had been struggling with slowing attendance at the Park and significant debt. The sale was to have allowed Six Flags to pay down some of its high-interest debt and possibly refinance all of its debt at more favorable terms.

be moved or demolished in the wake of a housing development. Efforts in the past had been successfully made to protect it as a historic site.

In 1978, Elitch Theatre had been designated a historic site on the National Register of Historic Places, one of the 59 buildings in Denver already on the register. To meet the standards of the National Register of Historic Places, a structure must qualify in at least one or more of these categories: it must be architecturally important, it must be historically significant, or it must constitute a notable cultural contribution. The Elitch Theatre met all three of these requirements.

> At the time of The Historic Elitch Gardens Theatre's designation on the National Register of Historic Places, no other summer stock theatre had equaled the number of years of its successful operation, nor the number of productions presented during a season. It is the oldest summer stock theater in the United States.[3]

In general, being on the National Register protects the building from the attacks of city developers and highway engineers. If someone wants to run a freeway through Elitch's lobby, they will have to contend with Washington.[4] To further strengthen its position, a concerted effort was made to designate Elitch Theatre as a Denver landmark. Landmark laws in Denver are a bit more stringent than federal laws and make it much more difficult if any effort is made to demolish the building.

Denver City Councilman, and later Denver City Auditor, Dennis Gallagher, who worked as a stagehand at the Theatre while attending Regis College, was committed to protecting the Theatre. His rallying cry was clear.

> Denver will not be a great city again until we renovate and restore Mary Elitch's Historic Theatre.
>
> I look forward to doing everything I can to turn this treasure back into a working theatre, full of the mystery and magic of its historic past.[5]
>
> Without Mary Elitch's Theatre, Denver is a city without a soul.[6]

On September 19, 1995, the Denver Landmark Preservation Commission voted unanimously to recommend to the Denver City Council that Elitch Theatre be designated a landmark.[7] The following month, the Denver City Council voted unanimously for the designation.[6]

There were plans considered by The Elitch Theatre Company to establish a non-profit corporation and a pledge drive to preserve the troubled Theatre. The drive was supported by actresses Debbie Reynolds and Cloris Leachman.

On July 17, 1996, the Elitch Gardens site was sold by the Gurtlers to Perry Affordable Housing, owned by developers Chuck Rose and Jonathan Perry, with the stipulation that the Theatre be preserved. Kevin Causey and Thomas Edmonds Hardy, who were consultants to developers Chuck Rose and Jonathan Perry, established the Historic Elitch Gardens Theatre Foundation whose mission was declared to be as follows:

> The Mission of the Historic Elitch Gardens Theatre Foundation is to restore and maintain the Historic Elitch Gardens Theatre, the Carousel Pavilion and the Theatre Plaza; to preserve the historic identity of the Theatre and the Carousel Pavilion; and to present quality programming in all three venues which will function as an arts, culture and community center for the City of Denver, and preserve part of its architectural heritage.* [3]

A campaign was undertaken by the Foundation to raise $14 million, $7 million allocated to renovate and restore the Theatre and the Carousel Pavilion and to construct the Theatre Plaza, 2 million to support programs ranging from children's arts education, productions of music, theater, dance and film and community programs, and $5 million for an endowment to support the maintenance of the historic sites and to provide additional programming support, and thereby protect its future.

A grant of $355,325 was awarded to the Foundation from the Colorado State Historical Fund, and $2.2 million from the city of Denver in tax-increment financing. A $200,000 matching grant was given by the Gurtler family. The land developers gave $600,000. Neighborhood fundraisers added an additional $100,000.

After considering several options for the property, a residential housing development was planned and later established, known as the Highlands Garden Village. The development encircled the Theatre, and the nearby Carousel Pavilion. The Carousel Pavilion was refurbished and a Theatre Plaza was constructed.

Work was in process for the Theatre. Plans for the renovation of the Theatre included the following:

> (a) Replacement of siding, weatherizing to turn the built-for-summer Theatre into a year round venue,
>
> (b) The removal and replacement of the outsized flyhouse (which houses the mechanical operations) with a facility more in scale with the Theatre. The new flyhouse would include offices, a shop, a warming kitchen, and renovated dressing rooms. The dressing rooms are on three levels beyond the "pagoda" boxes at either end of the stage.
>
> (c) Remaking the interior by reducing the number of seats to 800 and leveling a portion of the floor to accommodate events as well as performances, and addressing the need for disability access.

* The Elitch Pavilion's bell-shaped roof was a popular design for sheltering carousels. The Carousel itself was moved to the present Six Flags location in 1994, but the Pavilion was abandoned and not moved.

(d) Installation of air-conditioning and a heating system and wiring the Theatre for state-of-the-art multimedia and broadcast capabilities. Elitch Theatre had had no air conditioning or heating system. Swamp coolers were used, and fans when necessary.[3]

The Foundation will lease the Theatre from the developer for 99 years at $1 a year.

Kevin Causey was quoted as saying, "We want to take a great historical treasure and turn it into a contemporary and fully functioning theater and arts center. It is not a museum piece. (The goal is) to restore where we can and to replace in kind where we can't."[8]

In 2007 the outside of the Theatre was painted and otherwise restored. It was expected that the refurbishing of the interior of the Theatre was to be completed in early 2009, and it was to house what was to be called The Center for American Theatre. However, on September 2, 2007, the *Denver Post* reported that Kevin Causey resigned as executive director of the Foundation, but remained as a member of the Board. It also stated:

> All current programming, such as summer film series, outdoor theater and farmers' markets, will cease while the board refocuses on raising the $10 million it needs to rebuild the Theatre's interior.
>
> Though the news appears to be a huge blow in the long campaign to reopen the historic playhouse in northwest Denver as a community resource center dedicated to the study and production of American theater, Causey insists, "I don't want to give the impression the campaign is in jeopardy in any way - it's not ... We need to hire someone in this position whose sole focus and experience is in capital campaigns."
>
> As recently as January, the target date for reopening was 2009, but the projected cost has grown by $4 million since then. Now it might be four years before Causey has a facility to program.[9]

However, in an article dated March 28, 2008 by Paula Moore in the *Denver Business Journal*, it was reported that the Board of the Foundation was trying to decide how to revive itself and raise funds for the interior renovation of the Theatre.

> The board also will start looking at whether or not to replace the Foundation's former executive director, Kevin Causey, who left the post last fall.
>
> "The Foundation is operating on a more limited basis without an executive director ... We're looking at two options for that position - to replace Kevin or to step back and hire a consultant to analyze the highest probability for raising necessary funds," said Chuck Perry, Foundation

> board member and partner at Denver development firm Perry Rose LLC.
>
> The Foundation's fundraising efforts have been on hold since Causey left.[10]

The future of the Elitch Theatre was vague. However, the all-but-abandoned project is once again the subject of new energy. An article by John Moore, drama editor for the *Denver Post,* appeared in its February 14, 2010 edition captioned "Elitch jewel may rise again on modest hopes." It stated:

> It's been two years since we've heard a peep about the stalled campaign to rescue, renovate and revive the historic Elitch Theatre in northwest Denver.
>
> But a more modest (and therefore hopefully more attainable) new mission has been launched to save the 119-year-old former jewel that hosted some of the biggest names in show business.[11]

Denver attorney Paul R. Franke III has assembled and assumed the leadership of an eight-person neighborhood board, which includes University of Colorado of Denver assistant theater professor Jose Mercado. The goal is to reach $5 million to restore the interior and $1 million more for an operational budget. The *Denver Post* article stated that the former plan "to create an educational center dedicated to the production and study of American theater is long dead" ... (the goal now being to create) "a sustainable cultural center where arts, education, music, dance and theater can take place."

The funds to be raised are being sought from state grants, federal funding and by monthly ongoing grassroots fundraisers. For example, the article noted that a wine shop establishment had agreed to donate five percent of all its sales on a particular day to the Elitch campaign.

In an article that appeared in the October 2010 edition of the Denver magazine *5280,* it referenced different monetary amounts to achieve the goal of the Foundation. The article stated:

> Initial estimates call for up to $10 million to redo the interior, and some say it could cost even more. With the $50,000 in its coffers, according to chairman Paul Franke, at least one keystone donor would have to step forward with at least $1 million, which might then attract more money. So far this elusive benefactor has not yet emerged.

Since then the City of Denver's Office of Economic Development has awarded the Historic Elitch Gardens Theatre Foundation a grant of $425,000 toward restoring the interior of the Theatre; however, the funds are to be released only when 25% of the award is matched in contributions. As of April 13, 2012, the Foundation reported that it was about $20,000 away from the $106,250 needed to receive the $425,000 matching grant toward the restoration process.[12] Hopefully, the goal to create at the historic site a venue for the production, study, and celebration of performing arts while serving as a cultural center for the local community will be achieved. What is clear, however, is that the Theatre will never be the same as it was in its past, a past which shall always be remembered.

Voices of the Past

Following the final season and performance at the Elitch Theatre in 1987 until today, voices of the past that were closely associated with the history of Denver's famous summer playhouse were silenced by death.

Whitfield Connor died on July 16, 1988, at 7:30 a.m. at Norwalk Hospital, Norwalk, Connecticut not far from the home he lived in and maintained in Weston, Connecticut with Haila Stoddard, his wife of more than three decades following their marriage on January 26, 1956. He was 71 years of age. Connor had served as executive producer at Elitch for many years with his wife as associate producer, although ill-health curtailed most of his activities in 1985.

Arnold "Budd" Gurtler Jr., died on October 2, 1991. He was 71 years of age. He was interred in Mount Olivet Cemetery. He was married to Barbara Sandstrom in Denver on August 11, 1941. Sandy Gurtler, his son, had assumed management of Elitch Gardens Amusement Park and Theatre in 1985.

John M. "Jack" Gurtler, President of Elitch Gardens from 1962 until his retirement in 1979, died on September 16, 1993. He was 75. He was survived by his wife, four children, and seven grandchildren. He was born in Denver on September 19, 1917 and graduated from Regis High School in Denver and from Nichols College in Massachusetts. He was active in civic affairs, having served on the board of directors of the Denver Convention and Visitors Bureau, the Eisenhower-Evans Caddies Scholarship Foundation and the Denver Zoo. He was also President of the National Association of Amusement Parks, Pools and Beaches.

Harriet Louise Gurtler, the wife of John M. Gurtler died in Denver on March 5, 2000. She was 81 years of age. She was born in Denver and graduated from East High School. She was society editor at the *Denver Post* during the 1940s and wrote under the name "Harry Lou Johnson." In August 1944, she announced the engagement of "Miss Harriet Louise Johnson" in the *Denver Post* to Gurtler without revealing that it was her own engagement. They married on October 21, 1944 at Blessed Sacrament Church in Denver.

Haila Stoddard died on February 21, 2011, in Weston, Connecticut. She was 97. In the theater when one's hope is always to survive, she was never without work. She had an outstanding career. She and her husband, Whitfield Connor, brought star-studded productions from Broadway to Denver's Elitch Theatre from 1972 to 1987, the Theatre's final season.

A Precious Memory

John and Mary Elitch had a dream for all of Denver: the Gardens and, of course, the Theatre. Notwithstanding John's untimely death in 1891, Mary Elitch struggled and succeeded in keeping the dream alive.

In 1900, Father William O'Ryan, a priest and a longtime friend of Mary Elitch publicly paid tribute to her. His words echo within us today when we think of all that Mary Elitch, our "Lady of the Gardens," brought to Denver in keeping John and Mary's dream of Elitch Gardens and Theatre alive, and from which we have inherited an everlasting precious memory.

> All people of Denver recognize you, we salute you, we lift our hats to you in utter knowledge and respect and love, dear Mrs. Elitch. Denver owes you more than she knows; you and the Gardens will be held in the pleasant places of our memories. Some of us are growing old and the cares of life are many and heavy; but once we were young and loved and were loved, and the apple trees in the Gardens heard our vows and smiled upon us and blessed us with the blessing of blossoms.
>
> Thank God, "the Lady," the spirit of the place, is with us still. Though we may grow old and gray, the place in our heart's memory that enshrines "the Lady of the Gardens" will never grow old.[13]

While John and Mary Elitch's turn-of-the-century Theatre fell out of sync with the modern air-conditioned theaters of today, no matter how warm the place may have felt by intermission, it is and will always be dearly missed, while nurtured among our most precious memories.

Looking to the Future - Elitch Theatre - Its Restoration Process - Painting and Refurbishing

The Historic Elitch Gardens Theatre Foundation has committed to paint the exterior and to refurbish the interior of Elitch Theatre. The photos are indicative of the process. The Theatre will never be the theater of its past, a past that is embedded in the hearts and memories of its many patrons. The goal of the Foundation is "to create at the historic site a venue for the production, study, and celebration of performing arts while serving a cultural center for the local community."

Some Scenes of the Restoration Process - 2012

(above) The Gated Front - *(below)* The Newly Painted Building

Inside Elitch Theatre - the Stage From a Distance

Mary Elitch Long's Box Seat

Balcony Seats

Outside Stairway to Balcony Seating

The Main Entrance

Maude Fealy photograph on display
at an open house at Elitch Theatre in 2012

History Colorado - # 10038220

The Main Entrance - in Earlier Years - Part of Our Memories

Your support for the Historic Elitch Gardens Theatre Foundation will be appreciated.

Epilogue

During the research and writing of the history of Elitch Theatre, individuals approached the author from time to time to reveal their precious memories of the historic Elitch Theatre. It was as though the research awakened a personal and unforgettable day or event in their lives associated with Elitch Theatre, which they were anxious to share. It was apparent that the history of the Elitch Theatre will never be "complete," but rather always ongoing, always the subject of conversation and remembrance.

In an interview with Dennis Gallagher, Denver's City Auditor, he shared a remembrance of Elitch Theatre and Grace Kelly.

> I grew up a few blocks from Elitch Gardens in North Denver. I have always thought of Elitch Theatre as a sacred place. Of all the actors who trod the boards that summer at Mary's Theatre, Grace Kelly worked her magic with the skill of a priestess at Delphi. Grace Kelly rented a room next door to a friend of mine a block from where I lived. One morning Grace Kelly came to the student mass at Holy Family school where I attended. I sat two rows behind her and failed to respond to the sound of the cricket click from Sister Martha Ann, my wonderful teacher. I was obviously totally distracted by Grace's radiance. Sister Martha Ann walked up the aisle and told me, loud enough for Miss Kelly to hear, "Dennis Gallagher, you can kneel now and give your attention to the mass." Miss Kelly left right after communion, most likely to get to rehearsal. As she left the church, she glanced at me and whispered, "Thank you, Dennis Gallagher." I remember it as though it was now. Thank you Mary Elitch for inviting this future princess to your Theatre and allowing this moment to become a part of my life.

A contributor to the Internet recalled a day when he saw Victor Borge and his piano performance at Elitch Theatre. As Borge was playing a serious piece, he noted that one could faintly hear the sound of the Elitch train go by the Theatre with its familiar whistle. Without missing a beat, Borge segued from the classical piece he was playing into a few choruses of "I've Been Working on the Railroad."

Memories of Elitch Theatre have adorned its history from its very early days. In the book *Lady of the Gardens* by Caroline Dier, an event is recalled by Mary Elitch as follows:

> Theodore Roberts, the famous 'master of makeup'... became a devoted attendant at my bear pit. Early morning found him at the edge of the pits tendering choice breakfast fruits to the willing creatures below... While thus engaged Mr. Roberts one day realized the loss of a very highly-

> prized ring. It had been devoured, but the loss of this valued treasure did not dim the actor's enthusiasm for bears. When the loss was reported, Mr. Bellows, the director said: 'Well, now I suppose Theodore has had enough of bears and will report to rehearsal on time.' Not so - Theodore only seemed to grow fonder of Sam, who wore his ring internally.

And so it is that the names of John and Mary Elitch should be kept alive in people's hearts and minds for all they have contributed in making the Gardens a "respectable family resort" and its Theatre "one of the greatest cradles of drama in American history." Should the Historic Elitch Theatre Foundation succeed in refurbishing the interior of this historic site, as it surely will, and converting it into a sustainable communal center, may it set aside a special corner of the Theatre for individuals, lovers of Elitch, where a memory or two can be shared with others anxious to know as much as possible about the Theatre's nostalgic journey.

Appendix

An Index of Actors and Actresses

The opening of Elitch Gardens on May 1, 1890 offered vaudeville to its Theatre patrons. In 1891, the program consisted of vaudeville except for six weeks of light opera by the Boston Opera Company. In 1892, the program consisted of light opera by the Aborn Opera Company. In 1893, the Frank Norcross Stock Company was engaged to present a season of plays. Vaudeville was presented exclusively in 1894. In 1895, vaudeville was presented, as well as six weeks of comic opera by the Dunbar Pyke Opera Company. In the 1896 season of plays, the final two weeks of the season consisted of vaudeville. Several one-act plays were included among the 1897 presentations.

Until 1899, vaudeville acts were sometimes given in between acts of plays. Vaudeville continued at Elitch until 1901.

Consideration was given to creating an index that would identify all those actors and actresses who set foot on the boards of Elitch.

In reviewing the newspapers and articles throughout the years, frequently, the resident company had to be augmented by other actors, as in 1899 when the cast of *Cyrano de Bergerac* called for 76 speaking roles, with extras added, for about 100 people on stage, or the troupe of youngsters needed to make up the large cast of *Janie* in 1944, or a stage of naval personnel for *My Sister Eileen*, and in 1926, 200 performers who were needed on stage in a scene from *The Westerner*.

When minor supporting players or extras were needed to augment the regular players, they were often selected from the list of local amateurs (usually supplied by the acting schools of Margaret Fealy and Robert Bell) or from former professional actors who had moved to Denver to make their home.

To name every participant who appeared on stage would be a gargantuan task and is clearly not necessary to this work.

For the most part, the various chapters of the book identify those actors and actresses who were a significant part of the Elitch resident companies, particularly those performing in lead roles, as well as special guest performers.

A different consideration has been given to the more contemporary actors and actresses of stage, screen and television that appeared under the "star package system" from 1964 through 1987. Their names are summarized herein. However, the names of supporting cast members are not included.

An asterisk (*) represents that the performer appeared in a concert and/or cabaret-type entertainment and not in a play.

Abel, Walter - 1975
Adams, Edie - 1971
Alda, Robert - 1966
Allen, Steve - 1974
Allyson, June - 1966
Aumont, Jean Pierre - 1965
Amsterdam, Morey - 1968
Arden, Eve - 1965
Arquette, Cliff - 1966
Astin, John - 1973, 1974
Bain, Conrad - 1986
Baxter, Keith - 1985
Bean, Orson - 1980
Bel Geddes, Barbara - 1964
Benedict, Dirk - 1979
Booth, Shirley - 1968
* Borge, Victor - 1970
Bottoms, Timothy - 1982
Boyd, Stephan - 1967
Byrne, Gaylea - 1977
Byrnes, Edd - 1968
Caesar, Sid - 1971, 1974
Cagney, Jeanne - 1969
Calabro, Thomas - 1984
Carello, Robert - 1978
Carlisle, Kitty - 1965, 1970
Caron, Leslie - 1985
Cass, Peggy - 1964, 1976, 1978
Catlett, Mary Jo - 1985, 1987
Conaway, Jeff - 1984
* Cook, Barbara - 1987
Crosby, Kathryn - 1969
Curtis, Keene - 1975
Cummings, Robert - 1968
Dandy, Gary - 1984
de Wilde, Brandon - 1972
Dee, Sandra - 1976
Dennis, Sandy - 1974, 1982
Duke (Astin), Patty - 1973, 1974
Dullea, Keir - 1977, 1983
Dussault, Nancy - 1984
Ewell, Tom - 1966, 1969
Fairbanks, Jr., Douglas - 1971, 1973
Farrand, Jan - 1976
Feldon, Barbara - 1982
Ferrer, Jose - 1973
Fontaine, Joan - 1967, 1968
Ford, Paul - 1967
* Ford, Phil - 1965, 1968, 1970
Francis, Arlene - 1964, 1965, 1969
* Gaynor, Mitzi - 1987
Gingold, Hermione - 1965
Gobel, George - 1971
Graham, Ronnie - 1967
Granger, Farley - 1978, 1980
Grimes, Tammy - 1983
Grizzard, George - 1969
Harris, Julie - 1978
Harrison, Noel - 1970, 1983
Hatfield, Hurd - 1969
Heckart, Eileen - 1982
Helmore, Tom - 1965
* Hines, Mimi - 1965, 1968, 1970
Hingle, Pat - 1981
Hirsch, Judd - 1981
Holden, Hal - 1967
Hugo, Laurence - 1975
Hunter, Kim - 1975
Ireland, John - 1982
* James, Joni - 1966
* Jessel, George - 1967
Johnson, Van - 1977, 1979
Jory, Victor - 1976
Kaplan, Gabe - 1983
Kasznar, Kurt - 1976
Kert, Larry - 1985
Kiley, Richard - 1976, 1983
Kirk, Lisa - 1966
Lawless, James - 1982
Leachman, Cloris - 1983, 1986
Learned, Michael - 1987
Levene, Sam - 1969, 1970
Lord, Marjorie - 1964
Louden, Dorothy - 1971
Loy, Myrna - 1967, 1969
Lynn, Jeffrey - 1965
MacKenzie, Giselle - 1967
MacLeod, Gavin - 1986

Masiell, Joe - 1969
March, Hal - 1964, 1965
McBain, Diane - 1968
McArthur, James - 1982
McCallum, David - 1976, 1983
McGavin, Darren - 1964
McGuire, Michael - 1986
McKay, Scott - 1976
Meadows, Jayne - 1974
Meeker, Ralph - 1965
Merrill, Gary - 1974
Morey, Bill - 1966
Morgan, Henry - 1967
Morris, Chester - 1966
Munsel, Patrice - 1972, 1978
Mulhare, Edward - 1978
* Nabors, Jim - 1985
Nelson, Barry - 1968, 1969, 1971
Newmar, Julie - 1968
Nolan, Kathy - 1965
Nye, Louis - 1966
Nype, Russel - 1976
O'Brien, Eloise - 1980, 1981
O'Brien, Pat - 1980, 1981
O'Shea, Milo - 1985
O'Sullivan, Maureen -
1966, 1972, 1976, 1983
Palmer, Betsy - 1975
Pavan, Marisa - 1965
Pidgeon, Walter - 1964
Platt, Howard - 1984
Poston, Tom - 1969
Powell, Jane - 1981
Power IV, Tyrone - 1983
* Presnell, Harve - 1986
Price, Vincent - 1979
Prinz, Rosemary - 1968, 1977
Purl, Linda - 1984
Raitt, John - 1976, 1977, 1979
Rayburn, Gene - 1981
Redgrave, Lynn - 1975, 1977
Repole, Charles - 1980
* Reynolds, Debbie - 1986
Ritchard, Cyril - 1964
Rodd, Marcia - 1984
Rogers, Ginger - 1975
Romero, Cesar - 1964
Rooney, Mickey - 1972, 1974
Ross, Marion - 1986
Rush, Barbara - 1982, 1987
Seldes, Marian - 1968
Schreiber, Avery - 1984
Shatner, William - 1980
Shepherd, Cybill - 1982
Skaggs, Marsha - 1982
Skinner, Cornelia Otis - 1964
Smith, Roger - 1964
Smith, Sheila - 1984
Sothern, Ann - 1968
Stadlen, Lewis - 1975
Swanson, Gloria - 1967
Sydney, Sylvia - 1976
Thaxter, Phyllis - 1984
Thompson, Sada - 1980
Towers, Constance - 1969
Tucker, Forrest - 1968
Turner, Lana - 1977
Vance, Vivian - 1966
von Furstenberg, Betsy - 1969
Walker, Nancy - 1981
Whitehead, Paxton - 1979
Whiting, Margaret - 1984
Whitmore, James - 1969
Winters, Shelley - 1973, 1983
Wright, Teresa - 1976
Wyckoff, Eveyln - 1964
Young, Gig - 1973

Bibliography

The author has relied on many sources in preparing this manuscript of Elitch Theatre in addition to his own experience as a patron of the Theatre. He has discussed the Theatre with many who miss its presence in the theatrical world and who have encouraged this effort to preserve its history.

Newspapers

The author examined more than 100 years of newspaper articles in the *Denver Post* and *Rocky Mountain News* relating to Elitch Gardens and Theatre. Other newspapers consulted were:

Boulder Daily Camera
Colorado Sun
Daily News
Denver Catholic Register
Denver Express
Denver Republican
Denver Times
Intermountain Jewish News
Jefferson County Sentinel
Longmont Daily Times
North Denver News

Books

Arps, Louisa Ward, *Denver in Slices* (Swallow Press/Ohio University Press 1998)

Atkinson, Brooks, *Broadway* (Cassell & Company Ltd. 1970)

Barrett, Daniel and Beth R., *High Drama* (Western Reflections Publishing Company 2005)

Bach, Steven, *Dazzler (The Life and Times of Moss Hart)* (Alfred A. Knopf 2001)

Barnes, Clive (selections) and Gassner, John (individual play introductions), *50 Best Plays of the American Theatre* (Volume 4) (Crown Publishers, Inc. New York 1970)

Barnes, Clive (editor), *Best American Plays (Eight Series 1974-1982)* (Crown Publishers, Inc. 1983)

Bentley, Eric, *What is Theatre?* (Beacon Press 1956)

Bernheim, Alfred L., *The Business of the Theatre* (Benjamin Blum, Inc. 1964)

Binns, Archie, *Mrs. Fiske and The American Theatre* (Crown Publishers, Inc. 1955)

Blair, Edward, *Leadville: Colorado's Magic City* (Pruett Publishing Company 1980)

Blum, Daniel (editor), *Great Stars of the American Stage* (New York, Greenberg Publisher 1952)

Bordman, Gerald, *American Theatre: A Chronicle of Comedy and Drama, 1869-1914* (Oxford University Press 1994)

Bordman, Gerald, *American Theatre: A Chronicle of Comedy and Drama, 1914-1930* (Oxford University Press 1995)

Bordman, Gerald, *American Theatre: A Chronicle of Comedy and Drama, 1930-1969* (Oxford University Press 1996)

Bordman, Gerald, and Hischak, Thomas S., *The Oxford Companion to American Theatre* (Oxford University Press 2004)

Brewer, E. Cobham, (as revised by Ivor H. Evans), *Brewer's Dictionary of Phrase and Fable* (Harper & Row, Publishers 1970)

Burns, George (written with David Fisher), *All My Best Friends* (G. P. Putnam's Sons 1989)

Caesar, Sid (with Eddy Friedfeld), *Caesar's Hours* (Public Affairs 2003)

Clark , Barret H., *Representative One-Act Plays by British and Irish Authors* (Boston: Little Brown and Co. 1921)

Chaplin, Charles, *My Autobiography* (Simon and Schuster 1964)

Convery, William J., *Pride of the Rockies* (University Press of Colorado 2005)

Dardis, Tom, *Harold Lloyd* (Penquin Books 1983)

Deutsch, Helen and Hanau, Stella, *The Provincetown: A Story of a Theatre* (Farrer & Rinehart, Inc., New York 1931)

Dier, Caroline Lawrence, *The Lady of the Gardens* (Hollywood: Hollycrofters, Inc. Ltd. 1932)

Ellmann, Richard, *Oscar Wilde* (Alfred A. Knopf 1988)

Englund, Steven, *Grace of Monaco* (Doubleday & Company, Inc. 1984)

Fadiman, Clifton and Bernard, Andre (editors), *Bartlett's Book of Anecdotes* (Little, Brown and Company 2000)

Fort, Alice Buchanan and Kates, Herbert S., *Minute History of Drama* (New York: Grosset & Dunlap 1935)

Freedland, Michael, *Al Jolson* (Sphere Books Ltd. - Abacus Edition 1975)

Gardner, Herb, *A Thousand Clowns* (Penquin Books 1987)

Griffith, Richard and Mayer, Arthur, *The Movies* (Simon and Schuster 1957)

Gurtler, Jack and Hunt, Corinne, *The Elitch Garden Story* (Rocky Mountain Writers Guild Publication 1982)

Hafen, Leroy R., and Hafen, Ann, *The Colorado Story* (The Old West Publishing Company 1953)

Hancock, Ralph and Fairbanks, Letitia, *Douglas Fairbanks* (London: Peter Davies 1953)

Hartnoll, Phyllis (editor), *The Oxford Companion to the Theatre* (Oxford University Press 1951).

Hay, Peter, *Broadway Anecdotes* (Oxford University Press 1989)

Hodgson, Terry, *The Drama Dictionary* (New Amsterdam 1988)

Hosokawa, Bill, *Thunder in the Rockies* (William Morrow & Co., Inc. 1976)

Hull, Betty Lynne, *Denver's Elitch Gardens* (Johnson Books 2003)

Iverson, Kristen, *Molly Brown* (Johnson Books 2003)

Johnson, Forrest H., *Denver's Old Theater Row* (A Gem Publication 1970)

Katz, Ephraim, *The Film Encyclopedia* (Thomas Y. Crowell, Publisher 1979)

Kennedy, Dennis (editor), *The Oxford Encyclopedia of Theatre and Performance* (Oxford University Press 2003)

Kennedy, Harold J., *No Pickle, No Performance* (Doubleday Company, Inc. 1978)

Knight, Arthur, *The Liveliest Art* (Mentor Books 1957)

Lacy, Robert, *Grace* (G. P. Putnam's Sons 1994)

LoMonaco, Martha Schmoyer, *Summer Stock* (Palgrave MacMillan 2004)

Lynn, Kenneth S., *Charlie Chaplin and His Times* (Simon & Schuster 1997)

Mantle, Burns (editor), *Best Plays of 1928-1929* (New York: Dodd, Mead and Company 1929)

Mantle, Burns, and Sherwood, Garrison (editors), *Best Plays of 1909-1919* (New York: Dodd, Mead and Company 1929)

Martin, Nick and Porter, Marsha, *Video Movie Guide 1999* (Ballantine Books 1998)

Marshall, Logan, *The Sinking of the Titanic* (Hara Publishing 1998)(original 1912 classic abridged and edited by Bruce M. Caplan)

Morehouse, Ward, *Matinee Tomorrow* (New York: Whittlesey House 1949)

Morison, Samuel Eliot, *The Oxford History of the American People* (Oxford University Press 1965)

Pickering, David (editor) and Cass, Judith M. (picture editor), *International Dictionary of Theatre-3*, (St. James Press 1996)

Priestley, J. B., *An Inspector Calls* (Dramatists Play Service, Inc. 1945)

Schwartz, Bonnie Nelson, *Voices From the Federal Theatre* (University of Wisconsin Press 2003)

Shearer, Stephan Michael, *Patricia Neal (An Unquiet Life)* (The University Press of Kentucky 2006)

Smith, Richard Norton, *Thomas E. Dewey and His Times* (Simon and Schuster 1982)

Spada, James, *Grace* (A Dolphin Book - Doubleday & Company, Inc. 1987)

Stagg, Jerry, *The Brothers Shubert* (Random House 1968)

Stevenson, Isabelle and Somlyo, Roy A. (editors), *The Tony Award* (Heinemann 2001)

Swanson, Gloria, *Swanson on Swanson* (Random House 1980)

Temple, Judy Molte, *Baby Doe Tabor* (University of Oklahoma Press: Norman 2007)

Watt, Eva Hodges, *Papa's Girl* (Western Reflections Publications Company 2007)

Wilson, Edwin, *The Theater Experience* (McGraw-Hill Book Company 1976)

Wood, Richard E., *Here Lies Colorado* (Farcountry Press 2005)

Doctoral Dissertations*

Kline, Hebron Charles, *A History of Denver Theatre During the Depression Era 1929-1941*, Ph.D. Univ. of Denver, 1963, Volume 1.

Levy, Edwin, *Elitch's Gardens, Denver, Colorado: A History of the Oldest Summer Theatre in the United States (1890-1941)*, Ph.D. diss., Columbia University, 1960.

Nichols, Dean G., *Pioneer Theatres of Denver, Colorado,* Ph.D. diss., University of Michigan, 1938.

* Available at the Western History / Genealogy Department of the Denver Public Library

Magazines

Colorado Magazine
Colorado Prospector
Field and Farm
Rocky Mountain Life

Internet

The Internet is a useful research source for all authors. It was a useful reference of information in this broad area and topics of theatrical history.

Library Sources

History Colorado in Denver provided valuable material for the author to examine, much of which was included in the reference designated as "Elitch Theatre Collection." It was a broad and useful reference of information on the subject matter. It contained boxes upon boxes of file folders donated by the Elitch Gardens Management about the workings of the Theatre, equity contracts, the cost of productions, box office records, photographs, contracts and leases entered into when the management of the Theatre was taken over by Helen Bonfils and then by Whitfield Connor upon her demise, correspondence with actors and agents including letters from Grace Kelly as Princess of Monaco, reviews by drama critics and other source materials.

The Western History/Genealogy Department of the Denver Public Library had an abundance of files and folders with information on Elitch Theatre, including numerous photographs. Among the materials available for study were over one hundred years of newspaper accounts relating to Elitch Theatre and research papers on facets of theatrical history in Denver, the most comprehensive being that of Edwin Levy of the drama department of the University of Denver submitted as his doctorate dissertation to Columbia University.

Both sources had numerous and various copies of Elitch Theatre programs within the framework of its early years up to the final performance in 1987. Copies of *The Elitch Gardener* and *Elitch's Weekly*, publications by the Elitch Gardens Management, were also available.

The author also visited the Theatrical Division of the Lincoln Center Library in New York City where he obtained information available on the Elitch Theatre.

The Historic Elitch Gardens Theatre Foundation

The author also examined the Promotional Literature of the Historic Elitch Gardens Theatre Foundation relating to the efforts being made to preserve the Theatre and the hope of its playing a future role among theater historians and enthusiasts.

Notes

Explanation of Footnote References

To aid the reader in his or her understanding of the footnote references throughout the text, the following explanation is offered.

The same footnote reference (i.e., 3 or 1) may appear numerous times in the text and will refer to a specific source such as Hancock and Fairbanks, *Douglas Fairbanks* (London, Peter Davies 1953) and the appropriate pages such as 20; 41; 43; 55. Thus, if footnote 3 refers to the Hancock and Fairbanks source, the first time it appears in the text (as 3-1) will refer to the source on page 20, the second time (as 3-2) on page 41, etc. All other sources, such as periodicals and theater programs, will be treated in the same manner except that some references may be to dates instead of pages, such as the *Denver Post*, Jan 12; Jul 9; Aug 20, 1936. Thus, Jan 12 will be the first time the *Denver Post* appears in the text (as 1-1) and Jul 9 (as 1-2) the second time it appears, etc. Pages and dates in a given footnote will be numbered in the order in which they appear in the text and therefore may not be in numerical or chronological order. The references within each entry in the notes section will be separated by semi-colons. When necessary for clarity or to make a reference outside the above parameters, a specific footnote will be made. The same footnote, such as 3-1 or 3-2 above, may appear several times in the text, but the corresponding source, such as p. 20 or 41 above, will appear only once in the notes section.

Levy, *Elitch's Gardens, Denver, Colorado: A History of the Oldest Summer Theatre in the United States (1890-1941)*, Ph.D. diss., Columbia University, 1940 - is cited in the notes as "Levy at p. (appropriate page)."

Dier, *The Lady of the Gardens* (Hollywood Hollycrofters, Inc., Ltd. 1932) is cited in the notes as "Dier at p. (appropriate page)."

Bordman & Hischak, *The Oxford Companion to American Theatre*(Oxford University Press 2004) is cited in the notes as "Bordman & Hischak at p. (appropriate page)."

On occasion, the Internet has been cited as a reference. Because of the dynamic nature of the Internet, any web addresses or links contained in this book may have changed since publication and may no longer be valid.

* * * * *

Two

1. Liggett, "A Garden For Mary," *Rocky Mountain Life* (Jun 1947), p. 16.
2. *Denver Republican*, Mar 11, 1891, p. 1.
3. *Denver Post*, May 31, 1914, p. 8.
4. *Denver Post*, May 31, 1914, p. 8 and Dier at 29 (Note).
5. See Elitch Theatre program, 89th Year, Aug 4-16, 1980.
6. *Denver Republican*, Aug 7, 1886, p. 4.
7. *Colorado Magazine*, Vol. XX, No. 2, Mar 1943, p. 70; Vol. 22, No. 6, Nov 1945, p. 271.

8. Hull, *Denver's Elitch Gardens* (Johnson Books 2003), p. 3.
9. See generally http://denverinfill.com/blog/2008/09/highland-or-highlands.html.
10. Arps, *Denver in Slices* (Swallow Press/Ohio University Press 1998), p. 212. In another reference, the year of sale was stated as 1889. See *Denver Post*, Mar 19, 1932, p. 4 (the article states the year of sale to be 1889).
11. *Denver Post*, Mar 19, 1932, p. 4.
12. Dier at pp. 19; 20-21; 23; 22; 36.
13. Barrett & Barrett, *High Drama* (Western Reflections Publishing Company 2005), pp. 11-12.
14. Levy at pp. 5; 7; 4-5; 8-9; 177.
15. Elitch Theatre Program, for Jun 11, 1932, pp. 6, 32. Newspapers advertising the opening of the Gardens referenced the transportation. *E.g.*, *Rocky Mountain News*, April 30, 1890 stated: "Take Fifteenth Street Cable Cars for North Denver and ask Conductor for Transfer Ticket to the Gardens."
16. *Denver Post*, Jul 17, 1936, p. 1.
17. *Rocky Mountain News*, May 2, 1890, p. 6.
18. Forrest H. Johnson, *Denver's Old Theater Row* (A Gem Publication 1970), p. 36.
19. Dier at p. 22. And see *Rocky Mountain News*, Jun 15, 1941, p. 12.
20. Levy at pp. 327-328, citing with approval A.B. Gurtler, "Elitch's Yesterday and Today," *Billboard*, Dec 6, 1930, p. 95.
21. History Colorado, Denver, Elitch Theatre Collection 1364, Box 11, File Folder 934.
22. *Denver Post*, Nov 14, 1954, p. 3A.
23. *Rocky Mountain News*, Jun 12, 1981, p. 3C.
24. *Rocky Mountain News* (Now Section), Jul 24, 1977, pp. 26, 29.
25. Compare *Rocky Mountain News* (Now Section), Jul 24, 1977, pp. 26, 29 (48 seats) *with* Levy at p. 184 (60 seats).
26. *E.g.*, Ads appearing in the *Denver Republican* and *Rocky Mountain News*, Apr 30, 1890.
27. *Rocky Mountain News*, Jun 19, 1966, p. 5A.

Three

1. Arps, *Denver in Slices* (Swallow Press/Ohio University Press 1959), p. 212.
2. *Field and Farm*, Vol. 10, No. 19, Nov 8, 1890, p. 5.
3. *Denver Republican*, Nov 4, 1890; Mar 11; Mar 12, 1891.
4. *Denver Republican*, Mar 11, 1891, p. 1. See also Forrest H. Johnson, *Denver's Old Theater Row* (A Gem Publication 1970), p. 36.
5. *Rocky Mountain News*, Apr 29, 2006, p. 2D.
6. Dier at pp. 29; 68.
7. *Rocky Mountain News*, Jul 17, 1936, pp. 1, 13.
8. See *Colorado Prospector*, Vol. 8, No. 5, Apr 25 and May 4, 1891 and *Rocky Mountain News*, May 10, 1891, p. 17.
9. *Rocky Mountain News*, May 9; May 10, 1891.
10. Prospectus and By Laws of the Elitch Gardens Amusement Company, pp. 8, 13, 14. A copy of the prospectus is on file with History Colorado, Denver, Elitch Theatre Collection 1364, Box 10, File Folder 802.
11. Levy at pp. 196-197 (footnotes omitted).
12. *Rocky Mountain News* (Now Section), Mar 28, 1982, p. 4.
13. *Denver Republican*, Apr 22; Jul 12, 1891; Jul 24, 1892.

14. *Rocky Mountain News*, Jan 13, 1957, p. 57.
15. *Compare Denver Post* (Out West Section) article (2,000 seats) *with* untitled article (3,000 seats) in clippings file of Manhattan Beach in the Western History Division of the Denver Public Library.
16. *Rocky Mountain News*, May 10, 1891, p. 19.
17. *Jefferson County Sentinel*, Dec 29, 1966, p. 17.
18. *Rocky Mountain News*, Aug 12, 1894, p. 15.
19. *Denver Post*, Jan 28, 1900, p. 15.
20. *Denver Times*, Jun 23; Jun 30, 1901.
21. Hull, *Denver's Elitch Gardens* (Johnson Books 2003), p. 22.
22. *Rocky Mountain News*, Apr 3, 1953, p. 1F.
23. See *Rocky Mountain News*, May 3, 1953, p. 1F and *North Denver News*, Sep 7, 2004, p. 5.
24. *Intermountain Jewish News*, Aug 29, 1975, p. 8.

Four

1. Elitch Theatre program, 40th Year, the week beginning Jul 10, 1932, p. 10.
2. Arps, *Denver in Slices* (Swallow Press/Ohio University Press 1959), p. 221.
3. Levy at pp. 49-50; 50; 51; 11; 54-55.
4. See Elitch Theatre program, Jul 17, 1893, p 3.
5. Bordman & Hischak at pp. 115; 298.
6. See Iverson, *Molly Brown* (Johnson Books 1999), pp. 101-102 and Morison, *The Oxford History of the American People* (Oxford University Press 1965), p. 741.
7. Morison, *The Oxford History of the American People* (Oxford University Press 1965), p. 795.
8. Blair, *Leadville: Colorado's Magic City* (Pruett Publishing Company 1980), p. 174.
9. Levy at pp. 75-76, citing with approval the *Colorado Sun*, Sep 17, 1893, p. 4.
10. Levy at p. 50, citing with approval the New York Dramatic Mirror, XXX, Sep 2, 1893, p. 8.
11. *Denver Republican*, Apr 15, 1894, p. 12; May 26, 1895, p. 12.
12. Dier at p. 56.
13. *Daily News*, Jul 19; Aug 30, 1896.
14. Griffith and Mayer, *The Movies* (Simon and Schuster 1957), pp. 1 and 2; 2-3; 3.
15. *Denver Republican*, Aug 16, 1896, p. 24.
16. *The Daily News*, May 23, 1897, p. 5 and May 30, 1897, p. 12.
17. Elitch Theatre program, Jun 30, 1929, p. 32.
18. Bernheim, *The Business of the Theatre* (Benjamin Blum, Inc. 1964), p. 32.
19. Hodgson, *The Drama Dictionary* (New Amsterdam 1988), p. 317.
20. *Elitch's Weekly*, Volume VI, Number 5, Jul 9, 1912; Number 11, Aug 20, 1912.
21. Hull, *Denver's Elitch Gardens* (Johnson Books 2003), p. 23.
22. *Denver Post*, Jul 2, 1898, p. 6.

Five

1. Bernheim, *The Business of the Theatre* (Benjamin Blum, Inc. 1964), pp. 34; 53; 133. The book, an economic history of the American Theatre from 1750 to 1932, was first published in 1932 and was reissued by Benjamin Blum, Inc. in 1964. The book "supplies a great deal of information never before available in concrete form to the men who control the theatre." (Editor's note).
2. The *Oxford Encyclopedia of Theatre and Performance* (edited by Dennis Kennedy) (Oxford University Press 2003), p. 1353.

3. Bordman & Hischak at pp. 611; 571 and 611; 6.
4. For articles dealing with the arrival of theater during the early mining days of Colorado, see Cochran, "Jack Langrishe and the Theater of the Mining Frontier," *The Colorado Magazine*, Volume XLVI, Number 4 (1969), p. 324, McConnell, A Gauge of Popular Taste in Early Colorado, *The Colorado Magazine*, Volume XLVI, Number 4 (1965), p. 338 and Dean G. Nichols, *Pioneer Theatres of Denver, Colorado*, Ph.D. diss., Univ. of Michigan, 1938 (covers earlier periods).
5. Barrett and Barrett, *High Drama* (Western Reflections Publishing Company 2005), pp. 14-17.
6. Levy at pp. 104; 18; 125.
7. See May 26, 1913 of www.actorsequity.org/AboutEquity/timeline/timeline_firstyears.html.
8. LoMonaco, *Summer Stock* (Palgrave Macmillan 2004), p. 111.
9. See www.actorsequity.org/Benefits/benefitshome.asp.

Six

1. Wilson, *The Theater Experience* (McGraw-Hill Book Company 1976), pp. 279; 286; 286-287; 279-293.
2. Dier at pp. 57; 61; 69; 66-67; 76.
3. Interview with Ray Southard, Denver, Nov 8, 1952, by Edwin Levy. See Levy at pp. 82-83.
4. Levy at p. 85 (citing with approval the *Denver Times*, Jun 30, 1905, p. 7); p. 87 (citing with approval the *Denver Post*, Nov 30, 1897, p. 7); p. 197.
5. *Denver Times*, May 21, 1899, p. 18; May 21, 1899, p. 16.
6. *Denver Post*, Jul 20, 1899, p. 3.
7. Bordman & Hischak at pp. 156-57; 358 and 562; 87 and 168.
8. Elitch Theatre program for the week beginning Jun 3, 1899, p. 3.
9. Barrett and Barrett, *High Drama* (Western Reflections Publishing Company 2005), p. 16.
10. *Denver Times*, Jul 8; Jul 11; Nov 21, 1900; Jul 14, 1901.
11. *Rocky Mountain News*, Jun 19, 1966, p. 5A.
12. *Denver Post*, Jul 22; Feb 4, 1900; Jul 14; Jul 28; Aug 1; Aug 18; Jul 18, 1901; Jul 20, 1902.
13. Elitch Theatre program, 89th Year, Jul 7-19, 1980, pp. 27-28.
14. *Denver Republican*, Sept 22, 1901, p. 7 and Apr 24, 1902, p. 5. And see Dier at pp. 64-65.
15. *Denver Republican*, Apr 24; Aug 31, 1902.
16. See the *Denver Times*, May 16, 1902, p. 10, May 18, 1902, p. 3 and May 28, 1902, p. 3.
17. *Denver Times*, May 8; Jun 15; Jun 23; Jul 27, 1902.
18. *Rocky Mountain (Daily) News*, May 28, 1902, p. 6.
19. Levy at pp. 188, 190 (citations omitted).

Seven

1. Bordman & Hischak at pp. 156-157.
2. Dier at pp. 80; 82-83; 85-86.
3. *Denver Post*, Nov 10, 1971, p. 3.
4. *Denver Post*, Jul 5; Jul 12, 1903.
5. *E.g.*, Elitch Theatre program for week beginning Sunday, Aug 28, 1904, p. 3.
6. *Denver Post*, Jun 12; Jul 31; Jul 24; Aug 7; Aug 21; Aug 28, 1904.
7. Dier at pp. 86-87. See also Hartnoll, *The Oxford Companion to the Theatre* (Oxford University Press 1951), pp. 390-392, for more on Sir Henry Irving.
8. See Bordman & Hischak at pp. 495, 621 and Stevenson and Somlyo (editors), *The Tony Award* (Heinemann 2001), pp. xix-xxiii.

Eight

1. Dier at pp. 87; 91-92; 88; 88-89.
2. *Rocky Mountain News*, May 28, 1905, p. 7.
3. *Denver Post*, Aug 6; Jul 16; May 26, 1905; *Denver Times*, May 26, 1905.
4. Bordman & Hischak at pp. 627; 230-231; 230; 215.
5. Levy at p. 162 (from interview by Edwin Levy with Ernest Truex, at Amityville, Long Island, May 19, 1952).
6. Bordman, *American Theatre: A Chronicle of Comedy and Drama, 1869-1914* (Oxford University Press 1994), pp. 559-560 and 621; 589 and 629 and 732.
7. Katz, *The Film Encyclopedia* (Thomas Y. Crowall Publishers 1979), p. 325.
8. *The Elitch Gardener*, Vol. 5, No. 2, Jun 20, 1926, p. 2.
9. *Rocky Mountain News*, Nov 10 1971, p. 29 and *Denver Post*, Nov 10, 1971, p. 13.
10. *International Dictionary of Theatre-3*, by David Pickering (editor) and Judith M. Cass (picture editor) (St. James Press 1996), pp. 282-283 and see generally Bordman & Hischak at pp. 230-231.
11. *The Oxford Encyclopedia of Theatre and Performance* (edited by Dennis Kennedy) (Oxford University Press 2003), p. 469.
12. Hartnoll, *The Oxford Companion to the Theatre* (Oxford University Press 1951), p. 262.
13. *Denver Republican*, May 26, 1905, p. 2.
14. *International Dictionary of Theatre-3*, *supra* note 10.
15. *Denver Post*, May 20; Jul 29; Jul 8; May 25, 1906.
16. Forrest H. Johnson, *Denver's Old Theater Row* (A Gem Publication 1970), p. 36.
17. See generally Dier at pp. 95-98; 38.
18. Hancock and Fairbanks, *Douglas Fairbanks* (London: Peter Davies 1953), pp. 20; 40-41; 60-61; 62; 55; 43.
19. *Denver Catholic Register*, Jan 25, 1978, p, 18.
20. Hancock and Fairbanks, *supra* note 18 at p. 62. And see *Denver Post* (Roundup), May 16, 1971, p. 3.
21. Chaplin, *My Autobiography* (Simon and Schuster 1964), p. 222.
22. Katz, *The Film Encyclopedia* (Thomas Y. Crowell, Publishers 1979), p. 399 (Fairbanks) and p. 912 (Pickford).
23. Hay, *Broadway Anecdotes* (Oxford University Press 1989), p. 356.

Nine

1. Levy at p. 185.
2. Bordman & Hischak at pp. 231; 648 and 649.
3. *Denver Post*, Jul 21; Jul 14; Jul 3; Aug 18; Jul 27; Jul 28, 1907.
4. Atkinson, *Broadway* (Cassell & Company Ltd. 1970), pp. 51-53.
5. See generally Wilson, *The Theater Experience* (McGraw-Hill Book Company 1976), pp. 151-159.
6. Dier at p. 104.
7. *Rocky Mountain News*, Aug 2, 1923, p. 4 (Sherwin was identified in the article as a "noted playwright").
8. *Denver Post*, Nov 10, 1971, p. 3.
9. Elitch Theatre program, week beginning Sunday, Jul 26, 1908, p. 4.
10. *E.g.*, Elitch Theatre program for the week beginning Sunday, Jul 26, 1908, p. 17.
11. Dier at pp. 105; 106; 106-107; 108; 109.

12. *Denver Post*, May 24; May 30; Jun 22; Jun 29, Jul 12, Aug 9, 1908.
13. *Denver Post*, Jun 19, 1905, p. 2.
14. See generally Bordman & Hischak (2004) at pp. 648-649; and www.David Warfield-Wikipedia.
15. Levy at pp. 133 (citing with approval New York Dramatic Mirror LX Sep 5, 1908, p. 10); 91; 27.
16. See internet for Opera House/Denver (1908-2005) at http://www.operapronto.info/exhibitions.html.

Ten

1. *Rocky Mountain News*, Jan 30, 1994, p. 24A.
2. *Rocky Mountain News*, Aug 3, 1986, p. 32 (from *"Rocky Mtn. Memories"* article written by Frances Melrose).
3. See *Denver Express*, Mar 26, 1910, p. 8.
4. *Denver Post*, May 28; May 22; Jun 26; Jul 3, 1910.
5. *E.g.*, see *Denver Post* (Section Two), Jul 24, 1910, p. 4, advertising "Vaudeville in the Casino Beginning Today" and "Symphony Concerts Monday in the Casino."
6. *Denver Republican*, Jun 17, 1913, p. 10.
7. See *Denver Post*, May 30, 1920, p. 9; Aug 15, 1920, p. 9.
8. See, *e.g.*, *Denver Post* (Amusement Section), Aug 3, 1919 ("Cabaret in the Casino") and *Denver Post*, Jun 16, 1921, p. 14 ("Casino Cabaret").
9. Dier at pp. 32-33.
10. *Rocky Mountain News*, Aug 3, 1986, p. 32 and May 4, 1974, pp. 56, 65.

Eleven

1. *Denver Post*, Jun 6; Jul 11; Aug 8, 1909.
2. *Denver Post*, Jul 3; May 29; Jul 24; Aug 14; Aug 7, 1910.
3. Bordman & Hischak at pp. 117; 178.
4. Hays, *Broadway Anecdotes* (Oxford University Press 1989), p. 198.

Twelve

1. *Denver Post*, Aug 13; Jun 11; Jun 5, 1911.
2. See Bordman & Hischak at pp. 169; 129; 546; 669-670.
3. *Rocky Mountain News*, Jul 31; Jul 30; Jul 10; Aug 30, 1911.
4. Dier at pp. 121; 124-125; 125.
5. *Denver Post*, Jul 7; Aug 11; Aug 25; Jul 21, 1912.
6. Levy at pp. 114-115, citing with approval Ward Morehouse, *Matinee Tomorrow* (New York: Whittlesey House 1949), p. 98.
7. Levy at 115, citing with approval *Denver Post* Jul 22, 1912, p. 5; Levy at 115-116, citing with approval *Denver Post* Aug 12, 1912, p. 4.
8. Hartnoll, *The Oxford Companion to the Theatre* (Oxford University Press 1951), p. 660.
9. Levy at 116-117.
10. *Denver Post*, Jun 8; Jun 15; Jun 29, 1913.
11. *Rocky Mountain News* (Amusement Section), Aug 31, 1913, p. 6.

Thirteen

1. The letter appeared in the *Denver Post* (Section Two), May 24, 1914, p. 8.
2. See articles in *Denver Post*, May 31, 1914, p. 8 and (Section Two), Jun 2, 1914, p. 8 and (Section Two), Jun 14, 1914, p. 6.
3. See generally *Denver Times*, Jun 3, 1914, p. 3 and Jun 6, 1914, p. 5 and *Denver Post* (Section Two), Jun 7, 1914, p. 8 and Dier at p. 126.
4. Bordman & Hischak at pp. 400; 425-426.
5. *Denver Post*, Jul 6; Aug 24; Jun 22; Jun 29, 1914.
6. Dier at p. 126.
7. See Katz, *The Film Encyclopedia* (Thomas Y. Crowell, Publishers 1979), p. 190.
8. *Elitch's Weekly*, Volume VIII, Number 12, Aug 25, 1914, p. 1.

Fourteen

1. See Elitch Theatre programs, Jun 13-19, 1915; Aug 16-22, 1920.
2. *Denver Post* (Section Two), May 20, 1906, p. 1 (article by Frank W. White).
3. Bordman & Hischak at pp. 246 and 367.
4. Bordman, *American Theatre: A Chronicle of Comedy and Drama, 1914-1930* (Oxford University Press 1995), pp. 4; 63.
5. Levy at pp. 67-68; 217; 217-218.
6. *Denver Post*, Aug 1; Jul 11; Jun 13; Jul 25; Aug 1 and 8, 1915.
7. *Denver Post*, May 7 and May 14; May 14, 1916.
8. Convery, *Pride of the Rockies* (University Press of Colorado 2005), p. 95.
9. Gurtler and Hunt, *The Elitch Garden Story* (A Rocky Mountain Writers Guide Publication 1982), pp. 14-15.
10. *Rocky Mountain News*, Jan 15, 1930, pp. 1, 12.
11. Morison, *The Oxford History of the American People* (Oxford University Press 1965), pp. 852; 859-860.
12. *Denver Post*, Jun 3, 1917, p. 8 (the article mistakenly referred to "Glass" as "Cass"); Jun 17, 1917, p. 1.
13. *Denver Post*, Aug 22, 1920, p. 18 and Levy at pp. 218-219.
14. *Denver Post*, Jun 27; Aug 20 (the article noted that its final compilation "may bring changes" to the estimates); Jun 29; Jul 6; Aug 22, 1920.
15. *Denver Post*, Sep 14, 1920, pp. 1, 7 and *Rocky Mountain News*, Sep 14, 1920, p. 3.
16. Liggett, "A Garden For Mary," *Rocky Mountain Life* (Jun 1947), p. 27.
17. *Denver Post*, Jul 17, 1936, pp. 1, 7.

Fifteen

1. *Rocky Mountain News*, Jan 15, 1930, pp. 1, 12.
2. *Denver Post*, Jun 12; Aug 13 and 14, 1921; Jun 26; Jul 16; Aug 28, 1922.
3. Bordman & Hischak at p. 428.
4. Katz, *The Film Encyclopedia* (Thomas Y. Crowell, Publishers 1079), p. 135.
5. *Denver Post (Roundup)*, Jun 29, 1980, p. 3.
6. *Denver Post*, Jul 1; Jun 25, 1923; Jul 14; Jul 6; Aug 10; Aug 24 and Aug 25, 1924.
7. *Rocky Mountain News*, Jul 1; Jul 29; Aug 19; Aug 6, 1923.
8. Bordman, *American Theatre: A Chronicle of Comedy and Drama, 1914-1930* (Oxford University Press 1995), p. 160.

Sixteen

1. Bordman & Hischak at pp. 203; 513-514; 301-302.
2. See Katz, *The Film Encyclopedia* (Thomas Y. Crowell, Publishers 1979), p. 140.
3. *The Elitch Gardener*, Vol. VI, No. 13, Aug 28, 1927, p. 5; Vol. 5, No. 1, Jun 12, 1926, p. 3.
4. *Denver Post*, Aug 13; Aug 23; Aug 22, 1925.
5. Unless otherwise indicated, the contents of this section are supported by Wikipedia, the free encyclopedia, easily accessible on the Internet. Pulitzer Prize winners are identified in the Wikipedia reference. See also www.pulitzer.org/historyofprizes.
6. Comments and quotes in this section are supported by *The Elitch Gardener*, Vol. 5, No. 2, Jun 20, 1926, pp. 2-3; Vol. 5, No. 7, Jul 25, 1926, p. 4.
7. Gurtler and Hunt, *The Elitch Garden Story* (Rocky Mountain Writers Guild 1982), pp. 62-65.
8. Levy at p. 263.
9. *Denver Post*, Jul 18; Jul 16; Jul 17, 1926.
10. Martin & Porter, *Video Movie Guide 1999* (Ballantine Books 1998), p. 1082.
11. Wilson, *The Theater Experience* (McGraw-Hill Book Company 1976), pp. 13-15.

Seventeen

1. *Denver Post*, Jul 3; Aug 7; Jul 16; Ju1 1; Jul 4; Jul 9; Jul 17, 1927.
2. Interview with Fredric March, New York City, Mar 18, 1952 by Edwin Levy. See Levy at p. 260.
3. Bordman & Hischak at pp. 561-562.
4. See *Denver Post* (Amusement Section), Aug 14, 1927, p. 1, an interesting story about Miss Rittenhouse's pursuit of the role of Lize Burns.
5. This section is supported by an article that appeared in *The Elitch Gardener*, Vol. VI, No. 6, Jul 10, 1927, p. 3.
6. *The Elitch Gardener*, Vol. V1, No. 2, Jun 11, 1927, p. 3.
7. For the text and quotes that follow, see generally Freedland, *Al Jolson* (Sphere Books Ltd. - Abacus Edition 1975), pp. 111-119.
8. *Denver Post (Roundup)*, Jun 29, 1980, p. 3.
9. *Denver Post*, Aug 4; Aug 13; Aug 12; Aug 14; Jul 23; Jul 22, 1928.
10. *Denver Post*, Aug 14, 1928, p. 14 (the article was captioned "Well, Why Didn't You Leave the Theater?").
11. Fort & Kates, *Minute History of the Drama* (New York: Grosset & Dunlap 1935), pp. 96, 97 and Clark, *Representative One-Act Plays by British and Irish Authors* (Boston: Little Brown and Co. 1921), pp. 3 and 4.
12. Fort & Kates, *id.* at p. 97.
13. *Denver Post*, Apr 5, 1929, p. 1.
14. *Rocky Mountain News*, Jan 15, 1930, pp. 1, 12.
15. Knight, *The Liveliest Art* (Mentor Books 1957), p. 141.

Eighteen

1. Knight, *The Liveliest Art* (Mentor Books 1957), pp. 141-142; 147.
2. *Denver Post*, Aug 4 and 11; Jun 9; Apr 5; Mar 31; Jul 8; Jul 15; Jul 19, 1929.
3. *Rocky Mountain News*, Jan 15, 1930, pp. 1, 12.
4. *Denver Post*, Jun 25, 1928, p. 19.
5. *The Elitch Gardener*, Jul 7; Aug 18, 1929.

6. *Rocky Mountain News*, July 29, 1929, p. 5.
7. Bordman & Hischak at pp. 292.
8. *Denver Post* (Roundup), Jun 21, 1953, p. 17.
9. Bordman, *American Theatre: A Chronicle of Comedy and Drama, 1914-1930* (Oxford University Press 1995), p. 385.
10. See generally Kline, *A History of Denver Theatre During the Depression Era 1929-1941*, Ph.D. Univ. of Denver 1963, Vol. 1.
11. *Denver Post*, Jul 27; Jul 20; Jan 14; Jan 15; Aug 11; Jun 16; Aug 25, 1930.
12. *Rocky Mountain News*, Jan 15, 1930, p. 1. See also *Denver Post*, Jan 14, 1930, p. 1.
13. *Rocky Mountain News*, Jan 17, 1930, p. 3. See also *Denver Post*, Jan 15, 1930, p. 1.
14. The changes by Arnold Gurtler are discussed in Hull, *Denver's Elitch Gardens* (Johnson Books 2003), pp. 76-77.
15. See Levy at p. 332.
16. *Denver Post*, Aug 12, 1958, p. 52.
17. Katz, *The Film Encyclopedia* (Thomas Y. Crowell, Publishers 1979), p. 268.

Nineteen

1. *Denver Post*, Aug 24; Jun 4; Jun 8; Aug 17; Jul 26, 1931.
2. See May of 1931 of www.actorsequity.org/AboutEquity/timeline/timeline_1930.html.
3. Bordman & Hischak at p. 576.
4. *Denver Post*, Mar 6; Mar 19; Aug 8 and 4; Aug 8; Jun 20; Jun 26, 1932.
5. *Denver Post*, Feb 3; Jun 23; Aug 13; Aug 9, 1933.
6. Watt, Eva Hodges, *Papa's Girl* (Western Reflections Publishing Company 2007), p. 61.
7. *Rocky Mountain News*, Jun 11, 1933, p. 7, Jun 12, 1933, p. 4 and *Denver Post*, Jun 19, 1933, p. 8.
8. *Rocky Mountain News*, Jun 11, 1933, p. 7.
9. *Denver Post*, Jun 17, 1933, p. 6 and see Bordman & Hischak at p. 262.

Twenty

1. *Denver Post*, Jun 24; Jun 25; Jul 16; Jul 13; Jul 22, 1934; Jun 17; Aug 25; Jul 2, 1935.
2. *Rocky Mountain News*, Jun 17; Jun 15; Jun 16; Jun 25, 1934.
3. Bordman and Hischak at pp. 489; 220-221; 296.
4. Hay, *Broadway Anecdotes* (Oxford University Press 1989), p. 311.
5. Watt, Eva Hodges, *Papa's Girl* (Western Reflections Publishing Company 2007), pp. 20; 68-70.
6. See generally *Denver Post*, Feb 9, 1956, p. 1 and *Denver Post* (Empire Magazine), Aug 10, 1947, p. 4.
7. *Denver Post* (Section Three), Jul 22, 1934, p. 6 (as per Sir Guy Standing, the English stage and screen star).
8. Bordman & Hischak at pp. 15-16.
9. Fadiman & Bernard (editors), *Bartlett's Book of Anecdotes* (Little, Brown and Company 2000), p. 419.
10. Schwartz, *Voices from the Federal Theatre* (University of Wisconsin Press 2003), pp. XI and XII; XIII; 6; XVII.
11. See "WPA Federal Theatre Project - Encyclopedia Britannica" (on-line).
12. Hartnoll, *The Oxford Companion to the Theatre* (Oxford University Press 1951), p. 259.
13. See "Federal Theatre Project - Wikipedia, the free encyclopedia" (on-line).
14. See generally, Schwartz, *Voices from the Federal Theatre* (University of Wisconsin Press 2003).

15. Bordman & Hischak at p. 296 and Levy at p. 316n.9.
16. *Denver Post*, Feb 2; Jun 7, 1936.
17. Levy at p. 315, citing with approval *Rocky Mountain News*, Oct 21, 1936, p. 11.
18. *Rocky Mountain News*, Aug 25, 1936, p. 9.
19. See *ibid*, and Schwartz, *supra* note 10 at p. 147 and also pp. 52, 53, 144, 145.

Twenty-One

1. See *Denver Post*, Jul 16 and 17, 1936, p. 1 and *Rocky Mountain News*, Jul 17, 1936, p. 1.
2. *Denver Post*, Jul 21; Jul 17; Jun 14, 1936; Jul 21; Aug 11; Nov 13 and 14; Jul 26, 1937.
3. *Rocky Mountain Life*, Jun 1947, p. 16.
4. *The Elitch Gardener*, Vol. 5, No. 9, Aug 8, 1926, p. 4, quoting from an article written by Burns Mantle.
5. Bordman & Hischak at pp. 357-358; 190; 463; 667; 473.
6. *Rocky Mountain News*, May 18; Jun 24, 1936; Jul 8; Aug 27 and 30; Aug 30; Aug 27, 1937.
7. Elitch Theatre program, 45th year, Jul 4-10, 1937, p. 2.
8. Elitch Theatre program, 45th year, Jul 4-10, 1937, p. 10 and Jul 18-24, 1937, p. 2.
9. See Elitch Theatre program, 46th Year, July 10-16, 1938, p. 12.
10. *Denver Post*, Jun 30; Jun 12; Jul 11; Jul 27, 1938.
11. Elitch Theatre program,46th year, beginning with the week of Jun 19, 1938, p. 5.
12. *Denver Post*, Jun 16; Jul 31; Jul 27; Jul 17 and Jul 16, 1939.
13. Elitch Theatre program, 48th Year, beginning with the week of Aug 13, 1939, p. 8.
14. *Rocky Mountain News*, Jun 24, 1940, p. 5.
15. *Denver Post*, Jun 23; Jun 14; Jun 24; Aug 26; Aug 12, Jul 8; Jun 29, 1940.
16. Bordman & Hischak at p. 481 and *Denver Post*, August 12, 1940, p. 11.

Twenty-Two

1. See generally *Rocky Mountain News*, Jun 17, 1941, pp. 1, 6, for comments in this section. See also *Denver Post*, Jun 5, 1941, p. 4 and Jun 16, 1941, p. 8 and Jun 17, 1941, p. 21.
2. A copy of the program can be found in History Colorado, Denver, Elitch Theatre Collection 1364, Box 14, File Folder 1096.
3. *Rocky Mountain News*, Jun 17, 1941, pp. 1, 6.
4. *Denver Post*, Jun 17, 1941, p. 21.
5. Levy at pp. 355-356.
6. *Rocky Mountain News*, Aug 5; Aug 6, 1941.
7. *Denver Post*, Aug 25, 1941, p. 14.
8. *Denver Post*, Aug 22; Jun 14, 1942.
9. *Denver Post*, Jul 24; Aug 30; Aug 27 and 30; Aug 29; Aug 20, 1943.
10. Bordman & Hischak at pp. 414; 184; 340; 340-41; 483-484.
11. *Denver Post*, Jul 30, 1944, p. 4 and Bordman & Hischak at p. 620.
12. *Denver Post*, Aug 7, 1944, p. 10 and Aug 6, 1944, p. 41.
13. *Rocky Mountain News*, Jul 17, 1944, pp. 1, 5, 16 and July 18, 1944, p. 5.
    See also *Rocky Mountain News*, July 21, 1944, p. 8 (an inquest into the tragedy was conducted but "no further evidence on origin of the blaze has been discovered").
14. Morison, *The Oxford History of the American People* (Oxford University Press 1965), pp. 1041, 1045.

Twenty-Three

1. *Denver Post,* Jun 14; Aug 9; Aug 23, 1946.
2. Bordman & Hischak at p. 173.
3. *Rocky Mountain News,* Jun 21; Jun 1, 1947.
4. The information in this section is supported by references in her biography by Stephen Michael Shearer entitled *Patricia Neal (An Unquiet Life)* (The University Press of Kentucky 2006), pp. 41-48, 54-55 and 162.
5. For comments in this section, see generally *Denver Post,* Aug 4, 1947, p. 10.
6. *Denver Post,* Aug 31, 1947, p. 6B.
7. See Bordman & Hischak at pp. 21 and 432-433.
8. *Denver Post,* Jun 17, 1948, p. 14; Aug 15, 1950, p. 21.
9. *E.g.,* see *Denver Post,* June 19, 1951, p. 26 (opening Sunday evening - matinee on Wednesday only).
10. *Rocky Mountain News,* Jun 16; Aug 9; Aug 16; Aug 23; Jun 26, 1949.
11. Elitch Theatre programs, 59th Year, Jul 30-Aug 5; Aug 20-26; Jul 9-15; July 16-22, 1950.

Twenty-Four

1. *Denver Post,* Jul 22; Jul 13; Aug 20; Jun 25; Jul 9; Jul 23, 1951.
2. Elitch Theatre program, 60th Year, Jul 8-14, 1951, p. 6 and the *Denver Post,* Jul 22, 1951, p. 4E; Elitch Theatre program, 60th Year, Jun 24-30, 1951, p. 2.
3. See Internet search for - www's 1st Home of Harold Lloyd - The Biography of Harold Lloyd.
4. See Internet search for - www's lst Home of Harold Lloyd - A Guide to Addresses and Sites.
5. Dardis, *Harold Lloyd* (Penguin Books 1983), pp. 14 and 16-18; 8-9.
6. *Denver Post,* Apr 16, 2006, pp. 1A, 16A.
7. Elitch Theatre program, 60th Year, Aug 26-Sep 1, 1951, pp. 6, 32, and *Denver Post,* Aug 20, 1951, pp. 2 and 16.
8. Englund, *Grace of Monaco* (Doubleday & Company, Inc. 1984), pp. 18-19; 38.
9. Katz, The Film Encyclopedia (Thomas Y. Crowell Publishers 1979), p. 646 and Bordman, *American Theatre: A Chronicle of Comedy and Drama, 1930-1969* (Oxford University Press 1996), p. 285 ("Young Kelly was welcomed as a promising player").
10. History Colorado, Denver, Elitch Theatre Collection 1364, Box 11, File Folder 923 (see letter by Whitfield Connor dated Aug 16, 1983); Box 11, File Folder 854 (the original of the letter to Whitfield Conner by Grace Kelly is part of this file folder); Box 11, File Folder 859.
11. Lacey, *Grace* (G.P. Putnam's Sons 1994), pp. 113; 112-113; 122 and 234; 123.
12. See Lacy, *Grace* (G.B. Putnam's Sons 1994) and Spada, *Grace* (A Dolphin Book - Doubleday & Company Inc. 1987) and Englund, *Grace of Monaco* (Doubleday & Company, Inc. 1984).
13. *Denver Post,* Aug 27, 1961, p. 16.
14. Elitch Theatre program, 66th Year, Jul 28-Aug 3, 1957, p. 6.

Twenty-Five

1. *Denver Post,* Jun 23; Jul 11; Aug, 3, 1952.
2. Elitch Theatre program, 61st Year, Jul 6-12, 1952, pp. 32, 36.
3. Elitch Theatre programs, 62nd Year, Jun 21-27; Aug 16-22; Jul 5-11; Jul 12-18; Jul 19-25; Jul 26-Aug 1, 1953.
4. See Internet re "Haila Stoddard" at www.michenermuseum.org/bucksartists/artist.php?artist=268.

5. *Denver Post* (Empire Magazine), Feb 16, 1986, pp. 10, 12.
6. *Denver Post*, Jun 16; Aug 3; Aug 30; Aug 24; Jul 13; Jul 20, 1953.
7. See Hancock and Fairbanks, *Douglas Fairbanks* (London: Peter Davies 1953), p. 53.
8. Elitch Theatre programs, 63rd Year, Aug 1-7; Jul 25-31; Jul 4-10; Jul 18-24, 1954.
9. Elitch Theatre programs, 64th Year, Jul 31-Aug 6; Jun 26-Jul 2, 1955.
10. *Denver Post*, May 19, 1953, p. 28.
11. *Denver Post*, Jul 26; Aug 22; Dec 30; Nov 14, 1954.
12. See *50 Best Plays of the American Theatre* (Volume 4) (Crown Publishers, Inc., New York 1970), p. 88.
13. *Denver Post* (Roundup), Jun 29, 1980, p. 3.
14. *Denver Post*, Aug 24; Aug 28; Jul 22, 1955.

Twenty-Six

1. See generally *Denver Post*, Feb 9, 1956, p.1; *Rocky Mountain News*, Feb 9, 1956, p.5. See also *Denver Post*, Mar 22, 1957, p. 3 (dedication of plaque honoring Somnes placed on "theater wall" of General Rose Hospital memorial lounge).
2. *Denver Post*, Feb 10; Aug 20 (review of play); Jul 1 and 2 (review of play); Apr 22; 1956.
3. Elitch Theatre program, 65th Year, Jun 17-23, 1956, p. 5.
4. Elitch Theatre program, 61st Year, Jun 22-28, 1952, p. 32.
5. See generally Elitch Theatre programs, 65th Year, Jun 17-23, 1956, p. 36 and Jul 22-28, 1956, p. 40.
6. *E.g.*, Elitch Theater program - 65th Year, Jun 24-30, 1956, p. 44. The caveat appeared in future programs, as well. *E.g.*, Elitch Theatre program, 66th Year, Jun 30-Jul 6, 1957, p. 46.
7. *Denver Post*, Jun 17, 1956, p. 5AA (a clip-out ticket of admission appeared in the *Denver Post*).
8. See *Rocky Mountain News*, Jul 16, 1957, p. 42 (*Love Out of Town*) and Aug 6, 1957, p. 38 (*The Gimmick*).
9. Elitch Theatre program, 66th Year, Jun 16-22, 1957, p. 2.
10. *Denver Post*, Jul 7; Aug 4, 1958.
11. *Denver Post*, Feb 10; Jul 6, 1959.
12. References in support of the text relating to *Our Town* are found in the *Denver Post*, Aug 24, 1959, p. 26 and Bordman & Hischak at p. 483.
13. Watt, Eva Hodges, *Papa's Girl* (Western Reflections Publishing Company 2007), pp. 113-115; 12; 13; 172-173.
14. Watt, Eva Hodges, *supra* note 13 at p. 137. And see generally Hosokawa, *Thunder in the Rockies* (William Morrow & Co. Inc. 1976), pp. 396-398.

Twenty-Seven

1. For information contained in this section, see generally *Denver Post*, Jan 28, 1960, p. 2 and *Rocky Mountain News*, Jan 29, 1960, p. A7.
2. *Denver Post*, Jul 24; Jun 5; Jun 20; Jun 19; Jun 21; Aug 16; Aug 23; Aug 21, 1960.
3. *Denver Post*, Jun 17, 1963, p. 20.
4. *Denver Post*, Aug 2, 1960, p. 23 and see Bordman & Hischak at p. 188.
5. Elitch Theatre programs, 69th Year, Aug 15-20; Jun 27-Jul 2; Aug 1-6; July 25-30, 1960.
6. *Denver Post*, Jun 20; Jun 21, 1961.
7. *Denver Post*, Jul 25, 1961, p. 20 and Aug 22, 1961, p. 20. See also Bordman & Hischak at p. 392.
8. *Denver Post*, Jun 26; Aug 14; Jul 12, 1962.

9. The contents of this section are supported by an article in the Contemporary Section of the Sunday *Denver Post*, Aug 26, 1962, p. 9.
10. *Denver Post*, Jun 17; Aug 13; Jun 16, 1963.
11. *Rocky Mountain News*, Aug 20, 1963, p. 55.

Twenty-Eight

1. Watt, Eva Hodges, *Papa's Girl* (Western Reflections Publishing Company 2007), p. 154.
2. See *Denver Post*, Feb 5; May 4; Jun 24; Jun 21; Jun 22; Jul 14; Jul 29; Jul 28, 1964.
3. History Colorado, Denver, Elitch Theatre Collection 1364, Box 12, File Folder 943.
4. *Rocky Mountain News*, Aug 24, 1977, p. 53.
5. LoMonaco, *Summer Stock* (Palgrave Macmillan 2004), pp. 134-135; 135; 138-140 (see discussion of "star system economics").
6. *The Denver Catholic Register*, Aug 27, 1980, p. 15 (interview of Josephine Gonzales, a practical nurse on duty at Elitch for many years).
7. Interview of Sandy Hale, media director for Elitch Theatre for many years, who was responsible for attending to the needs of the stars and securing interviews in the press and on television and radio.
8. *Denver Post*, Dec 12; Jul 4; Jul 5; Aug 31 and Aug 22, 1965.
9. History Colorado, Denver, Elitch Theatre Collection 1364, Box 7, File Folder 649; Box 12, File Folder 943.
10. *Denver Post*, Aug 3, 1969, p. 5; May 7, 1967, pp. 14, 15, 17, 19.
11. Wilson, *The Theater Experience* (McGraw-Hill Book Company 1976), pp. 233-235; 235; 233.
12. See *Denver Post* (Empire Magazine), May 7, 1967, pp. 14, 15, 17 and *Denver Post* (Roundup), Aug 3, 1969, p.5.

Twenty-Nine

1. *Denver Post*, Jun 21; Aug 9; Jul 26, 1966.
2. *Denver Post*, Jun 20; Jun 18, 1967; Jun 21, 1975; Jul 7 and 11; Jul 19, 1967.
3. History Colorado, Denver, Elitch Theatre Collection 1364, Box 5, File Folder 568; 569.
4. Kennedy, *No Pickle, No Performance* (Doubleday Company, Inc. 1978), pp. 35; 34.
5. Swanson, *Swanson on Swanson* (Random House 1980), pp. 467; 468-469.
6. Burns and Fisher, *All My Best Friends* (G.P. Putnam's Sons 1989), p. 301.
7. *Denver Post*, Jun 16; Jul 23; Jul 30; Jun 25; Aug 13; Aug 4, 1968.
8. *Denver Post*, Jul 9, 1968, p. 59.
9. See drama critic's review in *Denver Post*, Aug 6, 1968, p. 50.
10. *Denver Post*, Jun 4; Aug 5; Aug 6; Aug 14; Aug 17; Aug 19; Aug 24, 1969.
11. As to the contents of this section, see generally article by Rena Andrews, staff writer for *Denver Post*, Aug 3, 1969, p. 5.

Thirty

1. *Denver Post*, Feb 20, 1970, p. 3. As to the death of Gurtler's first wife, the daughter of the Mulvihills, see *Denver Post*, Jan 28, 1960, p. 2.
2. *Denver Post*, Jun 30; Jun 28; Jul 28; Jun 16; Jul 14, 1970.
3. Bach, *Dazzler* (*The Life and Times of Moss Hart*) (Alfred A. Knopf 2001), pp. 287 and 289-290; 287 and 291.
4. History Colorado, Denver, Elitch Theatre Collection 1364, Box 7, File Folder 675; Box 11, File Folder 852; Box 5, File Folder 576.

5. Elitch Theatre program, 80th Year, Jun 21-Jul 3, 1971, p. 40.
6. Caesar and Friedfeld, *Caesar's Hours* (Public Affairs 2003), p. 16.
7. *Denver Post*, Jul 6, 1971, p. 16.
8. Katz, *Film Encyclopedia* (Thomas Y. Crowell, Publishers 1979), pp. 399-400; see also Hancock and Fairbanks, *Douglas Fairbanks* (London: Peter Davies 1953), pp. 224-233.
9. For the information contained in this section on Maude Fealy, see generally *Rocky Mountain News*, Nov 10, 1971, p. 29 and *Denver Post*, Nov 10, 1971, p. 3.
10. History Colorado, Denver, Elitch Theatre Collection 1364, Box 12, File Folder 943.
11. *Denver Post*, Jul 16; Aug 1; Aug 13; Jun 21; Jul 7; Jul 8; Jul 11; Jun 20, 1972.
12. Bordman & Hischak at pp. 223-224.

Thirty-One

1. *Denver Post*, Jun 21; Jun 26; Jul 22 and 24; Jul 25; Aug 22, 1973.
2. History Colorado, Denver, Elitch Theatre Collection 1364, Box 5, File Folder 600; Box 11, File Folder 870.
3. Bordman & Hischak at pp. 202; 387.
4. *Denver Post* (Empire Magazine), Feb 16, 1986, pp. 10, 11. And see the *Longmont Daily Times* (Weekend Section), Jun 13-14, 1981, p. 19.
5. *Rocky Mountain News* (NOW Section), Jun 30, 1974, p. 26.
6. *Denver Post*, Jul 9, 1974, p. 22 (a review of the play).
7. *Rocky Mountain News*, Aug 7, 1974, p. 66.
8. See article by Dennis Gallagher entitled "Theatre" at History Colorado, Denver, Elitch Theatre Collection 1364, Box 6, File Folder 621.
9. *Denver Post*, Jun 9; Aug 6; Jul 21 and 23; Aug 1; Jun 18, 1974.
10. *Denver Post*·(Empire Magazine), Feb 16, 1986, pp. 10, 15-16.
11. Kennedy, *No Pickle, No Performance* (Doubleday & Company, Inc. 1978), pp. 88-89.
12. *Denver Post*, Jun 24; Jul 8; Jun 21; Jul 22; Aug 5; Aug 19; Aug 10 and Aug 12, 1975.
13. Katz, *The Film Encyclopedia* (Thomas Y. Crowell, Publishers 1979), pp. 986-987 and *Denver Post* (Roundup), July 6, 1975, p. 7.
14. History Colorado, Denver, Elitch Theatre Collection 1364, Box 6, File Folder 629.
15. *Rocky Mountain News*, Aug 20, 1975, p. 43.

Thirty-Two

1. *Denver Post*, Jul 9, 1976, p. 25.
2. *Rocky Mountain News*, Jul 7, 1976, p. 56.
3. *Rocky Mountain News*, Aug 5; Jul 24; Aug 24, 1977.
4. *Denver Post*, Jul 15; Aug 23; Jul 26, 1977.
5. See photograph of celebration in the *Denver Post*, Aug 26, 1977, p. 25.
6. History Colorado, Denver, Elitch Theatre Collection 1364, Box 7, File Folders 656; 672.
7. *The Denver Catholic Register*, Aug 27, 1980, pp. 15-16.
8. The information as to compensation contained in this and the next section is supported by files at History Colorado, Denver, Elitch Theatre Collection 1364, Box 7, File Folders 647 to 656.
9. *Denver Post*, Aug 8, 1978, p. 23.
10. See Katz, *The Film Encyclopedia* (Thomas Y. Crowell, Publishers 1979), p. 498 and *Rocky Mountain News*(Center Section), Aug 4, 1978, p. 3C.

11. *Rocky Mountain News*, Aug 4 and Aug 9; Aug 22; Jun 11; Aug 23, 1978.
12. See article captioned "Harris triumphs as Dickinson" at History Colorado, Elitch Theater Collection 1364, Box 7, File Folder 666.
13. The contents of this section are supported by the review in the *Rocky Mountain News*, Jun 27, 1979, p. 65.
14. *Denver Post*, Jul 31, 1979, p. 10.
15. *Rocky Mountain News*, Jul 27; Aug 9; Aug 24; Aug 22; Nov 9, 1979.
16. *Denver Post* (Empire Magazine) Feb 16, 1986, pp. 10, 15.
17. History Colorado, Denver, Elitch Theatre Collection 1364, Box 7, File Folder 675.

Thirty-Three

1. *Denver Post*, Jun 24; Jul 22; Jul 7; Jul 13, Aug 20, 1980.
2. *Rocky Mountain News*, Jun 25; Jul 23; Jul 22, 1980.
3. History Colorado, Denver, Elitch Theatre Collection 1364, Box 8, File Folder 685.
4. Bordman & Hischak at pp. 88-89 and 505; 603.
5. *Denver Post*, Jun 17; Jun 19; Jun 24; Jul 8; Aug 19; Oct 21, 1981.
6. See *Best American Plays* (Eight Series 1974-1982) (edited by Clive Barnes) (Crown Publishers, Inc. 1983), pp. 158 and 161-162.
7. *The Denver Catholic Register*, Jul 23, 1980, pp. 1, 21.
8. *Denver Post*, Jun 21; Jun 28; Aug 12; Jul 28, 1982.

Thirty-Four

1. *Boulder Daily Camera*, Jun 30, 1983, p. 5B.
2. *Rocky Mountain News*, Jun 30; Jul 15, 1983.
3. *Denver Post*, Jul 1; Jul 14; Jul 11; Aug 11; Jul 25; Aug 25, 1983.
4. See article by Blair Chotzinoff at History Colorado, Denver, Elitch Theatre Collection 1364, Box 9, File Folder 737.
5. History Colorado, Denver, Elitch Theatre Collection 1364, Box 9, File Folder 737.
6. *Westport News*, Aug 3, 1983, p. 15.
7. *Denver Post* (Empire Magazine), Feb 16, 1986, pp. 10, 15.
8. Bentley, *What is Theatre?* (Beacon Press 1956), p. 235.
9. *Rocky Mountain News*, Jun 28, 1984, p. 79.
10. *Denver Post*, Jun 24; Aug 9; Aug 23, 1984.
11. See article captioned "Elitch's Musical Amounts to a Non-Experience" at History Colorado, Denver, Elitch Theatre Collection 1364, Box 9, File Folder 761.
12. See article by Marion Rex at History Colorado, Denver, Elitch Theatre Collection 1364, Box 9, File Folder 768.
13. Hischak, *American Theatre* (Oxford University Press 2001), p. 223.
14. *Denver Post*, Jun 13, 1985, p. 2C.
15. *A Woman's Point of View*, Jul 18-31, 1985, p. 12. The article is on file at History Colorado, Denver, Elitch Theatre Collection 1364, Box 15, File Folder 1126.
16. *Denver Post*, Jun 20; Jun 13, 1985.
17. *Rocky Mountain News*, Jul 4; Jul 17, 1985.
18. *Denver Post*, Aug 1, 1985, p. 3B.
19. Hull, Denver's Elitch Gardens (Johnson Books 2003), pp.116, 117.

Thirty-Five

1. History Colorado, Denver, Elitch Theatre Collection 1364, Box 12, File Folder 983.
2. Elitch Theatre program, 95th Year, Jul 7-19, 1986, p. 6.
3. History Colorado, Denver, Elitch Theatre Collection 1364, Box 10, File Folders 785 and 786.
4. See *Rocky Mountain News*, Jun 11, 1986, p. 78 and *Denver Post*, Jun 11, 1986, p. 1C.
5. *Rocky Mountain News*, Jun 22; Jul 6; Jul 10; Aug 4, 1986.
6. *Denver Post*, Jun 11, 1986, p. 1C.
7. *Rocky Mountain News*, Jul 6, 1986, p. 4E and *Denver Post*, Jul 25, 1983, p. 1C.
8. See letters to editor in *Rocky Mountain News*, Jun 1, 1986, p. 67.
9. *Denver Post*, Sep 1; Jul 23; Jun 25; Jul 8; Aug 6, 1987.
10. Copy of letter is on file with History Colorado, Denver, Elitch Theatre Collection 1364, Box 10, File Folder 802.
11. Copy of the Aug 24, 1987 press release is on file with History Colorado, Denver, Elitch Theatre Collection 1364, Box 12, File Folder 1001.
12. *Rocky Mountain News*, Aug 25, 1987, p. 38.
13. Copy of the letter is on file with History Colorado, Denver, Elitch Theatre Collection 1364, Box 10, File Folder 808.
14. *Denver Post* (The Lively Arts Section), Aug 24. 1986, p. 4.

Thirty-Six

1. Hull, *Denver's Elitch Gardens* (Johnson Books 2003), pp. 117 and 118; 123.
2. *Rocky Mountain News* (Sunday Magazine), Jun 23, 1991, p. 8M.
3. See promotional literature of Historic Elitch Gardens Theatre Foundation.
4. *Denver Post* (Roundup), Jun 11, 1978, p. 3.
5. Quoted in promotional literature of the Historic Elitch Gardens Theatre Foundation.
6. *Denver Post*, Oct 31, 1995, p. 3B.
7. *Rocky Mountain News*, Sep 20, 1995, p. 27A.
8. *Rocky Mountain News*, Mar 4, 2004, pp. 7D, 8D.
9. *Denver Post*, Sep 2, 2007, p. 20F.
10. See Internet article on the "Restoration of Elitch Theatre - Business First of Columbus."
11. The article appears in the *Denver Post* (Arts & Entertainment Section), Feb 14, 2010, p. 2E.
12. *Denver Post*, Apr 16, 2012, p. 2A.
13. Dier at p. 63.

Acknowledgments

My love of theater as an inspiration for me to undertake the task of writing this manuscript has already been expressed in the Preface to this book. But the writing of a book is never a solitary task. A writer must be surrounded by sources and friends who ease the road upon which one must walk.

Not enough can be said about the patience, cooperation and assistance by members of the staffs at the Denver Public Library and at History Colorado. They were very helpful and cooperative and always made an effort to make my life easier, particularly on days when I was exhausted from sitting at the microfilm machine struggling to read an article from the rather faded and small print of an 1896 edition of a newspaper. Coi Drummond-Gehrig of the Western History/ Genealogy Department of the Denver Public Library was of particular and effective assistance in aiding the author search for photographs and in preparing them for publication.

I learned a great deal from this experience, not only about the history of the Elitch Theatre and all those individuals who were an intimate part of its history, but also of other happenings associated with theater in general, and of the historical settings in which the Elitch Theatre functioned, as in the war years and the Depression years. These happenings and historical settings are included in the manuscript to give the reader a sense of the times in which the Elitch Theatre lived.

I acknowledge all the stars that walked the stage at Elitch. I acknowledge the directors that were satisfied with nothing less than the best in their productions. I thank the stage designers, stagehands, extras and others behind the scenes. I acknowledge and thank the patrons and friends of the Theatre who supported the summer seasons, even in difficult economic times.

I want to particularly acknowledge the work of the graphic artist selected to bring the book to publication. He was in charge of the layout of the book, the photos to be positioned, the book's front and back covers and all the other details designed to enhance the subject matter. His name is David Robison. This was more than an assignment for David. His work represented his love for Elitch Theatre and a belief in the subject matter of the manuscript. He made the tiring and detail work of the author easier.

Most of all, every author needs a friend with patience and understanding, one who doesn't mind being consulted on the spur of the moment, even late in the evening or on a Sunday day of rest, to resolve an issue in the manuscript - NOW! Such friends are understandably scarce. I was fortunate to have such a friend. He and his wife live in New Mexico. He loves the theater, has encouraged me in the project, carefully reviewed the manuscript, made corrections where needed and offered suggestions. His name is Bill Assini. I acknowledge him as a good friend, a wise editor and a factor that moved me forward when times were tiring. His sense of humor was always welcome in our discussions.

Certain liberties were taken with the manuscript. Drama critics tend to abbreviate or modify words like "thru" for "through" or capitalize a word that is best served in lower case. Editorial changes brought spelling, punctuation and capitalization in line with accepted English practices.

While I may boast of efforts made in recognizing the need for corrections, more than likely my manuscript may also suffer from the same flaws, considering the scope of years being covered by the project. I take full responsibility for any such errors, if any there be. Notwithstanding, however, I rest assured that no such errors will divert the stream of information that is being presented to the reader from making the impression intended. The manuscript, as the lawyers state, is substantially correct.

This project has been a labor of love. All the sayings that surrounded the Elitch Theatre are valid, such as "not to see Elitch, is not to see Denver" and that it was "the greatest cradle of the drama in American history" and so on. There is so much to record and remember about this showcase of stars. There is a need for this nostalgic journey in time.

Theodore A. Borrillo
Littleton, Colorado
October 2012

About the Author

Theodore A. Borrillo, the author, was born in the Bronx, New York, the younger of two children born to Michele and Incoronata Borrillo, immigrants from San Marco dei Cavoti in the Province of Benevento, Italy. He is a graduate of the City College of New York and St. John's University School of Law (*Magna Cum Laude*). After his military service in Verdun, France and Vicenza, Italy as a 1st Lieutenant in the Judge Advocate General Corps, he returned to the Bronx. He then enrolled in the Harvard Law School and received a Master of Law Degree. Upon graduation, Mr. Borrillo moved to Denver, Colorado.

After serving a few years as an Assistant Professor at the University of Denver School of Law, Mr. Borrillo became a member of the Office of the Denver District Attorney, where he served in the capacity of Chief Deputy. He and his late wife, Elfriede, raised their four children - Christopher, Angela, Thomas and Matthew - in Denver.

Mr. Borrillo has had an abiding interest in writing. His lengthy book, *Colorado Criminal Practice and Procedure*, was published by West Publishing Company. He has also written numerous articles for legal and non-legal publications as well as four books of poetry. He is frequently a speaker at various venues.

Mr. Borrillo has been retired from the practice of law for several years and resides in the small community of Bow Mar, Colorado, on the outskirts of Denver. His children live their separate lives in different areas of the country except that Angela works and resides in The Netherlands in Amsterdam. The children are all a cell phone call away. They have been and are blessings to him as they were to their mother.

Index

The author has structured the Index into categories in an effort to facilitate search by the reader. Since they are commonly referred to by the first and last names, actors, playwrights and other theatrical people are presented alphabetically using first names. The total number of these people as well as the plays presented in this work is far too large to include in this Index. The Table of Contents which identifies Chapter subheadings and an earlier Index of Actors and Actresses (see pages 361 to 363) also offer pathways into the various chapters. As for this Index, it is the author's belief that it sufficiently and substantially satisfies the categories identified. The categories are:

Actors
Directors
Drama Critics
Elitch Gardens
Elitch Theatre
John and Mary Elitch
Managers and Producers
Plays
Playwrights
Scene Designers
Stage Managers
Star Package System
The Remaining Subjects

Actors

Directors

Drama Critics

Elitch Gardens

Elitch Theatre

Plays

Playwrights

Made in the USA
San Bernardino, CA
24 July 2014